D0036002

BISON
BOOKS

The biographical sketches in this volume have been selected from among those published in the ten-volume set *The Mountain Men and the Fur Trade of the Far West*, under the editorial supervision of LeRoy R. Hafen (Glendale, Calif.: Arthur H. Clark Company, 1965–72).

MOUNTAIN MEN and FUR TRADERS of the Far West

Eighteen Biographical Sketches

Edited by LeRoy R. Hafen
Selected, with an introduction, by
Harvey L. Carter

University of Nebraska Press
Lincoln and London

Manufactured in the United States of America

First Bison Book printing: June 1982
Most recent printing indicated by the first digit below:
7 8 9 10

Library of Congress Cataloging in Publication Data
Mountain men and the fur trade of the Far West.
Selections.
Mountain men and fur traders of the Far West.
Reprinted from: The Mountain men and the fur trade of the Far West. Glendale, Calif. : A. H. Clark, 1965–1972.
Includes index.
1. West (U.S.) — History — To 1848 — Biography — Addresses, essays, lectures. 2. Trappers — West (U.S.) — Biography — Addresses, essays, lectures. 3. Fur traders — West (U.S.) — Biography — Addresses, essays, lectures. 4. West (U.S.) — Biography — Addresses, essays, lectures. 5. Fur trade — West (U.S.) — History — Addresses, essays, lectures. I. Hafen, Le Roy Reuben, 1893– . II. Carter, Harvey Lewis, 1904– . III. Title.
F592.M742 1982 978 81–21803
ISBN 0–8032–7210–3 (pbk.) AACR2

Published by arrangement with the Arthur H. Clark Company.

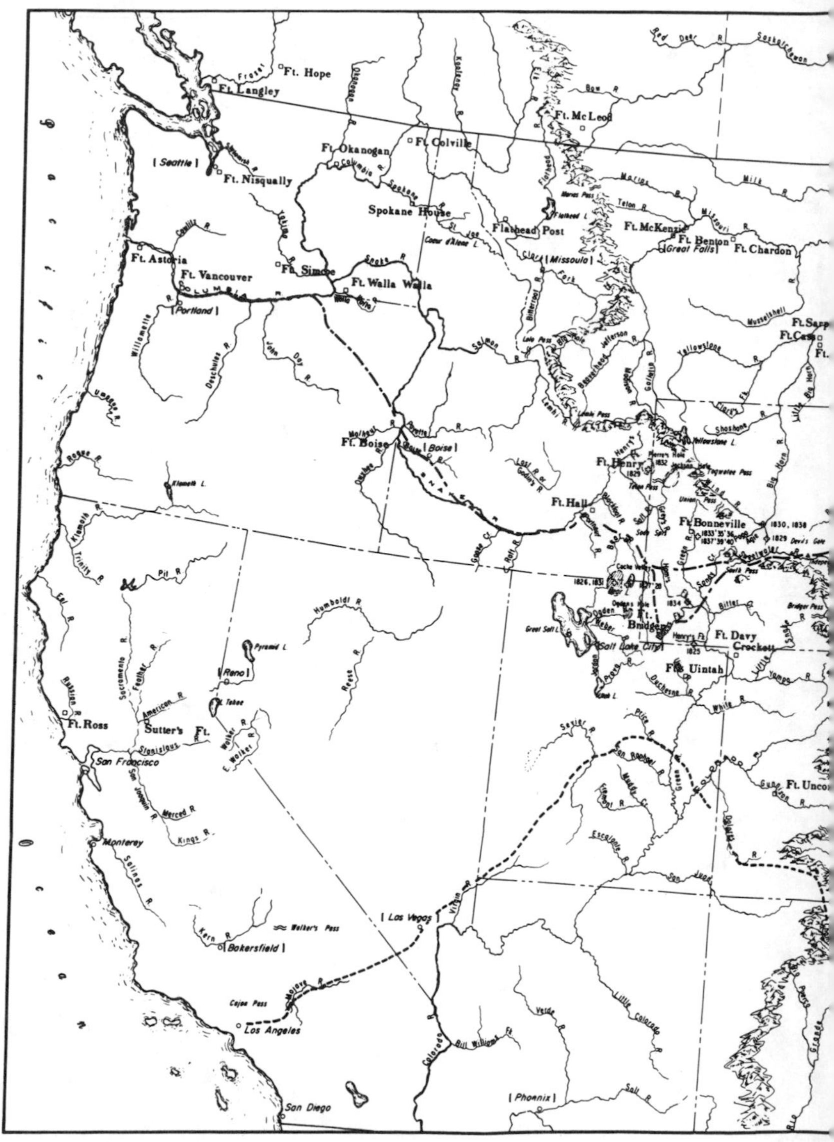

Ft. Hope
Ft. Langley
Fraser
Okanogan
Kootenai R
Red Deer R
Saskatchewan
Bow R
Ft. McLeod
Ft. Colville
Ft. Okanogan
[Seattle]
Ft. Nisqually
Columbia R
Spokane
Spokane House
Flathead
Flathead Post
Flathead L.
Marias
Marias Pass
Teton R
Milk
Missouri R
Ft. McKenzie
Ft. Benton
[Great Falls]
Ft. Chardon
Cowlitz R
Yakima R
Ft. Astoria
Ft. Vancouver
Ft. Simcoe
Snake R
Ft. Walla Walla
Walla Walla
[Portland]
St. Joe
Coeur d'Alene L.
Clark
[Missoula]
Fork
Bitterroot R
Musselshell
Ft. Sarpy
Ft. Cass
Willamette
Deschutes R
John Day R
Salmon R
Lolo Pass
Big Hole
Jefferson
Beaverhead
Madison
Gallatin R
Yellowstone
Little Big Horn
Umpqua R
Lemhi R
Lemhi Pass
Clark's Fk
Shoshone
Yellowstone L.
Malheur R
Payette R
Ft. Boise
[Boise]
Ft. Henry
Henry's
Pierre's Hole
1832
Jackson Hole
Togwotee Pass
Teton Pass
Union Pass
Wind R
Big Horn
Rogue R
Klamath L.
Owyhee R
Lost R or Godin's R
Ft. Hall
Blackfoot R
Portneuf R
Bear R
Soda Spr.
Salt R
Greys R
Ft. Bonneville
1833, '35, '36
1837, '39, '40
1830, 1838
1829
Devil's Gate
Klamath R
Trinity R
Pit R
Goose Cr.
Raft R
Cache Valley
1826, 1831
1827, '28
Green R
Sandy Cr.
Sweetwater
South Pass
Eel R
Humboldt R
Ogden's Hole
1834
Ogden
Weber
Ft. Bridger
Bitter
Bridger Pass
Great Salt L.
Henry's Fk
1825
Ft. Davy Crockett
Salt Lake City
Pyramid L.
Sacramento R
Feather R
[Reno]
Reese R
Jordan R
Provo R
Ft. Uintah
Utah L.
Duchesne R
Yampa R
Little Snake
White R
Russian R
Ft. Ross
American R
L. Tahoe
Sutter's Ft.
Walker R
E. Walker R
Stanislaus R
San Francisco
Sevier R
Price R
San Rafael R
San Joaquin R
Merced R
Kings R
Muddy Cr.
Fremont R
Gunnison R
Ft. Uncompahgre
Dolores
Monterey
Escalante R
San Juan
Salinas R
Virgin R
[Las Vegas]
Kern R
Walker's Pass
[Bakersfield]
Mojave R
Cajon Pass
Los Angeles
Little Colorado R
Verde R
Colorado R
Bill Williams Fk
[Phoenix]
Salt R
San Diego
Rio Grande
Pacific Ocean

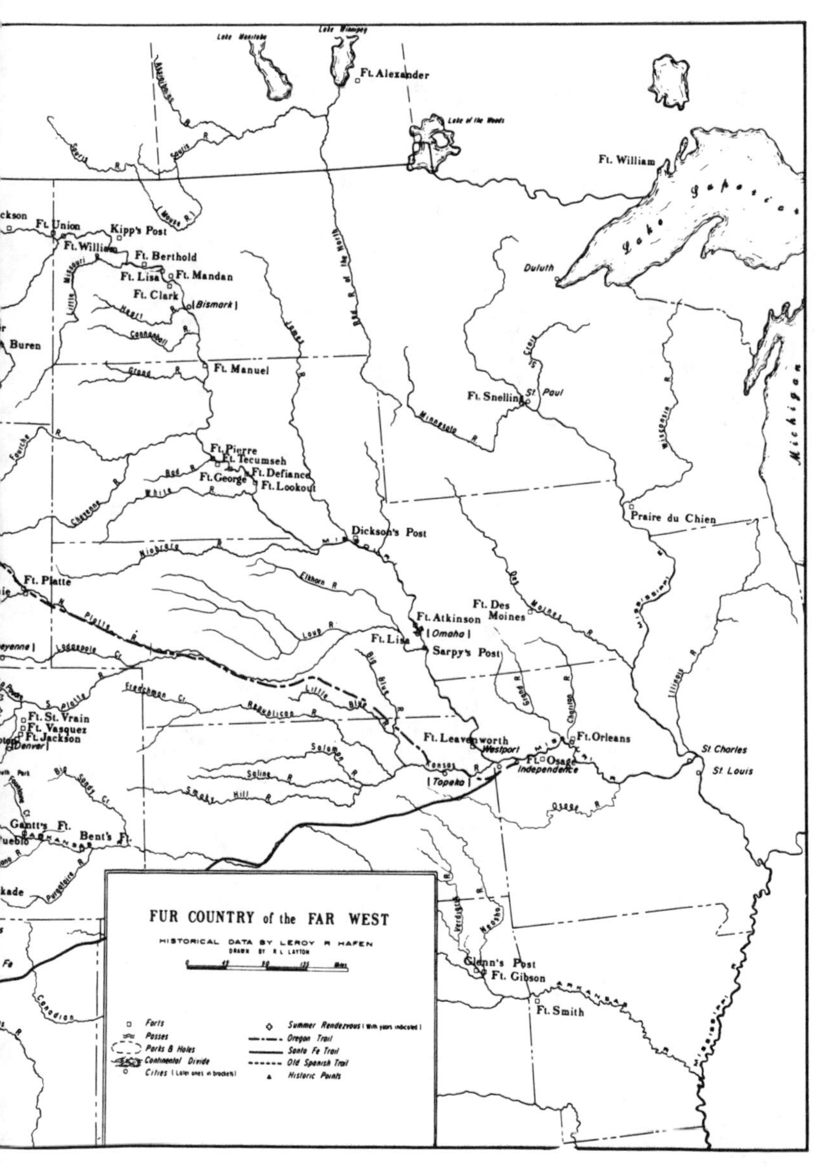
FUR COUNTRY of the FAR WEST
HISTORICAL DATA BY LEROY R HAFEN
DRAWN BY R L LAYTON
0 45 90 135 Miles
Forts
Passes
Parks & Holes
Continental Divide
Cities (Later ones in brackets)
Summer Rendezvous (With years indicated)
Oregon Trail
Santa Fe Trail
Old Spanish Trail
Historic Points
Lake Manitoba
Lake Winnipeg
Ft. Alexander
Lake of the Woods
Ft. William
Lake Superior
Duluth
Michigan
Ft. Union
Kipp's Post
Ft. William
Ft. Berthold
Ft. Lisa
Ft. Mandan
Ft. Clark
[Bismark]
Buren
Ft. Manuel
Ft. Snelling
St. Paul
Ft. Pierre
Ft. Tecumseh
Ft. Defiance
Ft. George
Ft. Lookout
Prairie du Chien
Dickson's Post
Ft. Platte
Ft. Des Moines
Ft. Atkinson
[Omaha]
Ft. Lisa
Sarpy's Post
Ft. St. Vrain
Ft. Vasquez
Ft. Jackson
[Denver]
Ft. Leavenworth
Westport
Ft. Orleans
Ft. Osage
Independence
St. Charles
St. Louis
[Topeka]
Gantt's Ft.
Pueblo
Bent's Ft.
Glenn's Post
Ft. Gibson
Ft. Smith
Souris R.
(Mouse R.)
Red R. of the North
James R.
Heart R.
Cannonball R.
Grand R.
Bad R.
White R.
Cheyenne R.
Fourche
Niobrara R.
Elkhorn R.
N. Platte R.
Loup R.
Lodgepole Cr.
S. Platte
Frenchman Cr.
Republican R.
Little Blue
Big Blue R.
Solomon R.
Saline R.
Smoky Hill R.
Kansas
Big Sandy Cr.
Osage R.
Minnesota R.
St. Croix
Wisconsin R.
Des Moines R.
Grand R.
Chariton R.
Illinois R.
Mississippi R.
Missouri
Little Missouri
Arkansas R.
Purgatoire R.
Verdigris R.
Neosho R.
Canadian

Contents

Introduction

The Mountain Men, as the fur traders and trappers who penetrated the Rocky Mountains and explored the American Far West in the first half of the nineteenth century are commonly called, were the counterparts of the astronauts of the second half of the twentieth century. Strange as it may seem to modern readers, the "western wilderness" of that day was as unfamiliar to the average person as the outer space that is being explored today. In their own day, the adventurous wayfaring of the Mountain Men was noted in contemporary newspapers; they attracted the gifted pen of Washington Irving, and one of their number, Kit Carson, became a national hero and a legend in his own time.

In the second half of the nineteenth century, however, the Mountain Men were eclipsed by the military heroes of the Civil War. In the Far West itself, the beaver trap was supplanted by the pick and pan of the gold seeker in the mountain streams and the lasso of the cowboy on the open range. The iron horse and the singing wire replaced the pack mule and the hard-riding courier. The muzzleloader gave way to the six-shooter, the Indian was relegated to the reservation, and the Mountain Man was forgotten.

The historian Frederic Logan Paxson, whose lectures sparked my interest in the frontier, had no chapter on the Mountain Men in his prize-winning *History of the American Frontier* (1924). Although Kit Carson, Jedediah Smith, Jim Bridger, and Thomas Fitzpatrick, the perennial candidates for the title of *primus inter pares* among the Mountain Men, each received a bare mention in Paxson's textbook, none was identified with the western fur trade.

Beginning in the decade of the twenties, however, the Mountain Men began a slow rise in public esteem, aided by the researches of LeRoy Hafen, Ralph Bieber, Charles Camp, and W. J. Ghent, and popularized by Stanley Vestal. By mid-twentieth century, works such as Bernard De Voto's *Across the Wide Missouri* (1947), Robert Cleland's *This Reckless Breed of Men* (1950), David Lavender's *Bent's Fort* (1953), and Dale Morgan's *Jedediah Smith and the Opening of the West*

(1953) had succeeded in arousing once more a considerable enthusiasm for the Mountain Men.

Two readable biographies of Carson appeared in 1962—Bernice Blackwelder's *Great Westerner* and M. Marion Estergreen's *Kit Carson: A Portrait in Courage*. Don Berry's *A Majority of Scoundrels* (1961) and David Lavender's *The Fist in the Wilderness* (1964) provided more reliable and better-told histories of the fierce competition for domination of the western fur trade that was won by the American Fur Company. When Dale L. Morgan produced his monumental *The West of William H. Ashley* (1964), the Mountain Men had become familiar figures once more and many historians began to feel that the western fur trade was no longer a field for historical investigation.

This judgment proved to be premature, for it was at this point that the Arthur H. Clark Company launched a project of herculean proportions, *Mountain Men and the Fur Trade of the Far West* in ten volumes, edited by LeRoy R. Hafen. It was published from 1965 to 1972, and contained 292 biographical sketches by 84 contributors; probably no one but Hafen could have undertaken such a work. Because contributors were allowed great latitude in the length of their sketches, some lesser figures received more space than some major ones, but it was justified by the amount of material brought to light concerning relatively unknown but deserving men. Janet Lecompte and I, each of us contributing sketches sufficient to fill a volume, were the wheelhorses of the project. Her work was of greater originality, being centered on the trappers of French origin who penetrated the Southwest, whereas many of my subjects were men already well known. LeRoy and Ann Hafen contributed between them about half a volume, and he contributed a summary history of the fur trade that fills half of the first volume.

The ten volumes edited by Hafen have been used chiefly by scholars; the present volume of eighteen sketches of leaders among the Mountain Men, reprinted without change from the original work, is intended to appeal to a large and growing number of readers among the general public. It is meant to be representative of the biographical approach to the history of the western fur trade in the early nineteenth century. The selection of such a list is obviously a matter of opinion, and other qualified persons might well have constructed a quite different list.

My list of representative Mountain Men stresses the importance of the rendezvous country. It may be regarded by some as placing too much emphasis on that area and too little on the southwestern fur trade centered at Taos; others will feel that the emphasis on the British fur trade based at Fort Vancouver is not sufficiently strong. The British are represented only by McLoughlin and Ogden; the Southwest only by St. Vrain, and in part by Carson, Smith, and Williams. Had it been possible to extend the list to twenty-five men, instead of eighteen, both the Southwest and the British Northwest might have been better represented.

Nevertheless, there are valid reasons, in my view, for emphasizing the rendezvous country. Despite the welcome additions to our knowledge of both the Southwest and the Northwest in Hafen's ten volumes and elsewhere, the area in which the rendezvous were held will remain the focus of attention because that is primarily where the action was. It was the region where beaver were not only most numerous but also of best quality. It was just beyond South Pass where the mountains were most easily crossed. It was the area that was least subject to Indian attack. It was the area where the British and the Americans had an equal right to be and where the Mexican authority was absent, even within the Mexican boundary. From this region both Oregon and California could be most easily reached. It was the region of greatest interest to the American government. For all these reasons, I believe that the present volume, in its selection of Mountain Men, presents the best historical overview of the western fur trade possible within the confines of a single volume of four hundred pages. This contention may become more acceptable if the list of biographies is examined briefly.

Manuel Lisa (1772–1820) launched the American fur trade on the Missouri River in 1807. The wily Spaniard, who knew all the tricks of the trade, needed them to survive until 1820. He provides a link with the fur trade that existed before American acquisition of Louisiana. His career shows the difficulties that had to be overcome by the early American expeditions. Pierre Chouteau, Jr. (1789–1865) went up the Missouri in the same year as Lisa but his long subsequent career was spent in St. Louis. A member of a great family of fur traders, he typifies the western businessman, surviving against great financial odds by his complete mastery of that aspect of the business. Wilson Price Hunt (1783–1842) was the little-known commander of the well-known Astorians. His inclusion points out the early interest of John Jacob Astor in the far western fur trade and sets the stage for competition with both the British companies and the American companies based in St. Louis. He also exemplifies the man of the counting house, who could become a good leader of men in the field.

The appearance of William H. Ashley (1778– or 1782–1838) on the scene introduces the rendezvous system and the replacement of trading by trapping, whereby he and his successors were able to survive against better-financed competition. His political career shows the importance of the fur trade in Missouri and in the Congress of the United States. His able right-hand man, Jedediah Smith (1799–1831) demonstrates the link between the fur trade and exploration. His visit to southern California preceded the approach from New Mexico, and his advent in the Pacific Northwest, even under disastrous circumstances, was a warning to British interests there of an American wave of the future.

John McLoughlin (1784–1857) took charge of operations on the Columbia River for the Hudson's Bay Company about the same time that Ashley held the first rendezvous at the eastern end of the Oregon country. His long tenure there indicates the well-entrenched position of the British in Oregon until political negotiations forced their retirement. Peter Skene Ogden (1794–1854) was the most durable and wide-ranging of the British field leaders. His clash with the Ashley men in 1825 near Great Salt Lake and his later trapping in California show that the British respected the Mexican boundary no more than did the Americans.

The Southwest is represented by Ceran St. Vrain (1802–70), an urbane gentleman whose trading activities began in 1824 at Taos, from which center he went westward to Arizona and northward to Wyoming in his early years. As a partner of the Bent brothers, he participated in the trade at Bent's Fort on the Arkansas River and Fort St. Vrain on the Platte. Kit Carson (1809–68), still America's favorite frontiersman, accompanied Ewing Young's expedition to California when but a youth and settled at Taos in his later years. In between, he spent several years in the rendezvous country and several more as a guide for the explorations of John C. Frémont. "Old Bill" Williams (1787–1849), though he ranged far and wide, spent much time in the Southwest. He provides the best example of the highly individualistic free trapper whose eccentricities did much to establish the popular but somewhat exaggerated notion of what a Mountain Man was like. Too crotchety to be a leader, he was a legendary figure, respected by the trappers of his day for his solitary wanderings.

William Sublette (1799–1845), equally capable of leadership in the field and perception in business, was astute enough to recognize that the supplying of goods to the rendezvous was the key to the fur trade. Hard-driving and ambitious, like Smith and Fitzpatrick, he died at the height of his achievements. Thomas Fitzpatrick (1797–1854) was one of the most able of the Mountain Men. He was active in all aspects of the business and a man who had risen from the ranks. As an Indian agent, he displayed a better grasp of that difficult role than many others who tried to fill the job. Jim Bridger (1804–81) was not only one of the best field leaders but also one of the few who could survive in the mountains after the height of the fur trade had passed. He eventually became the personification of the Mountain Man, rivaling Carson in some respects and Fitzpatrick and Smith in others. He outlived all the others on this list and was known for his tall tales of the mountains.

With the advent of Benjamin Bonneville (1796–1878) in the fur business in 1832 for a brief period, we are made aware of the thinly disguised interest of the government in the Oregon country. Although Bonneville had a cover of private investment for his fur-trading operation, it was not a successful business venture. The trappers ridiculed his fort on Horse Creek as Fort Nonsense, but it is notable that six rendezvous were held in its vicinity and that it was near the center of the rendezvous country as well as of strategic importance to the United States claim to Oregon. His chief lieutenant, Joe Walker (1798–1872) was an experienced frontiersman. Walker found a route to California from the rendezvous country that was soon followed by others. He undoubtedly knew the Great Basin better than any other man of his time. Nathaniel Wyeth (1802–56) was, like Captain Bonneville, an interloper in the fur trade for a time, beginning in 1832, although his interest represented private capital rather than governmental concern. Although Wyeth failed, his impact on the trade was considerable and his company's Fort Hall account books are a valuable historical record.

The final triumph of the American Fur Company is illustrated by Andrew Drips (1789–1869), a veteran brigade leader who dominated the closing years of the rendezvous system, ending in 1840. Drips was less openly aggressive than the men trained by Ashley, but his operations were no less efficient. We would expect a big company's field manager to exemplify the quiet authority shown by Drips. He continued to be active in various capacities until three years before his death. Joe Meek (1810–74) was slightly younger than Carson. Like Carson, he stayed in the rendezvous country as long as he could;

finally, in September 1840, he took his Indian wife and family and settled in Oregon, as did a number of other Mountain Men. Meek was as boastful as Carson was modest, but they were both loyal to friends and family. Meek not only typifies the common trapper but also represents the vanguard of American settlers on the Pacific coast.

Of the men sketched in this volume, Ashley, Ogden, Smith, and Wyeth kept journals, portions of which are extant and have been edited for publication. Meek and Carson dictated reminiscent accounts that were taken down by others and have helped to piece out the historical record. Bonneville and McLoughlin also left some useful information, and fugitive papers were left by several others on the list. It is of interest to note that half of the men on the list took Indian wives by whom they had children.

A word should be said in behalf of the biographical approach to history. It has been justly criticized for its tendency toward adulation or animosity rather than impartiality, for its oversimplified explanation of complex events, for its penchant for moral judgments and psychological explanations, for its preoccupation with trivial detail and anecdotal entertainment, and for its elevation of the personal above all other forms of causation. It is safe to say, however, that despite these readily apparent weaknesses, the biographical approach to history will continue to flourish in popular favor because no other approach can rival it in creating interest and holding attention. Yet readers should be cautioned that the biographical approach to history is a selective one and cannot present a complete view. If the entire list of biographies, or even a fair portion, had been changed, readers might receive a considerably different impression of the history of the western fur trade than they will receive from the list that is presented here. Nevertheless, men represented in this book probably give a reasonably accurate and faithful impression of the fur trade as a whole. This forms the most satisfactory basis for any attempt to learn history from biography.

Far from providing the capstone for a memorial under which the Mountain Men might be buried, the original ten-volume *Mountain Men* seems to have stimulated further publication by scholars of the subject. Dale L. Morgan and Eleanor Towles Harris's *The Rocky Mountain Journals of William Marshall Anderson* (1967) included sketches of several men not included in Hafen's larger work as well as some that were. My *"Dear Old Kit": The Historical Christopher Carson, with a New Edition of the Carson Memoirs* (1968) presents much new information on Carson as well as demonstrating that much of the old information was unreliable. David J. Weber (*The Taos Trappers*, 1971) unearthed a mine of material from the New Mexico archives that provided an entirely new perspective on the fur trade of the Southwest. Fred R. Gowans, in *Rocky Mountain Rendezvous: a History of the Fur Trade Rendezvous, 1825–1840* (1976), narrated that important subject from primary sources in a single convenient volume. Janet Lecompte's *Pueblo-Hardscrabble-Greenhorn: The Upper Arkansas, 1832–1856* (1978) presents a thoroughly researched prize-winning study of both sides of the southwestern political and cultural border that is also a splendid social history of a neglected area. Among new biographies may be mentioned Kenneth Holmes, *Ewing Young: Master Trapper* (1967), John E. Sunder, *Joshua Pilcher, Fur Trader and Indian Agent* (1968), Gloria Griffen Cline, *Peter Skene Ogden and the Hudson's Bay Company* (1974), and Richard Clokey, *William H. Ashley* (1980).

The inclusion of Richard J. Fehrman's "The Mountain Men—A Statistical View" in the index volume of Hafen's *Mountain Men* provided some impetus for other interpretative studies. Harvey L. Carter and Marcia C. Spencer's "Stereotypes of the Mountain Man," *Western Historical Quarterly* 6 (January 1975): 17–32, concluded that the stereotype of "heroic adventurer" was generally applicable because adventure was inherent in the occupation; that the "daring but degenerate" stereotype was of limited application in earlier years but increased in the later years of the fur trade; and that the "expectant capitalist stereotype" was highly valid for the leaders but of doubtful application to the rank and file of Mountain Men. Howard R. Lamar, in *The Trader on the American Frontier: Myth's Victim* (1977), drew a strong distinction between the Mountain Man as fur trader and the Mountain Man as fur trapper. The former was welcomed by the Indian and was not viewed as a threat; the latter was actually a threat to the Indian way of life and was so perceived by the red man. In *The Fur Trade of the American West, 1807–1840* (1979), David J. Wishart examines the fur trade as a system, but he overemphasizes, I believe, the destructiveness of the trade to both the environment and the native inhabitants.

William R. Swagerty, in "Marriage and Settlement Patterns of Rocky Mountain Trappers and Traders," *Western Historical Quarterly* 11 (April 1980): 159–80, concludes, on the basis of an able statistical study, that "mountain men were bicultural [but] not without prejudices. . . . Nor can the fur trade era be excluded from the list of factors which demoralized, depopulated, and eventually dispossessed the Indians. . . . The Mountain Men were, nevertheless, more open-minded and sensitive to other cultural viewpoints than any other social group entering the West during the nineteenth century."

Despite the enormous literature of the American fur trade, there is still no complete history that synthesizes the writings on the many aspects of the subject or that separates the reliable from the erroneous or the important from the inconsequential. Works like this volume, however, admirably capture a period in our national history that can never be lived again except vicariously by readers of the lives of the Mountain Men.

The sketches here presented are factual and well documented in scholarly fashion. This does not mean that they make dull reading. The narratives are reliable but they are also filled with personal adventures encountered in unusual places and over a vast field of operations. The phrase used by the astronauts of our time to designate those of their number who are able to take the rigorous training program in their stride without faltering might aptly be applied to the Mountain Men: "They had the right stuff."

HARVEY L. CARTER
Professor Emeritus of History
Colorado College
Colorado Springs, Colorado

Manuel Lisa

by RICHARD E. OGLESBY
University of California, Santa Barbara

On the 11th of August, 1820, at the sulphur springs immediately adjacent to the town of St. Louis, Missouri, a small group of distressed relatives looked on anxiously as the ailing man before them affixed a shaky signature to his recently completed last will and testament. Manuel Lisa, fur trading pioneer and fiery leader of the succession of Missouri Fur Companies, was dying. But even as life ebbed, the now enfeebled Spaniard still had his attention fixed upon the Missouri, and, with the optimism born of confidence, felt he was leaving as a legacy to his partners and successors the means of accomplishing his lifelong dream, a fur trading empire in the Rocky Mountains. "It is my wish," he had written,

> that the part I now have in the Missouri Fur Company shall be & continue as long as the articles of Association will permit . . . and . . . I hereby authorize and empower my Executors to carry into effect the aforesaid articles of association in as full and ample manner as I could – were I living.[1]

Toward evening the next day, the healing waters of the spa and the ministrations of the attending physician notwithstanding, Manuel Lisa passed away, in the words of his father-in-law, "without distressing struggles."[2] His departure marked the close of an era in the evolution of the fur trade which bore his personal imprint as its most distinguishing characteristic.

---

[1] St. Louis Probate Court File no. 497, Manuel Lisa, Deceased.

[2] Stephen Hempstead Diary, Saturday, August 12, 1820, Missouri Historical Society, St. Louis, Missouri.

Although death came quietly and with somber dignity, it was about the only thing in Lisa's stormy and significant career that did. From the date of his birth in New Orleans, September 8, 1772,[3] the son of Christobal de Lisa and Maria Ignacia Rodriquez had struggled against adversity, and did so with a tenacity that impressed his most bitter rivals. Even his last venture, another partnership under the name of Missouri Fur Company, had had its difficult moments during organization. Lisa's partners, his brother-in-law, Thomas Hempstead, Joshua Pilcher, Andrew Woods, Moses B. Carson, John B. Zenoni, and Joseph Perkins, were individuals not previously associated with the fur trade in any important capacity, and some of them had had no prior experience in the industry. The capitalization of the group, however, amounted to $70,000,[4] a far larger sum than any Lisa had ever had behind him, and enough, perhaps, to enable him to return to the rich fur country of the northern Rockies, an area from which he had been excluded, largely because of lack of financing, since the War of 1812.

As president of the company, Lisa had opened a new avenue of commerce for St. Louis by contracting with David Stone and Company of Boston to supply the requisite goods. Thomas Hempstead had journeyed east in the spring of 1819 to meet with Oliver Bostwick, acting partner for Stone and Company, and to conclude an agreement for the purchase of $25,910.98 worth of merchandise to be delivered in St. Louis in the spring of 1820.[5] Bostwick, worried over the extent of his commitment to the Missouri Fur Company, had come to St. Louis himself during the summer of 1820 to confer with company officials. Lisa, certain of the com-

[3] Although there is some doubt as to its accuracy, this is the date on Lisa's tombstone.

[4] Lewis C. Beck, *A Gazetteer of the States of Illinois . . .* (Albany, 1823), 329-30.

[5] Deposition of Thomas Hempstead, November 9, 1824, St. Louis Records, Book I, 447, Office of the Recorder of Deeds, City Hall, St. Louis, Missouri.

pany's potential, had agreed to mortgage his entire landholding in St. Louis as security for that first purchase.[6] This had satisfied Bostwick, and Lisa had looked forward to a lasting association with the eastern firm, one which, he felt, would produce great profits for both concerns. Death came before he was able to accomplish his goal.

This last effort was but the culmination of Lisa's previous experience in trade and commerce, an experience which dated back into the 1790s, when, as an itinerant trader, he had piloted his own vessel on the waters of the Mississippi and Ohio rivers. In 1796, Lisa established a frontier store in the American community of Vincennes, on the Wabash River, Northwest Territory.[7] There he became acquainted with Polly Charles Chew, a widow whose family, except for her infant daughter, had been wiped out in an Indian ambuscade. To take better care of his new family, Lisa moved westward to St. Louis, the northernmost Spanish outpost in Louisiana, where opportunities seemed superior.

After procuring one of the rather generous land grants freely dispensed to all newcomers to Spanish territory who indicated an intention of becoming permanent residents, Lisa attempted to break into local trading circles. By so doing, Manuel found himself confronted by the determined opposition of the old and well-established French families of the Mound City who had acquired, over the years, control of all the business monopolies granted by the Spanish government. Unsuccessful locally, Lisa, armed with a barrage of petitions and memorials signed by others in a similar predicament, went to the seat of government in New Orleans and endeavored to induce the authorities to open Louisiana to free trade.[8] Utterly frustrated in that effort, Lisa returned

6 *Ibid.*

7 Richard E. Oglesby, *Manuel Lisa and the Opening of the Missouri Fur Trade* (Norman, 1963), 10.

8 A. P. Nasatir, ed., *Before Lewis and Clark; Documents Illustrating the History of Missouri, 1785-1804* (2 vols., St. Louis, 1952), 647-48.

to St. Louis determined on a more direct course of action.

With a native's knowledge of the inner workings of Spanish bureaucracy, Manuel bid for the best of the monopolistic grants, the trade with the Osage Indians. Long sought after by French traders, the Osage trade had always been a lucrative, albeit dangerous, business, as the warlike proclivities of that tribe had kept the frontier in a constant state of unrest. Recognizing the opportunity, Auguste Chouteau, who had been one of the original founders of St. Louis, and his half-brother Pierre, had petitioned the Spanish government in 1794 for a six year monopoly of the Osage commerce. In return for such a grant, the Chouteaus had promised to build a fort among the Indians, and to convert their hostility to whites into friendship. This they had done, and, as a reward, had received a four year extension of their monopoly in 1800.[9] Thus Lisa was asking for a privilege that had long been the perquisite of St. Louis' oldest and most respected citizens.

But his instinct regarding Spanish government was unerring, and, after promising to build "a water mill to make flour as fine as that of the Anglo-Americans," and placing a "gift" of $1,000 in the royal treasury, Manuel Lisa, in partnership with F. M. Benoit, Gregory Sarpy, and Charles Sanguinet, received "for the precise term of five years . . . the trade with the Osage Indians," in June of 1802.[10] The grant was extremely unpopular in St. Louis, Lisa and his partners finding opposition everywhere, and profits, therefore, were difficult to obtain. Lisa, with his short and explosive temper, at once became embroiled in a series of disputes with Charles Dehault Delassus, the lieutenant governor in St. Louis, and even earned a brief jail sentence for his outspoken criticism of the governor's policies. All of these petty squabbles evaporated, however, with

[9] *Ibid.*, II, p. 591.

[10] *Ibid.*, II, p. 698.

the sudden shift of Louisiana from Spain to France, and, finally, to the United States.

Almost at once the dynamism so much a part of the early American republic became apparent in backward Louisiana. On the Illinois side of the Mississippi River, directly opposite the mouth of the Missouri, a small group of Americans assembled over the winter of 1803-04, and made preparations for one of the young nation's greatest adventures. Under the leadership of captains Meriwether Lewis and William Clark, these men were planning to embark upon an epic voyage up the Missouri, across the mountains, to the Pacific Ocean and return. Somnambulating St. Louis awoke with a start, and the business community hastened to give aid, both in necessary goods and in information, what little of it they possessed, of the country to the west. Manuel Lisa was one of those suppliers, and no doubt visited the bustling encampment and became acquainted for the first time with John Colter, George Drouillard, and the rest of that hardy band, knowing, perhaps, that they would become valuable sources of information upon their return, information which might point the future of St. Louis northwestward. Certainly they would be ideal contacts for a man interested in beating the competition. The doughty explorers pointed the prows of their clumsy keelboats upstream in the spring of 1804, and Lisa turned to other pursuits.

The leaven of American capitalism was beginning to work in Louisiana, and, to take advantage of it, Lisa moved to consolidate his assets by instituting a number of lawsuits designed to collect funds from all those in his debt. This process took the better part of two years. Once on a fairly sound financial footing, he projected a connection with his former countrymen in Santa Fe, far across the plains and deserts of the Southwest. Since the days of the Mallet brothers, traders from the Mississippi valley had periodically gone to Santa Fe to sell merchandise to the isolated settlers there, but, though the trade was profitable, the Spanish government usually had declared it illegal as well, and commerce was never put on a regular basis. Lisa joined with the fabulous Portuguese adventurer, Jacques Clamorgan, in an attempt to do just that. In 1806 the pair purchased from the Philadelphia firm of Giesse, Tayesse, and Snyder some $12,000 worth of merchandise, hired Louison Beaudoin, an experienced hand, to lead the expedition, and prepared to set out in the spring of 1807.[11]

Somehow this scheme fell afoul the operations of that noteworthy soldier of fortune, James Wilkinson, then acting governor of the Louisiana Territory. Wilkinson warned Lieutenant Zebulon M. Pike, then off on an exploring mission to the headwaters of the Arkansas River, of Lisa's arrangement, and ordered him to "take all prudent and lawful means to blow it up."[12] Manuel, not wishing again to become embroiled with government, disavowed his southwestern intentions and bent his efforts toward the Missouri. He kept his financial interest in the Santa Fe expedition, however, and Clamorgan himself took it west in 1807.[13]

Although he took no active part in that effort to open the Santa Fe trade, Lisa kept it always in his mind. When, almost by accident, opportunity again offered in that direction, he was quick to seize it, attempting this time to effect a connection with Santa Fe from the Upper Missouri country. In 1811, one of Lisa's best field men in the Rockies, Jean Baptiste Champlain, returned from a trapping foray on the upper reaches of the Platte River to report that the "Spaniards of Mexico" sent annual expeditions to the Arapaho Indians, the tribe inhabiting the Platte watershed

---

[11] Copy of Agreement, Feb. 19, 1810, Lisa Papers, Missouri Historical Society, St. Louis, Missouri.

[12] Zebulon M. Pike, *An Account of Expeditions . . .* (Philadelphia, 1810), Appendix, 38.

[13] J. J. Hill, "An Unknown Expedition to Santa Fe in 1807," *Mississippi Valley Historical Review*, VI (March 1920), 590-592.

region. Manuel quickly re-equipped Champlain for another journey to the Arapahoes, and authorized him to open negotiations with any Spanish representative he might meet for trading rights in Santa Fe.[14] The following year, having heard nothing from his emissary in the meantime, Lisa dispatched Charles Sanguinet from the newly constructed Fort Manuel on the Missouri to the Platte to find out what had happened to Champlain. Sanguinet carried with him a formal letter from Lisa to the Spanish indicating his desire to open trade, and a fair amount of merchandise to show that he was serious.[15] Sanguinet returned shortly with the distressing news that Champlain was dead, killed by the Blackfeet, at least so said the Arapahoes, and that hostility blocked the road to Santa Fe.[16] This completely dashed Lisa's hopes in the Southwest, and he never again made a major effort in that direction.

However thwarted in the Southwest, Lisa found his opportunity up the Missouri. The return of Lewis and Clark to St. Louis, and the wealth of information they brought back concerning the availability of furs in the Rocky Mountain region through which they had passed, excited the trading fraternity, but only Lisa took the initiative. Short of funds after his investment in Clamorgan's expedition, Lisa formed a partnership with two well-established Illinois merchants, Pierre Menard and William Morrison, both of Kaskaskia, to equip a party to ascend the Missouri to the mountains with the joint objects of trading with the Indians and trapping for furs. Recruits were readily available for such an undertaking as most of the former members of the Lewis and Clark expedition were still in town and looking for more adventure. George Drouillard was appointed the personal representative of Menard and Morrison, both of

---

[14] Herbert E. Bolton, "New Light on Manuel Lisa and the Spanish Fur Trade," *Southwest Historical Quarterly,* XVII (July 1913), 61-66. [15] *Ibid.*

[16] John C. Luttig, *Journal of a Fur Trading Expedition on the Upper Missouri, 1812-1813,* Stella M. Drumm, ed. (St. Louis, 1920), 103.

whom preferred the difficult, but impersonal, problems of finance at home to the very personal perils posed by the wilderness, and Benito Vasquez was hired as second in command.[17]

For goods and equipment the partners utilized the services of the St. Louis trader Myers Michaels to purchase most of their $16,000 outfit from G. Gillespie in Michilimackinac.[18] The merchandise was loaded on a pair of keelboats, and, with Lisa at the helm of the lead boat, some fifty to sixty men set off in the spring of 1807, their every action setting a precedent for voyages to follow, as did the annoying and unexpected difficulties which immediately arose to plague the party. One engagé, Jean Baptiste Bouché, failed to make the sailing from St. Charles, thereby causing the first of many aggravating delays. In fact, Bouché's numerous transgressions lent credence to Lisa's later charge that the creole was deliberately sabotaging the expedition.[19]

After the party left St. Charles, little word of their progress drifted downstream. In mid-May, a pirogue showed up at St. Charles with two of Lisa's men and the body of a third, Antoine Bissonette. As the story came out, Bissonette had deserted from the party at the mouth of the Osage River, some 120 miles from St. Louis. Lisa had ordered Drouillard to bring him back "dead or alive," which Drouillard had done, wounding Bissonette severely in the process. The engagé had been sent down for medical attention, but had died before reaching civilization. A murder complaint was quickly lodged against both Lisa and Drouillard, but their arrest, trial, and ultimate exoneration had to await their return.[20]

The following summer Lisa appeared in St. Louis carry-

---

17 Oglesby, *Lisa,* 40.

18 St. Louis Records, Book D, 375, Office of Recorder of Deeds, City Hall, St. Louis, Missouri.

19 Deposition of Manuel Lisa, March 18, 1811, Lisa Papers, Missouri Historical Society, St. Louis, Missouri.

20 Oglesby, *Lisa,* 6.

ing with him proceeds enough to ensure a modest profit for the first year's operations, and expectations for even greater gain in the future. The voyage, however, had not been an unqualified success. Aside from the Bissonette episode, the early part of the trip had gone well, and two experienced hands, Francois Le Compt, half-blood trader to the Kansas Indians, and John Colter, former hunter for Lewis and Clark, were picked up to augment the crew. The latter was a particularly fortunate addition as he had, after his early discharge from the Lewis and Clark expedition, joined two American hunters, Forrest Handcock and Joseph Dickson, in a fur trapping venture in the Rockies. That partnership had broken up in the spring of 1807, and Colter was headed home at the time he met Lisa on the river. The wilderness was in his blood, though, and when Lisa made an offer, Colter accepted, his knowledge of the country and sage counsel immediately became invaluable to the party.[21]

Real difficulties were encountered at the Arickara villages as the Rees, unpredictable and always dangerous, massed at the water's edge and forced the boats to land. Their aspect was hostile, but Lisa, with a judicious display of weapons and belligerency, cowed the natives, and managed to pass them in peace. One of the Mandan chiefs, farther upstream, also was disposed to be unfriendly, but was pacified without major incident. A large war party of Assiniboines was similarly intimidated by a show of strength as Lisa and his men successfully ascended the Missouri toward the mountains.[22] Strongly peppering his negotiations with demonstrations of power, Lisa gave his men an object lesson in Indian diplomacy, in the art of which he would continually prove a master.

---

21 The best account of Colter is contained in Burton Harris, *John Colter: His Years in the Rockies* (New York, 1952).

22 Henry M. Brackenridge, *Views of Louisiana, Together with a Journal of a Voyage up the Missouri River in 1811* (Pittsburgh, 1814) contains the story of this expedition.

With the season growing late, and probably prompted by the advice of Colter and Drouillard as well, Lisa left the Missouri at the mouth of the Yellowstone and followed that stream into the heart of Crow country. It was a wise decision, for the Crows already had learned of the white man's predilection for furs, had become adept at trapping, and were willing to trade.[23] At the confluence of the Yellowstone and Bighorn rivers temporary shelters were set up and the construction of Fort Raymond begun. By that time it was mid-November and the fall hunting season had been lost. To inform the Indians of his arrival, in hopes of obtaining by trade a portion of what he had lost to the lateness of the season, Lisa dispatched John Colter on his famous winter odyssey up the Wind River, over into Jackson's Hole, across the Tetons, and around present day Yellowstone Park back to Fort Raymond.[24] Colter located the main camp of Crows at the upper end of the Wind River Valley and the redoubtable Edward Rose was sent to them with a selection of goods to trade for their furs. Unfortunately, Rose gave way all his merchandise in the course of making himself popular, and returned to the post in the spring with empty hands.[25] Some trapping was done near the post during the winter, and much more in the spring, enough to earn a profit and to convince Lisa that he had been correct in utilizing white hunters rather than relying upon Indians to bring in furs.

This first experience satisfied Lisa that the methods he had initiated, together with some further refinements he had noted, would serve to extract a fortune in furs from the mountains. Needed now were trading posts along the Missouri to keep the natives pacified and the river open to

[23] Antoine Larocque, "Journal of Larocque . . . ," L. J. Burpee, ed., *Publications of Canadian Archives,* no. 3 (1910), 28.

[24] Harris, *Colter,* traces the route.

[25] Reuben Holmes, "The Five Scalps," Missouri Historical Society *Glimpses of the Past,* v.

traffic, and more trappers to force an entrance into the country of the hostile Blackfeet. More capital was obviously necessary, but Lisa, Menard, and Morrison were prepared to continue. As they made plans for another expedition, they extended the partnership to include George Drouillard, whose experience and ability certainly warranted the move.[26]

Lisa's initial success caused a change in attitude on the part of the old and established French traders in St. Louis. Heretofore they had considered Lisa an upstart interloper and had opposed his every move. Now, with their hegemony challenged, joining with the Spaniard seemed to be the only means of achieving a partial share in the northwest fur trade. As Lisa was looking for further backing, the two groups came together during the winter of 1808-1809. The result was the creation of the St. Louis Missouri Fur Company, a co-partnership of ten members, including Lisa, Menard, and Morrison, and Benjamin Wilkinson, Pierre Chouteau, A. P. Chouteau, Jr., Sylvestre Labbadie, Reuben Lewis, Andrew Henry, and William Clark.[27]

Although mutual interest brought the partners together, the articles of incorporation clearly indicated the distrust they evidently felt for one another. The activities of the company were severely restricted, and all of the partners, with the exception of the elected president, William Clark, were required to accompany the first expedition upstream in the spring of 1809. It was a true co-partnership they had formed, with all members bearing an equal share of the work, paying equal portions of the bills as they fell due, and dividing equally the profits as they came in. New capital was provided in the sum of about $40,000, and the future looked secure. There was, hopefully, a full season's catch

---

26 Bryan and Morrison Store, Kaskaskia Ledger D, 438, William Morrison Records, Reel 1, Microfilm, Illinois Historical Survey, Urbana, Illinois.

27 Oglesby, *Lisa,* 68.

waiting above as most of Lisa's original crew had remained in the mountains to trap, and, in addition, the company had concluded a contract with Governor Meriwether Lewis to return the Mandan chief, Shahaka, to his village, for which service they were to receive $7,000.[28] Thus a substantial income was expected that first year.

It was only that promise of ample and almost immediate returns which held the heterogeneous collection of traders together, and when the first voyage earned less than they had hoped, many lost heart. The first expedition of the St. Louis Missouri Fur Company seemed ill-fated from the beginning. Pierre Chouteau organized the 140 man militia contingent, charged with returning Shahaka and his entourage, while Lisa managed the trading section. About 350 men in all made up the combined party, the militia leaving St. Louis on May 17, about a month before the traders were ready to go. A substantial quantity of merchandise was procured, primarily from Pierre Chouteau, to stock the proposed posts along the Missouri. Lisa's trading party left in mid-June, very late in the year for river travel, and he was forced to push the men hard to make up time. The excessive labor demanded of the Americans caused them to desert in great numbers, and to stage at least one mutiny. Nonetheless, the first part of the voyage was successful. Shahaka was returned without difficulty, two posts were set up for the Sioux, one for the Arickaras, and company headquarters was erected at Fort Mandan, ten or twelve miles above the Gros Ventre village.[29]

However, the expected returns failed to materialize. Benito Vasquez met the company at the Mandan villages, and his was a gloomy report. The men had set out for beaver

[28] Articles of Agreement between Meriwether Lewis, Governor, and the St. Louis Missouri Fur Company, February 24, 1809, Chouteau Collection, Missouri Historical Society, St. Louis, Missouri.

[29] Letter, Pierre Menard to Adrien Langlois, October 7, 1809, Kaskaskia Papers, Missouri Historical Society, St. Louis, Missouri.

country immediately after Lisa's departure the previous summer, three men heading south to trap the "River of the Spaniards," while the rest, divided into small groups, pointed for the Three Forks of the Missouri, reputedly the richest beaver region in the West. Unhappily, it also was a region dominated by the ferocious Blackfeet Indians, antagonistic to all whites but particularly Americans after the incident in which Meriwether Lewis had killed two members of their confederation. The Indians had attacked in force, killing and robbing where they could, and had expelled practically all the trappers from the area.

The men had reformed at Fort Raymond, and, under the leadership of Charles Sanguinet and Jean Baptiste Beauvais, had gone south to trap the Green River. Vasquez had closed up the fort, caching all the equipment, and had gone to the Mandan villages carrying the proceeds for the year, fifteen beaver pelts and ten buffalo robes.[30] Champlain, trading with the Crows, was supposed to have about four packs of beaver, and perhaps the scattered hunters would bring in more, but it was not an altogether auspicious beginning.

But if the partners were discouraged, the men were undaunted. The four-member party, led by Casé Fortín, the last group known to be in the Three Forks region, had reported possession of twenty packs of beaver when last heard from in the fall of 1808, and Vasquez estimated they should have fifty if they were still alive. Those fifty packs of beaver, gathered in a single season, might be worth as much as $25,000, a fine fortune, even divided by four, so few of the men evinced a desire to turn back. The partners in council decided that Andrew Henry would take a land party directly to Fort Raymond, winter there, and move into Blackfoot country in force the following spring. Pierre Menard would take the boats and supplies to the same destination while Pierre Chouteau and Manuel Lisa re-

---

[30] *Ibid.*

turned to St. Louis to prepare the outfit for the following year.[31]

The partners arrived in St. Louis in the latter part of November 1809, and Lisa set out immediately to procure goods for the coming spring. No one on the river was more capable of selecting a trading outfit than Manuel Lisa. Through years of experience, he had acquired close knowledge of Indian needs and desires, and he fully understood the vagaries of Indian character. Thus Manuel was able to anticipate the yearly needs of the company with regard to each tribe, and his partners recognized this talent by always delegating that task to him. Lisa first went to Vincennes, where he picked up his friend, Touissant Dubois, and the pair continued on to Detroit. On the British side of the river, the two found goods readily available, but, due to President Jefferson's recently instituted embargo, they were not importable.[32] Thwarted at Detroit, Lisa continued on to Montreal in hopes of finding some way of getting the goods across the border, but was unsuccessful. He returned to St. Louis by way of Philadelphia and Pittsburgh in a vain effort to purchase suitable merchandise, but finally returned home empty handed. As a consequence, there was no company expedition in the spring of 1810, and the hunters in the mountains were left to their own devices.

It was an unfortunate situation all around. Not only were the trappers expecting new supplies, they desperately needed help. Andrew Henry, Pierre Menard, and the trappers guided by John Colter, had gone to Three Forks in the spring of 1810 as planned, and there had constructed a post. The Blackfeet met force with force and so harrassed the trappers that Henry was forced to abandon his fort. He took about eighty volunteers with him across the divide to the waters of the Columbia, while Menard took the rest back

31 *Ibid.*

32 Letter, Manuel Lisa to Pierre Chouteau, February 14, 1810, Chouteau Collection, Missouri Historical Society, St. Louis, Missouri.

to St. Louis. Menard's subsequent report, with its pessimistic outlook, the news of the loss of $12,000 in a fire which destroyed the post at Cedar Island,[33] and impending war between the United States and Great Britain, caused most of the partners to pull back, making things even more difficult for the men above.

Largely at Lisa's insistence, the company agreed, at a stockholders meeting September 10, 1810, to send a relief expedition upriver the following spring to aid Henry and his men, but the majority would permit no further expenditures to develop company holdings in the upper country. No more than $2,000 worth of goods was to accompany the relief upstream, not more than twenty-one men were to be hired for the voyage, and the total cost of boat, wages, provisions, etc., was to amount to no more than $4,750.[34] Lisa was distressed at this retrenchment, especially in view of the newly developed competition in St. Louis that winter. Wilson Price Hunt was in town recruiting men and purchasing supplies for John Jacob Astor's newly formed Pacific Fur Company, and was busy laying plans for a transcontinental expedition to establish a post at the mouth of the Columbia River. Although Hunt had no apparent designs on the territory claimed by the Missouri Fur Company, the presence of Ramsay Crooks and Robert McClellan, two old and bitter rivals of the Spaniard on the river, as partners in the Pacific Fur Company, caused Lisa to suspect that Astor was interested in the Rocky Mountain trade. After assessing the motley crew Hunt brought with him to St. Louis, Lisa was even more sure they were not going across the continent.

The severe competition for men and supplies over the winter drove prices upward and shortened tempers on both sides. Hunt got the jump by wintering most of his crew part

33 *Missouri Gazette,* May 10, 1810.

34 St. Louis Missouri Fur Company Ledger Book, 1809-1812, Missouri Historical Society, St. Louis, Missouri.

way up the Missouri, and got the rest away from St. Louis three weeks before the Missouri Fur Company was ready to sail, thus provoking one of the greatest keelboat races ever recorded. Lisa, traveling light and afraid his small party would be overwhelmed should the Sioux catch it on the river, intended to catch Hunt and travel in his company, making a combined force large enough to deter any marauding war party. Lisa also was worried that Crooks and McClellan might persuade their leader to incite the Sioux purposely against the Missouri Fur Company boat, something the two had claimed, without substantiating proof, Lisa had done to them a few years earlier.

By urging his men to almost superhuman exertions, working from dawn to late night, Lisa gradually gained on Hunt's slower moving five-boat flotilla. Arriving at the Omaha village the men were cheered to find they were only four days behind. Lisa sent an emissary ahead on horseback to ask Hunt to wait. Astonished to find his rival so close behind, the leader of the Astorians promised to wait at the Ponca village, but, fearing that Lisa might try to pass him and use the Indians to the advantage of the Missouri Fur Company, pushed ahead with all possible speed. Nonetheless, Lisa caught him on June 2, after an incredible two-month pull, and the joint party proceeded upstream. Although the first meeting was peaceful enough, trouble quickly developed as Lisa tried to persuade Pierre Dorion, Hunt's interpreter, to leave his employer and return to his former position with the Missouri Fur Company. The incident blew up all out of proportion, and bloodshed was only prevented through the intervention of two concerned bystanders, Henry M. Brackenridge, an American adventuring with Lisa, and John Bradbury, an English naturalist taking passage with Hunt. Nonetheless, all communication between the rival expeditions ceased, Lisa even sailing the opposite side of the river.

As they approached the Arickara villages some intercourse between the groups became imperative, and, again through the offices of Brackenridge and Bradbury, the leaders agreed to land their parties together and put up a show of friendship. The Rees brought the white men immediately into council, and Manuel was the first to speak. Allaying the fears of his adversaries, Lisa announced to the assembled Indians that the Astorians were his friends, and that he would consider any harm done to them as done to himself. Thereafter, tension between the parties decreased substantially, and Hunt, now planning to leave the river and strike overland, concluded an agreement whereby Lisa would purchase his boats and some of his equipment, part payment for which would be made in horses to be brought down from Fort Mandan. Lisa bade farewell to the Astorians, never expecting to see them again.[35]

In September, Andrew Henry and his haggard crew, or what was left of it, appeared with a number of packs of beaver and Henry related his doleful tale of trouble with the Blackfeet. Shortly thereafter the partners moved downstream, stopping at Cedar Island to rebuild the burnt-out post and reopen the trade with the Sioux. This post was most important in Lisa's plans as he saw the developing influence of the British along the Missouri and out into the plains, through the agency of the Shawnee, Tecumseh, and his brother, The Prophet. The hostility of the Missouri tribes, the Sioux in particular, could destroy the company's access to the upper country, and Manuel determined to keep those Indians loyal to the United States.

Shortly after his arrival at Fort Mandan, Lisa had dispatched Henry M. Brackenridge with a load of furs for St. Louis. Those proceeds, plus the beaver brought in by Henry's party, meant that the company's year had been

[35] A supplement to Brackenridge's account is in John Bradbury, *Travels in the Interior of America . . .* (Liverpool, 1817).

profitable, but the returns were nowhere commensurate with the risks involved. Yet the partners were unwilling to give up altogether, and decided upon reorganization as a means of solving their problems. Charles Gratiot was given the task of rebuilding and revitalizing the enterprise. The need for more capital was imperative, and Gratiot proposed to obtain it by offering a full partnership to John Jacob Astor, who had been long interested in striking up an association with a St. Louis firm. This suggestion failed to find favor, and Astor was not included when the articles of a new, limited partnership with a board of directors of three men, were signed on January 24, 1812. William Clark was elected president of the new board, with Manuel Lisa and Sylvestre Labbadie named the other directors. Public shares were issued to the amount of $23,000, but, to the dismay of the directors, the shares were never taken up.[36]

A further difficulty was encountered as agents of the company found that they could no longer make purchases on credit, and the directors called upon the membership to provide "Four hundred dollars Cash, and a credit of Six hundred dollars." The response to this appeal was negative, so William Clark and Manuel Lisa were forced to put up notes for $10,000, and Sylvestre Labbadie a note for $1,000, to keep the company solvent.[37] Lisa then mortgaged a large portion of his landholdings to Antoine and Pierre Carraby of New Orleans for $3,000 in cash to enable him to make a few purchases of merchandise. On top of financial difficulties, the company also had to meet the competition of another group outfitting in St. Louis that winter, the firm of Robert McKnight and James Baird, planning a foray to Santa Fe. Nonetheless, an expedition was organized, and Lisa prepared to lead it upstream in the spring of 1812.

It was a small party, two boats and $11,000 worth of trade

---

36 The articles of Agreement were published in the *Missouri Gazette*, February 2, 1812.

37 Oglesby, *Lisa*, 122-123.

goods, but the threat of war was real, and the partners hesitated.[38] The trip upriver was routine by this time, and proved uneventful. The Sioux showed their obvious pleasure at the arrangement Lisa had made with them the previous autumn, and, to keep them in an amicable mood, a new post was constructed and stocked with over $4,000 in merchandise. At the Arickara villages Lisa ran into trouble as the chiefs protested his proposal to remove the trading house from the villages because of the poor profit it had produced over the past season. He persisted, and the Rees finally agreed to the construction of a new establishment about twelve miles above them.

Lisa found the general situation on the upper river extremely volatile. British agents had made further inroads into the loyalties of the Missouri tribes during the previous winter, and, while the Rees remained friendly, the rest of the Indians were severely agitated. The usually agreeable Gros Ventre had killed two American hunters and had run off twenty-six company horses. Manuel made a special trip to recover the lost horseflesh, but the Gros Ventre chief, Le Bourgne, refused to make restitution. This was indicative of the whole atmosphere of hostility which hung about Fort Manuel the entire winter.

Aside from sending Charles Sanguinet to find Champlain, Lisa sent out two trapping parties: seventeen men, led by Reuben Lewis, to the Little Horn; and Louis Lorimier, with four companions, to the Wind River country, and they, too, found antagonism wherever they traveled. A large number of Indians from various tribes camped continually outside the gates of the fort, but despite their numbers, trade was not particularly brisk. The Indians were sullen, and grew more so as winter began to melt into spring. Ulti-

38 The narrative of this voyage is in John C. Luttig, *Journal of a Fur Trading Expedition on the Upper Missouri, 1812-1813*, Stella M. Drumm, ed. (St. Louis, 1920).

mately, in early March, Lisa was forced to abandon the post and fall back downriver.

Upon his return, Manuel found the atmosphere in St. Louis no less hostile. Keenly disappointed at the few returns which had come down from above during the year, the partners, in Lisa's absence, had decided to curtail operations. Lisa had been removed from the board of directors and replaced by Pierre Chouteau, and the majority had decided that any additional risk of capital would be foolish. That meant they would use no more new funds but only the profits, if any, to finance future voyages. As the skins Lisa brought down to St. Louis did not even cover the costs of the previous year, let alone provide for a new expedition, a two-thirds majority of members, as required by the articles of incorporation, voted to call a meeting to dissolve the company. The proceedings finally were concluded, and the Missouri Fur Company came to an official end January 17, 1814.[39]

But while a majority of the partners saw no further possibilities on the Missouri, Lisa clearly grasped the fact that a fortune awaited the man who could sustain an effort in the Rocky Mountain fur country, and sought backing to prove it. He formed a partnership with a newly arrived Kentuckian, Theodore Hunt, and, using at least his old portion of the company's posts and equipment, planned another assault on the river in the fall of 1814. William Clark, as Indian agent, was delighted to see Lisa on the river, and quickly appointed him sub-agent for all the Missouri tribes above the Kansas,[40] and charged him with keeping those Indians, particularly the Sioux, loyal to the United States. With $1,335 in merchandise provided by the government, Lisa headed north in late August. By the time he reached

39 Missouri Fur Company Ledger Book, 1812-1814, William Clark mss., Kansas State Historical Society, Topeka, Kansas.

40 Letter, William Clark to John Armstrong, August 20, 1814, Clark Collection, Missouri Historical Society, St. Louis, Missouri.

the Omaha village, site of his own post, now called Fort Hunt, ice had closed the river and Lisa was forced to winter there.

While at this post, Manuel literally wedded the Omahas to the American cause by taking to wife Mitain, dusky daughter of one of the principal Omaha chiefs. This act, of course, also insured the majority of Omaha trade to his post. The following spring Lisa met with the Teton and Yankton Sioux, and those tribes agreed to launch an attack on their brother Santees, who had joined the British, as soon as practicable. The campaign was not exactly a success, but it did keep the Santees home guarding their rear flank, and rendered them useless for British service. Lisa then brought back to St. Louis several of the chiefs and principal men of the various tribes. From there the Indians were taken to Portage des Sioux where treaties of friendship were signed with the United States.[41]

Manuel completed his important services to the government, which many said were crucial in keeping the western tribes loyal to the United States during the War of 1812, by the spring of 1816, and he once again attempted to find the funds with which to return to the mountins. On June 29, 1816, Manuel advertised in the Missouri *Gazette* for "Those gentlemen desirous of hearing Proposals for a Company for trading up the waters of the Mississippi and Missouri" to attend a meeting he had called for that night.[42] The appeal fell upon deaf ears, and Lisa's association with Hunt continued for another season. It proved to be a good one, as Lisa brought into St. Louis in June 1817, $35,000 in peltries, but the Hunt-Lisa combination terminated by prior agreement that same month.

Although Lisa now appeared to be on his own, and so operated during the 1817-1818 season, a new organization

[41] Richard Peters, ed., *The Public Statutes at Large of the United States of America*, VII (Boston, 1861) has copies of these treaties.

[42] *Missouri Gazette*, June 29, 1816.

was being formed to tap the trade of the Upper Missouri, and Lisa hoped it would be the vehicle to take him back to the mountains. The firm, known as Cabanné and Company, included two old line St. Louis merchants, Jean Pierre Cabanné and Bernard Pratte, William Clark's nephew, John O'Fallon, the partnership of Berthold and Chouteau, Theodore Hunt, and Manuel Lisa. Highly capitalized, on paper, this organization proved to be a highly temporary affair as O'Fallon early made arrangements to drop out in the spring of 1819. Lisa, put in charge of his first love, field operations, took the company expedition northward in the fall of 1818, bidding farewell to his recent bride, Mary Hempstead Keeney. The first Mrs. Lisa had died February 20, 1818, and, in the frontier manner, Lisa quickly had remarried. He returned, however, in the spring of 1819, unhappy over the terms of agreement, particularly the value of the Lisa-Hunt partnership absorbed into the larger entity. Manuel apparently wanted some compensation for the excellent reputation he carried among the Indians, and Cabanné was loath to give it. In any case, Manuel was divested of his position and the upriver command was offered to Michael Immel, a longtime Lisa employee. Immel, and a number of other Missouri Fur Company men, refused to be a part of the organization without Manuel, so Cabanné and Company was dissolved by mutual consent in June 1819.[43]

From this distressing experience, Lisa moved into the formation of his last effort, one more Missouri Fur Company. Leaving the details of the arrangement with Stone and Company to Hempstead and Pilcher, Manuel went upriver with what supplies he had to the post with the Omahas, and spent some time preparing the Indians for the arrival of the government's ill-fated Yellowstone Expedition. The federal contingent got as far as Council Bluffs, where it

[43] Oglesby, *Lisa*, 168-70.

went into winter quarters, and the traders and soldiers entertained each other with dinners, dances, and other affairs until spring. These were noteworthy as the traders provided white women as hostesses. Mary Lisa and an unknown companion had accompanied Manuel, thus becoming the first white women to ascend the Missouri.[44]

Lisa returned to St. Louis in the spring suffering from some malady serious enough to cause him to hire a lawyer to put his papers in order. Whatever the illness, it grew worse as the summer progressed, and he finally sought relief at the sulphur springs, where the illness proved fatal. He was interred in the Hempstead burial plot, now a part of Bellefontaine Cemetery, St. Louis. The company struggled on for a few years after his death, but never was able to overcome the many obstacles it encountered.

In his long and active career, Manuel Lisa made numerous significant contributions to the development of the fur trade and the American West. His services to the United States during the War of 1812 were invaluable in keeping the western tribes peaceful and friendly, and the exploratory work of his men, John Colter and George Drouillard in particular, provided much of the early geographical knowledge of the Northwest. But more than that, Lisa laid down the principles for the successful operation of the fur trade in that area. Trade with the river tribes was essential to keep their friendship and thus keep the great Missouri highway open to traffic, but the real profits, he saw, were in the mountains. There groups of white trappers, working out of permanent posts, would bring in valuable pelts, while yearly expeditions supplied them from St. Louis. In his debt stand all those men who later utilized these principles to glean the fortune he so long sought.

[44] Mrs. Eliza Hempstead Cooke, "Account of Mrs. Manuel's Trip up the Missouri," typescript, Missouri Historical Society, St. Louis, Missouri.

Pierre Chouteau, Junior

by Janet Lecompte
Colorado Springs, Colorado

Pierre Chouteau, Junior, was born January 19, 1789, at St. Louis, the second son of Pierre Chouteau and the grandson of the founder of St. Louis, Pierre Laclède Liguest. For at least a century the Chouteaus were the leading family of St. Louis – a clan whose many intermarriages produced a tight core of social and business eminence. If one wished to make a name or a fortune in St. Louis, it was best to be born a Chouteau, and to marry another, as did Pierre Chouteau, Junior.

Young Pierre's mother was Pelagie Kiersereau, an orphan and only child reared by her grandfather, Joseph Taillon. She married Pierre Chouteau on July 26, 1783, and died ten years later, leaving four children, Auguste Pierre, Pierre Junior, Paul Liguest and a daughter Pelagie. A year after his wife's death in 1793, her widower married Brigitte Saucier who presented him with five more sons, François Gesseau, Cyprian, Louis Pharamond, Charles and Frederick.[1] Most of them became fur traders, which is not surprising for at that time the fur trade was the town's only business.

Of Pierre Chouteau's eight sons, it was young Pierre who inherited his father's name as well as his nickname "Cadet," referring to a second-born son. He also inherited his father's shrewdness and diligence, and his lust for wealth and

[1] Frederic L. Billon, *Annals of St. Louis in Its Territorial Days* (St. Louis, 1888), 168-69.

power.[2] But the son's ambition came not altogether from the father, nor in any part from the placid, frivolous creole society of his heredity. It came from the new materialism of the nineteenth century, and from its first behemoth exponent, John Jacob Astor. The interest in Chouteau's character lies in the conflict between the gentle, home-loving creole he was, and the grasping American tycoon he became.

Educational advantages in the village of St. Louis were meager, but young Cadet managed to learn whatever mathematics were necessary for a fur trader, and to write a handsome and legible hand. He also learned to read and speak English, but he so much preferred his native French that he stubbornly wrote all his letters in that language, to the annoyance of his non-Gallic correspondents. At maturity he looked and acted the aristocrat he was – tall, erect, black-eyed and black-haired. In repose he was often grave and contemplative, but in conversation, animated and cheerful. His personality was well-integrated. Seldom does his correspondence reveal a flash of temper or a sough of self-pity. His manner was unfailingly gracious, easy and affable with everyone, from the political leaders of the country to the lowliest boatman, yet he was resolute and, when necessary, politely ruthless. He commanded deference from all who knew him and a well-founded fear from those who opposed him.[3]

At about the age of fifteen, or since "earliest manhood" as he says in his Last Will and Testament, young Cadet en-

2 For contemporary estimates of the senior Chouteau's character, see James Wilkinson's letter of Nov. 26, 1805, and Albert Gallatin's of Aug. 20, 1804, in Donald Jackson, *The Journals of Zebulon Montgomery Pike* (Norman, 1966), I, pp. 209, 251; and other letters in *The Life and Papers of Frederick Bates,* ed. Thomas Maitland Marshall (St. Louis, 1926), I, pp. 45-47, 86-92.

3 Biographical sketch of Pierre Chouteau, Junior, by Pierre Chouteau, ms., Chouteau Collection, Missouri Historical Society, St. Louis; William Hyde and Howard L. Conard, eds., *Encyclopedia of the History of St. Louis* (New York, 1899), I, pp. 363-64; "Address of Hon. Elihu B. Washburne . . .", Jefferson City, 1881, Missouri Hist. Soc.

gaged in the fur trade, first as a clerk in his uncle Auguste's office [4] and then as a trader to the Osage Indians, among whom his father had traded since youth and made a small fortune. Cadet was at the Little Osage village as early as September 1806, when he sold Zebulon Pike a horse. As "Peter Chouteau jr" he was issued a license on September 26, 1807, to trade with the Great and Little Osage and went up the Missouri and Osage rivers with two boatloads of merchandise to spend the winter with these Indians. In the spring he returned, his trade no great success.[5]

While Cadet was thus engaged, his father and elder brother Auguste accompanied an expedition up the Missouri to return to his village the Mandan Chief Shehaka, brought east by Lewis and Clark. The expedition was turned back by hostile Arikaras and the project abandoned until 1809, when a successful attempt to return the chief was again led by Cadet's brother and father. In their absence, Cadet was left in charge of his father's business, which he handled with great seriousness. He even presumed to write the Secretary of War a respectful but firm letter defending his father from charges of dereliction of duty as Osage Indian Agent in undertaking the mission up the Missouri.[6]

In early spring 1810, Cadet left St. Louis to go five hundred miles up the Mississippi to the present site of Dubuque, Iowa. There Julien Dubuque had bought land from the Fox Indians in 1788 and mined lead with their labor. The Span-

---

[4] J. Thomas Scharf, *History of Saint Louis City and County* (Phila., 1883), I, p. 183; but H. M. Chittenden, *The American Fur Trade of the Far West* (N.Y., 1902), I, p. 382, says he started out in his father's office.

[5] Jackson, *Z. M. Pike,* I, p. 312n; *Life of Bates,* I, pp. 202-03; Richard Edwards and M. Hopewell, M.D., *Edwards's Great West and her Commercial Metropolis* (St. Louis, 1860), 537.

[6] Letter of Pierre Chouteau *fils* to the Secretary of War, Sept. 1, 1809, in Clarence Edwin Carter, ed., *The Territorial Papers of the United States,* XIV (Wash., D.C., 1949), 312-19. See Nathaniel Pryor to William Clark, St. Louis, Oct. 16, 1807, in Donald Jackson, ed., *Letters of the Lewis and Clark Expedition* . . . (Urbana, 1962), 432-37, for evidence that Pierre Jr. was not on the first expedition up the Missouri, as several historians have assumed.

ish government had granted Dubuque the land in 1796 and Auguste Chouteau had bought half of it, or 72,324 acres, in 1804, with the provision that on Dubuque's death all the property would revert to Chouteau and his heirs. Cadet, intending to manage his uncle's share of the business, found on arrival in April that Dubuque had died three weeks earlier. He was greeted with respect and affection by the Indians, and continued to live there off and on until the start of the War of 1812, when he returned to St. Louis. He retained an interest in the lead mines and the acreage around them until the United States courts denied his claim to them in 1845 and an appeal ended unfavorably in 1854.[7]

In 1813, at the age of twenty-four, Cadet opened a store in St. Louis with Bartholomew Berthold, a highly-educated gentleman from the Italian Tyrol who had come to the United States as a merchant in 1798 and had kept a store in St. Louis from 1809 until 1812. On May 1, 1813, Berthold & Chouteau began selling crockery, hardware, dry goods and groceries purchased at Baltimore and Philadelphia, in a two-story building at 11 North Main (St. Louis's first brick building).[8] It was no coincidence that Cadet's partner was his brother-in-law (Berthold had married Pelagie Chouteau in 1811), for creole St. Louisans regarded their relatives with the greatest loyalty and affection and kept their businesses closely held within the family. Not until Cadet

7 "Petition to the Senate and House of Representatives of the U.S. setting forth rights of claimants to tract of land known as Dubuque Mines," Jan. 10, 1837, Chouteau Coll.; Carter, *op. cit.*, XIV, pp. 73-75; "Dubuque Claim. Memorial to the Hon. the Senate and House of Representatives of the United States of America . . . Praying for the confirmation of the title to a tract of land granted to Julien Dubuque by the Baron de Carondelet . . . on the 10th of November, 1796. St. Louis, 1845," Chouteau Coll.; Richard Herrmann, *Julien Dubuque, His Life and Adventures* (Dubuque, 1922), 47, 56. Scharf and Chittenden place Cadet at the lead mines in 1806-1808; Stella Drumm, in 1808, (in her sketch of "Pierre Chouteau," *Dictionary of American Biography,* IV (1929), pp. 93-4); and Charles P. Chouteau's obituary, in 1806, (*St. Louis Globe-Democrat,* Jan. 6, 1901).

8 Billon, *op. cit.*, 127, 129, 234; Scharf, *op. cit.*, 150, 196; Carter, *op. cit.*, XIV, p. 791, and XV (1950), p. 85.

had been in business for many years and suffered many disappointments did he choose business associates outside his family.

Nor was there any need for Cadet, in a family with as many connections as the Chouteaus, to seek a wife of another lineage; and he chose his first cousin. On June 15, 1813, six weeks after the opening of the new store, he married Emilie Anne Gratiot, twenty-year-old daughter of Charles Gratiot and Victoire Chouteau,[9] and in so doing strengthened his relationships with useful men on his wife's side of the family – her sister Julie's husband, Jean P. Cabanné, who was to be Cadet's partner for many years, and Emilie's brother Charles who was to be a general in the United States Army and of great value to Cadet during his lobbying years in Washington.

Unfortunately we have no portrait of Emilie Gratiot Chouteau. She may have been beautiful like her sister Isabelle DeMun, or she may have been elegant and charming like her sister Julia Cabanné. Even if she were neither beautiful nor stylish, Emilie was a delightful woman. Bouncy and good-natured, she was blooming with health and seldom affected by the constant illnesses that attacked nearly everyone else in that era, and particularly her husband. Friends and family were her exclusive concern, and they kept her busy. Wrote her son-in-law Sanford in 1838 with affectionate amusement: "Mother is now occupied in arranging her new carpets – all Bustle and if it was not that, it would be something else *equally pressing*. Occupation. Occupation. Action! Action! I cannot imagine what would become of her without it."[10] Above all, Emilie was the soul of kindness and her family adored her. "Go often to kind Emilie's,"

[9] Billon, *op. cit.*, 170. Stella Drumm in the *Dictionary of American Biography* sketch says they were married in the church on Aug. 13, 1814, the earlier marriage being a civil one.

[10] John F. A. Sanford to P. Chouteau Jr., Jan. 12, 1838, Chouteau Coll.

wrote Jules DeMun to Isabelle in 1816,[11] and in a letter addressing Emilie as "My Dearest Mother," Sanford thanks her for her "unvarying kindness to me & mine." [12] To Cadet she was "my beloved wife and companion" for nearly fifty years of marriage.[13] They had five children born in the family home at Main and Vine, three of whom survived infancy: Emilie, born February 3, 1814; Julia, born February 18, 1816; Pierre Charles born December 25, 1817, died 1818; Charles Pierre, born December 2, 1819; and Benjamin Wilson, born August 17, 1822 and died soon after.[14]

The little firm of Berthold & Chouteau was the foundation of the great fur company that dominated the west for half a century. For the first year or so, it was merely a store on the main street of St. Louis. Then, inevitably, it slipped into the fur trade. In 1814 the company sent traders to the Otoes, Pawnee Loups and Pawnees on the Platte and Missouri rivers,[15] and in 1815 it outfitted Cadet's older brother Auguste Pierre and brother-in-law Jules DeMun for an expedition to the Rocky Mountains at the sources of the Platte and Arkansas rivers, to trade with the Arapahos, Comanches and other Indians. The expedition ended in such financial misery that Cadet never again trusted the mountain part of the fur trade.[16]

A. P. Chouteau and Jules DeMun returned to St. Louis in September 1817, and established the firm of Chouteau, DeMun & Sarpy, the latter being John B. Sarpy, nineteen-year-old cousin of the Chouteaus. By September 1818, DeMun had dropped out and Chouteau had borrowed a

11 *Bulletin,* Mo. Hist. Soc., XXVI, no. 1 (Oct. 1969), 29.

12 Sanford to Emilie Chouteau, Feb. 22, 1839, Chouteau Coll.

13 Last Will and Testament of Pierre Chouteau, Jr., 17 August 1865, copy in Mo. Hist. Soc.

14 Oscar W. Collet, *Index to St. Louis Cathedral and Carondelet Church Baptisms* (St. Louis, 1918); Billon, *op. cit.,* 171.

15 Carter, *op. cit.,* XIV, p. 791.

16 See sketch of "Jules DeMun," this *Series* vol. VIII.

large sum of money from Berthold & Chouteau to continue business as Chouteau & Sarpy in Berthold & Chouteau's new brick building. Chouteau & Sarpy was dissolved in 1821, but A. P. Chouteau never paid his debt to Berthold & Chouteau. In 1838 Cadet sued his brother for everything he owned, and won.[17] What bitterness and disillusionment surrounded this break in family relations will probably never be known, for if there were family letters about it, they seem to have disappeared.

In the early years, Berthold & Chouteau's principal opponent in the St. Louis mercantile business was Jean P. Cabanné & Co., whose senior partner was related to the partners of Berthold & Chouteau. Family gatherings in this era must have been carefully controlled affairs to maintain peace among the guests. When Bernard Pratte, grandson of Cadet's aunt Pelagie joined Cabanné in 1816, a family merger would seem to have been indicated, but it was six years in coming. On January 30, 1819, a newspaper advertisement announcing the dissolution of Cabanné & Co. was signed by "Pr. Chouteau Jr.",[18] but Cabanné did not immediately join Berthold & Chouteau, except for one brief, dismal venture. In 1819 a large expedition led by Manuel Lisa was financed by Berthold & Chouteau and by Cabanné, among others. The expedition returned before reaching the mountains because its leader was afraid his partners were doing him out of his just profits in his absence. Berthold & Chouteau had put in $22,286.45 and Cabanné $14,929, most of which was lost, and the joint venture came to an abrupt end.[19]

After that, competition in the fur trade based at St. Louis

---

17 Notice of dissolution of partnership, Sept. 14, 1818, in *Missouri Gazette,* Oct. 2, 1818; Billon, *op. cit.,* 129, 143, 152; Scharf, *op. cit.,* I, pp. 582-83; #1439 (Auguste P. Chouteau), Probate Court, St. Louis County, Mo.

18 "Reminiscences of General Bernard Pratte, Jr.," *Bulletin,* Mo. Hist. Soc., VI, no. 1 (Oct. 1949), 59-61; newspaper advertisement, Lisa Papers, Mo. Hist. Soc.

19 Richard Edward Oglesby, *Manuel Lisa and the Opening of the Missouri Fur Trade* (Norman, 1963), 168-71.

grew like weeds in a vacant lot. The vacuum created by the demise of Cabanné & Co. was quickly filled by the Missouri Fur Company whose principals, all intelligent and forceful men, were Lisa, Joshua Pilcher, Lucien Fontenelle, Andrew Drips, William Vanderburgh and Charles Bent. This company was highly successful at charging up the Missouri and establishing trading posts.[20] Berthold & Chouteau, rising timidly to the challenge, sent Joseph Brazeau ("Cayowa") to establish a post near Cedar Island in present South Dakota, but the rest of its posts in 1819 were far closer to home: François Chouteau's near the mouth of the Kansas River, Paul Liguest Chouteau's at the Osage village, Robidoux's and Papin's at the Nishnabotna, Sylvestre Pratte's and Baronet Vasquez's near the Omaha village.[21] By 1823 the company had other little posts on the Missouri besides Fort Cayowa – at the Poncas (under Pascal Cerré), at the Arikaras (under Citoleux) and among the various Sioux divisions, the Saones (under Sire and Brazeau), Oglallas (under Gratiot), Yanktons (under Pescay) and Santee (under Defont) – which altogether that winter turned out 877 packs of buffalo robes and 1355 pounds of beaver.[22]

Opposition continued to mount. In 1822 William Ashley began sending his annual company of trappers to the Rocky Mountains with increasing success, and by 1824 high-priced beaver brought in traders' wagons from Santa Fe began reaching the St. Louis market. But worst of all – or best, as it turned out for Cadet, was the competition of John Jacob Astor. Since 1816, Astor's agents had bought a few furs from Cabanné & Co. and from Berthold & Chouteau, but it was not until 1822 that Astor's American Fur Company

20 For information about the Missouri Fur Company and other fur trade matters of general knowledge and interest not hereafter footnoted, see H. M. Chittenden's *American Fur Trade,* published in 1902 but still the best treatment, and LeRoy Hafen's useful summary in vol. I, this *Series.*

21 "Trade and Intercourse," *American State Papers,* Indian Affairs, vol. II, p. 202.

22 "Tableaux ou l'on expose la quantité de peleteries que chacque post a traite dans l'hiver 1823 au 1824," Chouteau Coll.

established a strong Western Department in St. Louis, which meant to sell all the goods and buy all the furs in the west.[23]

Thus it happened that Cadet began his lessons in cutthroat competition from one of its all-time masters, John Jacob Astor. On February 9, 1822, Bernard Pratte, now a partner in the reorganized firm of Berthold, Chouteau & Pratte, signed an agreement with Ramsay Crooks to sell to the American Fur Company buffalo robes at $2.75 apiece and deerskins at 33½¢ per pound, and to buy goods from it for a period of one year.[24] The arrangement was highly profitable for Cadet. On December 7, 1822, he received a book profit of $25,097.76, of which $16,053.65 was his third share of profits earned by Berthold, Chouteau & Pratte.[25]

From this time forward, year by year, Cadet and his associates would learn Astor's techniques: upon dissolution of a rival company, Cadet would take over its posts and men, territories and trade, allowing no fragment of the defunct company to attach to other rivals; opposing local suppliers would be confronted with vicious price wars; competition that could not be smashed, such as William Ashley's unique ventures, would be supplied with either goods or backing and the profits shared; political influence would be fully exploited, and liquor shamelessly sold to the Indians when necessary; traders would work on shares, so that the company would profit both from selling them goods and buying their furs, and their territories would be carefully divided. These were the principles behind successful fur trade management, and Cadet violated them only at his peril.[26]

By May 1823, J. P. Cabanné had joined Berthold & Chouteau, and the name of it was henceforth Bernard Pratte & Co. Cabanné took over the post at Council Bluffs as man-

[23] R. Crooks Letter Book, 1816-1820, Chouteau Coll; Kenneth Wiggins Porter, *John Jacob Astor, Business Man* (Cambridge, 1931), II, pp. 692-93, 717-18.

[24] Agreement in the Chouteau Coll.

[25] Journal D, Chouteau Coll.

[26] Some of these principles are elucidated in Porter, *Astor,* 815-38; others become evident in the present sketch.

ager of the lower Missouri trade; Berthold ascended the river in the fall of 1824 to take charge of upper Missouri posts; Bernard Pratte handled the external affairs of the company; and John B. Sarpy settled down in the counting house where he handled the St. Louis books and correspondence for the rest of his life. But over them all as general superintendent, his growing ability the crown and glory of the firm, was Pierre Chouteau, Junior.[27]

In the fall of 1824, Cadet and Emilie left their children in St. Louis and went to New York in their carriage with Bernard Pratte, undoubtedly to explore the possibility of a closer association with Astor's firm. After a three-week trip over foul and dangerous roads, Emilie found New York and its people very pleasant, and she would often accompany her husband there in the future. In the city they spent much time with Ramsay Crooks, who was soon to marry Bernard Pratte's daughter, Emilie, thereby earning the right to address Cadet as "mon cher cousin" in a warm and affectionate correspondence that lasted twenty years. Cadet and Emilie also went to Niagara Falls, which, if not entirely for business purposes, was apparently the last vacation Chouteau allowed himself. But no arrangement with the American Fur Company resulted from this journey.[28]

Astor would not have benefitted from an association with B. Pratte & Co. at this time. The St. Louis firm had still not mastered the mechanics of competition, and its traders were always lagging behind. The ineffective Cayowa had been replaced by Berthold as head of the upper Missouri operations, but Berthold was a weak and gentle person who was ignored by his clerks. Cabanné on the lower Missouri was neither cool enough nor quick enough to outguess the bright competition leaders. Only the traders among the Osages –

27 B. Pratte & Co. to O. N. Bostwick, St. Louis, May 26, 1823, and Cabanné to Chouteau, May 26, 1823, both in Chouteau Coll.

28 Crooks to P. Chouteau, Jr., Nov. 1, 1824 and Dec. 6, 1824, and Pierre Chouteau to P. Chouteau, Jr., Dec. 14, 1824, in the Chouteau Coll.

Cadet's brothers A. P. Chouteau and Paul Liguest Chouteau, and his cousin Pierre Melicourt Papin – were without serious competition, and only because fine peltry was scarce in their territory. Elsewhere the company was short of men with nerve and experience. To make profits it was forced to share ventures with other traders – with the Missouri Fur Company and with slippery old Joseph Robidoux, who, in the sheep's clothing of a B. Pratte & Co. employee, made his own expeditions in direct or indirect competition.[29]

B. Pratte & Co.'s worst mistake was its "Taos Adventure." In the fall of 1824, the company bought 1500 pounds of beaver trapped in the southwest, a pale fur that to their surprise sold better than the dark northern variety. Excited but cautious, the partners bought a one-third interest in Ceran St. Vrain's small outfit for trading with trappers in New Mexico in 1825, which earned them little. The following summer the company sent Sylvestre S. Pratte, Bernard's son, to Taos to take charge of nearly 120 free trappers who spread out in different parties hunting for two years from the Rio Grande to the Gila and as far north as the Platte River and Lake Utah. The business was a calamity, one of the parties under Michel Robidoux being massacred and the others bringing in few furs. Young Pratte died in the mountains in October 1827, but not before he had signed what Cadet disconsolately referred to as "these inexhaustible fur-drafts" which the company was forced to honor.[30] Historian H. M. Chittenden's judgement that Chouteau turned to profit everything he touched was far from true, especially in these early years.[31]

But his time was coming. In June 1826, Ramsay Crooks

29 See correspondence of J. P. Cabanné, Chouteau Coll; sketch of "A. P. Chouteau," this volume; Dale L. Morgan, *The West of William H. Ashley . . .* (Denver, 1964), 154, 156-67; J. Robidoux to P. Chouteau, Jr., March 15, 1825, Chouteau Coll.

30 W. B. Astor to O. N. Bostwick, Nov. 11, 1824, Chouteau Coll; David J. Weber, "Sylvestre S. Pratte," this *Series*, vol. VI.

31 *American Fur Trade*, I, p. 383.

was again in St. Louis proposing to all the partners of B. Pratte & Co. – Pratte, Cabanné, Berthold and Chouteau – a merger with the American Fur Company. They also discussed means of eradicating their most persistent competition, the Columbia Fur Company, a band of energetic Britishers including Kenneth McKenzie, William Laidlaw, Daniel Lamont and James Kipp, with an American named Tilton as front man. In 1822 this company began trading at St. Peters and by 1826 had worked westward to the Mandans, threatening the American Fur Company on the upper Mississippi and B. Pratte & Co. on the upper Missouri. The combined power of the two companies would be needed to stop the intruders.[32]

In the fall of 1826 Chouteau, after buying goods in Philadelphia and selling furs in New York, signed an agreement dated December 20, 1826, with John Jacob Astor, making B. Pratte & Co. the sole western agent of the American Fur Company. They agreed to make a joint concern of their two St. Louis fur companies, sharing equally in profit and loss. The American Fur Company would furnish all supplies, collecting 7% interest on all disbursements and 5% commission on all goods imported from England, and on all charges, including transportation and insurance and the 60% duty charged on woolen goods. No commission was to be charged on American goods. B. Pratte & Co. would offer its whole collection of furs to the American Fur Company. If Astor did not choose to buy them, they would be sold by Astor at a commission of 2½%. If not sold by September 25 of each year, they would be offered at public sales held in October or at reduced prices in April. Pierre Chouteau, Junior, was to be agent of the American Fur Company, general superintendent of the business and director of affairs in the Indian country at an annual salary of $2000 and travel-

32 Porter, *Astor,* 745-53.

ing expenses. Bernard Pratte was to act in his stead in case of illness (Cadet was frequently and severely ill during this period) or absence from St. Louis. Berthold and Cabanné were to remain in charge of the Sioux country and Council Bluffs respectively at a salary of $1200 apiece. The new company would begin on July 1, 1827, or with the outfit for that year, and continue for four years, or until the returns of 1831.[33]

Now the little family company of Berthold & Chouteau, a French creole organization of limited imagination and effectiveness, was backed by the country's biggest monopoly. The power and wealth of Pierre Chouteau, Junior, may be said to have begun in 1827, even though he had already been in the fur business for twenty years.

The immediate advantage of Chouteau's 1826 association with the American Fur Company was the acquisition of strong and capable men to lead his enterprises. In the summer of 1827 the Columbia Fur Company succumbed, even though their traders had out-maneuvered B. Pratte & Co. traders all along the river that spring. The American Fur Company took it over intact with its men and trading posts; henceforth it was called the Upper Missouri Outfit ("U.M.O."), and operated from the mouth of the Big Sioux River to the mountains. Kenneth McKenzie was paid $2000 a year as its head. William Laidlaw, James Kipp and Daniel Lamont each managed a trading post and its trading parties, and they were all excellent men. In September 1828, the Missouri Fur Company fell apart. Joshua Pilcher remained in the mountains; Charles Bent soon afterward abandoned the upper Missouri for the Arkansas; but Lucien Fontenelle, Andrew Drips and William Vanderburgh signed up with the American Fur Company and became partisans or bri-

[33] Articles of agreement, with letter of P. Chouteau, Jr., New York, Dec. 21, 1826, to B. Pratte & Co., Chouteau Coll.

gade leaders of trappers in the mountains, and they, too, were all excellent men.[34]

There was still William Ashley who, as Chouteau wrote, "is always in my way."[35] In 1826 Ashley had brought more beaver out of the Rocky Mountains than anyone knew existed. When Ashley made Chouteau a proposition for the summer of 1827 to furnish goods and buy furs for Ashley's successors, Smith, Jackson & Sublette, Chouteau accepted. The expedition was highly profitable and Chouteau, for a time, forgot his distrust of trapping and was eager to send a party like Ashley's to the mountains under Kenneth McKenzie. But prudence or fear prevailed, and McKenzie remained on the Missouri to build a post (later called Fort Union) at the mouth of the Yellowstone as a base of operations and a headquarters for his outfit.[36] During the 1830s there were many hundreds of American Fur Company men divided into outfits – at Fort Union, Fort Clark, Fort Pierre; among the Oglalla, Huncpapa, Saone, Yancton, Yanctonnais and Brulé divisions of the Sioux; at the Sacs, Iowas, Osages, Kansas, Poncas, Otoes and Rees; at White River, Cherry River, Bois Blanc, Platte and Vermillion.[37] And there were traveling salesmen who sold goods to free trappers in the mountains. In the summer of 1829 McKenzie sent Etienne Provost to gather in trappers at a predetermined rendezvous to trade their furs for goods with William Vanderburgh. Thus began ten years of such "mountain business" which Cadet thought was a waste of men and money from beginning to end. The company never arrived on time at the rendezvous with its goods, thereby losing most of the trade, and some of its finest men, including

34 Chittenden, *op. cit.*, I, p. 330n; Cabanné to Chouteau, Oct. 14, 1828, Chouteau Coll.

35 P. Chouteau, Jr., New York, Dec. 21, 1826, to B. Pratte & Co., St. Louis, Chouteau Coll.

36 P. Chouteau, Jr., to McKenzie, Sept. 28, 1827, and Crooks to Chouteau, July 2, 1828, Chouteau Coll.

37 Journal v, Chouteau Coll.

Vanderburgh, were killed by Indians. These expeditions, as Chouteau wrote Astor in 1833, were an annual financial loss, but they were continued until 1839, for the company could not afford to abandon the mountains to its rivals.[38]

The concomitant of a healthy business is rivals, and Cadet's company always had its share. One was Joseph Robidoux, whom Cabanné bought out in 1828, paying him $1000 a year to stay in St. Louis for two years.[39] A shaky little organization known as Papin & Co., or the French Fur Co., was bought out in October 1830, for the sum of $21,000. To keep its leaders from forming another company, two of them – Pascal Cerré and Honoré Picotte – were hired for $1000 a year, a generous salary for men whose fidelity the company had no reason to trust.[40] The most dangerous competition of these years was Smith, Jackson & Sublette (after 1830 the Rocky Mountain Fur Co.) whose experienced partisans were followed by Drips, Fontenelle and Vanderburgh to their secret sources of beaver, or sometimes to a nest of murderous Blackfeet, as when Vanderburgh was killed.

As general superintendent of the company, Chouteau had other matters to deal with as well. One was his own frequent illness, which in late 1827 was so debilitating that he asked Crooks to replace him as St. Louis agent of the company. Crooks could not leave New York, and by February 1828, Chouteau was feeling well enough to face other problems of the year, such as Bartholomew Berthold. In the fall of 1827, Berthold had lied to the customs people about some imported beads. Because of this and Chouteau's illness, the other partners briefly considered dissolving the company.

38 Chittenden, *op. cit.*, I, pp. 365-66.

39 Cabanné to P. Chouteau, Jr., Oct. 14, 1828, Chouteau Coll.

40 Theodore Papin to P. M. Papin, Feb. 24, 1831, Chouteau Coll. Crooks warned Chouteau of the "endless number of spies you have around you – there are perhaps more Papins and Picottes in your service than you are aware of. . ." (Crooks to Chouteau, Feb. 23, 1834, Chouteau Coll.).

There were other worries – the settlement with the Columbia Fur Company which dragged on because the appraisal of their upper Missouri inventory had been too high, and the company's new retail store in St. Louis which was built cockeyed – the architect miscalculated the ground level.[41]

Along with the burdens of a growing business, Chouteau occasionally garnered his share of glory. In 1830 the inventive Kenneth McKenzie proposed a steamboat to haul goods to and from the upper Missouri (one was already making the run between St. Louis and Fort Leavenworth). Chouteau adopted the idea with alacrity, bought a boat in Pittsburgh for $7000 or $8000 and boarded it, all enthusiasm, when it left St. Louis for the upper Missouri on April 16, 1831. Although the boat was optimistically named the "Yellow Stone," low water kept it for days at the Ponca post and it went no farther up the river than Fort Tecumseh. Undismayed, Chouteau again boarded it next spring in company with his future son-in-law John F. A. Sanford, then upper Missouri Indian Agent, and the painter George Catlin. The boat left St. Louis on March 26, 1832, reaching the condemned Fort Tecumseh two months later, at which time Chouteau christened its successor "Fort Pierre." The boat went on to Fort Union at the mouth of the Yellowstone, finally justifying its name, and returned to St. Louis by July 7, doing a hundred miles a day. It was proclaimed a stunning achievement by the press and Chouteau was widely congratulated. Next season another boat, the "Assiniboine," went up the river and from then on there were always steamboats on the upper Missouri, until the railroads did the job more cheaply.[42]

---

[41] Letters from Ramsay Crooks to P. Chouteau, Jr., dated Feb. 15, 1828, Feb. 29, 1828, April 6, 1828, July 2, 1828, all in the Chouteau Coll.

[42] Chittenden, *op. cit.*, I, pp. 339-41; P. Chouteau, Jr., to William Renshaw, Pittsburgh, Nov. 25, 1831; P. Chouteau, Jr. to Gen. B. Pratte, Poncas River, May 31, 1831; J. J. Astor to P. Chouteau, Jr., Sept. 28, 1832; all in the Chouteau Coll., George Catlin, *Letters and Notes on the Manners, Customs, and Condition of the North American Indians* (London, 1841), I, p. 14.

Company steamboats gratuitously carried many scientists, artists and European adventurers to the upper Missouri region – Prince Maximilian of Weid-Neuweid in 1833 and 1834, J. J. Audubon in 1843, the Swiss artist Rudolph Friederich Kurz in 1850 and others, all of whom praised the generosity of the company in newspaper interviews and published reports. It was as good public relations as Chouteau could have hoped for in that era.

In the fall of 1831, Cadet and his wife went east not only to buy a steamboat and goods for the trade but also to see their daughter Emilie, who was ill at her convent school in Georgetown. The trip was miserable; Chouteau wrote home that he had caught a cold in Philadelphia and was homesick and worried about his daughter. When young Emilie was well enough to travel, they returned in a new coach and horses bought in Washington, arriving home in February. By November Emilie had recovered sufficiently to marry John F. A. Sanford. Two years later Sanford resigned as Indian Agent, and went to work for his father-in-law, who soon came to value the young man's loyalty and tactful handling of delicate affairs and angry opponents. Emilie died April 27, 1836, leaving a son, Ben, who became Cadet's favorite and badly-spoiled grandchild. John F. A. Sanford remained Cadet's right hand until Sanford's death twenty years later.[43]

Like all fur traders, the American Fur Company sold liquor to Indians, sparingly on the Missouri below the Mandans, abundantly above, to compete with the Hudson's Bay Company. William Clark, the sympathetic Superintendent of Indian Affairs at St. Louis, regularly issued the company

[43] P. Chouteau, Jr., to William Renshaw, Philadelphia, Jan. 6, 1832; P. Chouteau, Jr., to J. B. Sarpy, Washington, Feb. 6, 1832; Crooks to P. Chouteau, Jr., New York, Jan. 3, 1832, and Feb. 10, 1832; and P. M. Papin to P. Chouteau, Jr., Nov. 12, 1832; all in the Chouteau Coll. Marriage announcement in the *Missouri Republican,* Nov. 27, 1832; John F. A. Sanford to the Commissioner of Indian Affairs, Feb. 4, 1834, in Letters Received by the Office of Indian Affairs from the St. Louis Superintendency, National Archives; Emilie's obituary in the *Missouri Republican,* April 28, 1836.

permits for ample supplies of liquor "for the use of the boatmen." Then in July 1832, a bill passed Congress excluding spirituous liquors from the Indian country, whether intended for boatmen or Indians. In August 1832, government agents at Fort Leavenworth ignored William Clark's permit and destroyed over a thousand gallons of whiskey on board the "Yellow Stone." At the same time a rival trader named Leclerc passed Fort Leavenworth in his boat and was not thoroughly searched. Furious at this inequity, Cabanné sent his own men after Leclerc, who stopped the trader and seized his liquor. Leclerc returned to St. Louis to report the illegal arrest and seizure and sue the company. Chouteau finally settled with Leclerc for $9200, and Cabanné was banned from the Indian country for a year.[44]

In 1833 there was no liquor to be had on the Missouri. In desperation, McKenzie set up a distillery at Fort Union and made his own. Rival traders passing Fort Union on their way to St. Louis reported the distillery, and by the end of 1833, Chouteau was in Washington trying to explain to Indian Commissioner Elbert Herring that McKenzie had been making wine from the wild pears and berries of the region – an innocent botanical experiment and nothing more. Nobody was fooled, but such was the power of the company that the affair was dropped, after Chouteau promised he would conform to the law, as he had no intention of doing.[45] As he explained later, "it could not be expected that the traders should be very observant of the law, when the officers appointed to enforce [it] neglected to do so."[46]

In the spring of 1834, discouraged by ill health, John

[44] John Dougherty to William Clark, Nov. 10, 1831, in Letters Received, OIA from St. Louis Superintendency, which contains many documents describing this affair.

[45] Crooks to P. Chouteau, Jr., Feb. 23, 1834; Kenneth McKenzie to Crooks, Dec. 10, 1833, Fort Union Letter Book and other letters in the Chouteau Coll.; P. Chouteau, Jr. to William Clark, Nov. 23, 1833 and other letters in Letters Received, OIA from St. Louis Superintendency.

[46] P. Chouteau Jr. & Co. to Messrs. T. H. Harvey and T. G. Gantt, Jan. 12, 1842, in Letters Received, OIA from St. Louis Superintendency.

Jacob Astor retired from the American Fur Company, of which he owned 90% of the stock (Crooks and Robert Stuart owned 5% each). Crooks bought the Northern Department and called it the American Fur Company. B. Pratte & Co. bought the Western Department and called it Pratte, Chouteau & Co. The name change was long due. Berthold had died in 1831; Cabanné, though still a partner, had lost his status after the Leclerc debacle; Bernard Pratte was eastern agent for the company until he died in 1836; but it was plainly Pierre Chouteau, Junior, as the new St. Louis manager, who deserved to have his name on the door. The terms of the agreement were proposed by Ramsay Crooks in September and accepted by the middle of December:

> The American Fur Company will import from Europe, and purchase in the United States, all the supplies you require for your trade, the former at 12 months and the latter at the usual credit, for which we will charge you a commission of 2½ percent. We will sell all the Furs, skins and other property you may send to New York, or we will ship the same for sale abroad, for either of which modes of disposing of your goods, we will charge you a commission of 2½ percent. We will accept your Bills to such an amount as your business may require, and will charge you a commission of one percent on such part as you do not provide funds to meet. If you wish the sales of your goods guaranteed, we will do so, at the established customary rates. You will understand that the present proposition is provisional on the expectation of doing all your business . . . a limited portion of your affairs I would not engage to transact on these terms.[47]

So Astor bowed out, and without his guidance Cadet began making mistakes that would cost the company dearly. When Cadet was in New York in February 1834, he bought out the Missouri River forts and equipment of Sublette & Campbell, a company which had been organized in December 1832, with unlimited credit from William Ashley and Robert Campbell for both the Missouri River and moun-

[47] Crooks to Pratte, Chouteau & Co., Sept. 6, 1834 and December 20, 1834, American Fur Company papers in the New York Historical Society.

tain trade. After one unprofitable season on the Missouri, Campbell offered to sell out to McKenzie at Fort Union, if McKenzie would stay out of the mountains for a year. McKenzie refused, certain of his ability to drive Sublette & Campbell off the field, but when Sublette went to New York in February 1834, Chouteau accepted his offer. Chouteau promised Sublette to retire from the mountains for a year, which made it impossible for his company to supply Drips and Fontenelle, their mountain leaders. Cabanné was not quick enough with his offer of other employment, and at that year's rendezvous, Drips and Fontenelle joined with James Bridger, Thomas Fitzpatrick and Milton Sublette in Fontenelle, Fitzpatrick & Co., a formidable opposition. Chouteau's company was forced to buy them out at the 1836 rendezvous, after which the joint company became the Rocky Mountain Outfit which lost money for Pratte, Chouteau & Co. every year until it was dissolved in 1839.[48]

In 1835, Chouteau reorganized the business, and not to everyone's satisfaction. Out of the Upper Missouri Outfit territory he created a Sioux Outfit headed by Honoré Picotte, and he notified William Laidlaw at Fort Pierre not to send an outfit to the Platte, which now was in Sioux Outfit territory. Outraged at having his territory curtailed, Laidlaw quit and sold his share of the Upper Missouri Outfit to Jacob Halsey. Daniel Lamont also quit the company, sold his share to D. D. Mitchell in 1835, and then went into business with Peter and Joseph Powell as Powell, Lamont & Co., buying robes and beaver from the upper Arkansas River and Santa Fe, and providing stiff competition for Chouteau in those areas. Laidlaw also joined Powell, Lamont & Co., but sometime after Lamont's death in 1837 he

[48] J. C. Cabanné to Fontenelle, April 9, 1834, Drips papers, Mo. Hist. Soc.; Dale L. Morgan and Eleanor Towles Harris, eds., *The Rocky Mountain Journals of William Marshall Anderson* . . . (San Marino, 1967), 309-10.

returned to work for Chouteau.[49] Because of these and other signs of disaffection, Chouteau's administration was reported in 1836 to be "highly unpopular with the principal persons in the interior." Benjamin Clapp in the New York office attempted to analyze the difficulty: "I am inclined to believe that Mr. Chouteau has allowed his fears to be operated on by his opponents, that he has temporized, & undertaken to conciliate until he has gotten himself into pretty much of a snarl." [50]

Part of the trouble may have been Chouteau's preoccupation with Indian treaties, which caused him to spend much of his time away from St. Louis and from the direct management of his business. In the 1830s the government was eager to move Indians west of the Mississippi and give their lands to settlers, which it accomplished by treaties promising the Indians an annuity in cash or goods for their lands, and payment of their debts to traders. Since the debts to traders were those which fur companies had long ago written off as uncollectable, payment of them was like a donation from public funds, and well worth Chouteau's time and energy. He made a trip to the upper Mississippi to be witness on September 28, 1836, to a treaty with the Sacs and Foxes which allowed his company payment of a debt of over $20,000. This was the only treaty at which Chouteau was present, but some member of his firm attended all other treaties with Indians owing the company money, and their efforts eventually bore rich fruit. The Sioux treaty of 1837 allowed $90,000 for payment of all the traders' debts, and the Winnebago treaty of 1837 allowed $200,000. But actual payment of the debts was often years away from the signing

[49] Laidlaw to P. Chouteau, Jr., March (or May) 14, 1836 and Jacob Halsey to P. Chouteau, Jr., June 16, 1836, Chouteau Coll.; Annie Heloise Abel, ed., *Chardon's Journal at Fort Clark, 1834-1839* (Pierre, 1932), 219, n.67.

[50] Benjamin Clapp to Ramsay Crooks, Sept. 28, 1836, American Fur Company papers in the New York Hist. Soc.

of the treaty, and that was where Chouteau's work began.[51]

Directly after returning from the Sac and Fox treaty conference in September 1836, Cadet went east. In Pittsburgh he bought a new steamboat replacing the "Assiniboine" which had burned in 1835; in Philadelphia he bought goods; in Washington he petitioned for confirmation of title to the Dubuque claim.[52] He also lobbied for Senate confirmation of the Sac and Fox treaty – but in vain. In March 1837, he returned home. Scarcely a month later he was called east again to meet a crisis. In April 1837, the country was suffering a financial panic. Drafts were called in, companies failed, banks suspended specie payments. As a result, the Commissioner of Indian Affairs was threatening to pay Sac and Fox annuities not in specie as the treaty of 1832 specified, but in bank notes or merchandise. Chouteau objected with all his strength and voice. When he advised the Indians to accept nothing from the government but hard money, the government retaliated by threatening to legislate against traders' rights to advise Indians. Chouteau and Crooks talked in Washington with Indian Commissioner Harris in June, but they could not alter his intentions. On June 14, Chouteau started home again, to tell the Sac and Fox chiefs waiting in St. Louis that they would not receive their annuities in cash that year. Nor did the company receive payment of its Indian debts, either that year or until 1842, when a new Sac and Fox treaty allowed the company $112,109.47 for traders' debts.[53]

51 Charles J. Kappler, *Indian Affairs: Laws and Treaties* (Washington, 1904), II, pp. 476-78, 493-94, 498-500, 549.

52 J. Throckmorton to P. Chouteau, Jr., Pittsburgh, April 20, 1837, and "Petition to Senate and House of Representatives . . . setting forth rights of claimants to . . . Dubuque Mines," Jan. 10, 1837, Chouteau Coll.; John B. Whetten, New York, to Pierre Chouteau, Jr., Philadelphia, Mar. 9, 1837 (#2437); *Calendar of the American Fur Company's Papers,* American Historical Association, *Annual Report, 1944* (Washington, 1945), II, p. 276.

53 Pratte, Chouteau & Co. to American Fur Co., May 22, 1837 (#2605); Pratte, Chouteau & Co. to American Fur Co., May 29, 1837 (#2641); Henry H. Sibley to

On November 21, 1837, Chouteau left St. Louis for the third time that year, to spend four months lobbying in Washington for payment of debts owed the company by Sioux and Winnebagos, as provided for in treaties now awaiting Senate confirmation.[54] But it was years before the treaty money was appropriated and paid, and in the meantime Chouteau made many uncomfortable journeys in rocking, jolting coaches, and spent many months of many years in Washington and New York, talking endlessly to friends and enemies of the treaties and using every means, fair or foul, to achieve his ends. One of his friends whom he used shrewdly was Missouri Senator Thomas H. Benton. In March 1843, Senator Benton, who had strongly opposed the Sioux treaty confirmation, suddenly relaxed his opposition and voted for it – after talking to Chouteau and borrowing $1000 from him on favorable terms.[55] Benton served Chouteau in other ways, and not without profit. In 1851 he succeeded in obtaining payment of the claim of A. P. Chouteau and Jules DeMun against the Mexican government for $30,000 worth of goods confiscated in 1817. For Chouteau, who was beneficiary of the claim by this time, Benton got $81,772; for himself, 10% of that amount.[56]

The firm of Pratte, Chouteau & Co. terminated by limitation with the peltry returns of 1839. When Bernard Pratte

---

American Fur Co., Oct. 7, 1837 (#3277); American Fur. Co. to Joseph Rolette, June 9, 1837(#2674); American Fur Co. to Pratte, Chouteau & Co., June 17, 1837 (#2701); Pratte, Chouteau & Co. to American Fur Co., June 30, 1837 (#2768); all in *Calendar, A.F.C. Papers,* II, pp. 293, 297, 301, 304, 312, 360; Kappler, *Indian Affairs,* II, pp. 546-49.

54 Pratte, Chouteau & Co. to American Fur Co., Nov. 24, 1837 (#3560); American Fur Co. to Charles H. Gratiot, Dec. 30, 1937 (#3754); P. Chouteau, Jr., to Ramsay Crooks, Feb. 22, 1838 (#4022); *Calendar, A.F.C. Papers,* II, pp. 387, 403, 427.

55 William Nisbet Chambers, *Old Bullion Benton, Senator from the New West* (Boston, 1956), 263. Chouteau was in the east from May to July, 1839, from spring through the summer of 1841, and from November 1842, to March 1843. Chouteau Coll.

56 "Account of Money Received from the United States Government for Claim against the Mexican Gov^{t}. St. Louis June 12, 1851." Chouteau Coll.

died on April 1, 1836, Chouteau assumed full management of the company. Bernard Pratte, Junior, kept his father's interest until 1838, when he left the company to serve in the Missouri legislature. By 1838, other partners were John P. Cabanné, John B. Sarpy, J. F. A. Sanford, Pierre Menard and Felix Vallé. The new company, organized in May 1839, was known as P. Chouteau Jr. & Co. until it was sold in 1865. It was capitalized at $500,000, of which Cadet and his father (who lived until 1849) owned a little more than half. Other partners were, for once, of Chouteau's own choosing – Joseph A. Sire, John F. A. Sanford and John B. Sarpy, who each owned stock worth $80,000. Sire, long a steamboat captain on the upper Missouri, continued to manage that part of the business. Sanford was company lobbyist in Washington from 1837 to 1840 and manager of the New York office when it opened in 1841. Sarpy remained in St. Louis, in charge of accounts. In 1842 Kenneth McKenzie and Benjamin Clapp also became partners, but both had withdrawn by 1853.[57]

The organization of P. Chouteau Jr. & Co. in 1839 marked the end of the closely-held family business. Jean P. Cabanné withdrew from the company and applied that fall to Crooks in New York for goods to pursue the Indian trade in partnership with Bernard Pratte, Junior, in opposition to P. Chouteau Jr. & Co. His plans did not mature and he died in 1841 at odds with Chouteau's firm, but with good Emilie Chouteau at his bedside. Shortly after his death, his son John Charles Cabanné formed a company with Bernard Pratte, Junior, which opposed P. Chouteau Jr. & Co. on the Missouri and North Platte until 1845.[58]

[57] Pratte Chouteau & Co. to Crooks, July 9, 1839 (#6519), *Calendar, A.F.C. Papers*, II, p. 664; John E. Sunder, *The Fur Trade on the Upper Missouri, 1840-1865* (Norman, 1965), 5-6, 69. At the time of Sire's death in 1854 and Sarpy's in 1857, each owned 26% of the stock of the company (Sanford had retired from the firm in 1853) *ibid.*, 161. Just as Chittenden's work is my general source for the fur trade up to 1840, Sunder's book is my source for these later years.

The biggest change Cadet made in the company's operations was in finally terminating the mountain business with the returns of 1839. No longer could his trappers compete with those of the Hudson's Bay Company who ranged from the Pacific Ocean to within fifteen days' travel of St. Louis trading duty-free goods that were cheaper and better than American goods. And beaver, the principal crop of the mountains, was not only scarce but in small demand, as nutria and silk had all but replaced beaver in the tall hats then in fashion.[59]

The company's business henceforth was mainly in buffalo robes. Besides the upper Missouri, centers of that trade were the North and South Platte and the Arkansas, where Bent, St. Vrain & Co. traders had dominated since 1834. In 1836, P. Chouteau Jr. & Co. got a foothold on the North Platte by acquiring Sublette & Campbell's Fort Laramie (Fort William; Fort John) and in 1838 made a friendly pact with Bent, St. Vrain & Co. to stay off the South Platte if the other company would stay off the North Platte. Before long Bent, St. Vrain & Co. was buying its supplies, selling its furs and paying its employes at the St. Louis store of P. Chouteau Jr. & Co. Much of the company's income depended upon this independent subsidiary which regularly produced quantities of buffalo robes and a little Santa Fe beaver through the lean 1840s.[60]

The full force of the panic of 1837 hit the west in 1841. In June, Chouteau's London agent wrote desperately, "the

58 Bernard Pratte, Jr. to Crooks, Oct. 7, 1839 (#6898), and Geo. Ehninger to Bernard Pratte, Jr., Oct. 28, 1839 (#6990), *Calendar, A.F.C. Papers,* 698, 707; Sanford to P. Chouteau, Jr., & Co., June 28, 1841, Chouteau Coll.

59 Advertisement in the *Missouri Republican,* May 10, 1839, announcing termination of the mountain business; *Niles National Register,* Oct. 3, 1840, p. 68, c. 1.

60 Agreement between H. Picotte of Pratte, Chouteau & Co., and Ceran St. Vrain of Bent, St. Vrain & Co., July 27, 1838, Chouteau Coll.; ledgers CC, Z and DD all have records of goods bought by Bent, St. Vrain & Co. in 1838 and 1839, and ledger AA has a list of Bent men paid at P. Chouteau Jr. & Co. in St. Louis, as do subsequent ledgers.

fur trade is dead,"[61] for small-pox had ravaged the Indians, fur markets abroad were closing, prices had plummeted, money was tight, credit non-existent. Suddenly everybody wanted out of the business. From New York, Crooks wrote that his health demanded a change of occupation. From Prairie du Chien, Hercules Dousman wrote that he and his partners Joseph Rolette and Henry H. Sibley would like to sell their Western Outfit to Chouteau on agreeable terms. From St. Louis, Chouteau wrote that he wished to withdraw his personal supervision from the company, leaving it in younger hands.[62]

Crooks achieved his change of occupation the hard way. On September 10, 1842, the American Fur Company suspended payment under pressure of bad times and bad debts, and the great monopoly was no more. Dousman and Sibley (Rolette had died) solved their problem by selling their Western Outfit to Chouteau on July 18, 1842, in New York.[63] But Cadet's own wish took longer to fulfill, for the "younger hands" he had in mind were still a bit too young. Chouteau was certain, however, that his boy Charles would indeed take over the business in time.

Educated by the Jesuits at Florissant as a child, Charles was sent to the Peugnet School in New York City in 1834, at the age of fourteen, along with some Berthold and Cabanné boys and Crooks' three little girls. Crooks and his wife entertained the boys once a fortnight, lecturing them on the value of education. At eighteen, Charles' formal education ended, and in the summer of 1838 he left New York with Crooks to visit the company's posts at St. Peters and Prairie du Chien. When the arduous journey was finished,

---

61 C. M. Lampson to American Fur Co., June 16, 1841, (#11,044), *Calendar, A.F.C. Papers*, III, p. 1076.

62 Crooks to P. Chouteau Jr. & Co., Jan. 27, 1841, Chouteau Coll.; Hercules L. Dousman to American Fur Co., Jan. 20, 1841 (#10,137), *Calendar, A.F.C. Papers*, III, p. 993; Crooks to Chouteau, Jan. 27, 1841, Chouteau Coll.

63 *Niles National Register*, Oct. 1, 1842, p. 80, c. 1; American Fur Company to Charles W. Borup, July 18, 1842 (#12,973), *Calendar, A.F.C. Papers*, III, p. 1247.

Crooks pronounced Charles "an excellent young man." Back in St. Louis, Charles began four years of training in the firm of Chouteau & McKenzie, a wholesale mercantile house started in May, 1838, by his father and Kenneth McKenzie (who had sold out of the Upper Missouri Outfit, apparently to F. A. Chardon). Then Charles worked for a year in his father's New York office and two years in London and on the continent. He returned to St. Louis in 1845 and married his cousin Julia Gratiot, daughter of General Charles Gratiot. By 1845 Charles was twenty-five years old, but it was another five years before he took over P. Chouteau Jr. & Co., and freed his father from direct supervision of the business.[64]

Chouteau's focus for the next four years, when he was not doing business in New York or Philadelphia, or lobbying in Washington, was the elimination of liquor in the fur trade. Although the fur market hit its depths during the winter of 1841-1842, opposition traders swarmed over the upper Missouri, North and South Platte country. Their liquor, principal weapon in the war for furs, was dissolving the Indians' family and tribal relationships and (far more alarming to Chouteau) their ability to hunt buffalo and make robes. In 1841, Chouteau decided to dry up the competition by enforcing the long-ignored law prohibiting liquor in the Indian country. With the cooperation of the Indian Department, Chouteau worked out a plan to send an agent with a supporting company of dragoons to tour the Indian country, destroying liquor and arresting vendors.[65]

All sorts of things went wrong. The agent chosen was

---

64 Hyde and Conard, *Encyclopedia of History of St. Louis,* I, pp. 361-62; B. Pratte to P. Chouteau Jr., Oct. 11, 1834; Crooks to P. Chouteau Jr., Jan. 24, 1836; Crooks to P. Chouteau, Oct. 17, 1838, all in the Chouteau Coll.; obituary of Charles P. Chouteau, *St. Louis Globe-Democrat,* Jan. 6, 1901. Chouteau sold his share of Chouteau & McKenzie to McKenzie in the spring of 1840. Another short-lived mercantile partnership of Chouteau's was started in late 1838 with J. C. Barlow, a merchant of Louisville married to Chouteau's niece, Virginia, daughter of A. A. Chouteau.

65 John F. A. Sanford to Andrew Drips, July 10, 1842, Drips Papers, Mo. Hist. Soc.; D. D. Mitchell to T. Hartley Crawford, Oct. 25, 1841, Letters Received, OIA from St. Louis Superintendency.

Chouteau's faithful partisan, Andrew Drips, who could not have escaped the charge of partiality for his old employers even if he had been more scrupulous than he was. The company of dragoons was not allowed, and Drips' only deputy was recalled after a season, so that for over two years Drips' finger was the only plug in the dike. But the Sioux cooperated in keeping liquor out of their country and Chouteau's traders were sternly denied liquor. By 1845 Drips was able to say – and agonized cries from the upper Missouri traders bore him out – that "illicit whiskey has entirely disappeared from the Upper Missouri country." The competition also disappeared. In 1845 both Pratte & Cabanné and the Union Fur Co. gave up. Drips had done his work well – too well, in fact, for in the fall of 1845 Chouteau's company wrote its associate Henry H. Sibley in Minnesota asking if liquor desperately needed for the Assiniboine and Blackfeet could be smuggled in from the north (Sibley said no). Drips was removed in the spring of 1846 and next season all was back to normal – opposition traders everywhere and the Indian country awash in alcohol.[66]

Chouteau had been successful in drying up the competition if only temporarily, but the sins of his own traders were not forgiven. In 1846, spurred on by accusations of an opposition trader and former employe, seven separate suits amounting to $25,000 were instituted in the St. Louis District Court against P. Chouteau Jr. & Co. for selling liquor to Indians. After two years of delays, disappearing witnesses

[66] D. D. Mitchell to T. Hartley Crawford, Feb. 27, 1843, and endorsements, Letters Received, OIA from St. Louis Superintendency; H. Picotte to P. Chouteau Jr. & Co., Jan. 4, 1844, Chouteau Coll.; Jos. V. Hamilton to D. D. Mitchell, March 7, 1844, Letters Received, OIA from Upper Missouri Agency, National Archives; Thomas H. Harvey to T. Hartley Crawford, July 9, 1844, and Andrew Drips to Thomas H. Harvey, June 1, 1845, *ibid.;* H. H. Sibley to P. Chouteau Jr. & Co., Feb. 23, 1846, Chouteau Coll.; Picotte to P. Chouteau Jr. & Co., March 10, 1846, Fort Pierre Letter Book, Chouteau Coll.; Report of T. P. Moore, Sept. 21, 1846, *H. Exec. Doc. 4,* 29 Cong., 2 sess. (Ser. 497), 288-96. Both Sunder (*op. cit.,* 47-84) and Abel (*op. cit.,* 259) have a far more sinister viewpoint of Chouteau's motives.

and conflicting testimony, the court accepted a compromise suggested by the company that it forfeit $5000 and costs. In a letter summing up the trial, the company admitted that its subordinates had sold liquor to Indians every year they had operated, but only in violation of company instructions and positively without the knowledge of partners in the firm, a pious deceit. In 1848, the letter stated, "the liquor trade has now no existence in the Indian country" – but the company knew as it wrote those words that as long as there was competition in the fur trade, there was liquor also.[67]

In 1846 the Mexican War broke out, and by the time it was over in 1848, Bent, St. Vrain & Co. were ruined, along with the fur business of the southwest. The Santa Fe Trail was jammed with soldiers, teamsters and emigrants, all with their guns pointed at whatever moved in the brush, be it rabbit or friendly Indian. Soon there were no more friendly Indians. The South Platte business which had been Bent, St. Vrain & Co. territory was abandoned, and the North Platte fell victim to more soldiers and emigrants. Fort Laramie was sold to the Army in 1849, and from then on P. Chouteau Jr. & Co., managed by Charles Chouteau, operated only on the upper Missouri, where it held undisputed sway for another fifteen years, although declining year by year. The company was sold in 1865 to J. B. Hubbell of Mankato, Minnesota, who styled his business "The Northwest Fur Company" and carried it on to extinction.[68]

Though his company was finally in "younger hands" from 1849 on, Pierre Chouteau, Junior, was a decade away from retirement. As long ago as 1835, Chouteau had attended a meeting to discuss the possibility of a railroad from St. Louis to Fayette, and to the iron and lead mines in the

[67] P. Chouteau Jr. & Co. to William Medill, Dec. 5, 1848, and P. Chouteau Jr. & Co. to T. H. Harvey and T. G. Gantt, Jan. 12, 1849, both in Letters Received, OIA from St. Louis Superintendency. See also Sunder, *op. cit.*, 113-16.

[68] See Sunder, *op. cit.*, for a detailed account of these last years.

southern part of Missouri. Railroads were to be the playthings of his old age. In 1849 he established in New York the firm of Chouteau, Merle & Co. in partnership with a New Orleans merchant with whom the company had done business since the 1830s. Later Chouteau's son-in-law joined the company which then became Chouteau, Merle & Sanford, and was engaged in selling railroad iron.[69]

In 1849, Chouteau became a partner with François Vallé and James Harrison in the American Iron Mountain Co., dedicated to mining Iron Mountain and developing 25,000 acres around it. The mine was forty miles over hills and hollows from Ste. Genevieve, and had been unproductive because of difficulty in transporting ore. In 1851, the company built a twelve-foot wide plank road – the wonder of its day – between Iron Mountain and Ste. Genevieve. Seven years later a branch of the Illinois Central, established by Chouteau and others and named the Iron Mountain and Southern Railroad, put the plank road out of business, but greatly increased the value of the Iron Mountain property. In 1858, Chouteau, Harrison & Vallé took over a blast furnace built in 1853, and later another at Irondale, twelve miles north. Two thousand men were employed at Iron Mountain in its heyday, and millions of dollars worth of ore was extracted from it, mostly after Chouteau's death. Chouteau, Harrison & Vallé tried to develop the place as a summer colony, as well. From New York in 1858, Chouteau wrote Dr. Maffitt, Julie's husband, urging him to see that "Mama" visited "our Saratoga or Newport" during the summer. The company also established the Laclede Rolling Mill within the city limits of St. Louis.[70]

---

69 Scharf, *op. cit.*, I, p. 181; advertisement for sale of railroad iron by Chouteau, Merle & Co., Sept. 3, 1850, Chouteau Coll.; John F. A. Sanford to Charles P. Chouteau, April 2, 1852, Chouteau Coll.; Edwards and Hopewell, *op. cit.*, 356.

70 Last Will and Testament of Pierre Chouteau, Jr., Aug. 17, 1865; "The Passing of Iron Mountain," St. Louis, July 29, 1906, clipping in Missouri Historical Society; "Reopening of Iron Mountain Workings. . .", *St. Louis Star*, Aug. 31, 1923; P. Chouteau, Jr. to Dr. William Maffitt, Aug. 9, 1858, Chouteau Coll.

Chouteau, Merle & Sanford reorganized in 1852, becoming Pierre Chouteau Jr., Sanford & Co. Sanford had become ever more important to Chouteau through the years. Their relationship was very close; Chouteau allowed Sanford and Ben $5000 a year in addition to the large income Sanford had from his share of P. Chouteau Jr. & Co. and Pierre Chouteau Jr., Sanford & Co. When Sanford, a widower for sixteen years, married again in 1852, Chouteau, in the gracious family tradition, took the lady to his heart and made the Sanford home his headquarters in New York when Emilie was not with him. When "Mama" was in New York, she too went to dine with Belle Sanford and her two little children twice or three times a week. Sanford withdrew from P. Chouteau Jr. & Co. in 1853 to manage Chouteau's growing interests in other fields, such as the Ohio and Mississippi Railroad which Chouteau had helped incorporate in 1851, and the branches of the Illinois Central Railroad which he was developing.[71]

After 1850, Chouteau reluctantly spent more time in New York than in St. Louis, but whatever the press of business, his love and need for his family back in St. Louis was apparent in his letters. He worried over Julie's expected confinement; he shopped for Emilie's furs and corsets, and expressed his serious concern that her new teeth fit no better than the last set.[72] Sanford was probably correct in stating to Charles that the family should have made its home in New York years earlier, where there was a better field for business.[73] But Pierre Chouteau, Junior, was very much a product of the creole village of St. Louis, now grown to a metropolis but still the little pond where he was a big fish.

[71] John H. Thompson to Dr. Maffitt, July 11, 1859, and July 29, 1859; John F. A. Sanford to Charles Chouteau, April 2, 1852; P. Chouteau, Jr. to Emilie Chouteau, July 25, 1854; all in Chouteau Coll.; Scharf, *op. cit.*, II, p. 1180; agreement between Chouteau, Sarpy and Sire, Aug. 30, 1853, Chouteau Coll.

[72] Letters of P. Chouteau, Jr. to his wife and Julie dated Sept. 8, 1854, Nov. 27, 1854, and Oct. 4, 1856, Chouteau Coll.

[73] John F. A. Sanford to Charles P. Chouteau, April 2, 1852, Chouteau Coll.

And he was perplexed. A letter to Julie in 1852 reveals a lifetime of doubts about his purposes and ideals:

> As to business, I, who would like to withdraw from it, find myself drawn in deeper than ever. Rail Road Iron, Bonds of the state, of the town, of the Railroad, i.e., Central Railroad of Illinois, coal mines; so you see, my dear Julie, that I do just the contrary of what I would like. . . . As long as I have been in business I have never been as sanguine of clearing so much in so few years. You will doubtless ask, why all these speculations, why risk the substance already won, when we have enough on which to be happy if we know how to enjoy it. This question on your part would be perfectly just and reasonable if a man has enough moderation, enough judgement to comprehend it, but whether it be ambition or advantage or even perhaps a little vanity, he lets himself be subjugated. He does not like to be stationary when everything around him seems to go forward.[74]

The year 1857 was the beginning of the end, a time when Chouteau had to be stationary and watch everything around him go forward, or backward. In April when he was in New York, he heard of the death in St. Louis of John B. Sarpy and was greatly upset. He was hardly less so when his son-in-law, Dr. Maffitt, refused to accept an interest in the fur business and take over Sarpy's job.[75] A worse blow came in May when John F. A. Sanford died.[76] In 1858, Maffitt was struck with a paralysis which did not finish him off until 1862. Later in 1858 Chouteau himself became ill and spent much time at Hot Springs for an ailment that affected his sight. Early in 1859 he became incurably blind, and was doomed to spend the last six years of his life in total darkness.[77] His beloved Emilie died on August 24, 1862, and was

74 Pierre Chouteau, Jr. to Julie, July 8, 1852, Chouteau Coll., translated by Mrs. Max Myer.

75 P. Chouteau, Jr. to Dr. William Maffitt, April 6, 1857, and April 24, 1857.

76 He died on May 5, 1857, supposedly driven insane by his involvement in the Dred Scott case. See biography of John F. A. Sanford in this volume.

77 Many letters in the Chouteau Collection trace the progress of Pierre Chouteau, Jr.'s blindness and Dr. Maffitt's paralysis.

buried in Calvary Cemetery. He died three years later on September 6, 1865, aged 76, and was buried beside her.[78]

What Chouteau's estate amounted to can only be estimated; one historian has guessed "several millions."[79] He left over four hundred thousand dollars in railroad bonds alone;[80] he had very large interests in the Indian country; a third of the Laclede Rolling Mill and the Iron Mountain property of Chouteau, Harrison & Vallé; valuable real estate in the towns of St. Paul, St. Anthony and Hastings, Minnesota, and even more valuable lots in downtown St. Louis.[81] He died rich but not universally beloved. His detractors, then and now, have with some justification called him a master of fraud, debaucher of Indians, corrupter of government officials, abuser of public funds. He was, indeed, one of the great manipulators in the history of United States commerce.

But in the memories of his family and the depths of his being he remained to the end a simple French creole.

---

78 Last Will and Testament of Pierre Chouteau, Jr.; obituary of P. Chouteau, Jr. in the *St. Louis Republican,* Thursday, Sept. 7, 1865.

79 Stella Drumm, "Pierre Chouteau," *Dictionary of American Biography,* IV, p. 94. Chouteau left $5000 in his will for the Catholic orphans of St. Louis, the only bequest to other than his heirs, which illustrates a facet of his life: he was ever openhanded with his family, but to no one and nothing else would he give either time or money. His civic achievements were paltry. I have found only that he served as delegate to the Missouri Constitutional Convention in May, 1820, and as commissioner to locate a site for the St. Louis courthouse in 1822 (Scharf, *Saint Louis,* I, pp. 571, 728).

80 #7159 (Pierre Chouteau, Jr.), Probate Court, St. Louis County, Mo.

81 Last Will and Testament of Pierre Chouteau, Jr.

Wilson Price Hunt

by WILLIAM BRANDON
Monterey, California

Wilson Price Hunt was John Jacob Astor's field marshal in the founding of Astoria, and is consequently a figure of some consequence in western history. As leader of the overland Astorians in 1811 he is credited with first tracing the route between the Snake and the Columbia that was to become a key part of the western section of the Oregon Trail. He was never, however, a "Mountain Man" finding his glory in the wilderness – he was a business man who made one long and vastly adventurous trip West and never thereafter left his counting room; he was a business man first, last, and always, and that he once happened to find himself in mountain-crossing business was coincidental.

He was born March 20, 1783 [1] at Asbury, New Jersey, the son (probably the second son) of John P. and Margaret (Guild) Hunt.[2] He was "bred to mercantile pursuits" [3] and

[1] From information furnished the Missouri Historical Society in 1948 by Mrs. W. P. Hunt of Normandy, Mo., who takes this birth date from the Hunt family Bible. A brief biographical sketch in the Missouri Historical Society *Collections*, III, p. 325, gives the date of birth as March 29, 1783. Further biographical data may be found in the Hunt Collections in the Missouri Historical Society, St. Louis. See also T. C. Elliott, "Wilson Price Hunt, 1783-1842," in *Oregon Historical Quarterly*, XXXII (1931), 130-34.

This article, except for the annotations, appeared in a somewhat revised form in the July 1968 issue of the *American West*.

[2] Hunt's parents are named in T. B. Wyman, *Genealogy of the Name and Family of Hunt* (Boston, 1862-3), 149. A brother named John Guild Hunt, as well as two sisters, are named in the Wilson Price Hunt will, in the collections of the Missouri Historical Society and reprinted in Elliott, "Wilson Price Hunt."

[3] Alexander Ross, *Adventures of the First Settlers on the Oregon or Columbia River* (London, 1849), 11. This work is reprinted as Vol. 7 of *Early Western Travels*, edited by Reuben Gold Thwaites (Cleveland, 1904).

at the age of twenty-one went west to St. Louis and opened a store in partnership with John Hankinson, under the firm name of Hunt and Hankinson.[4] This was in 1804, the year that St. Louis passed under the sovereignty of the United States as part of what was then called the Upper Province of Louisiana. Hunt, as a young native-born American citizen, could scarcely have gotten any closer to the ground floor in thus setting up shop in this new American annex.

John Jacob Astor, in need a few years later of just such a young native-born American merchant in St. Louis, invited Hunt to join the venture into the western fur trade that was to become the Astoria enterprise. Hunt left St. Louis in November, 1809, to go to New York and confer with Astor; he then went on to Montreal to join a couple of ex-North West Company fur-traders Astor had lured into the new company, Alexander McKay and Donald McKenzie, to begin the work of organizing the western expedition.[5]

The Louisiana Purchase and the Lewis and Clark report of the wealth of beaver in the great West that had now become United States territory turned a considerable chorus of Yankee attention on the western fur trade, which until that time had been largely in the hands of Canadian traders. Astor, the leading fur merchant of the United States, organized the American Fur Company in 1808 and conceived a grandiose plan involving a chain of fur-trading posts along the route of Lewis and Clark and a monopoly coastwise trade on the Northwest Coast with the Russians at Sitka. These operations would be supplied both overland from St. Louis and by sea to a main depot at the mouth of the Columbia, and the furs thus gathered would be carried on across the Pacific by the same supply ships to China, the best market for fine peltries; these ships would then return

---

[4] Frederic L. Billon, *Annals of St. Louis from 1804 to 1821* (St. Louis, 1888), 193.

[5] Kenneth W. Porter, *John Jacob Astor, Business Man* (Cambridge, 1931), I, 183.

with goods from the China trade for Boston and New York, to be met by other Astor ships arriving from Europe with fresh cargoes of cheap Birmingham goods for the Indian fur trade, to begin the cycle all over again. The profits at each step would be huge and the cumulative profits enormous; nor was the possible political effect in a West still to be won from British competition lost on Astor and the government officials (including President Jefferson) with whom he consulted.[6] Astor told Washington Irving that he considered his "projected establishment at the mouth of the Columbia as the emporium to an immense commerce; as a colony that would form the germ of a wide civilization; that would, in fact, carry the American population across the Rocky Mountains and spread it along the shores of the Pacific, as it already animated the shores of the Atlantic."[7]

This plan was to be put into motion with two simultaneous expeditions, one by sea carrying men and material to establish the main depot at the mouth of the Columbia River; the other to travel to this new Columbia post overland "winning the confidence of the Indians, and ascertaining the points at which trading posts might most properly be located,"[8] along the route of Lewis and Clark.

Hunt was to be in command of the overland expedition, and was to be in charge at the Columbia River establishment on the Pacific Coast. The choice of the inexperienced Hunt as commander of the overland party, in preference to

[6] Porter, *op. cit.*, 164-73. That Astor was keenly aware of the political inferences of the Astoria project is remarked on by Porter, who points out, 242-243, that Astor, asking Washington Irving to present him to posterity in the story of Astoria, his one resounding failure, evidently preferred to be remembered as a "dreamer of empire" rather than as merely the most successful money-maker of his time.

[7] Washington Irving, *Astoria, or Anecdotes of an Enterprise beyond the Rocky Mountains*, 2 vols. (Philadelphia, 1836), and many subsequent editions. The superlative edition edited and with an Introduction by Edgely W. Todd (Norman, Okla. 1964) is the edition that will be cited throughout these notes; in that edition the quotation reprinted here is on page 32. Irving had the account of the genesis of the Astoria undertaking, which make up Chapters 2 and 3 of *Astoria*, from Astor himself.

[8] Porter, *op. cit.*, I, p. 183.

various of the ex-Nor'westers who had had long experience in the mountains, seems curious; however, Astor regarded Hunt as his chief lieutenant in the entire venture, and, in view of fur trade prejudices and regulations in the new American West, he may also have wanted a native-born United States citizen in title of command.[9]

One contemporary source relates that Hunt and McKenzie (a wilderness veteran) were, at first, co-leaders of the overland expedition, and that a letter from Astor put Hunt in sole command only after the expedition was fairly under way.[10] This interesting plot-point, repeated by a number of authorities, has come under some doubt in recent years.[11]

Several experienced French-Canadian voyageurs were signed on in Montreal and several more at Mackinaw, the famous old French trading post on Michilimackinac Island, in the strait between Lakes Michigan and Huron; here also a young Canada Scot turned Missourian whom Hunt had invited by letter[12] came to join the new company as a partner. This was Ramsay Crooks, later to become a most weighty nabob in the American fur trade. It is possible that Hunt had discussed the Astoria project with Crooks, and Crooks' partner as a Missouri River trader, Robert McClellan, before leaving St. Louis.[13]

---

9 *Astoria* (Todd, ed.), 36-37: "As this gentleman [Hunt] was a native born citizen of the United States, a person of great probity and worth, he was selected by Mr. Astor to be his chief agent, and to represent him in the contemplated establishment."

10 Ross, *op. cit.,* 178. Ross, however, was not with the overlanders, being one of the group that went to Oregon by sea.

11 David Lavender, *The Fist in the Wilderness* (New York, 1964), 555, *n.*11, cogently states this doubt. *Astoria* (Todd, ed.), 123, says "The conduct of this expedition . . . was assigned to Mr. Wilson Price Hunt, of Trenton, New Jersey . . ." Ross himself is ambiguous, inasmuch as earlier remarks tend to imply that Hunt was not only in sole command of the expedition from the start but was "a person every way qualified for the arduous undertaking" (169); except for Ross there is little other support for any notion of such friction. In later years McKenzie reopened a correspondence with Hunt in the friendliest terms: see below, *n.* 108 and 109.

12 *Astoria* (Todd, ed.), 129-130.

13 Lavender, *op. cit.,* 108-113, and 441, *n.* 11, indulges in unsupported but reasonable speculation to this effect.

Formal documents organizing the new fur company, to be called the Pacific Fur Company, were drawn up in New York, June 23, 1810, providing for an established one hundred shares, fifty for Astor, five each for Alexander McKay, Donald McKenzie, Duncan McDougall,[14] David Stuart,[15] Crooks and Hunt; two and a half shares each to Robert McLean (sic), and Joseph Miller,[16] the remaining fifteen shares reserved for "the use or benefit of the several parties interested in the said Company." Astor was to advance all the capital, and retained a right to nominate four new partners and to transfer his shares if he wished to the American Fur Company, the parent company which Astor owned outright. Wilson Price Hunt was specified as the resident agent of the company on the Pacific Coast.[17]

The seaborne expedition, consisting of several partners, clerks and voyageurs, and a cargo of materials for trade and construction, sailed from New York on September 8, 1810, in the ship "Tonquin," Jonathan Thorn, master. Two other Astor vessels, the "Beaver" and the "Enterprise," were already in the Pacific, having sailed during the previous year for the Northwest Coast and Canton, and a deal with the Russian government giving Astor an exclusive on the Russian Sitka trade was in the works;[18] Astor had also coppered all bets by confidential offers to negotiate with the North West Company for cooperation rather than competition in the fur trade of the interior and the Pacific Coast.[19]

---

14 McDougall too was an ex-Nor'wester, according to Porter, *op. cit.*, 181, and 210, *n.* 41.

15 Philip Ashton Rollins, ed., *Discovery of the Oregon Trail, Robert Stuart's Narratives* (New York, 1935), xxxvii, states that David Stuart and his nephew, Robert, were both ex-employees of the North West Company.

16 Miller and McClellan joined the expedition later; McClellan's name is always spelled McClelan in Porter, *op. cit.*

17 An original copy of these articles of agreement is in the Accounts Case of the Hunt Collections, Missouri Historical Society, St. Louis. The full text of the agreement is reprinted in Grace Flandrau, *Astor and the Oregon Country* (St. Paul, n.d. [1926?]), 24-41.

18 Porter, *op. cit.*, I, pp. 172-79, 192-93.

19 *Ibid.*, I, p. 171, 193-94; and *Astoria* (Todd, ed.), 34.

The overlanders, forming under Wilson Price Hunt during the summer of 1810, left Michilimackinac in August and traveled by "the usual route"[20] of Green Bay and the Fox and Wisconsin Rivers to Prairie du Chien, and then down the Mississippi to St. Louis, arriving there early in September. After taking on more men in St. Louis (notably a new partner, Joseph Miller, an experienced wilderness hand) they left St. Louis on October 21st and went up the river some 450 miles to establish a winter camp – this to save money,[21] it being cheaper to winter in a distant camp where "five or six hunters can easily provide for forty or fifty men"[22] than among the fleshpots of St. Louis. The expedition was considerably behind its original schedule, due (reports Irving) to delays occasioned by the machinations of rival fur-trading companies in Michilimackinac and St. Louis.[23] Also, at St. Louis it was decided to increase the size of the party from thirty men to sixty, and finding so many qualified men, with or without villainous machinations of rivals, took time.[24]

There are a number of well-known contemporary accounts of the journey of the overland Astorians.[25] Wash-

---

20 *Astoria,* 131. 21 *Ibid.,* 136.

22 John Bradbury, *Travels in the Interior of America in the Years 1809, 1810, and 1811 . . . etc.* (second edition, London, 1819), reprinted as Vol. 5 of Thwaites' *Early Western Travels;* the pagination of this latter edition will be cited here, in which the remark quoted appears on page 37.

23 *Astoria,* 128, 135. 24 *Ibid.,* 130.

25 Besides Irving, principal accounts are Gabriel Franchere, *Narrative of a Voyage to the Northwest Coast of America,* originally written in French and published in Montreal in 1820, an English translation, by J. V. Huntington, published in New York in 1854, and published as the last part of Vol. 6 of Thwaites' *Early Western Travels;* the accounts of Alexander Ross (hearsay, as far as the overland expedition is concerned, as is Franchere's) and of John Bradbury, an English botanist botanizing on the Missouri frontier who accompanied the Astorians on the Missouri River leg of their journey, have been previously cited; and Ross Cox, *The Columbia River,* 2 vols. (London, 1832), another hearsay account, since Cox, like Franchere and Ross, came out to the Columbia post by sea. Wilson Price Hunt's own journal of the trip has been lost but a French translation was published in J. B. Eyriès and Malte-Brun, eds., *Nouvelles Annales des Voyages . . . etc.* Tome 10 (Paris,

ington Irving's *Astoria,* the chief of these, written from conversations with the participants as well as from contemporary records, is one of the few great classics of America's westward movement, and has been shown by its modern editor to be as sound and accurate as most historical documentation, if not more trustworthy than some[26] – its mandarinism, snobbery, arrogant Yankee prejudices, as in its frequent disparagement of French Canadians, were tics of the age, not of the author. In all these contemporary accounts, so far as I can determine, Wilson Price Hunt is generally well spoken of, not only as an organizer and administrator but also as an able and courageous field commander, combining the "mildest"[27] and most "amicable"[28] of dispositions with, when needed, firmness or boldness.[29]

Some later writers have been critical of Hunt, for example Chittenden, who concluded that his "conduct of the overland expedition was not efficient" and that he "was not

1821); a none too perfect English retranslation is included as part of Appendix A (pp. 281-308) in Rollins, *op. cit.* Ramsay Crook's narrative of the overland expedition is in the *Missouri Gazette,* issue of May 15, 1813, and reprinted in *Niles Register* for June 26, 1813, and is included in Appendix III (pp. 228-34) of Bradbury, previously cited. Henry Marie Brackenridge, the later historian, went along as a young man of twenty-five with Manuel Lisa's keelboat crew that chased the Astorians up the Missouri; his story of the trip was published as *Journal of a Voyage up the River Missouri . . . etc.* (Baltimore, 1816), and is reprinted as the first part of Vol. 6 of Thwaites' *Early Western Travels,* which edition is used here.

[26] Edgely W. Todd, in his edition of *Astoria* often referred to in these notes, speaks at length of Irving's reliability in this work, and of the questions about the book's authenticity that have been raised by later writers: Introduction, xxxii-xli. He concludes: "Working closely with *Astoria* and the hundreds of pages of its sources, the researcher comes in time to respect what Irving says and learns that he should not lightly impugn Irving's accuracy." Todd cites several instances in which modern scholarship authenticates certain passages in *Astoria* previously believed to be romancing on the part of the author. A further such instance is provided in Kenneth Spaulding, ed., *On the Oregon Trail: Robert Stuart's Journey of Discovery* (Norman, 1953), which includes as Appendix II a letter by Elisha Loomis relating a Lyceum talk given by Stuart in 1831 which incidentally provides authority for a hitherto questionable passage on pages 383-84 of *Astoria.*

[27] Bradbury (Thwaites, ed.), 75.

[28] *Astoria* (Todd, ed.), 123.

[29] See for example Bradbury, 91, 103, 107-108, 112, 122; and Ross, *Adventures,* 276.

the man for the place."[30] Bancroft was hotly critical of the entire Astoria undertaking (and particularly of Washington Irving's account of it).[31]

The expedition's winter camp was at the mouth of the Nodaway River, a few miles below the junction of the present day borders of Kansas, Nebraska, and Missouri. Ramsay Crooks's ex-partner, Robert McClellan, joined the Astorians here as a partner in the company, being granted two and a half shares. At least one other American hunter, John Day, was recruited at this winter camp. Hunt returned to St. Louis for the winter and signed on more personnel there, including one expert of great value, Pierre Dorion, a half-breed Sioux interpreter. However, during the winter a number of American hunters previously signed on at St. Louis deserted the expedition, and presumably Hunt had to hire Canadians in their stead.[32] According to Alexander Ross (who went out by sea and saw Hunt only in Oregon), Hunt, ". . . grave, steady, and straightforward . . . detested the volatile gaiety and ever-changing character of the Canadian voyageurs . . ."[33] and preferred American hunters; but the American hunters were touchy when it came to company discipline, and quick to go over the hill.

One of the Americans who left the expedition at the winter camp on the Nodaway was probably Caleb Greenwood – "Old Greenwood" as he was later known when he became a man of renown in the mountains. Several other later celebrities in the literature of the West had some connection brief or otherwise with this early expedition – for example, Edward Rose and Samuel Chambers.[34]

---

[30] Hiram Chittenden, *The American Fur Trade of the Far West,* 2 vols. (Stanford, 1954), I, p. 232.

[31] Hubert Bancroft, *History of the Northwest Coast,* 2 vols. (Vols. 27 and 28 of *The Works of Hubert Howe Bancroft,* San Francisco, 1884), II, 138*n.*, 145*n.*, 169*n.*, 172*n.*, 221*n.*, 222 *n.*, 223*n.* Chittenden, above cited, discusses Bancroft's denunciations in I, 244-46. These charges are further discussed in the Editor's Introduction to *Astoria* (Todd, ed.), xxxviii-xxxix.

[32] *Astoria,* 142-43.

[33] Ross, *op. cit.,* 171.

The overlanders, as they headed up the river from their winter camp on April 21, 1811, consisted of almost sixty people in four boats – forty Canadian engagés, "several" American hunters, the interpreter Dorion and his wife (an Iowa Indian girl)[35] and two children, a clerk named John Reed ("a rough, warm-hearted, brave, old Irishman")[36] and five partners.[37] They were also accompanied, for the first leg of the trip, by the touring English naturalist John Bradbury and the young botanist Thomas Nuttall.

During the following weeks of pushing up the river, enjoying back-breaking toil and some tense encounters with menacing bands of Sioux, a few more men quit – quit openly or deserted between dark and dawn without taking leave – and various wandering hunters or trappers were hired to take their places. Two of these new men were Ben Jones and Alexander Carson, who had been working the headwaters of the Missouri for two years past; three others were Missouri Fur Company veterans from Andrew Henry's detachment on Henry's Fork of the Snake – John Hoback, Jacob Reznor, and Edward Robinson. All these experts agreed that the Lewis and Clark route Hunt had intended to follow would not be as good as a more southerly route, which would offer both an easier crossing of the mountains[38] and safety from the hostile Blackfeet who ruled the most northerly reaches of the Missouri.[39] Accordingly it was decided to

[34] Kenneth W. Porter, "Roll of Overland Astorians, 1810-12," in *Oregon Historical Quarterly,* Vol. 34 (1933), 103-112, used two account books kept by Hunt, now in the Astor Papers at the Baker Library at Harvard, as basic sources in compiling a list of all the people who had any connection at all with the expedition, including several who were just passing by and in one way or another got their names inscribed in these account books. A total of some 86 persons are thus listed, of whom six were non-members of the Astorians, twenty left the expedition at some time during the trip, fourteen were killed or died either during the trip or during subsequent operations in Oregon, and one disappeared.

[35] Bradbury, 63.

[36] Cox, *op. cit.,* 154.

[37] This breakdown of the personnel at this point is as given in *Astoria,* 155.

[38] Bradbury, 99-100.

[39] *Astoria,* 177-78.

leave the river at the Arikara towns, some 450 miles sooner than originally planned.

A week or so before reaching the Arikara towns (in present South Dakota, near the North Dakota line), the Astorians were overtaken by a party under the command of Manuel Lisa, king of the Missouri River fur traders, who had left St. Louis nineteen days after Hunt's departure and had now caught up with him after two months of fast and furious keelboating.[40] Each party suspected the other of some design of treachery in concert with this or that Indian group, and there were a few old grudges as well to add friction, to the point that fists, knives and pistols were unlimbered, and Hunt even challenged Lisa to a duel.[41] All was made sweetness and light, however, when Lisa spoke up on behalf of the Hunt party among the Arikaras, with whom he was reputed to have great influence.

Lisa thereafter assisted Hunt in trading for horses with the Arikara people, and himself furnished fifty or so horses from his Missouri Fur Company trading fort – located seven miles beyond the Mandan towns, which in turn were some one hundred and eighty miles farther up the river[42] – in exchange for several of the boats the Astorians were here abandoning. With eighty-two horses, all loaded with baggage except for riding mounts for the company partners and Dorion's wife – this long pack train gives an indication of the wealth in supplies and merchandise – the overlanders headed west across country from the Arikara towns on July 18th, guided for the Crow country by Edward Rose.[43] At this point, according to Hunt's journal, the party numbered sixty-five, including Dorion's wife and two children.[44]

---

40 Walter B. Douglas, *Manuel Lisa,* annotated and edited by Abraham P. Nasatir (New York, 1964), 266-67; Richard E. Oglesby, *Manuel Lisa* (Norman, Okla., 1963), 109-14.

41 Bradbury, 122; *Astoria,* 190.

42 Bradbury, 147.

43 Hunt, "Journal," in *Nouvelles Annales,* 31; and *Astoria* (Todd, ed.), 214-16.

They traveled southwest to cross Rampart or (present-day) Oak Creek,[45] which joined the Missouri a few miles below the Arikara towns, and after two or three days picked up the present Grand River, known to the Astorians as Big River or Ouenned-Poréhou.[46] Here they ran across a camp of Cheyennes where Hunt bought thirty-six more horses. The Little Missouri was reached on August 14th, and on the 23rd Powder River was crossed. A week later, as they traveled the Big Horn Mountains, a camp of Crow Indians was found and here Edward Rose remained, to Hunt's relief for he found Rose a "villainous and audacious rogue" and was ready to suspect him of all manner of dastardly plots.[47]

They followed the Bighorn River and Wind River[48] into the Wind River Mountains where they crossed the Continental Divide (probably by the pass nowadays called Union Pass) to pick up Green River, called by them the Spanish River.[49] From a band of Snake Indians encountered on Green River, they bought a large supply of buffalo jerky to add to the already large supply their hunters had been making. They turned west on a stream now named Hoback River[50] to reach the Snake (called Mad River by the trappers) on September 27th, and immediately began searching for trees large enough to turn into canoes. The Snake was known to be a principal tributary of the Columbia, but it was not known by Hunt's people that it writhed its way to the Columbia by means of some of the most impassable cañons and unshootable rapids in the West.

A couple of days were spent searching for canoe-wood

---

44 *Nouvelles Annales, loc. cit.* Rollins, ed., *op. cit.,* discusses the number of persons and of horses very fully, citing variant figures in contemporary newspaper accounts, various articles in the journal literature, etc., 312, *n.* 44.

45 Rollins, 312, *n.* 47; and *Astoria,* 218-19, *n.* 5.

46 *Nouvelles Annales,* 32. Rollins identifies the route in rather careful detail in his annotation to Hunt's journal.

47 *Nouvelles Annales,* 38-39.

48 Rollins, 316, *n.* 105.

49 *Ibid.,* 317, *n.* 125; and *Nouvelles Annales,* 43.

50 Rollins, 317, *n.* 135.

and felling sample trees – all too small – until a scouting party reported the river ahead not yet navigable. Two Snake Indians who had been with them since the country of the Crows told them the same thing. Therefore, they continued overland to Henry's fort (then deserted) on Henry's Fork of the Snake, near the present St. Anthony, Idaho.[51] Here they found cottonwoods large enough to make pirogues, and here the river, a hundred to a hundred and fifty yards wide, appeared (hopefully) tame enough to carry them. Canoes were fashioned forthwith[52] and the expedition took to the water.

This decision to abandon the horses and trust to the river was made, says Irving, after a consultation among all the partners, in which the vote "was almost unanimous for embarkation."[53] Irving then insists that partner Joseph Miller ("being troubled with a bodily malady that rendered travelling on horseback extremely irksome")[54] was displeased because they didn't embark precipitately enough and that as a consequence, when the party was at last ready to embark, Miller resigned his partnership and went away (on horseback) with a party of trappers being detached to work out from Henry's fort.[55] Presumably someone related this story to Irving with an equal insistence. Since Miller was the only one of the partners except Hunt (and one of the few members of the entire expedition) whose experience had not been in riverine travel and trading, it might be supposed he would be exactly on the opposite side in this issue. And since this issue, the decision to leave the horses and take to boats, was all-important in bringing the expedition to disaster, an air of special pleading perforce clings to this Joe Miller story. Something, anyway, rings of brass here, even without the bodily malady, which in itself does seem a touch too much.[56]

---

51 *Ibid.*, 169, *n.* 16.

52 Irving says fifteen canoes – *Astoria*, 271.

53 *Ibid.*, 264.

54 *Ibid.*, 266.

55 *Ibid.*, 266-70.

Furs had been traded for or hunted all the way along the route, wherever occasion offered, but now detachments were dropped off to make full-scale fall hunts and pack their catch to the headquarters post at the mouth of the Columbia, or to Henry's fort, which would be taken over as an outpost. Four men (one of them Alexander Carson) were thus left on the Hoback River, and five, including Miller (and Hoback, Reznor, and Robinson, who had been here before), on Henry's Fork.[57] The rest, by inference fifty-five souls, cached their saddles and left the horses[58] in the care of the two young Snakes and shoved off down the river, on October 19th.

Ten days later, after the death of one voyageur and the loss of several boatloads of goods, they found any further progress down the river absolutely stopped. Here, between the modern little towns of Milner and Murtagh[59] a few miles east of present Twin Falls, Idaho, the expedition spent ten more days exploring this way and that, conferring, caching everything except essentials to be carried on their backs, and splitting into splinter groups under the various partners and clerk John Reed. The purpose of these splinter parties was to travel various directions in search of Indians who might furnish provisions, horses, and information, the expedition being nearly out of food.[60]

Hunt's detachment numbered twenty-one, including Dorion's family (whose wife, by the way, was in the last months

---

56 Miller returned to St. Louis in 1813 and nothing further seems to be known of his life – Rollins, ci.

57 Rollins, 320, *n.* 184, discusses these and other detachments in detail.

58 *Ibid.*, 318, *n.* 158, discusses the number of the horses here abandoned – seventy-seven, according to Hunt's journal. Miller's detachment, which was meant to remain in this locality, was apparently furnished with four horses – one wonders why not more? Even granting Miller's malady, horses here were of great value as objects of trade, and a few more would have presumably been as well taken care of in the possession of Miller's detachment as in the custody of the two young Shoshones.

59 *Ibid.*, 320-21, *n.* 187; but also see *Astoria*, 277, *n.* 21.

60 *Nouvelles Annales*, 56.

of pregnancy); Crook's detachment twenty; McKenzie's five; McClellan's four; and Reed's four.[61] A couple of Reed's men returned to join Hunt after several days and report that the river ahead remained hopeless for travel. McKenzie and McClellan, finding no information or provisions or horses or Indians, decided it was pointless to report back to Hunt,[62] and joining together their parties, together with Reed and his companion, kept on toiling westward. Hunt and Crooks, after spending a week or so caching the last of the stocks of merchandise, set out on separate routes with their separate bands on November 9th.

Hunt had better luck than Crooks in finding Indians (Shoshone camps) and getting from them some horses and sustenance,[63] but during much of the last week of November and the first week of December Hunt also met no Indians, and on December 6th, after themselves enduring great privation and hardship in difficult mountains and heavy snow, Hunt's people met again the Crooks detachment. This meeting seems to have been near the present town of Homestead, Oregon, Crooks on the Oregon side of the Snake, Hunt on the Idaho side.[64] Crooks and all his men were in desperate straits from hunger, discouragement and fatigue, having existed for the last nine days on "one beaver, a dog, a few wild cherries, and some old mockason soles. . ."[65]

Crooks reported that the mountains ahead were deep in snow and quite impassable, impassable at least for men so weak as he and his people now were. Hunt spent a long night in bitter reflection, and decided to turn back in order

---

61 Rollins, 321-22, *n.* 190.

62 *Astoria* (Todd, ed.), 322.

63 Crooks's narrative in Bradbury, *op. cit.*, 231.

64 The geography of these wanderings has to be based on Hunt's journal in *Nouvelles Annales,* which is pretty vague, but a great deal of ingenious detective work has been done on it by scholars familiar with the region. Notes in the volumes edited by Rollins and Todd, respectively, are very helpful; and see especially J. Neilson Barry, "The Trail of the Astorians," in *Oregon Historical Society Quarterly,* XIII (1912), 227-39.

65 Crooks in Bradbury, *op. cit.*, 232.

to help the Crooks detachment reach the salvation of the last Indian camp, passed some days up the river. One of Crooks's voyageurs, Jean Baptiste Prevost, out of his mind from starvation,[66] was drowned in the river in the course of this back-tracking. By December 21st, when Hunt was ready once more to push on westward (with the two detachments combined) he had retreated to the vicinity of his encampment of November 26th, apparently near the junction of the presentday Weiser River with the Snake.[67]

But by heroic persuasion he had recruited three Shoshone guides, who now led the way across the Snake and directly northwest to the Columbia along the route that was to become an important link of the Oregon Trail,[68] leaving the Snake at the point future emigrants would call Farewell Bend, and traversing Baker Valley, Grande Ronde Valley, and the Blue Mountains.[69] On the way another voyageur, Michael Carriere, was lost,[70] and Dorion's wife gave birth to her baby, which died a few days later, although she kept up with the line of march, and apparently without complaint.[71] (Marguerite Dorion proved a better mountain man than many of her companions on other occasions still,[72] and outlived most of them to boot, dying in Oregon in 1850.)[73]

On January 8, 1812, they reached a large Indian camp on (probably) the Umatilla River,[74] rested among these Indians[75] for six days, and arrived on the banks of the Columbia on January 21st. They reached Astoria February 15th. Six men left behind along the way, including Ramsay Crooks and the hunter John Day, did not appear until many weeks afterward.

66 *Ibid.*, 232-33.

67 Rollins, ed., *op. cit.*, 324, *n.* 227, 230, 233.

68 *Astoria*, 306, *n.* 2.

69 Rollins, 325, *n.* 237-52.

70 From starvation, says Crooks, in Bradbury, 233; but Hunt's journal says he vanished and may have lost his way: *Nouvelles Annales*, 75-76.

71 *Astoria*, 308.

72 See for example *Astoria*, 499.

73 See J. Neilson Barry, "Madame Dorion of the Astorians," in *Oregon Historical Quarterly*, XXX (1929), 272-78.

74 Rollins, 326, *n.* 253; *Astoria*, 310, *n.* 18.

75 The identity of these Indians, called by Hunt Sciatogas, is uncertain.

The McKenzie-McClellan-Reed party had made it to Astoria, after "unheard-of difficulties,"[76] on January 18th.[77] On the way they had happened upon one of the untold sagas of the West, meeting and taking along with them a young man named Archibald Pelton. He was a survivor of the Blackfoot attacks on the Andrew Henry fur brigade of 1810; he had lost his mind and for almost two lunatic years had wandered wild unknown mountains with bands of Shoshones.[78]

At Astoria, Hunt learned of the loss at Nootka of the "Tonquin" with all hands, including her captain whose arrogant behavior caused the tragedy, and the company partner Alexander McKay. This catastrophe was a sensational news event among the Indians too, and Hunt heard Chinook reports of it long before reaching the fort.[79] Also, in the spring and summer of 1812, McClellan and then Crooks resigned their partnerships and left for the East. But Astoria, founded in April 1811, before the "Tonquin" sailed on to perish, was in business all the same. Early in May 1812, another supply ship, the "Beaver," under Captain Sowle, arrived. Various detachments had by that time set forth on spring trips, to supply or man trading posts, to trap, or to carry dispatches overland to Astor. A number of Hunt's trail companions lost their lives in such occupations during the next year or two, including among others Dorion, John Reed, Hoback, Reznor, and Robinson, all these murdered by Nez Percé Indians (according to the belief of some of the Astorians) in revenge for the death of a Nez Percé hanged by John Clarke for the theft of a silver cup. Clarke was a newly appointed partner who had come out on the "Beaver."[80]

[76] *Nouvelles Annales*, 27.

[77] *Ibid., loc. cit.;* Franchere (Thwaites, ed.), 268; Ross, *Adventures*, 182, says January 10th.

[78] *Nouvelles Annales*, 29; Franchere, 271; Cox, *op. cit.*, 61-62.

[79] *Nouvelles Annales*, 82; *Astoria*, 319.

[80] *Astoria*, 449-450, and 499-500.

Hunt departed on the "Beaver" to see to the next step of the operation: the Russian trade at Sitka. This project was fraught with its own peculiar perils, for the fierce old Russian governor, Count Baranoff, would only talk business to the music of uproarious drinking bouts, and might, in his jolly way, have a visitor whipped around the pickets if he couldn't stand the pace.[81] Hunt's talents were apparently equal to the challenge. At any rate the trade he came for was brought off handsomely, the "Beaver" disposing of its cargo for nearly 75,000 seal skins, worth at that time in Canton six or seven times the cargo's value.[82] These furs had to be picked up at one of the Russian seal-fisheries in the Pribilof Islands, a detour of six weeks. The "Beaver" had planned to stop again at Astoria to pick up the furs being baled there, but in view of the delays already in her schedule this stop was omitted, and Hunt dropped off at the Hawaiian Islands while the "Beaver" made directly for China. It was Hunt's intention to return to Astoria on the next supply ship, expected to touch at Oahu in the spring of 1813.[83] The next supply ship, however, did not arrive, the War of 1812 interrupting Astor's plans and defying all his emergency maneuvers.[84]

Hunt, when he learned of the war, succeeded in chartering a ship at Oahu, the "Albatross," Captain Smith, and arrived at Astoria with some trading supplies and provisions in August, 1813.[85] He came too late. The company partners at Astoria, under the leadership of Duncan McDougall, learning of the war and finding themselves left unsupplied

---

81 *Astoria,* 466-67.

82 Porter, *John Jacob Astor,* I, 206-207.

83 *Astoria* (Todd, ed.), 470. Irving makes much of this omitted stop, but it is not easy to see what difference it could have made in the final outcome, except for saving from the clutches of the North West Company such furs as were then ready to ship.

84 Porter, *John Jacob Astor,* I, pp. 214-20, describes Astor's desperate maneuvers, which included trying to send his own man-of-war secretly from England.

85 *Astoria,* 472.

and without means of sending out the considerable stocks of furs they were accumulating, had decided to abandon the whole enterprise and leave the country.[86] Hunt objected but was argued down, and since the "Albatross" could not wait long enough to load Astoria's furs and people, Hunt left in her to find another ship.[87]

While he was gone word came to Astoria, via North West Company men, that a vessel of the British Navy was en route to seize Astoria (which indeed one was) and all other American property on the Northwest Coast. McDougall thereupon hastily sold Astoria, all its dependencies, and all its riches of gathered furs to the North West Company for a fraction of their value. Controversy has surrounded this deal ever since,[88] McDougall partisans claiming the forced sale was necessary to keep Astoria and its goods from falling an outright prize to the expected English man-of-war; McDougall detractors (among them Astor, Irving, and Hunt) claiming that he had been guilty of double-dealing and had "virtually given away"[89] the property in exchange for a partnership in the North West Company – which, in fact, he did secretly accept while the negotiations of sale were still in progress.[90]

A British sloop-of-war appeared at the end of November, operating under the orders (so he claimed) of a North West Company partner who was on board,[91] and sailed away on

[86] *Ibid.*, 452-54, 473.

[87] *Ibid.*, 473-74.

[88] Porter, *John Jacob Astor,* gives a thorough and objective discussion of this controversy, I, pp. 226-35; and at 245, *n.* 32, cites the detailed discussion in Bancroft, *Northwest Coast,* II, pp. 221-25, 229, 234; and in Chittenden, *op. cit.,* I, pp. 232-35, and 244-46. *Astoria* gives a strong anti-McDougall case in 452-54, 484-86, 494-95, and 495, *n.* 3. Among witnesses on the scene, Ross, *Adventures,* 262, is rather pro-McDougall, while Franchere, 303-316, 317, is rather anti.

[89] *Astoria,* 486.

[90] *Ibid.*, 495. See also T. C. Elliott, "Sale of Astoria, 1813," in *Oregon Historical Quarterly,* XXXIII (1932), 43-50. Much detail on the events of this time is to be found in Vol. 2 of Elliott Coues, ed., *New Light on the Early History of the Greater Northwest: Manuscript Journals of Alexander Henry, . . . and David Thompson* (New York, 1897).

[91] Porter, *John Jacob Astor,* I, p. 231.

December 31st. Hunt then returned to Astoria at the end of February, 1814, in the brig "Pedler," bought in the Hawaiian Islands, and learned with "indignation"[92] of the sale of Astoria and its furs, although, as Porter points out, if the furs had not been previously sold, the British warship could presumably have seized them for nothing.[93] In any case, Hunt concluded the transaction of Astoria's sale, and on April 3rd left in the "Pedler," taking along four clerks who wanted to go home by sea.[94] Some of the Pacific Fur Company people stayed on in the employ of the North West Company, either voluntarily or under duress,[95] and some went back east overland, among these two disaffected voyageurs who said they were going to Montreal to sue the Pacific Fur Company for their back wages.[96] The story behind this familiar sort of big-business quarrel is unclear, since by the terms of Astoria's transfer the North West Company accepted the obligation of paying wages due Pacific Fur Company employees.[97] A half dozen or so of Hunt's original overlanders stayed to eventually become permanent Willamette settlers.[98] Thus ended the Pacific Fur Company and Astor's Astoria.[99]

Thus ended, too, Wilson Price Hunt's brush with fortune. Doggedly faithful to the last, he gathered up for his employer what nickels and dimes he could on the way home, spending nearly two years (alternately arrested by both the

---

92 *Astoria*, 494.

93 Porter, *loc. cit.*

94 *Astoria*, 497, and *n.*; Franchere, 316, says April 2nd.

95 *Astoria*, 494, *n.* 2.

96 Porter, "Roll of Overland Astorians."

97 *Astoria*, 485, and *n.*

98 Joseph Gervais, Etienne Lucier, Louis La Bonte, Alexander Carson, Joseph St. Amant, Jean Baptiste Ouvre – plus, of course, Dorion's widow and two children. Archibald Pelton was killed by Indians in 1814. See Porter, "Roll of Overland Astorians," and see especially, J. Neilson Barry, "Astorians Who Became Permanent Settlers," in *Washington Historical Quarterly*, XXIV (1933), 221-31, 282-301.

99 A list of works touching upon Astoria's significance in the history of the Northwest would be long, and can scarcely be attempted here. Oscar O. Winther, in *A Classified Bibliography of the Periodical Literature of the Trans-Mississippi West, 1811-1957* (Bloomington, Ind., 1961), lists more than two dozen items dealing rather directly with Astoria in the journal literature alone.

Spanish and the Russians) in the chancy Pacific Coast trade, sailing with his gains to China to trade for a cargo of silks, china, and teas, and at last returning to New York in October, 1816.[100]

Home again in St. Louis in 1817 Hunt bought several thousand acres of land on Gravois Creek, about eight miles southwest of town. A grist mill was built here, and the place was known for years as "Hunt's Mill."[101] He was a candidate for delegate to the constitutional convention in 1820 and was defeated, although his party won "a signal victory" in the same election.[102] He was appointed postmaster at St. Louis in 1822, a rather important political plum in those days, and as a consequence – the postmaster then serving as a collector for newspaper subscriptions – his correspondence contains some interesting notes concerning such subscribers as Joshua Pilcher, George C. Sibley, Colonel Kearny, or General Clark (" I hope shortly to collect that of General Clark who says he will pay so soon as convenient which will be I suppose as soon as Government forward him funds of the Indian Department . . .")[103] Otherwise he settled down to the life of a provincial merchant.[104]

---

100 See Kenneth W. Porter, "Cruise of Astor's Brig *Pedler*, 1813-1816," in *Oregon Historical Quarterly*, XXXI (1930), 223-30.

101 Elliott, "Wilson Price Hunt," and the Missouri Historical Society *Collections*, III, p. 325. Astor may have held a mortgage on this land, as appears from a letter from Hunt to Astor, St. Louis Nov. 16, 1836, giving Astor a deed "(for which the same land was formerly mortgaged)" to 4002 arpents and excepting some three hundred acres for a "little farm" for himself – Missouri Historical Society, Hunt Collections, Wilson Price Hunt Letterbook.

102 *Dictionary of American Biography*. W. J. Ghent, in the article here on Wilson Price Hunt says Hunt was "humiliated" by this defeat, but a better view of Hunt's political feelings is given in a letter of January 20, 1830, in Missouri Historical Society, Hunt Collections, Wilson Price Hunt Letterbook.

103 Hunt to H. Niles, Esquire, June 13, 1836, in Missouri Historical Society, Hunt Collections, Wilson Price Hunt Letterbook.

104 W. G. Lyford, *The Western Address Directory . . . etc.* (Baltimore,

He brought out from New Jersey in 1829 a nephew, John H. Wilson, to take care of his farm.[105] He married in 1836 the widow of his cousin, Theodore Hunt (who long before had followed Wilson Price Hunt's example in moving West),[106] and acquired thereby a readymade family of a stepson and two stepdaughters.[107]

Donald McKenzie opened a cordial correspondence with Hunt in the 1820s – speaking of where he might live when retired from the fur trade (". . . the prospect of living near yourself would furnish . . . no small inducement for me to bend my weary steps toward the Missouri. . .")[108] and saying in a later letter, ". . . abler pens will hand the names of my friends to after times. In this event suffer me to add my good Sir that yours shall honorably be enrolled high among the number."[109]

Very possibly the most far-reaching effects of the whole Astoria adventure flowed ultimately from the influences of Washington Irving's heroic statuary group, *Astoria,* in which Hunt was cast as the chief hero. Hunt, alas, was not impressed at being thus immortalized. He wrote Astor, upon the book's appearance in 1836, that he had just had a glimpse of it and had "had time only to see some things that would have been well to have been otherwise expressed," namely that Irving's description of St. Louis in 1810

1837), lists Hunt, page 421, as a dealer in furs and peltries with office at the North West corner of Front and Chestnut Streets, St. Louis.

105 Elliott, "Wilson Price Hunt."

106 See Theodore Hunt's biographical sketch in Vol. IV of this *Series.*

107 In Hunt's will, his stepson, Charles L. Hunt, was left $100; his nephew John H. Wilson was left half of the Hunt farm and several slaves; and another nephew $400.

108 Letter dated at "Rocky Mountains, Columbia River," March 1, 1820, from McKenzie to Hunt, in Missouri Historical Society, Hunt Collections, Wilson Price Hunt Letterbook.

109 McKenzie to Hunt, from Hudson's Bay, July 30, 1822, quoted in T. C. Elliott, "Letters of McKenzie to Wilson Price Hunt," in *Oregon Historical Quarterly,* XLIII (1942), 10-13, and 194-97.

did not render the town genteel enough. "I am sorry my name is blended with a discription of merely the Boatmen, Motlies, etc."[110]

Hunt served as Astor's western representative when he could be of use, and a letter written to a lawyer in Belleville, Illinois, only a few months before Hunt's death shows him still loyal, come what may: ". . . I have ascertained that the trespasses on the land of John Jacob Astor of New York have been committed by Joseph Fagotte, widow Shumate and her son George, [and] Louis Lecompte. The name of the first I left with you to bring suit. Please add the two other names Shumate and LeCompte and bring suit for $1000 against each of the three. It is a very disagreeable thing to bring a suit against a widow but it is not at my discretion to pass her by. . ."[111]

He died April 13, 1842,[112] at his residence at 7th and Olive, and was interred in the "Episcopal burying grounds," St. Louis.[113]

---

110 Hunt to Astor, St. Louis, Nov. 16, 1836, in Missouri Historical Society, Hunt Collections, Wilson Price Hunt Letterbook.

111 Hunt to Gustavus Koerner, Esq., August 13, 1841, in Missouri Historical Society, Hunt Collections, Wilson Price Hunt Letterbook.

112 Missouri Historical Society *Collections*, III, *loc. cit.*

113 Elliott, "Wilson Price Hunt."

William H. Ashley

by Harvey L. Carter
Colorado College, Colorado Springs

Considering his relatively brief period of active association with the fur trade of the Rocky Mountains, no individual can be said to have left so strong a mark upon its development as did William Henry Ashley. Born in Chesterfield County, Virginia, and growing up in neighboring Pawhatan County, he migrated as a young man to what was to become Missouri, and his career was closely associated with the development of that territory and state. Neither the date of his birth nor the year of his migration is certainly known. Ashley himself stated, in 1831, that he had resided in Missouri for twenty-nine years and the Reverend W. G. Eliot stated in a memorial address, delivered a few weeks after Ashley's death in 1838, that he came to St. Genevieve at the age of twenty.[1] If we accept both of these statements, the year of his birth was 1782 and that of his migration was 1802.[2]

However these matters may be resolved, it is certain that

1 Letter of William H. Ashley to Nathan Kouns, September 20, 1831, in Dale L. Morgan, *The West of William H. Ashley* (Denver, 1964), 205-7; W. G. Eliot, *An Address on the Life and Character of the Life of the Late Hon. Wm. H. Ashley; Delivered in St. Louis, Missouri, June 6, 1838, at the Request of the Committee on Arrangements* (St. Louis, 1838).

2 My own judgment is that these are the most probable dates. However, Eliot, *op. cit.*, gives the date of birth as 1785 and the date of migration as 1803. These dates are inconsistent with his previously quoted statement. William F. Switzler, "General William Henry Ashley," in *American Monthly Magazine* (April 1908), XXXII, pp. 318-30, gives the date of birth as 1778. This is a more probable date than 1785, and Dale L. Morgan, the greatest contributor of fugitive information concerning Ashley, is inclined to accept it. However, the earliest record of Ashley at St. Genevieve to have been found by Mr. Morgan is dated 1805 and it seems unlikely that he would have been there as early as 1798 without some indication of the fact having been turned up.

Ashley was a resident of St. Genevieve in the summer of 1805 and that he witnessed the marriage of Andrew Henry, later his partner in the fur trade, in that year. Between 1808 and 1811, according to Eliot, Ashley made trips to New York and brought supplies by pack horse to St. Genevieve and by ship to New Orleans, but these trading speculations were more financially disastrous than otherwise. While still based at St. Genevieve, and probably within this trading period, Ashley was married to Mary, daughter of Ezekiel Able, holder of a large Spanish land grant.[3] Ashley acquired some land claims by his marriage, soon became involved in land speculation, and seems to have resided for a time on a plantation near Cape Girardeau.

About 1811, he seems to have removed to Potosi, where he operated both a lead mine and a saltpetre mine. In these ventures, he was associated with Andrew Henry and with Lionel Browne. The mining of saltpetre led naturally to the business of manufacturing gunpowder, which was carried on until the death of Browne in 1819. The occurrence of several explosions during these years, with resultant damage to property and loss of life, may also have influenced Ashley to abandon the enterprise.[4]

Ashley was active in the Missouri Territorial Militia from an early date and during the War of 1812 he became lieutenant colonel of a regiment, with Andrew Henry as his 1st major. It was not until 1821 that he became a brigadier general of militia, thus acquiring the title of General Ashley, by which he was thereafter always known.[5] In the year 1812,

[3] Louis Houck, *A History of Missouri* (Chicago, 1908), III, p. 168.

[4] *History of Franklin, Jefferson, Washington, Crawford and Gasconade Counties* (Chicago, 1888), 480-2, 490, 494, contains some account of these activities. Potosi is located in Washington County. Both Ashley and the beginning of mining seem to have preceded the organization of the town itself in the history of Washington County.

[5] Morgan, *The West of Ashley,* xix. I would like here to acknowledge my indebtedness to this great source book of Ashley material, without which this sketch would be much less complete. However, I have made use of all other primary sources cited, depending on Morgan chiefly for materials not readily available to me.

Ashley is said to have marched with the Missouri Militia expedition under General Howard, which destroyed the Indian village on the site of Peoria, Illinois, whence raids had been organized by the Indians against the Missouri settlers.[6]

In 1819, Ashley removed to St. Louis, where he extended his real estate operations and entered politics. In 1820, he was elected to the office of lieutenant governor of the new state of Missouri. The office was not a demanding one and Ashley formed a partnership with his old friend, Andrew Henry, to engage in the fur trade of the Rocky Mountains, in which Henry had already had considerable experience. Ashley's first wife died November 7, 1821, and he did not re-marry until 1825. It was during these years that he made a name and a fortune for himself in the fur trade, only taking time out to run unsuccessfully for governor in 1824.[7]

It was on February 13, 1822, that Ashley first ran his famous advertisement for one hundred enterprising young men to ascend the Missouri River to its source and to be employed from one to three years.[8]

Henry acted as the field commander of their first expedition and Ashley undertook the part of supplying him. Henry started up the Missouri River in April 1822, and reached the mouth of the Yellowstone by October. He began construction of a fort there at once. Ashley started up the river a month after Henry, had the misfortune to lose his cargo by the upsetting of his boat and returned to St. Louis, where he obtained more supplies on credit. With these he reached

6 "Unsigned article of April 14, 1838, from the *Missouri Saturday News,* edited by Alphonso Wetmore and Charles Keemle," reprinted in *Bulletin of the Missouri Historical Society* (July 1968), XXIV, pp. 348-54. This anonymous article was probably based on the recollections of Charles Keemle and is very imprecise in most of its information. It is the only source I have found which mentions Ashley as a member of the Peoria Expedition.

7 Morgan, *op. cit.,* xxii-xxiii, discusses these matters in some detail.

8 *Ibid.,* 1, where the advertisement, which ran originally in the *Missouri Gazette and Public Advertiser,* is reproduced. It was later carried by other Missouri newspapers.

the Yellowstone in October 1822, and returned almost at once, leaving Henry to carry on trade and trapping from the fort.[9]

In March 1823, Ashley ascended the Missouri again with seventy men, recruited by means of another advertisemnt and by the personal exertions of James Clyman, who had taken employment with Ashley and was given this task as his first assignment. Among those recruited were William L. Sublette, David E. Jackson and Thomas Fitzpatrick. Already serving with Henry on the Yellowstone was Jedediah S. Smith. It is clear that Ashley's advertisement had succeeded in attracting many of the enterprising young men whom he sought. A further examination of the known employees would reveal many recruited by Clyman from the grog shops of St. Louis, who were not so enterprising, but who knew or adapted to the life of the trapper well enough.[10]

Ashley reached the Arickaree villages where, after friendly negotiations, he was treacherously attacked on April 2, 1823, and forced to withdraw down the river with a loss of twelve dead and twelve wounded, three of whom died later of their wounds.[11] The Arickarees had not taken into account the fact that Ashley was a politician. As such, he was able to summon to his aid a punitive force consisting of the 6th U.S. Infantry under Colonel Henry Leavenworth. He was also joined by Joshua Pilcher at the head of a party of trappers of the Missouri Fur Company, and his own partner, Andrew Henry, came down the river to his aid. Time was required to get organized but by August 9, 1823, Leavenworth with 230 men, Ashley and Henry with 80, and Pilcher with 50, were joined by about 700 Sioux Indians and an assault on the Arickaree villages was made.

[9] See *ibid.*, 1-19, for documents bearing on the activities of 1822.

[10] Charles L. Camp, *James Clyman, Frontiersman* (Portland, 1960), 7.

[11] For Ashley's three accounts of the Arickaree fight, see Morgan, *op. cit.*, 25-31; Clyman's account is given in Camp, *op. cit.*, 8-13.

The objectives of the U.S. Army were different from those of the trappers and the Sioux and after some fighting and some attempted negotiations, the Arickarees were allowed to abandon their villages under cover of night on August 14th. Ashley seems to have accepted this unsatisfactory result with more equanimity than Pilcher. Despite his losses, Ashley was in a position to attempt the renewal of his business while the Missouri Fur Company was not, because of the deaths of Jones and Immel at the hands of the Blackfeet and because its financial losses were about five times those sustained by Ashley and Henry.[12]

Nevertheless, Ashley was not in good shape financially, for few furs had been gathered by Henry. He lost men by desertion, although the number is difficult to ascertain. Henry's return to the Yellowstone brought the information that the Indians of that area were increasingly hostile. Ashley was forced to discover some alternate route by which the beaver filled waters of the continental divide could be reached. Accordingly, he dispatched a small force of his best men, under Jedediah Smith, by an exploratory overland route which eventually reached the Green River by way of South Pass.[13] Word was brought by Thomas Fitzpatrick to Ashley in 1824 of the great plenty of beaver to be found in the Green River country.

Ashley himself returned to St. Louis in the fall of 1823 after Smith's party had set out for the mountains. Henry, meanwhile, had cut loose from the fort on the Yellowstone and led a party to the Wind River country with some success but, on his return to St. Louis, decided to withdraw from the partnership.[14] The breakthrough had been made and Ashley alone prepared to take advantage of it.

12 The documents bearing on the punitive campaign against the Arickarees and on the subsequent controversy are assembled in Morgan, *op. cit.*, 35-67.

13 See Camp, *op. cit.*, 15-28. Clyman's reminiscences are the chief source for this important expedition.

Accordingly, his unsuccessful campaign for governor behind him, and armed with a new license, Ashley set out with a fresh party to join his men on Green River. He left Fort Atkinson on November 4, 1824, and followed the Platte and then the South Platte, until he came in sight of the Rocky Mountains. Winter forced him to make camp for three weeks in February on the Cache la Poudre River.[15]

Resuming his journey, Ashley led his party across the front range of the Rockies and emerged on the Laramie Plains. On March 25, 1825, they skirted the northern limits of the Medicine Bow Range and descended to camp next day on the North Platte River.[16] They now crossed the Great Divide Basin, passing near present Rawlins, Wyoming, hampered only by a loss of seventeen horses, stolen by the Crow Indians, and by blustery weather. April 19 found them camped on Green River at a point where it was both wide and deep and where there was a view of the Uinta Mountains to the south and west.

Not much time was wasted in getting organized for more trapping. On April 22, Ashley divided his party into four sections. Parties under James Clyman, Zacharias Ham, and Thomas Fitzpatrick were dispatched in various directions, while Ashley himself with seven men set off down Green River in bull boats. Arrangements had been made to "randavoze for all our parties on or before the 10th July next" upon the tributary of Green River flowing into it from the

---

14 Henry's expedition is described in the informative letter of Daniel T. Potts, one of the trappers, written from "Rocky Mountains, July 16, 1826." It is reproduced in Donald McKay Frost, *General Ashley, the Overland Trail, and South Pass* (Barre, Mass., 1960), 56-60.

15 Ashley's trip, up to this point, is described in a narrative which he wrote to General Henry Atkinson. It is reproduced in Morgan, *op. cit.,* 100-104.

16 Ashley's diary, covering the period from March 25, 1825, to June 27, 1825, has survived and is reproduced in Morgan, *op. cit.,* 104-17. It was given to Colonel Frank Triplett by Thomas Eddy, one of the last survivors of the Ashley men. Triplett erroneously supposed it to be a diary of William Sublette but must be credited with having preserved it.

west above the Uinta Range, soon to be known as Henry's Fork.

Ashley's trip down Green River was productive of beaver at first but became less so as they passed through Flaming Gorge, Lodore Canyon, and the other awesome natural features of the stream. Although Ashley does not record it, he painted his name and the date on the walls of Red Canyon, where the inscription was discovered by Major J. W. Powell in 1869. Farther down river at the lower end of Son of a Bitch Rapids, Ashley's boat was pulled ashore by cables when it seemed in danger of being sunk after hitting a rock, on May 14, 1825.[17] Three days later they encountered two of Etienne Provost's trappers from Taos, who told Ashley that four of their companions had descended the river still farther and found it destitute of game. Ashley continued on Green River to a point below its junction with the Duchesne (Uinta) in an effort to effect a meeting with Provost. He met a party of Ute Indians who led him to the Frenchman's camp, which was reached on June 7, 1825. Relying on information furnished by Provost, Ashley continued up the Duchesne-Strawberry Trail, passed around the Uinta Range on the west, and reached a point on Big Muddy Creek near present Carter, Wyoming, by June 27, when his diary suddenly breaks off.

From here he continued on toward the appointed place of rendezvous, which actually took place about twenty miles up Henry's Fork from its junction with Green River.[18] About 120 men were at rendezvous by July 1, including

[17] This is the incident inaccurately reported by James P. Beckwourth, *The Life and Adventures of James P. Beckwourth. . . , written from his own dictation by T. D. Bonner* (New York, 1856), 58-60. Beckwourth was not with Ashley at the time and so could not have saved the general's life as he claimed to have done.

[18] The location of the rendezvous has been questioned by some writers but, in the opinion of the writer, who traveled over the area in question in 1948, it was on Henry's Fork in the vicinity of present Burnt Fork, Wyoming. The appointed place was at the mouth of Henry's Fork.

those under Ashley's trusted captains, John H. Weber and Jedediah Smith. The latter had returned from a visit to the Flathead Post of the Hudson's Bay Company. Twenty-nine deserters from Peter Skene Ogden's Hudson's Bay men from the vicinity of Great Salt Lake were also on hand. Ashley took Smith in as a junior partner and field captain and by July 2 was ready to start back to St. Louis with nearly 9,000 beaver pelts, a good part of which he had bought from his own free trappers at two or three dollars per pound, depending on the condition of the fur.[19] He set out with fifty men, headed for some navigable point on the Bighorn River, which he reached on July 7. Here half of his men remained to trap and the other half, including Jedediah Smith, descended the Bighorn to the Yellowstone and then went down that river to its junction with the Missouri. At the mouth of the Yellowstone, Ashley met General Henry Atkinson and Indian Agent Benjamin O'Fallon, with a considerable body of soldiers and five keelboats equipped with paddle wheels, "the Mink, Beaver, Muskrat, Elk and Rackoon." General Atkinson agreed to transport Ashley's furs back to St. Louis for him and so Ashley and his men descended the Missouri with less worry than they otherwise would have had.[20]

Ashley arrived back in St. Louis in early October and set about equipping a party for Smith to lead back to the mountains as soon as possible. By the end of the month Smith was off, but was forced to winter among the Pawnees of the Republican River. Ashley waited until early spring, but on March 8, 1826, set out with a party of his own, and overtook Smith in April on the Platte River at Grand Island. They continued their way westward together, this time following

19 Ashley's accounts with the trappers at this first rendezvous are given in Morgan, *op. cit.*, 118-29. Ashley paid $5 per pelt at the rate of $3 per pound.

20 See "Journal of the Atkinson-O'Fallon Expedition, 1825," edited by Russel Reid and Clell G. Gannon, in *North Dakota Historical Quarterly,* (Oct. 1929), IV, pp. 1-40.

the North Platte and the Sweetwater to South Pass, a route that was to become famous as the Oregon Trail. They proceeded to Cache Valley, where the second rendezvous was held in accordance with previous agreement. Sixty or seventy trappers, who had remained in the mountains, joined them with a good catch of beaver. Also present were a considerable number of Iroquois who had left the service of the Hudson's Bay Company. David Jackson and William Sublette were encountered on Bear River shortly after the two week rendezvous had ended and it was apparently at this time that Ashley sold out to Smith, Jackson, and Sublette, agreeing to act as supplier of goods to them.[21]

Having settled this business, Ashley loaded 123 packs of beaver on pack horses and mules and returned overland to St. Louis, arriving there during the last week in September 1826.[22] Presumably he returned by the route he followed coming out but of this nothing very definite is known.

Between his two successful trips to the Rocky Mountains, Ashley married for the second time, the wedding date being October 26, 1825. His bride was Eliza Christy and for her Ashley now built a fine mansion in St. Louis. The second Mrs. Ashley died June 1, 1830. During the years of his second marriage Ashley continued to have some connection with the fur trade as a supplier of trade goods and provisions to Smith, Jackson and Sublette.

The death of a Missouri congressman in a duel, in August 1831, gave him an opportunity to enter politics once more.

---

[21] Very few details of Ashley's second trip to the mountains have survived. A little can be gleaned from Beckwourth, *op. cit.*, 90-98. The most reliable source is a reminiscent account by Robert Campbell, the original of which is in the Missouri Historical Society Library, St. Louis, Missouri. I have relied upon Morgan, *op. cit.*, 142-50, which makes skillful use of Campbell's recollections in reconstructing the events of 1826. The articles of agreement between Ashley and the new firm are reproduced in *ibid.*, 150-52.

[22] *Missouri Republican*, Sep. 21, 1826. Ashley is reported "within the settlements" but had not yet reached St. Louis. Ashley probably returned with about 1500 more beaver pelts in 1826 than he had brought back in 1825.

He was elected to the House of Representatives as an independent candidate and re-elected in 1832 and again in 1834. Meanwhile, in October 1832, he had married Elizabeth Moss Wilcox, an attractive widow, the daughter of Dr. James W. Moss, of Boone County, Missouri. Originally a Jacksonian Democrat, Ashley broke with that party over the question of a re-charter for the second Bank of the United States and ran once more for the governorship of Missouri in 1836, as a candidate of the Whig party. In this contest, he was defeated by the Democratic candidate, Lilburn W. Boggs.[23]

Ashley was making plans to run again for Congress on the Whig ticket when he died of pneumonia on March 26, 1838. He was buried in an Indian mound on the farm of his father-in-law, Dr. Moss, at his own request. His grave, on a bluff overlooking the Missouri River was unmarked until 1939, when a suitable stone was provided by the Daughters of the American Revolution. He left an estate of upwards of $50,000 but had no children by any of his three marriages.[24]

No portrait of Ashley is known to be in existence. He was described by Frederick Billon, who knew him well, as "a man of medium height, say about five feet nine inches, of light frame, his weight might have been from one hundred and thirty five to one hundred and forty pounds; thin face, prominent nose, not Roman, but aquiline or Grecian, so that a profile view of his face presented a projecting nose and chin with the mouth drawn in."[25]

Of a restless and active disposition, Ashley was a good

---

23 Details of his political career and of his second and third marriages will be found in Morgan, *op. cit.*, xxii-xxv.

24 His widow subsequently married Senator John J. Crittenden of Kentucky. She died in 1873.

25 J. Thomas Scharf, *History of St. Louis City and County* (Phila., 1883), I, pp. 196-7.

type figure of the business enterpriser and risk taker of early 19th century America. Often on the verge of financial ruin, he rose to triumph over adverse circumstances almost by sheer will power and perseverance. As a congressman, he was a good representative of the interest of his state.

Few individuals can be said to have exercised a greater influence on the course of the fur trade of the Far West. His advertisements attracted some of the ablest younger men to the business and his own success was a pattern for them to emulate. The innovations that he introduced can be said to have revolutionized the business. The first rendezvous was held at his direction and was so successful that it replaced the earlier method of maintaining a fort as a trading post. His decision to gather most of the furs by the employment of trappers rather than to rely on the Indian trade was responsible for the rapid development of the business and was to lead ultimately to its decline.

Ashley's employment of free trappers rather than *engagés* at a fixed annual wage offered more incentive to the trappers. The prices paid to trappers for beaver and the prices charged for goods supplied to them by Ashley were both sufficiently competitive to force the Hudson's Bay Company to revise its prices in order to stay in business. Before the British company realized what it was up against it had lost many employees, although some of the deserters returned after the British policy was revised.

Not particularly interested in exploration, Ashley was sufficiently curious about the country to make his first trip to the mountains by a new route. His voyage down Green River was also a notable achievement. Both of these departures from more traveled paths were occasioned by his desire to uncover new beaver territory. In the end, his common sense prevailed over his desire to explore and his use of the South Pass-Sweetwater-North Platte route both going out and returning on his second trip had much to do with establishing that route as the most practical one available.

Finally, it was by conducting business along the lines laid down by Ashley that his successors were able to remain in business as long as they did. Ashley's place in history is that of a man of energy and action, to whom the making of decisions came easily and naturally. The decisions that he made greatly influenced the development of the fur trading frontier.

Jedediah Smith

by HARVEY L. CARTER
Colorado College, Colorado Springs

First to find and recognize the natural gateway to the Oregon country; first overland traveler to reach California; first to cross the Sierra Nevada; first to traverse the Great Basin on its most direct and desert route; first to travel overland from California to the Columbia! That one man should have accomplished all these achievements is remarkable, but that these things should have been done, recognized at the time, and then forgotten, only to be recognized again a century later, is more remarkable still.

The two preeminent reputations among the Mountain Men of the Far Western fur trade are those of Kit Carson and Jedediah Smith. The contrast in their characters is marked but equally diverse are their pathways to lasting fame. Carson, a typical but undistinguished trapper, was singled out by adventitious circumstances, became a legend in his own time, a folk hero whose deeds were so exaggerated by an admiring public that his fame was made secure in later times only by the realization that his sterling qualities, as Pericles said of the Athenians, were superior to the commonly circulated reports. Jedediah Smith was an acknowledged leader, a blazer of trails and a maker of history, whose importance had to be painstakingly reestablished by the labors of later historians after years of undeserved neglect.[1] However dissimilar the two routes to remembrance,

[1] The pioneer work in restoring to Jedediah Smith his proper place in history was Harrison C. Dale, *The Ashley-Smith Explorations and the Discovery of a Central Route to the Pacific, 1822-1829* (Cleveland, 1918). The next important step was taken by Maurice S. Sullivan, *The Travels of Jedediah Smith* (Santa Ana, 1934), followed by Maurice S. Sullivan, *Jedediah Smith: Trader and Trail Breaker* (New York, 1936). A more complete biography, thoroughly researched and ably written

the results were justified in both cases. Nor could the two men have emerged so well, if the circumstances of their rise to the top of their profession had been interchanged. The verdict of history is sometimes established in mysterious ways.

Jedediah Smith was far from being a typical fur trader and trapper in three respects. He was a New Yorker by birth and a New Englander by derivation, an unusual background for a Mountain Man. He was strongly religious, which could be said of only a small minority of his fellow trappers. He also had a keener sense of the importance of exploration than most of his associates, although his education was not more comprehensive than that of a good many others. He had undoubted qualities of leadership and a strong desire to make money but these were qualities that marked many of the more successful traders and do not particularly set him apart from his rivals or his partners.

Jedediah Strong Smith was born at Bainbridge (then called Jericho) in Chenango County, New York, on January 6, 1799. His parents, Jedediah and Sally Strong Smith both of old New England colonial stock, had settled in the upper Susquehanna Valley about five years earlier. About 1811 the family moved to Erie County, Pennsylvania, and by 1817 they were pioneering in the Western Reserve of Ohio. Little is known of Jedediah's early years, beyond the fact that he was influenced by a family friend, the frontier physician Dr. Titus Gordon Vespasian Simons, who was probably responsible for his interest in the Far West.[2]

---

is Dale L. Morgan, *Jedediah Smith and the Opening of the West* (Indianapolis, 1953). Alson J. Smith, *Men Against the Mountains* (New York, 1965) is another well written work on Smith's explorations, but scarcely adds to the knowledge amassed by Dale, Sullivan, and Morgan.

[2] See Sullivan, *Jedediah Smith,* 5-7, and Morgan, *Jedediah Smith,* 23-26. Jedediah was the sixth of fourteen children. The brothers and sisters who survived him were Sally (b. 1791), Ralph (b. 1794), Betsey (b. 1796), Eunice (b. 1797), Austin (b. 1808), Peter (b. 1810), Ira (b. 1811), Paddock (b. 1813), and Nelson (b. 1814). Ralph Smith and Eunice Smith married children of Dr. T. G. V. Simons.

When Jedediah made his appearance in St. Louis in the spring of 1822, after about a year spent in northern Illinois, it was with the deliberate intention of seeking employment that would take him into the Oregon country where he was confident he could make his fortune as a trapper.[3] His arrival in St. Louis coincided with General W. H. Ashley's famous advertisement for enterprising young men to go to the headwaters of the Missouri and Jedediah had no difficulty in persuading Ashley that he could fill the requirements. His first trip up the Missouri River was begun in late June with Ashley himself in command of the boat. They reached the mouth of the Yellowstone on October 1 and Jedediah remained there under Andrew Henry, while Ashley returned down river. Jedediah had the opportunity of ascending the Missouri as far as the mouth of the Musselshell and spent the winter near there.[4]

In the spring of 1823, Smith was sent down river by Henry with an urgent message to Ashley concerning the need for horses and encountered Ashley before he reached the Arikaree villages with his two keelboats of supplies and about ninety men.[5] In the ensuing treacherous attack by the lower Ree village on Ashley's party, on June 1, 1823, Jedediah was conspicuous for his bravery under fire that cost the lives of thirteen of Ashley's men. He further distinguished himself by volunteering to go to the mouth of the Yellowstone to secure help from Andrew Henry.[6] Within about a month Smith returned with Henry and his reinforcements, joining Ashley at the mouth of the Cheyenne. Colonel Leavenworth of the United States Army now organized Ashley's men and those of Joshua Pilcher, of the Missouri

[3] "Captain Jedediah Strong Smith: A Eulogy of that most Romantic and Pious of Mountain Men, First American by Land to California," in *Illinois Magazine* (June 1832) is reprinted in Alson J. Smith, *Men Against the Mountains*, appendix c. The unknown author of this eulogy states that Jedediah told him of his design in March 1831. See also Sullivan, *Travels of Smith*, 1.

[4] *Ibid.*, 2-10.

[5] Morgan, *Jedediah Smith*, 50.

[6] *Ibid.*, 51-58.

Fur Company, into the Missouri Legion and advanced on the Arikaree villages. Jedediah Smith was appointed captain of one of the two companies of Ashley men in the Legion.[7] In the campaign which followed, the Rees got off too lightly to satisfy Pilcher, whose company was in bad financial straits. Ashley and Henry had also lost, but not so heavily and were eager to recoup their losses by getting back to the beaver country. Henry was sent back to the Yellowstone but Jedediah Smith was singled out for a small independent command. In his party of about a dozen men, however, were William Sublette, Jim Clyman, Thomas Fitzpatrick, Thomas Eddy, and Edward Rose. Captain Smith was to endeavor to find and open up new beaver country south of the Yellowstone. What we know of their operations comes from Jim Clyman almost exclusively.

This history-making expedition left the Missouri at Fort Kiowa and went westward overland through the Sioux country starting about the last of September 1823. Somewhere west of the Black Hills but before they reached Powder River, Captain Smith was fearfully mauled by a grizzly bear. The wounds were chiefly on his head and face. Under Smith's direction, Clyman sewed them up as well as he could, reattaching one ear.[8] Smith was scarred for life and always wore his hair long thereafter in order to minimize the scars. They fell in with a party of friendly Crows with whom they wintered in Wind River Valley near present Dubois, Wyoming. They also made contact here with Charles Keemle and William Gordon, of the rival Missouri Fur Company, and with a party under Captain Weber, which included Daniel Potts and which had been sent by Andrew Henry up the Yellowstone.[9] The Crows told them of a river beyond the Wind River Mountains that was teeming with beaver and directed them how to reach it by pass-

[7] Dale L. Morgan, *The West of William H. Ashley* (Denver, 1964), 52.

[8] *James Clyman, Frontiersman,* edited by Charles L. Camp (Portland, 1960), 15-18.

[9] Morgan, *West of Ashley,* 78-79.

ing around the southern extremity of the Wind River Range. The winds were high and the weather bad when, in late February 1824, they moved down to the Sweetwater but, about mid-March, they were able to move over the Continental Divide to westward flowing waters and, by March 19, they reached the Siskeedee, or Green River, near the mouth of the Big Sandy. This crossing soon came to be known as South Pass, to distinguish it from Lewis and Clark's crossing far to the north.[10] Captain Smith led half his party down river and sent the other half upstream under Fitzpatrick. Both groups took many beaver. Clyman became detached from the reunited party on the Sweetwater, and made his solitary way to Fort Atkinson, whither also came Fitzpatrick after being forced to leave the beaver cached at Independence Rock. Smith remained in the mountains and Fitzpatrick rejoined him from Fort Atkinson, after sending news down river to Ashley concerning the events of the past year.[11]

This news brought Ashley to the mountains as fast as he could get there to join his field captain, who meanwhile was discovering that the Hudson's Bay Company had penetrated to his beaver paradise from the northwest. In mid-September 1824, near present Blackfoot, Idaho, Jedediah encountered Pierre Tevanitagon and his Iroquois hunters, who had split off from the main British party under Alexander Ross. The Iroquois were in dire peril from the Shoshones and turned over to Smith their entire catch of 105 beaver on condition that he would give them safe escort to the Flathead Post, located on Clark's Fork of the Columbia. This Smith was glad to do, much to the irritation of

[10] Clyman, *op. cit.*, 21-25, 30. This was the effective discovery of South Pass, which had been traversed by the returning Astorians in 1811. In the same way, Zebulon M. Pike made the effective discovery of Pikes Peak in 1806 and Christopher Columbus made the effective discovery of America in 1492. In all three cases there had been prior knowledge which had been put to little use. There are many variant spellings of the Siskeedee, the Indian name for Green River, which meant Prairie Hen River.

[11] Clyman, *op. cit.*, 29.

Ross, who regarded the Americans as interlopers, despite the fact that Great Britain and the United States had signed a joint occupation agreement regarding the whole of the Oregon country in 1818.[12]

Peter Skene Ogden arrived to replace Ross in charge of Flathead Post just ahead of Ross and Smith on November 26, 1824. He and William Kittson headed a British trapping party into the Snake River region and Jedediah and his small party of seven accompanied him. They left Flathead Post, on December 20, 1824, and parted company, in April 1825, on Bear River. Jedediah's movements during this time can only be traced through the journals of Ogden and Kittson.[13]

During May, Jedediah made contact with some Ashley men under Captain J. H. Weber, who had wintered in Cache Valley and Ogden encountered a party from Taos under Etienne Provost. There was considerable intermingling of the parties for a time and Johnson Gardner, a free trapper, took it upon himself to inform the British that they were trespassing on American soil. Actually all were trespassing on the Spanish domain. Some British trappers were persuaded to desert to the Americans but it is doubtful if this was by deliberate inducement on the part of Smith or any American leaders; more probably it was a consequence of higher prices and wages paid by the American companies.

Meanwhile, Ashley reached Green River on April 19 and sent out his trappers in all directions while he himself undertook to explore down river. However, word was given to rendezvous on the fork of Green River just above the Uinta Mountains (Henry's Fork) and here all the Ashley men, including Smith and Weber, met about the first of July.

---

[12] Alexander Ross, *Fur Hunters of the Far West* (2 vols., London, 1855), II, pp. 128-29. See also Morgan, *Jedediah Smith,* 126-30.

[13] *Ibid.,* 133-42. Morgan provides a good summary from the British accounts and points out that Smith was forced to sell beaver at low prices to the British leaders in order to replenish his ammunition and other supplies.

Now the accumulated 8,829 pounds of beaver had to be taken to St. Louis and Jedediah accompanied Ashley, going by way of the Bighorn, the Yellowstone, and the Missouri. They arrived in St. Louis October 4, 1825, and in less than a month Jedediah was on his way back to the mountains, not only as field captain but with a partner's interest in the business.[14]

He was forced to winter among the Pawnees of the Republican River and was overtaken by Ashley, at Grand Island, on the Platte, in the spring. Together they moved west, pioneering the route that became the well-known Oregon Trail. At the rendezvous in Cache Valley in the summer of 1826, Ashley soon left with a haul of beaver more than equal to that of the previous year. Before he left, however, he made arrangements to sell out to Jedediah Smith, David E. Jackson, and William L. Sublette. The precise terms are not known, but Ashley agreed to act as supplier of goods to the new partners and to them alone.[15]

Sometime in August, Jackson and Sublette headed north for the fall hunt, but the senior partner, taking seventeen men, set out to ascertain whether there was new beaver country to be uncovered south and west of Great Salt Lake.[16] Jedediah later avowed that he had no intention of going to California when he started from Cache Valley about August 15, 1826. There is no reason to question his veracity, so we may accept his statement that, since he did not find good beaver streams, he kept going until his party was in such

14 *Ibid.*, 171-75.

15 See Morgan, *West of Ashley*, 142-52, for the route, the probable terms, and an interesting list of trade goods conveyed by Ashley to the new firm.

16 The seventeen men were Arthur Black, Manuel Eustavan, Robert Evans, Daniel Ferguson, John Gaiter, Silas Gobel, John Hanna, Abraham La Plant, Manuel Lazarus, Martin McCoy, Nepassang (probably an Indian), Louis Pombert (who does not appear in the records until after California had been reached but there is no other way to account for his presence), Peter Ranne (described as a "man of color"), James Reed, John Reubascan, Harrison Rogers (clerk and second in command), and John Wilson. Manuel Eustavan and Neppasang do not seem to have reached California. They may have deserted along the way.

want of supplies that he had no choice but to cross the desert to the California missions. At the same time, it is certain that, having done so, he had an intelligence keen enough to consider that his travels might be turned to some profit if he published an account of them and that the government might find his geographical findings of interest and utility.

From Cache Valley into the valley of the Great Salt Lake and thence south to Utah Lake, they went in a week's time. Then south until they struck the Sevier River which they followed upstream until they turned west up Clear Creek, then over "Sandy plains and Rocky hills" until they found a small westward flowing stream, the Beaver, which they crossed and ascended the Rim of the Basin. Here they found a creek leading to the Virgin River, whose increasingly tortuous course they followed with difficulty to its junction with the Colorado River.[17]

They had met Utes near Utah Lake and saw a few Paiutes as they moved through their country, but now they passed down the east side of the Colorado until they reached the Mojave villages where they spent two weeks and were well received. Smith had now succeeded in supplying the link between the 18th century explorations of Fathers Domínguez and Escalante, from New Mexico, and those of Father Garcés, from California. Half his horses had been lost and his supplies exhausted. He decided to visit the California missions, crossed the Colorado and advanced up the Mojave River about November 10, 1826. On November 26, they descended into the San Bernardino Valley by the Mojave Trail south of Cajon Pass. Jedediah rode ahead to Mission

[17] The letter of July 17, 1827, written by Jedediah Smith to General William Clark from the Bear Lake Rendezvous summarizes the course traveled. It is reprinted in Dale, *Ashley-Smith Explorations,* 186-94. The names bestowed by Smith upon the rivers he found have not survived. Sevier River he named Ashley's River; Beaver River he appropriately called Lost River; the Virgin River he named Adams River in honor of the President in 1826. The Colorado he recognized as the Siskeedee and called it by that name.

San Gabriel, dispatched a letter to the governor in San Diego, and sent back word for his men to come in to the mission. Father José Sánchez made them welcome and was particularly solicitous toward Captain Smith and his clerk, Harrison Rogers.[18]

Relations with Governor Echeandia were on no such easy basis. Jedediah was informed that his presence was required in San Diego. He complied but could not persuade the governor to permit him to go northward in search of beaver and visit the Russian post on Bodega Bay. Captain Cunningham, a Yankee trader, and other masters of sailing vessels in San Diego Harbor convinced the governor that Jedediah was innocent of political intentions adverse to the republic of Mexico, and he gave permission for the Americans to leave California provided that they returned by the way they had come. Captain Cunningham sailed him to San Pedro and he rejoined his men after an absence of a month. By January 18, 1827, Smith had his party well equipped with new horses and supplies and was ready to leave. Two troublemakers, Ferguson and Wilson, were left behind. Smith retraced his route over the San Bernardino Mountains but then skirted the edge of the Mojave Desert and crossed the Tehachapi range into the valley of the San Joaquin River. Here they found beaver at last.[19]

Late in April we find the party camped on the American River with more than fifteen hundred pounds of beaver. Smith was now ready to leave California and get his beaver back to summer rendezvous. But the snow lay deep on the Sierra Nevada and when they tried to cross by following the

---

18 The first of two journals kept by Harrison Rogers is the authority for the period of their stay at San Gabriel Mission. It extends from Nov. 27, 1826, to Jan. 27, 1827, and is reprinted in Dale, *op. cit.*, 198-228.

19 *Ibid.* Smith may have considered both the Mojave Desert and the San Joaquin Valley to be outside the California governor's jurisdiction since there were no settlements in either. However, he was certainly aware that both were within the limits of Mexico and that he was not complying strictly with Echeandia's orders.

American River, in early May, they were forced to turn back. They went into camp on the Stanislaus. Rumors reached Jedediah here that the San José Mission and the governor, who was now in Monterey, were disturbed at reports they had received of the American activities, and Smith wrote letters to both to explain. The governor sent troops to apprehend Smith. Late in May they found the camp but the captain had departed. Smith had taken two men, Robert Evans and Silas Gobel, and set out to cross the mountains, leaving Rogers in charge and promising to be back in four months. The beaver was necessarily left behind.[20]

The three men, with seven horses, left on May 20, 1827. They ascended the north fork of the Stanislaus and crossed by Ebbetts Pass, coming down south of Walker Lake.[21] The route from this point across the present state of Nevada followed roughly the course of the modern highway, U.S. 6, and required three weeks, at the end of which time several of their horses had been eaten as they gave out, and the three men were in dire lack of water. The portion of Smith's "Journal" that has survived takes up the story on June 22, at the Nevada-Utah line, near present Gandy, Utah. Three days later Evans gave out but the other two persisted, found water at the Skull Valley Springs, and Jedediah took a kettle of water back to Evans, who revived. Two days later they sighted and recognized the southern end of Great Salt Lake. By July 2, they were in Cache Valley once more and learned from Indians that rendezvous was at Bear Lake, a day's ride away. When the travelers rode in, it caused quite a commotion, for they had been given up as lost. A small

20 See Smith, *Men Against the Mountains*, 138-43, where Smith's letter to Father Duran at San José Mission is reprinted. Smith called the Stanislaus River the Appelamminy. He had a fight with the Mokelumne Indians, whom he calls the Macalumbry.

21 See *Ibid.*, 144-47, where other possible routes are discussed and rejected.

cannon brought out from St. Louis was fired in their honor.[22]

By July 13, Captain Smith with eighteen men had left the rendezvous and was headed for California once more. Silas Gobel was among them, but Robert Evans was not.[23] Smith took the Bear River-Weber River route to Utah Lake, but from there he followed the trail he had made the year before except that he avoided the worst of the Virgin River canyon by turning up Santa Clara River and pioneering the route of present U.S. highway 91. He heard rumors and saw signs of another party of whites that had been along his trail.[24] When he reached the Mojave villages, these Indians appeared friendly as before. Smith remained among them three days and then set about crossing the Colorado, probably about August 18, 1827. Leaving his horses and half his men on the east bank, Jedediah loaded part of his goods on rafts and pushed off on the river. At this moment the Mojaves struck. The men on shore were all killed, the two women captured along with the horses. The men on the rafts survived the attack with only five guns and with Thomas Virgin clubbed on the head. As they moved on, they were followed but they hastily forted up among some trees and repelled a second attack after which they were not molested. Their condition was precarious, however, and Jedediah feared he would have to avail himself again of the hospi-

22 See Sullivan, *Travels of Smith,* 19-26, where Smith's "Journal," covering these events, is reprinted.

23 The other men were Henry ("Boatswain") Brown, William Campbell, David Cunningham, Thomas Daws, François Deromme, Isaac Galbraith, Polette Labross (described as a mulatto), Joseph La Pointe, Touissant Maréchal, Gregory Ortago (identified as a Spaniard), Joseph Palmer, John Ratelle, John Relle ("a Canadian"), Robiseau ("a Canadian half-breed"), Charles Swift, John Turner, and Thomas Virgin. There were also two Indian squaws along.

24 There is a strong probability that this was a party headed by Ewing Young and contained some survivors of another party which included Miguel Robidoux and James Ohio Pattie. Young had trouble with the Mojaves and this may account for their changed attitude toward Smith, to whom they had been friendly in 1826. See Robert G. Cleland, *This Reckless Breed of Men* (New York, 1952), 182-83. However, if this was the party in question, James Ohio Pattie's dates are wrong.

tality of Father Sánchez at San Gabriel Mission. However, he was able to procure supplies at a ranch in the San Bernardino Valley and merely wrote to the Mission. Isaac Galbraith liked the country and was permitted to stay; Thomas Virgin was left behind to recover from his wounds; Jedediah and the rest retraced their route of 1826 to the camp on the Stanislaus, where they arrived September 18, 1827.[25]

Jedediah now became bogged down in what Dale Morgan has aptly termed the California quagmire. Father Duran at San José Mission was not friendly when Jedediah and three of his men appeared there. He was charged with trying to claim for the United States the country over which he had trapped. The governor sent a military escort which took him to Monterey as a prisoner and wished to send him to Mexico City, but Jedediah balked when he learned he was expected to pay his own expenses or else wait until a Mexican vessel was available. Governor Echeandia asked Smith to write and have his men come in but Jedediah wrote in such a way that he was sure Rogers would go to Bodega with the furs instead. It was finally agreed that Rogers should go to San Francisco. It was the shipmasters who once more came to Smith's rescue. William Hartnell, an English trader, persuaded the governor to adopt a practice used under British law when no consul was available, which was that four ship captains could appoint an agent to act as consul in an emergency. All agreed and Captain John Rogers Cooper, a former Bostonian, was appointed. Smith gave Cooper his bond for $30,000 that he would carry out his agreement with the governor. Echeandia issued Smith a passport for himself and his men and 250 horses and mules. Smith agreed to

[25] The men killed by the Mojaves were Brown, Campbell, Cunningham, Deromme, Gobel, Labross, Ortago, Ratelle, Relle, and Robiseau. See Sullivan, *Travels of Smith,* 30-35, where Smith's "Journal," describing these events, is reproduced. Also Morgan, *Jedediah Smith,* 337-43, which reproduces "A Brief Sketch of accidents, misfortunes, and depredations . . ." submitted by Smith, Jackson, and Sublette to General William Clark, Dec. 24, 1829.

leave by way of Bodega. He sold his beaver at $2.50 a pound to Captain John Bradshaw, who took him, on his ship the "Franklin," to San Francisco where he rejoined his men. He now obtained permission to go to San José where he could buy horses and mules. Here Isaac Galbraith came in with some beaver but did not rejoin the party. A week later Thomas Virgin appeared. It was now Christmas 1827, and Smith was ready to go but could find no boat to take him across to the north shore of San Francisco Bay, so he set off from San José on December 30 by land with twenty men and 315 horses but with only forty-seven traps. The horses he intended to sell in the Rocky Mountains and thus recoup his losses.[26]

The party moved east and north to the San Joaquin River and trapped its lower tributaries during January 1828. Moving north, they crossed the American River on February 22, trapped up it for some distance, then trapped the Yuba and Feather rivers to some extent and turned west, striking the Sacramento River somewhat below present Chico on March 28.[27] This was good beaver country, and Smith relinquished his plans to visit Bodega. They saw many Indians but had little trouble with them. The grizzly bears were more dangerous. Rogers was badly wounded by one on March 8, and Smith and La Point had narrow escapes.

In the vicinity of Red Bluff, Smith decided it would not be possible to follow the Sacramento River much farther and he veered to the west and northwest about April 16, striking a river which they followed. It was the Hayfork of the Trinity which joins the South Fork, which joins the main river, which flows into the Klamath River. The coun-

[26] *Ibid.*, 224-56. His beaver amounted to 1,568 pounds and brought $3,920. This was needed to outfit his men, purchase new supplies, and invest in horses and mules. Smith was not molested once he set out, but Governor Echeandia complained to Mexico City and the complaints were passed on to the American minister there. Smith had added a vagrant Englishman, Richard Leland, to his party.

[27] Smith's names for the American, the Yuba, the Feather, and the Sacramento rivers were the Wild, the Hen-neet, the Ya-lu, and the Buenaventura.

try was so difficult that they made often only a couple of miles in a day. The horses became lame. It took until May 3 to reach the Klamath, and until May 19 before the ocean was in sight.[28]

With incredible difficulty they made their way up the coast, often necessarily at some distance inland, and often, when following the shore line, they were forced to take to the water. They reached Rogue River on June 27 and, on July 3, they rescued from some Indians, a captive from the Willamette Valley, a boy about ten years old, whom they called Marion. On July 12, they crossed the Umpqua River at the point where it is joined by its north branch, which has since been called Smith's River. Next day they moved about four miles and encamped. They had been trading with Indians for beaver and sea otter skins and getting directions for reaching the Willamette.

On the morning of July 14, Smith set out, with Turner and Leland, to select the best route to travel. He instructed Rogers not to allow any Indians to come into the camp. But Rogers, for some unknown reason, permitted a large number of Kelawatset Indians, with whom they had had relations recently, to enter. These Indians, in revenge for recent incidents which they resented, suddenly fell upon the whites and began a butchery from which only Arthur Black was able to escape into the woods. When Smith and his companions returned, they were fired upon by the Indians but managed to escape and satisfy themselves that the other men had been massacred.[29]

---

[28] Until May 10, 1828, the only source is Smith's "Journal," reproduced in Sullivan, *Travels of Smith*, 53-89. From this date until the Umpqua Massacre we have Smith's "Journal" (until July 3) in *ibid.*, 90-105, and the second "Journal" of Harrison Rogers (until July 13), which is to be found in Dale, *Ashley-Smith Explorations*, 237-71. Smith called the Trinity by the name of Smith's River. It was the first time he had named anything for himself.

[29] Those killed in the Umpqua Massacre were Daws, Gaiter, Hanna, La Plant, La Point, Lazarus, Maréchal, McCoy, Palmer, Ranne, Reubascan, Rogers, Swift, Virgin, and the Indian boy, Marion. Reed and Pombert had deserted in California. Of the survivors, Turner and Leland chose to remain in Oregon.

On August 8, Arthur Black reached Fort Vancouver and told his story to Dr. John McLoughlin, the Hudson's Bay Company factor. He thought he was the sole survivor, but on August 10, Smith, Turner, and Leland came in. The Hudson's Bay Company could not afford to let such an occurrence as the massacre pass without notice. McLoughlin sent out a party under Alexander McLeod to recover Smith's goods as far as possible. Smith accompanied the expedition. A fair amount of beaver was recovered and a few of the horses.[30] This required about three months.

Sir George Simpson was at Fort Vancouver when Jedediah returned there and he offered to buy such beaver as had been recovered at $3.00 per skin and also to buy the horses. The deal was made for Smith had little choice. Altogether he received $2,369.60. It was better than nothing, and he had been hospitably treated.

Smith remained at Fort Vancouver until March 12, 1829, when, accompanied by Arthur Black, he began the ascent of the Columbia River by boat to Fort Colville. Once there, they went overland to the Flathead Post and thence to the Flathead River, above the lake of the same name, where he rejoined his partner, David E. Jackson, whom he knew, from British reports, to be in that vicinity.

Smith and Jackson did not get back in time for the rendezvous of 1829 in July on the Popo Agie. William Sublette was there, back from Missouri with trade goods, and he crossed over to Pierre's Hole where he met his partners on August 5. The work for the coming year was laid out as follows: Jackson to trap the Snake River country, Sublette to take the furs back to Missouri, and Smith to take a large party into the Blackfoot country with Jim Bridger as pilot.

They made an extensive hunt from Powder River to Tongue River to the Little Bighorn, through Pryor's Gap to

30 See Sullivan, *Travels of Smith,* 112-35, where McLeod's "Journal," covering this expedition, is reproduced. It was McLeod who determined that the Kelawatset Indians were the perpetrators of the massacre.

the Yellowstone, then to the Musselshell and finally to Judith River before returning through Pryor's Gap again and up the Bighorn to Wind River where they raised a cache of furs made in December 1829.[31]

The rendezvous was at the junction of the Popo Agie with Wind River in 1830. Sublette arrived on July 16, with his wagons. Before the rendezvous had ended, the partners had sold out to Fitzpatrick, Milton Sublette, Bridger, Fraeb, and Gervais, who formed the Rocky Mountain Fur Company. It was a sudden and unexpected action since no evidence has been found that they had considered it for any length of time.[32]

Back in St. Louis, Smith bought a house, but he was early engaged with his partners in planning a caravan to Santa Fe. Two of his brothers, Austin and Peter, were to go along, as was Jonathan Trumbull Warner, who had sought his advice about going west, and Samuel Parkman, a young man he had employed as a clerk.[33] The whole party was comprised of seventy-four men. Half of the twenty-two wagons belonged to Smith, the rest to Jackson and Sublette. Fitzpatrick appeared at the last minute demanding goods for the new firm, and it was agreed that he should go to Santa Fe with them and be outfitted there.

They left St. Louis on April 10, 1831, and by May 27 were on the dry stretch between the Arkansas and the Cimarron Rivers and had been three days without water. Smith and Fitzpatrick rode ahead and found a water hole that was

---

31 Frances Fuller Victor, *River of the West* (Hartford, 1870), 82-89. Meek's recollection, as given by Mrs. Victor, is substantiated to a considerable extent by Robert Newell's contemporary note.

32 The terms of the transaction are not known, but they were no doubt similar to those that Ashley had made in 1826. There is no doubt that the partners had made money, but it is difficult to arrive at a figure. Jedediah Smith's share of the net proceeds of the last year of operation amounted to $17,604.33, which was not paid until after his death. See Morgan, *Jedediah Smith,* 323-24.

33 Samuel Parkman made the transcription of Smith's "Journal," which has been preserved, the original having been lost.

dry. Fitzpatrick waited there for the wagon train and Smith rode on still looking for water. He was never seen again.

When the train reached Santa Fe, Indians were seen there with a pair of pistols, a rifle, and other things recognized to have belonged to Smith. They told this story. About twenty Comanches were concealed at a water hole waiting for buffalo when Smith rode up. Ignoring his peaceful gestures, they started to surround him. His horse shied and some Comanches fired. Jedediah was hit, but killed the leader of the party with the one shot he had time to get off before the rest were upon him with their lances.[34]

Jedediah Smith was not yet thirty-three years of age when he died, yet for eight years, he had led the way for others to follow and had ranged far in that time. His contributions to geographical knowledge were great and would have been greater had he lived to publish what he had learned.[35]

Jedediah had the habit of command and was usually called Mr. Smith or Captain Smith by others. He did not use tobacco or liquor, though he would drink a glass of wine socially. He kept himself clean shaven and was over six feet tall and rather spare.

His well known Bible reading habit helped him to bear adversity but his efforts to live as a practising Christian led him to be too trusting of Indians. He can bear no blame for the Umpqua Massacre but in the case of the Mojave attack and in the case of his own death, it is certainly possible that

---

34 The place where Smith was killed was formerly called Fargo Spring, later called Wagon Body Spring, and is near the western line of Seward County, Kansas. The spring is no longer active. See Morgan, *Jedediah Smith,* 436. At pp. 363-64, Morgan prints the letter of Austin Smith to Ira Smith, written from Walnut Creek on the Arkansas, Sept. 24, 1831, in which he gives such details as he had been able to learn concerning their brother's death.

35 The findings of Dale L. Morgan and Carl I. Wheat, *Jedediah Smith and His Maps of the American West* (1954) are conveniently summarized in Alson J. Smith, *op. cit.,* 263-65.

a less trusting man would have avoided or circumvented the danger.

Devoid of humor, he was all business and impatient with any delay or distraction. Yet for all his business ability and acumen, it must be said that Jackson and Sublette contributed more to the money made by the firm than did Smith. It should also be said that, if they ever complained of this, there is no record of it. In justice to Jedediah, it must also be stated that his recuperative powers of the spirit were marvelous, and he appears at his best when reorganizing to carry on after disasters that would have discouraged others. His confidence was great, his fearlessness undoubted, his persistence remarkable, his leadership unquestioned. Among the Mountain Men, in many ways he stands alone, and it was alone that he died.

> But where he died
> His brothers, even, didn't rightly know,
> Recalling, with already seasoned woe,
> How he went hunting water for the train,
> And how they watched until the lonely plain
> Went empty in the shimmer of the sun
> Forever.[36]

[36] John G. Neihardt, *The Song of Jed Smith* (New York, 1941), 110. Jedediah Smith had made his will before leaving St. Louis for Santa Fe, but his whole life on the frontier had been lived in such a way that he was ready for death whenever it might come.

John McLoughlin

by Kenneth L. Holmes
Oregon College of Education, Monmouth

The Scripture writer, hearkening back to ancient times, wrote, "There were giants in the land." A modern writer, harkening back to the second quarter of the nineteenth century in the Old Oregon Country, might declare, "There was a giant in the land." During that time when the land was dominated by the Hudson's Bay Company, John McLoughlin presided like a feudal king over some 670,000 square miles of wilderness – an area larger than Alaska, more than twice the size of Texas, or seven times as large as Great Britain. Within the region lived the greatest concentration of Indian peoples north of present Mexico. And the man was a giant himself. His big-boned frame reached to "six feet six or seven inches in height," according to a contemporary. Emil Ludwig's words about Bismarck, in *Genius and Character,* would describe the "Big Doctor" as well: "Wherever he went, he was the biggest man present . . . all were impressed to see him stoop as he came through the door and then draw himself up again to his full height." Add to the massive frame a great head of white hair and a tall beaver hat, and John McLoughlin must have towered above everyone who came into his presence.[1]

---

1 How tall was John McLoughlin? Most secondary sources give his height at six feet four inches. Frances Fuller Victor, in the first volume on Oregon in Hubert Howe Bancroft's *Pacific States* (page 30, footnote 6), quotes a contemporary, Stephen Fowler Chadwick, in giving the figures we use here. The late Dr. Burt Brown Barker told this author in 1967 of interviewing a man who had once helped to move the remains of McLoughlin to a new grave. Barker said that the bones were found to be "magnificent," gigantic in size, and that those who studied and measured them found the skeleton to be six feet four inches long. We have also consulted with

The oft-quoted and most vivid description of the man, written by Governor George Simpson of the Hudson's Bay Company, pictures him in his wilderness context as the two met on the trail in western Canada on September 26, 1824:

> He was such a figure as I should not like to meet on a dark Night in one of the bye lanes in the neighbourhood of London, dressed in Clothes that had once been fashionable, but now covered with a thousand patches of different Colours, his beard would do honour to the chin of a Grizzly Bear, his face and hands evidently Shewing that he had not lost much time at his Toilette, loaded with Arms and his own herculean dimensions forming a tout ensemble that would convey a good idea of the high way men of former days.[2]

He was born at Rivière-du-Loup, about 120 miles down the south shore of the St. Lawrence from Quebec, on October 19, 1784, to "cultivateur" John McLoughlin, an Irishman, and his wife Angélique, and was christened Jean Baptiste McLoughlin. The mother was the former Angélique Fraser, daughter of Colonel Malcolm Fraser, of the great Scottish clan, whose wife was a French Canadian whose maiden name had been Marie Allaire. Young John grew up the son of two cultures in a bilingual home.[3] If later he would show an aptness for getting along with French Canadians, who were the backbone of the British fur trade, there was a good reason for it.

Following in the steps of his mother's brother, Simon Fraser, John McLoughlin decided at about the time of his fourteenth birthday to study medicine. This led to a successful apprenticeship with a Quebec doctor, James Fisher.

Professor R. G. Harrison, of the Department of Anatomy of Liverpool University, England. He is a world authority on the study of human remains in aiding archaeologists. Although reticent to draw conclusions without access to the remains, he suggests "If his skeleton was 6 feet 4 inches long from the top of his skull to the bottom of his feet he was almost certainly greater in height in actual life than this by several inches." The tendency is to under-estimate the thickness of the flesh. Ludwig's book was published in New York in 1927, the quote being from page 42.

2 Frederick Merk, *Fur Trade and Empire* (Cambridge, Mass., 1931), 23.

3 Information about the McLoughlin family is from Burt Brown Barker, *The McLoughlin Empire and its Rulers* (Glendale, Calif., 1959), *passim*.

On May 3, 1803, the lieutenant governor of Lower Canada certified the nineteen-year-old youth to practice "Surgery and Pharmacy or as an Apothecary."[4]

The new physician then followed the path of another uncle, Alexander Fraser, and joined the forces of the North West Company, vigorous opponent of the Hudson's Bay Company in the fur trade of western Canada. His first post was at Kaministikwia, soon to be renamed Fort William, the key fur-trading depot at the head of Lake Superior.[5]

It was as a doctor that he spent his first years with the fur company. His activities centered at Fort William, but he turned up at other posts as well. The winter of 1807-1808 was spent at Sturgeon Lake, where he treated Daniel W. Harmon, the well-known trader. On November 9, 1807, Harmon wrote in his journal, "The Doctor . . . is an excellent companion, and fond of conversation; and I trust that a friendly intercourse will mutually cheer our spirits and that we shall spend the winter in a manner that will be pleasant and profitable."[6]

McLoughlin continued his medical studies on his own. In contemporary letters he mentions scientific books, including the works of such eminent French chemists as Antoine Fourcroy and Antoine Lavoisier.[7] In his first letter of many to his doctor uncle he says he is sending along "a piece of petrified fir."[8] His interest in the life of the Indians is revealed in an undated paper from these years, "An account of the Indians from Fort William to Lake of the Woods."[9] Although throughout his career the press of fur trade business prevented his giving much to the pursuit of scientific

4 T. C. Elliott, "John McLoughlin, M.D.," in *Oregon Historical Quarterly,* XXXVI (June 1935), 182-86.

5 W. Kaye Lamb, in his introduction of *Letters of John McLoughlin, First Series, 1825-38,* E. E. Rich, editor, in *Publications of the Hudson's Bay Record Society,* vol. IV (London, 1941), xxxii.

6 Elliott, *op. cit.,* 185.

7 Barker, *op. cit.,* 144. Letter 2, Kaministiquia, July 16, 1805.

8 *Ibid.*

9 Original in McGill University Library, Montreal. Microfilm at Oregon Historical Society, Portland, Oregon.

interests, he later played a significant part in encouraging botanical exploration of the West, aiding visiting naturalists such as David Douglas, John Scouler, and Meredith Gairdner. He was awarded a silver medal by the Horticultural Society of London on May 11, 1826, "for his assistance rendered Mr. David Douglas, whilst making his collections in the countries belonging to the Hudson's Bay Company in the Western part of North America."[10] There are two of his letters among the manuscripts at the Royal Botanic Garden at Kew, in which he discusses seeds he is sending to William Jackson Hooker, the eminent director of that institution.[11] He also sent meteorological reports from Fort Vancouver in the 1830s to the Academy of Sciences in Paris and these were published in the journal of that academy, *Comptes Rendus Hebdomaires des Seances.*"[12]

During his early years with the North West Company, he was often dissatisfied, especially with his pay, and thought several times about leaving the fur trade, once declaring in a letter that he planned to settle in Detroit.[13] By 1811, however, he was made a partner. The next winter, 1811-1812, he wintered at Vermilion Lake. He was offered a chance to go to the lower Columbia River region in 1812, but he turned it down and instead served as a wintering partner at Lac la Pluie (Rainy Lake) a strategic post because of its proximity to the as-yet unmarked American border. He stayed there for two winters.

The troubles with Lord Selkirk, a dominant figure in the Hudson's Bay Company at that time, found McLoughlin back at Fort William. Although he was not present at

10 Erwin F. Lange, "Dr. John McLoughlin and the Botany of the Pacific Northwest," in *Madroño,* XIV (Oct. 1958), 270.

11 William Jackson Hooker Letterbooks, LXIII: 317, McLoughlin to Hooker, Vancouver, Oct. 10, 1843; 318, Oct. 17, 1842.

12 July 13, 1835, vol. I, pp. 266-68; Jan.-June, 1838, vol. VI, pp. 120-21.

13 Lamb, *op. cit.,* xxxv.

the killing of some Hudson's Bay Company people by Nor'westers, he was indicted and tried as an "accessory after the fact" of the "murder of Robert Temple, 19th June 1816." The trial did not take place until the autumn of 1818 at Montreal. He and the other accused men were out on bail during this time and Fort William was again the center of his activities. The jury trial took place on October 30, 1818, and it ended the next day when the verdict was "not guilty." [14]

McLoughlin was in England, and quite ill, during the negotiations that merged the two fur companies. He and Angus Bethune were there to represent the wintering partners, but they were left out of the final arrangements. It was William and Simon McGillivray and Edward Ellice, the North West Company agent in England, who carried the burden of the negotiations, and Ellice was the only one to become a member of the governing Committee of the new Hudson's Bay Company. The agreement, signed in March 1821, did, however, provide that North West Company partners would become traders and factors in the new plan.

McLoughlin sailed for New York on an American ship, the "Amity," on March 21, arriving on May 10. A few days later he was in Montreal.

He was dissatisfied with the new arrangement as is revealed by Simon McGillivray in a letter to Ellice from Montreal, dated June 2, 1821. "Dr. McLoughlin continues his scruples about executing his agreement, and he shall not be asked to do it, for after all his decision is a matter of no great importance. *He* has got more than he is entitled to, and if he quarrels with his own advantage, be it so." [15] Years later McLoughlin wrote to his friend Edward Ermatinger,

14 Sir Peregrine Maitland Papers, Public Archives of Canada, Ottawa, 13 August, 1818, to 4 November, 1828. Proceedings against the North West Company, 1819 (vol. 327).

15 Ellice Papers, National Library of Scotland. Microfilm at Oregon Historical Society, Portland, Oregon.

> My compliments to Mrs. Ermatinger and tell her that I hope to give you a call some of these days after I retire. I dare say some day it would be time – if I and the other N.W. had not been so outrageously wronged at the Coalition and for which I blame both parties – and my N.W. Stock Accounted to me as a sale when it was an investment I would have been able to retire long ago.[16]

During this period of his life he was suffering some severe illness. He wrote his uncle, Simon Fraser, from Fort William on October 10, 1817, "I have been very unwell all this summer indeed at one time I thought I would have gone to the other world – now I am recovering but far from being so well as I was when I left Montreal this spring."[17] His bodily troubles followed him on his trip to England in 1821. He returned to Europe in late 1821 and visited his brother Dr. David McLoughlin, an eminent practitioner in Boulogne and Paris by that time.[18] Governor George Simpson wrote him from York Factory, "I shall be glad to learn that you are long ere now recovered from your severe illness and hope to have the pleasure of seeing you early here next Season."[19] With health much improved he was able to return to Canada in 1822, "Out via Liverpool and New York, March, 1822."[20] He went to Lac la Pluie once more and worked at that strategic border post through the seasons of 1822-1823 and 1823-1824.

When the Council met at York Factory in July 1824, McLoughlin learned that he had been given charge of that huge domain, the Columbia District, and by the end of the month he was on his way with his family to the mouth of the "Great River of the West." He had taken as a wife Marguerite Wadin, who had been deserted by Alexander McKay, a Nor'wester, who in 1811 had died on the Pacific Coast, where he had gone as a member of the Astor party.

[16] Walter N. Sage, "A Note on the Origins of the Strife between Sir George Simpson and Dr. John McLoughlin," in *Washington Historical Quarterly*, XXIV (1933), 259.

[17] Barker, *op. cit.*, Letter 27, p. 169.

[18] *Ibid.*, "Dr. David McLoughlin," pp. 81-94.

[19] Lamb, *op. cit.*, xlix.

[20] *Ibid.*, xl.

She was the daughter of a Swiss fur trader and an Indian woman. The date when they started living together "after the manner of the country" is not known, but their first child, John, Jr., was born on August 12, 1812. Young John was now left behind in Montreal for schooling. A nine-year-old daughter, Elizabeth, was left to the care of the Ursuline Convent in Quebec. Two younger children, six-year-old Eloisa and three-year-old David, accompanied their father and mother.[21]

He arrived at his new center of operations, Fort George, the famous post known to the Americans as Astoria, at the mouth of the Columbia on the south side. McLoughlin's first assignment was to work with Governor George Simpson, who had accompanied the overland party, in finding a new locale for company operations on the Pacific slope. The instructions from London read as follows:

> As the Americans are to have possession of Fort George whenever they please You will immediately proceed in erecting a Fort on the North side of the River taking care to select the most convenient Situation & remove from the south side of the River with everything belonging to the Company.[22]

The two leaders chose a spot known as Belle Vue Point, so-named by William Broughton, Vancouver's lieutenant who had explored the river in 1792. Well upstream from the Pacific, the new post, at the site of present Vancouver, Washington, was completed at least in part in 1825, to be added to a great deal through the following years, and it was named Fort Vancouver. Simpson described it thus:

> The place we have selected is beautiful as may be inferred from its name and the country so open that from the Establishment there is good travelling on Horseback to any part of the interior; a Farm to any extent may be made there: the pasture is good and innumerable

21 Barker, *op. cit.*, 44 and *passim.*

22 Instructions "To the Gentlemen Chief Factors in Charge of the Columbia Department," from London, 21 July, 1824. John Stuart Papers, Bank of Scotland, The Mound, Edinburgh. Microfilm at Oregon Historical Society, Portland, Oregon.

herds of Swine can fatten so as to be fit for the Knife merely on nutricious Roots that are found here in any quantity and the Climate so fine that Indian Corn and other Grain cannot fail of thriving; it is much better than that of the Coast say [namely] at Point George being less exposed to the Sea Air. The distance from the harbour is the only inconvenience but that is of little importance being now a secondary establishment; the small Vessel however can run up a considerable way and a Leighter or large Batteaux can work or drift down in a couple of tides.[23]

It was here opposite the confluence of the Columbia and the Willamette that John McLoughlin was to reign as a kind of *laird* or *seigneur* over a fief of massive dimensions, the Old Oregon Country. The extent of the trade he described once as extending "from St Francisco in Latd 38 to Latitude 54 North and the Interior as bounded by the Rocky Mountains."[24]

The move took place in April 1825. On the 19th of that month the botanist, David Douglas, wrote in his journal, "On my arrival a tent was kindly offered, having no houses yet built."[25]

McLoughlin's touch was felt in trade with Russians in present Alaska, with Spaniards to the south in California, and in the trans-Pacific commerce centering in the Hawaiian Islands. The company developed a vigorous coastal shipping trade and probed every bay, fjord, and river valley along the Northwest Coast, establishing trading posts at strategic localities. To the south of the Columbia the lush Willamette Valley was the route to rich beaver sources in the Coast Range, the Cascades, through the Cascade passes to the high interior country, and up the Willamette, across its upper divides to the tree-lined valleys of the Umpqua and Klamath rivers. By the 1830s the trapping parties were spilling over the Siskiyous to streams infested with beaver in the water-

23 Arthur S. Morton, *Sir George Simpson* (Portland, Oreg., 1944), 146.

24 Barker, *op. cit.*, Letter 96, p. 232.

25 W. Wilks, editor, *Journal Kept by David Douglas* (London, 1914), 107.

sheds of the Sacramento and San Joaquin rivers in the great Central Valley of California and in the water-logged land of the delta where these rivers flow jointly into San Francisco Bay. It was from this direction, too, that American trappers came – Jedediah Smith in 1828, and Ewing Young in 1834, the first a derelict to be rescued, the second to be the first successful American competition in the region near Fort Vancouver, but not as a fur trader. It was only when Young, the lank Tennessean, settled to become a successful farmer, cattleman, and lumberman, that he became the harbinger of advancing settlement that would cause the retreat of the fur trade. At first Young and McLoughlin, the western American frontiersman versus the feudal overlord, representatives of two worlds, faced each other in a stand off. Later they came to respect each other.[26]

There was a conflict, too, in the Snake River Valley with American trappers. There party after party of Mountain Men from the south met the Hudson's Bay brigades. The supply lines and trading routes were vastly over-extended in that high inland region. The Americans considered the area to be their own domain and the British to be interlopers, sometimes hoisting the Stars and Stripes in defiance.[27] McLoughlin sent Peter Skene Ogden and others at the head of parties into the Snake country season after season. As early as August 10, 1825, he wrote in a circular letter to the "Chief Factors & Chief Traders" that by the treaty of 1818 (Joint Occupancy) the land west of the Rockies was free to persons of both nations

> and by this you will see we are justified in resisting to the utmost of our Power any attack on our Persons and Property or any assumption of authority over us by the Americans indeed so confident am I of our being Justified in this that had we a party sufficiently strong – strong to defend itself from the Natives that could be depended on, I would

26 Kenneth L. Holmes, *Ewing Young, Master Trapper* (Portland, Oreg., 1967), 112-13, 145-46.

27 Lamb, *op. cit.*, lxii.

> have no hesitation in making another attempt in that quarter if it was merely for one year to defy them to put their threats into execution. . .[28]

Of course he won. A string of forts penetrated like a dagger from the Columbia to the heart of the Snake country – Fort Walla Walla, Fort Boise, and Fort Hall, which was purchased from the American, Nathaniel Wyeth, in 1837.

A new facet of American advance appeared on the scene in 1834 with the arrival of several Methodist missionaries over the fur-trade route soon to be known as the Oregon Trail. They were led by the Rev. Jason Lee. McLoughlin was all kindness to them. At the same time, he cagily, but gently, suggested that the mission be established in the Willamette Valley, *south* of the Columbia. He still expected, and would for some time, that the division of the Oregon Country between the two nations would be at the Columbia River, and that everywhere south and east of the great river as far upstream as the 49th parallel would become American territory. A similar policy is shown when McLoughlin persuaded Dr. Marcus Whitman and the Rev. Henry Spalding of the American Board of Foreign Missions in 1836 to establish their missions *east* of the Columbia farther inland.

The missionaries, too, were a vanguard of settlement, and the Willamette Valley with its deep fertile soil became the magnet drawing wagon train after wagon train over the trail in the 1840s and after. McLoughlin was torn between his loyalty as a company man and the crying needs of the immigrants, who often lacked the bare necessities of life. They found that they could count on the Chief Factor to aid and abet them as they struggled down the lower Columbia River and took up claims, each one mile square, in Oregon. They often wrote east telling of his generosity, as in the following quotation from the *Bradford Reporter* of Towanda, Penn-

---

28 John Stuart Papers, *op. cit.*

sylvania (December 4, 1844), written by an unnamed correspondent, newly arrived in Oregon:

> I cannot speak too highly of this excellent man, for his kindness to us all. – He sent several boats loaded with provisions to meet the emigrants last fall, and continued to distribute little luxuries amongst us as we remained in reach of him – he is always on the lookout for an opportunity to bestow his charity, and bestows with no sparing hand.

John McLoughlin was a complex person. He could be kindly one day, violent another. He was often at odds with the Hudson's Bay Company leaders in London, and with Governor George Simpson. At the time of settlement of the Oregon Question in 1846, he was fed up with several things. He retired from the service to become an American citizen in the new community of Oregon City, at the Falls of the Willamette. In anticipation of his retirement he bought out the company's interest in a claim at the falls, and that is where he settled. It was perfectly legal under the joint occupancy agreement and under the laws of the Oregon Provisional Government for him to do so, as it was for others, citizens of both Britain and the United States. The Provisional Government was not an American one, but partly a product of the joint occupancy situation. Oaths taken by its officers as late as June 1845 were sworn to by each man as "a citizen of the United States, or a subject of Great Britain."[29] John McLoughlin had every right to stake out a claim as a British subject, and then to keep it as an American citizen. At the Falls he built a magnificent home, still standing as a National Historical Site,[30] and there he lived out his years, the "Big Doctor," the "White Headed Eagle," the "Father of Oregon." He died on September 3, 1857.

---

[29] Oregon Territorial Papers, Oregon Archives, Salem. McLoughlin's own statement of what happened between the Company and himself, a defense of his position, is found in "Dr. John McLoughlin's Last Letter to the Hudson's Bay Company, as Chief Factor, in charge at Fort Vancouver, 1845," in *American Historical Review,* XXI (Oct. 1915), 104-34.

[30] Burt Brown Barker, *The Dr. John McLoughlin House, A National Historic Site* (Oregon City, 1949).

Peter Skene Ogden*

by TED J. WARNER
Brigham Young University

Peter Skene Ogden was a leading character in the Anglo-American struggle for fur trade and empire in the great Pacific Northwest. As a brigade leader for the Hudson's Bay Company he conducted an annual expedition into the Snake River country, seeking to create a "fur desert" between United States territory and the southern approaches to the Columbia River. The British implemented this policy to discourage American trapper penetration and the consequent entry of the pioneer farmer.[1]

Ogden was described by a contemporary as "humorous, honest, eccentric, law-defying, short, dark and exceedingly tough, the terror of the Indians and the delight of all gay fellows."[2] He was born in Quebec City in 1794, the son of Tory parents who had fled New York to England during the American War for Independence. His father, a judge in the royal service, after several years' residence in England accepted appointment to a Canadian judgeship in 1788. The year Peter was born his father was transferred to Montreal, and it was in this place that he spent his boyhood. His family hoped that he would enter the ministry or the legal profession in his father's and grandfather's footsteps, and he appears to have received some legal training. This type of life, however, did not appeal to him and at an early age he

* This sketch is based on the writer's master's thesis, "Peter Skene Ogden and the Fur Trade of the Great Northwest," Brigham Young University, 1958.

1 Frederick Merk (ed.), *Fur Trade and Empire, George Simpson's Journal, 1824-1825* (Cambridge, 1931), 252.

2 Ross Cox, *The Columbia* (Norman, 1957), 249-50.

abandoned his studies and sought employment as a clerk with Astor's American Fur Company, at that time operating in the Great Lakes region.[3] At the age of fifteen or sixteen he joined the North West Company, a Canadian concern operating in direct violation of the Crown monopoly granted to the Hudson's Bay Company.[4]

From 1810 to 1817 Ogden served as a clerk at several North West Company posts in the Hudson Bay region and in the latter year received appointment to command the company trading post at Ile-a-la-Crosse.[5] In 1818 the company officials found it expedient to transfer him from the Athabasca region to the then all-but-inaccessable Columbia, or Northern Department, in the Pacific Northwest.[6] From Fort George on the Columbia River he led trapping parties into the country between that river and Puget Sound and around the harbors north of the Columbia.[7] The company was sufficiently impressed with his ability to reward him with promotion to the rank of brigade leader on July 12, 1820. He conducted trapping expeditions out of Spokane House and Thompson's River Post between 1819 and 1821.[8]

The year 1821 was a turning point in Ogden's career. In that year a "voluntary" merger of the North West with the Hudson's Bay Company, ordered by the Crown, was effected. Ogden had been an outspoken opponent of the Hudson's Bay Company and had alienated its officials. In 1818 they had been instrumental in persuading the Crown to issue an indictment against him for murder.[9] In the West he likewise proved a severe irritant to the Company, so in the 1821 merger his name, along with those of other out-

[3] E. E. Rich (ed.), *Peter Skene Ogden, Snake Country Journal 1824-25 and 1825-26* (London, 1950), p. xvi.

[4] *Ibid.*

[5] *Ibid.*, p. xvii.

[6] T. C. Elliott, "Peter Skene Ogden, Fur Trapper," *The Quarterly of the Oregon Historical Society*, XI (September, 1910), 236.

[7] *Ibid.*, 240.

[8] Rich, *Peter Skene Ogden*, p. xx.

[9] Elliott, "Peter Skene Ogden, Fur Trader," 236.

spoken foes of the Company, was excluded from the list of Nor'westers who were to be retained in service. Ogden thus found himself, after devoting more than eleven years to the fur trade, without a position. He decided to journey to London and discuss his future with high officials of the Company.[10] Apparently he favorably impressed certain "gentlemen" and upon the recommendation of Sir George Simpson, the newly appointed governor of the Northern Department, Ogden was reinstated as Clerk of the First Class in the Northern Factory, with a salary equivalent to the amount of a Chief Trader's share.[11]

Ogden returned to the Oregon Country and was placed in charge of the Spokane House District. From this post he dispatched Alexander Ross on an expedition into the Snake Country. Governor Simpson, however, was not impressed with Ross. According to the governor:

> The Snake Country Expedition has hitherto been considered a forlorn hope the management of it the most hazardous and disagreeable office in the Indian Country. . . This important duty should not in my opinion be left to a self-sufficient empty-headed man like Ross who feels no further interest therein than as it secures to him a Saly of L 120 p Annum and whose reports are so full of bombast and marvellous nonsense that it is impossible to get at any information that can be depended on from him.[12]

Accordingly when Ross returned to Spokane House on November 25, 1824 he was handed a letter appointing Ogden to command of the Snake Country expeditions and Ross to take charge of Spokane Post.[13]

Between 1824 and 1830 Ogden was to make six so-called "Snake Country expeditions." On his first, he was ordered to proceed "directly for the heart of the Snake Country

[10] Rich, *Peter Skene Ogden,* p. xx.

[11] *Ibid.,* p. xxiii.

[12] Merk, *Fur Trade and Empire,* 45-46.

[13] T. C. Elliott (ed.), "Journal of Alexander Ross; Snake Country, 1824," *The Quarterly of the Oregon Historical Society,"* XIV (December, 1913), 371.

towards the Banks of the Spanish Rio Colorado, pass the Winter & Spring there and hunt his way out by the Umpqua and Wilhamet Rivers to Fort George."[14] The brigade, consisting of Ogden, his clerk, two interpreters, seventy-one men and boys, together with wives and children of the trappers, and equipped with 372 horses, 364 beaver traps, and eighty guns, departed Flathead Post on December 20, 1824. According to Alexander Ross this was "the most formidable party that has ever set out for the Snakes."[15] Accompanying the brigade were seven unwelcome American trappers, brought by Ross to that post from his expedition to the Snake Country, who were now on their way back to the Green River for a rendezvous with their compatriots of the Ashley organization.[16]

For five weeks the party proceeded in a southeasterly direction. They crossed the continental divide via Gibbon Pass to the sources of the Missouri River. This region was very rich in both beaver and buffalo, but the hunting was exceedingly hazardous, as the region was infested with the treacherous Blackfeet Indians. In addition, the British were now trespassing on American soil and doubtless Ogden realized this, but no mention of it was made in his journals. The brigade turned back to the Oregon Country and reached the Salmon River waters. Delayed by heavy snows in the passes of the Salmon River Mountains, they were at a standstill for twenty days, but on March 20 the mountains were finally breached and on April 2, 1825, they reached the Snake River. Trapping operations began at once, and though of "tolerable success" were of "short duration" due to the murder of a trapper who was scalped by the Blackfeet. This death caused Peter considerable difficulty with his men,

---

[14] Merk, *Fur Trade and Empire,* 46.

[15] Elliott, "Journal of Alexander Ross," 385.

[16] Frederick Merk, "Snake Country Expedition, 1824-25. An Episode of Fur Trade and Empire," *The Quarterly of the Oregon Historical Society,* xxxv (June, 1934), 112-13. The leader of this group was Jedediah Strong Smith.

who were reluctant to continue farther into the Snake Country; but with cajolery and threats he persuaded them to proceed. When the expedition reached Bear River on April 26, 1825, the Americans separated from the British brigade, "they in ascending Bear River, and we in descending." [17]

Difficulties continued with the trappers, especially after Piegan Indians stole twenty horses, but again promises and threats induced the trappers to continue.

On Cub River, a tributary of the Bear, near present Franklin, Idaho, Ogden encountered a party of forty Snake Indians who informed him that a large party of Americans had wintered there and had left early in the spring but without many beaver.[18] Inasmuch as the Americans had worked the lower portions of the various streams, Ogden found it necessary to work higher up in the foothills and canyons. As a result, he pushed southward along the face of the Wasatch Mountains, through the present sites of Smithfield, Logan, and Hyrum, Utah; and entered Ogden Valley (the present Huntsville area, and not present Ogden City) by the way of Paradise Canyon.[19]

---

[17] Basic to any understanding of Ogden's movements in the Utah region are the carefully edited portions of Ogden's journal and his clerk, William Kittson's journal, by Dr. David E. Miller of the University of Utah. According to Dr. Miller the fact that the Americans headed upstream while Ogden and his brigade turned downstream is of significance in view of the fact that it virtually excludes Jedediah Smith from any claim he may have to the honor of having discovered Great Salt Lake. Several men saw it before he could have arrived at its shores. David E. Miller, "William Kittson's Journal Covering Peter Skene Ogden's 1824-25 Snake Country Expedition," *Utah Historical Quarterly,* XXII (April, 1954), 125-42 and the same writer's "Peter Skene Ogden's Journal of His Expedition to Utah, 1825," *ibid.,* XX (April, 1952), 159-86.

[18] According to Professor Miller, this is a highly important entry in the Ogden-Kittson journals because it definitely locates for the first time the camp of John Weber's Rocky Mountain trappers, known to have been in the region that winter. It was probably from this American camp near present Franklin, Idaho, that Jim Bridger made his famous "bull boat voyage" down Bear River to discover Great Salt Lake either in the fall of 1824 or winter of 1825. Either date would antedate Ogden's arrival anywhere near the lake.

[19] Miller, "Kittson's Journal," 135-36. Ogden did not see nor visit the site of the present city which bears his name.

After trapping more than six hundred beaver in Ogden Valley, the British pushed southward "over a rugged hill" (near present Snow Basin) and were soon on the Weber River, just west of the present location of Mountain Green. This river was also described as "falling into the Large Bear Lake already mentioned." [20]

Ogden was now approaching events which were to cause him much humiliation, the Hudson's Bay Company much concern, and historians considerable debate. On May 23, the British encampment was visited by two Hudson's Bay Company deserters accompanied by three Canadians, a Russian and an old Spaniard, "this party under the command of one Provost." [21] Shortly after the arrival of this group another one of twenty-five to thirty Americans commanded by Johnson Gardner camped nearby. Gardner visited Ogden in his tent and an exchange between the rival leaders concerning the ownership of the territory they were in ensued. Gardner claimed it was American territory and that the British were trespassers; Ogden asserted that they were in territory jointly owned by the British and American governments.[22] In reality, since they had passed the forty-second parallel, they were both trespassing deep into Mexican territory.

In the region of joint occupation, two theories of trading were in operation: one the monopoly, the other unrestricted competition. The HBC represented the monopoly and, as such, worked under the handicap of being an English corporation and having to exercise full diplomatic restraint in order to prevent conflict; the free-wheeling Americans, under no restraint, had the advantage of thinking they were on home grounds. Gardner ordered Ogden to "return from whence they came without delay" and Ogden replied that when he received orders from the British government to

20 *Ibid.*, 137.

21 This was Etienne Provost who was operating from a Santa Fe base and had wintered on the Green River.

22 Merk, "Snake Country Expedition, 1824-25," 109-10.

abandon the country he would, but not until then. Gardner then warned the British that they remained at their peril.[23]

A general sense of oppression was felt by the British trappers that year. They were paid low prices for their furs and charged exceedingly high prices for their provisions and equipment at the Hudson's Bay Company stores. Consequently they remained year after year heavily in debt – a sort of debt peonage. They had long looked for an opportunity to desert and, now believing they were in American territory, many of Ogden's trappers crossed over to the side of the high-paying Americans. Eventually twenty-three trappers, carrying with them about seven hundred furs, defected to the American side.[24]

When the Hudson's Bay officials reviewed this situation they came to the conclusion that:

> We can afford to pay as good a price as the Americans and where there is risk of meeting their parties it is necessary to pay as much or something more to avoid the risk of a result similar to that of Mr. Ogden. By attempting to make such expeditions too profitable the whole may be lost.[25]

Consequently, prices to be paid for furs were increased and prices for provisions were lowered. These changes were to have a salutary effect upon the morale of the trappers and were to assist the British mightily in their objectives in the Snake Country.

Ogden arrived back at Fort Nez Perces on November 2, 1825, with only four hundred skins, which was "certainly far from what we had a right to expect." [26]

He had written to Governor Simpson on June 27, 1825:

> You need not anticipate another expedition ensuing Year to this Country, for not a freeman will return, and should they, it would be to join the Americans.[27]

23 *Ibid.*

24 *Ibid.*, 112.

25 Merk, *Fur Trade and Empire*, 286-87.

26 Merk, "Snake Country Expedition, 1824-25," 118-19.

27 *Ibid.*, 115-16.

However, the British reappraisal of their operations and the reforms instituted resulted in Ogden's dispatch into the Snake Country on his second expedition to that region, only twelve days subsequent to his return.

Ogden's orders were to proceed straightaway to the "River discovered by Silvaille (supposed to be a Branch of the River said to Fall in the Ocean South of the Umqua) thence towards Lac Sale make a Circuit West and come Out about the Clamet river."[28] The brigade, thirty-seven strong, proceeded down the Columbia from Fort Nez Perces to the Deschutes River, up that stream to near its sources, and thence eastward in the direction of the Snake Country. This part of Oregon had never been trapped by white men, but as it lay to the south of the Columbia it was included in the area to be trapped thoroughly. A Snake Indian who had spent many years among the Cayuse was secured as a guide, but he gave Ogden considerable difficulty. Great hardships were suffered from cold and hunger. Many horses were consigned to the pot and for ten days they had only one meal every two days.[29]

On February 2, 1826, they crossed the Blue Mountains and arrived on the South Branch (Snake River) of the Columbia. The men had been on short rations so long that they resembled "so many skeletons." They reached the Malade, or Sickly River, on March 3. On the twelfth, after five days without food, the hunters returned to camp with thirteen elk. "Never did men eat with a better appetite; many did not stop to go to bed till midnight."

On Raft River many of his trappers became sick from eating beaver meat. Ogden submitted himself as a guinea pig and ate some of the meat. Although he did not imme-

[28] E. E. Rich (ed.), *The Letters of John McLoughlin from Fort Vancouver to the Governor and Committee, First Series, 1825-38.* (London, 1941), 33.

[29] The information concerning this expedition is taken from T. C. Elliott (ed.), "Journal of Peter Skene Ogden; Snake Expedition, 1825-26," *The Quarterly of the Oregon Historical Society,* x (December, 1909), 331-65.

diately become sick, four days later he was seriously ill. The British were surprised at this illness. They knew that Sickly River got its name because of illness induced by trappers' eating beaver of that river. That was due to the beavers' eating certain roots which tainted the meat; the beaver on the Raft ate wild hemlock which caused a similar illness.

By the last day of March the brigade had trapped a thousand beaver. Three thousand skins were considered necessary for a successful expedition, and Ogden hoped to secure this number in spite of the many hardships and difficulties encountered. On April 2, they reached the Portneuf Fork and encamped. This was excellent beaver country, and Ogden speculated that if the Indians would leave them alone, they would do well there. A week later, however, the situation which Ogden dreaded most developed. His brigade had another encounter with an American trapping party. This group of twenty-eight men, which included some of his deserters of the previous year, entered the British camp and displayed some surprise at seeing the crusty Ogden again in the Snake Country. They believed, evidently, that the results of the first expedition and the threats made at the first meeting would keep the British out of the area. But they underrated Ogden. His fear of a second general defection was allayed when he learned that his deserters were already tired of their new masters. Several of them, indeed, made payments in beaver to be credited to their old company accounts. The next day the two groups separated. None of the British trappers appeared the least inclined to desert.

On July 17, 1826, Ogden reached Fort Vancouver, thus ending his second Snake Country expedition. Despite the severity of the winter and obstacles encountered, which left them only three of the eight months for actual trapping, his returns exceeded all expectations. He had collected 3,800 beaver and otter skins, yielding a profit of 2500 pounds. More important than this, however, was the knowledge Ogden gleaned of the region:

> From the Country we explored this year we obtained only 100 Beaver . . . however, we have the satisfaction to know that the Southside of the South Branch of the Columbia has been examined and now ascertained to be destitute of Beaver.

With this knowledge the British could now concentrate greater efforts on the rivers and streams facing St. Louis.

Two months elapsed before Ogden returned to the Snake Country.[30] He departed on September 12 and by November 1, 1826, the expedition was at Malheur and Harney Lakes in Southeastern Oregon. They reached Pauline Mountain, crossed it and arrived at East and Pauline lakes. West from Pauline Lake was the Des Chutes River which they reached on November 18. For two months the brigade had wandered through unexplored terrain and had secured only five hundred beaver, not due to lack of exertions of the trappers but because of the poverty of the country. From the Des Chutes the British proceeded southward to streams which drained into Klamath Lake. Southwestern Oregon also was not rich in beaver. Early in December they reached Lower Klamath Lake. On February 10, 1827, the brigade was in northern California, probably on the Pit River. On February 12, trapping operations were commenced on the Klamath River. There were many beaver along this stream, although extremely shy, because the Indians hunted them for food. On February 14, Ogden named a mountain in the vicinity "Mt. Sastise" (Mount Shasta) from the tribe of Indians in that locality.

By the end of February conditions were again bad, due to scarcity of food. Ogden complained:

30 The information for this expedition is taken from T. C. Elliott (ed.), "Journal of Peter Skene Ogden; Snake Expedition, 1826-27," *ibid.*, XI (June 1910), 201-22.

> This life makes a young man sixty in a few years. Wading in cold water all day they earn 10 shillings P. beaver. A convict at Botony Bay is a gentleman at ease compared to my trappers.

Over two thousand beaver had been taken by April 22. From May 14 to 24, Ogden traveled eastward and proceeded to the main stream of "Salt Lake River" (Malheur River). This second crossing of Oregon was attended likewise by severe hardships. They suffered greatly from lack of water, and thieving Indians stole fifty-six horses, although all but seven were later recovered. Their camp of the previous November, on Malheur and Harney lakes, was reached on June 6. For the past six months they had been wandering in heretofore unexplored country. The Snake Indians lurked constantly around the camp, waiting for opportunities to steal horses. According to Ogden, the natives in this region had destroyed upwards of sixty thousand beaver, not one of which had reached a Hudson's Bay Company factory.

The brigade reached the Snake River just below the Malheur on July 16, 1827. Ogden left the trappers and, with four men, made his way to Fort Nez Perces to make preparations for the arrival of the main body. After accomplishing this at Nez Perces he journeyed to Fort Vancouver, where he arrived on August 5. The fur returns amounted to almost 2500 skins – short of what was considered a successful expedition, but certainly far in excess of what might have been expected in such barren country as they had operated in that season.[31]

This expedition, although not a financial success, was still important, for it proved this region to be unprofitable for trapping operations, and future effort could be expended in other directions.

On September 5, 1827, Ogden and his brigade departed

[31] Rich, *The Letters of John McLoughlin*, 49-50.

Fort Nez Perces, once again bound for the Snake Country.[32] They crossed over to the Powder River, and on September 18 "encamped on River Brule" (Burnt River). On the Weiser River, Ogden's trappers reported many American traps. The presence of a large body of Americans blasted Ogden's hopes of taking many animals there. He advanced southward on the Snake River until he reached Reed's River (Boise River) on October 6; American trappers were already there. Ogden trapped this stream for two days and produced only eight beaver. He then decided to abandon that quarter. On the Weiser, Payette, and Boise he had expected big returns; as it turned out these streams yielded only 140 skins.

On Christmas Eve, at Snake River, an American party of six men, commanded by Samuel Tullock, joined the British. That night around the campfire the Gardner-Ogden affair of 1825 was discussed. Tullock said his company would readily enter into an agreement regarding the deserters because Gardner's conduct had not been approved by his superiors. "I shd. certainly be shocked if any man of principle approved of such conduct as Gardner's," was Ogden's indignant notation in his journal that night.

Snowshoes were the key to mobility in the deep snow, and the Americans were highly desirous of obtaining them from the British. Ogden issued orders that none should be sold or traded to the Americans. Ogden had good reason for trying to prevent the Americans from reaching their rendezvous.

> I dread their return with liquor. A small quantity would be most advantageous to them but the reverse to me. I know not their intentions but had I the same chance they have, long since I would have had a good stock of liquor here, & every beaver in the camp would be mine.

---

32 The information concerning this expedition is taken from T. C. Elliott (ed.), "Journal of Peter Skene Ogden; Snake Expedition, 1827-1828," *The Quarterly of the Oregon Historical Society,* XI (December, 1910), 361-79.

Ogden evidently held a different idea of trafficking in liquor with the Indians than did the Company. By January 27, 1828, the Americans succeeded in making their own snowshoes, which Ogden felt they should have done in the first place, yet these were "poor make-shifts & will give them trouble." Ogden figured it would be at least a month before the Americans could cross the mountains and return with reinforcements and then, he gloated, "there will be no beaver skins left among the Snakes."

When a group of deserters from the American firm of Smith, Jackson and Sublette, to whom they were heavily in debt, joined the British brigade, Ogden was considerably worried lest the American leaders indiscriminately seize British furs to apply to the defectors' accounts. Ogden stated that he knew nothing of their indebtedness, but that it was clearly the American leader's duty to secure both his men and the debts they owed. Ogden reminded the Americans that his present conduct was "far different from theirs . . . four years since." The Americans remarked that the episode was to be regretted, but that at that time there was no regular American company, otherwise he should have received compensation for the losses he sustained. To this Ogden recorded in his journal: "It may be so. At all events, dependent on me, they cannot acknowledge less. I have acted honorably and shall continue so."

From the Portneuf River Ogden proceeded to the Snake, which he reached on April 1. By April 24 his men had trapped two thousand beaver. On April 27 they crossed the Blackfoot Hills and on May 6 began the trip home. They reached Fort Nez Perces on July 19. Ogden's fourth Snake expedition fur returns far exceeded his expectations.

Ogden's fifth Snake Country expedition should have brought to him the honor of having one of the West's important rivers named after him. He was the first to arrive on the banks of the Humboldt River and the first to follow it from its source to its sink. The river has been known by various names – Mary's River, Unknown River, Swampy River, and Ogden's River. It remained for the ubiquitous John C. Frémont in 1843 to attach to it the name of the great German geographer and scientist, Baron Alexander von Humboldt. The Baron never saw the river which now bears his name and, according to Thomas Ambrose Cramer, "it does him little credit here. He was filled with wisdom and goodness; it only with mineral and vegetable poisons."[33]

Ogden remained at Fort Vancouver two months before departing on his fifth Snake expedition. On September 22 he left Fort Nez Perces, following his track of the previous year.[34] By November 9, he was on the Humboldt River and his trappers were out in all directions. The beaver were extremely shy because the Indians trapped them. These natives were the most "miserable looking wretches" Ogden had yet encountered. "A race of animals less entitled to the name of man" would be impossible to find, he said.

The weather was mild until November 25, when snow fell. The party followed the stream eastward until the frozen "Unknown River" dwindled into a small streamlet, then struck east across country. On December 18 they were in the Utas country and on the 26th Ogden wrote in his journal:

> Had a distant view of Salt Lake. Heavy fogs around it. Country is covered with cedars. From the tracks, buffalo must be abundant. At present none. On the eve of camping we were surprised to see our guide come in with a cheerful countenance. He informed us he had seen an Indian who reported buffalo, not far off. I trust this is true, as we are wretched reduced to skin & bone. Hunters killed 3 antelope.

---

33 Dale Morgan, *The Humboldt* (New York, 1943), 6.

34 The information for this expedition is taken from T. C. Elliott (ed.), "Journal of Peter Skene Ogden: Snake Expedition, 1828-1829," *The Quarterly of the Oregon Historical Society*, XI (December, 1910), 381-99. See also Gloria Griffen Cline, *Exploring the Great Basin* (Norman, 1963), 112-25. Dr. Cline had the benefit of the original Ogden journal to trace his course on this expedition.

This will assist, tho' poor food at this season, but far preferable to horse flesh that die of disease.

On December 30, they reached the plain of the Malade River, a tributary of the Bear. For two months they trapped the Malade, the Portneuf, and Bear in southern Idaho and northern Utah.

Silent partners in the fur trade were the trappers' Indian wives, who usually accompanied the trapping expeditions and endured all the hardships, fatigue, famine, and drudgery of the journey, but who are rarely mentioned in the journals or official records. Mountain Man Joe Meek in his reminiscences relates an incident concerning the "wife of Ogden" which illustrates the character of these women. Meek writes that the American trapping party to which he was attached had trapped the Blackfoot and Snake Rivers and had then proceeded south to Ogden's Hole. Here they encountered Peter Skene Ogden's brigade. Immediately the Americans began bartering with the Indian employees of the British for furs. They made no progress until they opened a keg of whisky and under its influence extracted most of the furs from Ogden's Indians. Naturally this was disagreeable to Ogden as well as unprofitable, and a hostile feeling prevailed between the rival camps.

While matters were in this stage a stampede occurred one day among the British horses. Two or three of the animals ran into the American camp. Among them was the horse of Ogden's wife, with her baby hanging to the saddle. The mother followed the horse into the hostile camp and retrieved it. At this moment she saw one of the Hudson's Bay Company pack horses loaded with beaver which had also run into the American camp. The Americans had already begun to exult over this circumstance, as they considered this chance load of beaver as theirs according to the laws of war. Ogden's wife disagreed. She mounted her horse, seized the pack horse by the halter, and led it out of the camp. At this action some of the trappers cried out, "Shoot her, shoot her!" but a majority interferred, exclaiming: "Let her go, let her alone; she's a brave woman; I glory in her pluck." While the clamor continued Ogden's wife galloped away with her baby and the pack horse.[35]

In late March Ogden divided his party and sent one division to Fort Nez Perces through the Snake Valley, in his track of 1826. With fourteen men he retraced his steps to Unknown River. Reaching the river and following it, by May 27 they encamped within a mile of a large lake called by Ogden "Unknown Lake." From here the brigade journeyed to the Pit River in northern California. Since this region was now considered to be McLeod's territory, Ogden decided to return to Fort Nez Perces. He left the brigade on July 6 and with two men proceeded for Nez Perces to make arrangements for arrival of the brigade. From the standpoint of fur returns this expedition was considered highly successful, with over four thousand furs taken.

Ogden's sixth and last "Snake Country" expedition (1829-30) carried him from Fort Vancouver on the Columbia River to the "Gulph of California," hence up the entire length of California's San Joaquin and Sacramento valleys and across Oregon back to the Hudson's Bay Headquarters.

On August 10, 1828, Jedediah Smith, fresh from the Umpqua Massacre, had arrived at Fort Vancouver. His arrival made the British increasingly aware that they had neglected a potential threat on their southern flank.[36] Chief factor John McLoughlin, ever on the search for new trapping grounds, was at that moment outfitting a reconnais-

35 Francis F. Victor, *The River of the West; Life and Adventure in the Rocky Mountains and Oregon* (Hartford, 1870), 95-96. Meek said this episode occurred in 1830 at Ogden's Hole. Inasmuch as Ogden was not in this vicinity that year it probably occurred during the Fifth Snake Expedition, in 1829.

36 Dale Morgan, *Jedediah Smith and the Opening of the West* (Indianapolis, 1953). This is the best study of Smith and his peregrinations in the West.

sance expedition for the California region. That this was Mexican territory did not bother him. In the pursuit of furs "the operations of its Expeditions, may be considered as extending as far in a Southerly & Westerly direction as Beaver can be found." [37] And Governor Simpson wrote:

> In regard to the Territorial rights of the Mexican Republic, we follow the example of the Spanish functionaries on the Coast, and opponents from the United States, by making no enquiries about them.[38]

While Ogden was at Fort Vancouver recuperating from his fourth Snake expedition and preparing for his fifth, he had renewed his acquaintance with Jedediah Smith. The two had met previously in the autumn of 1824 when Smith and his six companions attached themselves to the Alexander Ross Snake brigade and accompanied him back to Flathead Post to spend the winter. In the spring of 1825, taking the benefit of Ogden's protection from that post to the Snake Country, Smith had separated from the British brigade on March 19, 1825, on Bear River. The seven Americans had been unwelcome travelers with Ogden, who attributed the misadventures which later befell him on the trip to the knowledge the Americans had of his movements.[39]

During the two weeks prior to Ogden's departure for the Humboldt he became "intimately acquainted with poor Smith," and it was from this association that Ogden became interested in a southwestern and California expedition. When he returned on July 24, 1829, he was immediately outfitted for an excursion to the California waters, since the British were eager to reach and trap these streams before American trappers were informed of Smith's explorations.

So in September, 1829, with thirty men, Ogden departed

[37] E. E. Rich (ed.), *Part of Dispatch from George Simpson Esqr., Governor of Rupert's Land to the Governor & Committee of the Hudson's Bay Company, London* (London, 1947), 52. [38] *Ibid.*

[39] Merk, "Snake Country Expedition, 1824-1825," 112.

on an expedition that was to carry him to southern California.[40] After leaving the Columbia the brigade journeyed a month through sterile country, on a march accompanied by days-on-end without food, water, or wood for fuel. Many horses starved to death and the men were "compelled to eat the emaciated carcasses and as a last resort, to quench their thirst with their blood." When they reached Unknown River they found it choked with ice and snow, a situation which "blasted all hopes of a fall hunt." [41]

The Brigade reached the "Great Sandy desert of Great Salt Lake "in January, 1830.[42] The desert was traversed after much suffering, and then they "had a range of rocky Mountains to cross." They struck the Sevier River, which they followed to its discharge into a salt lake. This country they found destitute of beaver. From this point they probably followed Smith's track, possibly guided by one of the survivors of Smith's party. At any rate they at least had the advantage of an account of the region written by Smith.

Following a southwestern course in February, 1830, the British party reached the "South Branch of the Rio Collarado." Then "after three days' further traveling, over a country as barren as ever Christians traversed" they arrived among a tribe of Indians living on the Colorado and which Ogden "strongly suspected" to be the Indians who had

---

40 The journals of this expedition were lost on July 3, 1830, at the Dalles when Ogden's boat was upset and his papers, five hundred skins and the lives of nine men were lost. To piece together the course of this expedition it has been necessary to rely upon John Scaglione, "Ogden's Report of His 1829-1830 Expedition," *California Historical Society Quarterly*, XXVIII (June, 1949), 117-24 and the book written by A Fur Trader (Peter Skene Ogden) *Traits of American Life and Character* (London, 1833). There is some question as to Ogden's authorship of this book but the incidents related do correspond closely with portions of his career. Alice Bay Maloney, "Peter Skene Ogden's Trapping Expedition to the Gulf of California, 1829-30," *California Historical Quarterly*, XIX (December, 1940), 308-16, is also helpful. Gloria Cline's *Exploring the Great Basin*, 125-27 has additional new material.

41 Scaglione, "Ogden's Report of His 1829-1830 Expedition," 121.

42 *Ibid.* Gloria Cline, *Exploring the Great Basin*, does not believe that this was in Utah. See pp. 126-27.

treacherously attacked Smith in 1828. Ogden placed his men on the alert to guard the horses, and ordered them to be ready with guns and spears. He allowed some Indians into his camp in order to keep an eye on them and perhaps dissuade them from attacking. His strategy did not work, however, because presently one of the guards was wounded and the alarm given that the Indians were securing the horses. Ogden ordered a general discharge, to be followed by a charge with the spears, but the first was sufficient. The rest of the Indians fled the field when they observed that twenty-six of their fellows "in a single moment were made to lick the dust."

From the Mojave Indian villages the British continued down the Colorado "till nigh the Gulph of California."[43] From the Gulf, Ogden turned northward, but since he had no desire to encounter Mexican authorities and to answer embarrassing questions, he kept well to the east of the Mexican missions and settlements. He followed the "South Branch of the Bonaventura" (San Joaquin River) and trapped that stream from its source to San Francisco Bay, collecting a thousand skins along the way. An American brigade from Santa Fe, under Ewing Young, caught up with Ogden at San Francisco. Since Ogden had preceded the Americans, their returns were meager. The Yankees traveled with the British for ten days and separated when they reached Pit River. From this point the British followed the trail back to Fort Nez Perces, where they arrived on June 30, 1830.

The results of this expedition, as far as the net returns of fur were concerned, were very disappointing, being "one third less than last year."[44] McLoughlin described the California waters as the "poorest in Furs" that Ogden had thus far explored, "but as it was a new country we could not

[43] Rich, *The Letters of John McLoughlin,* 86.

[44] Scaglione, "Ogden's Report of His 1829-1830 Expedition," 122.

know it was Stocked in Beaver till he had explored it."[45] From a geographical standpoint, however, considerable knowledge concerning the California hinterland was gained.

Upon Ogden's return from his California expedition he found at Fort Vancouver a letter which relieved him of his Snake Country command and appointed him to establish a fur trading post at the mouth of the Nass River, some ten degrees north of Fort Vancouver.[46] That Ogden was not enchanted by such an assignment may be noted in the following:

> I have been a wanderer far and near, my perverse fate never permitting me to sojourn long in the same spot; but driving me about without cessation, like a ball on a tennis-court. While in the heyday of youth, this vagrant kind of life was not without its charms to one of my unsettled disposition; with advancing years, however, soberer tastes, and less adventurous desires have crept over me, until I could heartily wish for a life of greater tranquillity. The potentates who rule my destiny seem, however, otherwise inclined, and I now discover, to my overpowering chagrin and discomfort, that what I began willingly, and regarded as amusement, I must continue in earnest and against the grain, like physic administered to one who might with it "to the dogs" – "le flux, m'amena le reflux m'meme." When, oh, when, will this life of involuntary peregrination cease?[47]

In April, 1831, Ogden's party departed Fort Vancouver and arrived at their destination on May 11. A new post was erected and christened "Fort Simpson." For three years Ogden conducted trading and trapping operations in this Nass River region.[48]

In 1834 another British expedition, with Ogden in command, was organized to establish a trading post on the Stikine River. At the mouth of this stream the British found a

[45] Rich, *The Letters of John McLoughlin,* 86.

[46] T. C. Elliott, "Peter Skene Ogden, Fur Trapper," 251.

[47] Ogden, *Traits of American Life and Character,* 34.

[48] Hubert Howe Bancroft, *History of the North West Coast, 1800-1848,* (San Francisco, 1884), 629.

Russian blockhouse and a Russian corvette and two fourteen-oared boats which forbade entrance into the river. A considerable controversy ensued. Ogden and his men could not legally settle the matter, nor did they have the physical means to force their entry into the Stikine. He therefore retired from the scene.[49]

Ogden was later chagrined to learn that it was insinuated he had acted with "too much caution or in other words with cowardice." He demanded that Governor Simpson clear his name of the "foul stigma" of these charges by asserting that he had acted to the "ultimate interest of the Concern." [50] When the British government received word of the Russian violation of the spirit of the Convention of 1825, they vigorously protested. The result was that the Russian government eventually paid damages amounting to 20,000 pounds sterling, ceded Fort Wrangel, leased to the British the shore strip which was the basis of the controversy, surrendered the Stikine post, and also gave permission to build an establishment still farther to the north on the Tako River. In view of the concessions ultimately made by the Russians it is evident that Ogden's caution was vindicated and that the restraint he exercised resulted in far greater gains for the Company and the Empire than would have been realized had he provoked the Russians into a shooting war.

Peter Skene Ogden was promoted to chief factor, the highest field grade in the fur business, on January 1, 1835. This promotion was accompanied by his assignment to the command of the New Caledonia District at Fort St. James on Lake Stuart. For nine years (1835-1844) Ogden remained in charge of this district [51] and enjoyed a career here comparable to Chief Factor John McLoughlin's career in the Columbia Department.

---

49 *Ibid.*, 630-33.

50 Elliott, "Peter Skene Ogden, Fur Trapper," 253-54.

51 *Ibid.*, 255-56.

In the spring of 1844, Ogden took a year's leave of absence, his first vacation in twenty-two years. He attended to business matters conected with the estate of his mother, who had recently died, and also visited relatives and friends in Canada, New York, and in Europe. He returned to Canada in the spring of 1845 and was at the Red River encampment on his way back to Oregon when Governor Simpson assigned him to take charge of the Warre-Vavasour expedition to the Columbia Country.[52]

The Warre-Vavasour expedition had its origin at a critical point in the Anglo-American controversy over Oregon. The British Cabinet was alarmed over the situation, especially with American expansionists proclaiming Manifest Destiny, and with the election in 1844 of James K. Polk, who had campaigned on slogans of "Fifty-four Forty or Fight" and "The Reannexation of Oregon," and who had proclaimed that American title to Oregon was "clear and unquestionable." The British felt that they too had clear title to Oregon and decided to dispatch a reconnaissance mission to obtain "a general knowledge of the capabilities of the Oregon territory in a military point of view, in order that we may be enabled to act immediately and with effect in defense of our rights in that quarter, should those rights be infringed by any hostile aggression or encroachment on the part of the United States." Ogden convoyed Lt. Henry J. Warre and Lt. M. Vavasour to Oregon, Governor Simpson noting that his knowledge and experience would "guard against privation, inconvenience or danger along that route." Ogden greatly assisted the lieutenants in their reconnaissance, but the reports of Warre and Vavasour reached the British government too late to influence the negotiations. The 49th parallel was accepted as the boundary in June, 1846.

[52] See Joseph Shafer (ed.), "Documents Relative to Warre and Vavasour's Military Reconnaissance in Oregon, 1845-6," *The Quarterly of the Oregon Historical Society,* x (March, 1909), 1-99.

Ogden did not return to Fort St. James and the command of the New Caledonia District upon completion of his assignment with the Warre-Vavasour expedition. He was, instead, assigned to Fort Vancouver, where he shared the management of the Columbia District with Chief Factor James Douglas until 1849. From 1849 to 1852 he was the only chief factor on the Columbia. In the latter year, Dugald MacTavish was sent to assist him.[53]

In June, 1846, with the establishment of the Anglo-American boundary, a perplexing problem arose concerning the properties of the Hudson's Bay Company within United States territory. By that treaty the Company was given certain rights south of the boundary line, including permission to navigate the Columbia River south of the 49th parallel. Fort Vancouver continued to be the supply point for the Company's forts along the coast and for the Sandwich Islands, and trade with Oregon settlers and the Indians of the interior continued to be large. As manager of this largest business concern in the country, the responsibilities of Ogden were varied and great. While some American settlers were rather hostile to the Company, and this hostility helped to form the Oregon Provisional Government at Champoeg on May 2, 1843, Ogden's tact and diplomacy held him in high esteem with the majority of Americans in Oregon. He came to be called "Governor Ogden" by the settlers and was described as "a short man, dark complexioned, witty and lively in conversation and distinguished in appearance."[54]

The Whitman Mission massacre of November 29, 1847, gave Peter Skene Ogden the opportunity of performing his greatest service to the pioneer settlers of Oregon. In addition to the sixteen people murdered by the Cayuse Indians at Waillatpu (six miles west of the present city of Walla

[53] Elliott, "Peter Skene Ogden, Fur Trapper," 262.

[54] *Ibid.*, 263.

Walla), the natives took prisoner forty-seven others – five men, eight women and thirty-four children.[55] The murder of Marcus Whitman, his wife, and the others, posed a complicated problem for Ogden, who was among the first to learn of the disaster. He represented a foreign corporation located in United States territory. Should he take the initiative and attempt a rescue, or simply report it to the Americans then meeting in their provisional legislature in Oregon City, twenty-five miles away?

Although the legislature was the recognized American authority in the territory, it was practically powerless to begin and prosecute a war with the Indians. On the other hand, the Hudson's Bay Company had the necessary forces. Ogden was a skilled and forceful negotiator among the natives, but for him to attempt the rescue and fail could incur the wrath of both the people of Oregon and the American government toward him, his company, and the British government. But the situation was desperate. Early on the morning of December 7, Ogden set off en route to the scene of the massacre. He traveled with his usual complement of men, without display of arms, and at normal speed, in order not to arouse the suspicions of the natives. It required twelve days to reach his destination. On December 24, he assembled the chiefs of the Walla Walla, Cayuse, and Nez Perces tribes for a conference. He made no promises to them, but pointed out that if the Americans were aroused they would wage war which would not end until "every man of you is cut off from the face of the earth." He appealed for the release of the captives, offering to pay a small ransom. Chief Tiloukaikt of the Cayuse replied:

> Chief, your words are weighty, your hairs are gray. We have known you a long time. You have had an unpleasant journey to this place. I cannot therefore keep the families back. I make them over to you, which I would not do to another younger than yourself.

[55] *Ibid.*, 276-77.

Seven days of anxious waiting followed before the captives being held at Lapwai were turned over to Ogden. The Americans were conducted to Fort Vancouver and thence to Oregon City, and none too soon. Word was received that some of the Oregon Volunteers had arrived at the Dalles, and the Cayuse War had begun.

In December, 1851, Ogden left Fort Vancouver for Montreal for a leave of absence. There is some indication that he considered retirement from the fur trade at that time. Had he followed the inclinations of others and the desires of his eastern relatives he would have settled down to a life of ease in the society of congenial and well-to-do people in Montreal. But his first love was the great Pacific Northwest, and he determined to spend his last days there. He remained in the East for almost a year and then returned to Oregon, where he again undertook the management of the Hudson's Bay Company business which still flourished. The constant exposurse during his career in the field had whitened his hair and brought on some of the infirmities of age. Still, he was active in the fur business until a few months before his death. When poor health finally forced him to retire, he went to Oregon City, where at the homestead of a son-in-law, Archibald McKinley, he spent his last few months, an invalid, but fondly cared for by his wife and a daughter. Although the best of medical treatment and attention were available to him at Fort Vancouver, he preferred to die in the companionship of his family, and in this public manner gave confirmation of his affection and loyalty to his Indian wife of many years.[56]

During this illness Dr. McLoughlin was a regular visitor and he urged Ogden to permit a formal marriage ceremony with his wife. Ogden refused, stating that if his many years

[56] T. C. Elliott, "Remarks at Unveiling of Memorial Stone to Peter Skene Ogden At Mountain View Cemetery, Oregon City, October 23, 1923," *The Quarterly of the Oregon Historical Society,* XXIV (December, 1923), 382.

of open recognition of their relationship and of their many children were not proof enough, then the empty words of man would not add anything of value. Unfortunately, this refusal caused delay and trouble in the settlement of his estate, because members of his family in Canada and England instituted proceedings to break his will on the ground that there was no legal proof that he ever married. A compromise was finally arranged by Sir George Simpson, who was the executor of the estate, which amounted to at least fifty-thousand dollars.[57]

Peter Skene Ogden died on September 27, 1854, in his sixtieth year. He had been baptized into the English Episcopal Church, and the funeral service was read by the Reverend St. Michael Fackler, the first resident Episcopal rector of Oregon. The body was laid to rest in Mountain View Cemetery at Oregon City.

For nearly seventy years the last resting place of this man who had served so long and well in Oregon was largely forgotten. It was not even marked by a tombstone.[58] Finally, on October 23, 1923, as a result of the combined efforts of three organizations, the Oregon Historical Society, the Oregon Pioneer Association, and the Sons and Daughters of Oregon Pioneers, a fitting granite marker was erected over his grave.

57 Elliott, "Peter Skene Ogden, Fur Trapper," 273-74.

58 Frederick V. Holman, "Address at Unveiling of Memorial Stone to Peter Skene Ogden at Mountain View Cemetery, Oregon City, October 23, 1923," *ibid.*, 378.

Ceran St. Vrain

by HAROLD H. DUNHAM
University of Denver

Ceran St. Vrain (May 5, 1802-October 28, 1870) was recognized by his contemporaries as one of the outstanding Mountain Men of the American Southwest. From fur trapping and trading, he progressed to a position of business, military and political prominence that made him one of New Mexico's leading citizens. His personal qualities, which included kindliness, courage, reliability and reserve, indicate that he was a true gentleman. The fact that only a few of his personal and business papers seem to have survived helps explain why he has not yet been portrayed in a full-scale biography.[1]

Ceran's father, Jacques Marcellin Ceran de Hault de Lassus de St. Vrain, was born in French Flanders in 1770, and migrated to St. Louis, Missouri, in 1795, five years after his own father had fled the early stages of the French Revolution.[2] By 1796 Jacques had married Marie Felicite Dubreuil and settled down in a home near Spanish Lake, St. Louis County. There, in this predominantly French community, on May 5, 1802, Ceran St. Vrain, the second of ten children, was born to the couple. Unfortunately, very little is known of Ceran's early life. To be sure, his father was well acquainted with some of the leading French families of the town. He held minor political office and owned a generous land grant in southeastern Missouri, along with

[1] The life of C. St. Vrain is sketched in D. Lavender, *Bent's Fort* (1954), *passim;* N. Mumey, "Black Beard," in *Denver Westerners Monthly Roundup,* XIV, no. 1 (Jan. 1958), 4-16; and *Dictionary of American Biography* (1928-36), XVI, pp. 305-06.

[2] P. A. St. Vrain, *Genealogy of the Family of De Lassus and St. Vrain* (1943), 15.

smaller grants near St. Louis, so the family must have lived in fairly comfortable circumstances.

Ceran may well have received some formal education in a town school.[3] While the grammar and spelling of his known letters, beginning with the mid-1820s, reveal numerous deficiencies, Ceran's writing was in English, rather than French, and it displayed at times rather elegant penmanship. Possibly the death of his father in 1818, when Ceran was in his mid-teens, prevented the latter from receiving a more complete schooling, such as that provided for Bernard Pratte, Jr., and Charles Bent, two of Ceran's friends.

The father's death probably meant that the large family became a burden to Madame St. Vrain, so Ceran went to live with the Bernard Pratte, Sr., family. It was during this period that Bernard, Jr., transferred to a school in Kentucky to complete his education. Pratte, Sr., served as a partner in two fur trading companies before forming Bernard Pratte and Co., in 1823.[4] It was perhaps inevitable that as a youth living with the Prattes, Ceran should have become a clerk in the company's St. Louis store, progressed to managing fur shipments, and then entered into the trade of the company's Missouri River posts.[5] From such experiences, he progressed into the Santa Fe trade in his early twenties, yet just how this shift occurred is not clear.[6]

In any case, by 1824 St. Vrain had formed a partnership

[3] The reference to St. Vrain's formal schooling is based on inference from several sources, rather than any direct source. At least one of his younger brothers went on to college.

[4] *D.A.B.*, xv, pp. 180-81; and J. T. Scharf, *History of St. Louis City and County* (1883) I, pp. 196 fn., and 674.

[5] James Conklin recalled in 1877 that St. Vrain was a clerk in St. Louis for B. Pratte, Berthold and Co., merchants. R.I. 1723. Ritch Collection, Huntington Library, San Marino, Calif.

[6] The family genealogy states that St. Vrain entered the Santa Fe trade when he was about twenty-one. St. Vrain, *Genealogy,* 20. Conklin, cited in the previous footnote, asserts that St. Vrain left for New Mexico in 1823.

with Francois Guerin, secured from Pratte a supply of goods for the New Mexican and the Indian trade, and about November 1824 left St. Louis for New Mexico.[7] His trip proved to be a long and troublesome one lasting five months, for he did not reach Taos until March 20, 1825.

Five weeks later, St. Vrain reported to Pratte, Sr., that since he had reached Taos he had sold few goods; furthermore, merchandise was selling at reduced prices. He therefore considered two possible alternatives. First, he hoped to be able to sell out all his wares, primarily to Provost and Le Clerc when they came in from their spring hunt, and secondarily, to other trappers. He expected that he could make "verry profitable buisness" deals in that manner. On the other hand, should there be no such transactions, he planned to buy up articles that would suit the market in Sonora, and go there to purchase mules.

In some undisclosed manner (St. Vrain declared that the "reasons were two teajus to mention") the partnership of St. Vrain and Guerin was dissolved by April 1825. St. Vrain paid Guerin $100 in cash, gave him two mules, and pledged himself for the full amount owed Pratte and Co. At the same time, St. Vrain sent east with Guerin a small shipment of beaver skins, the receipts from which were to be placed partly to his own account. Shortly thereafter St. Vrain took on a new partner, for by the summer of 1825 the firm of St. Vrain and Baillio had been formed.[8]

The new partners outfitted a party of hunters and trap-

[7] Letter from C. St. Vrain to B. Pratte, dated on its face at Taos, Apr. 7, 1824, but on the outside, in St. Vrain's handwriting, "29, 1825." A further notation on the outside shows that it was received June 10, 1825. Chouteau Collection, Missouri Historical Society, St. Louis.

[8] Two letters from Lt. Col. A. R. Wooley to "St. Vrain and Ballio, Merchants," dated Ft. Atkinson, Sept. 14, 1825. Records of the War Dep't, U.S. Army Commands, 6th Infantry Letterbooks, Record Group 98. National Records and Archives, Wash., D.C. Re Baillio at Ft. Osage, see A. H. Favour, *Old Bill Williams, Mountain Man* (1936), 51-2.

pers, with expectations of a large profit.[9] This party may have been one to which Thomas L. (later called Peg-leg) Smith belonged, although there is some conflict of dates here in the record.[10] By July 1825 St. Vrain wrote his mother from Taos that he had sold out the greater part of his merchandise very profitably. This success ruled out the necessity for the Sonoran venture, although he still retained a small stock of goods on hand. This latter he hoped to dispose of to fur trappers who had not yet returned to Taos from their spring hunt.

St. Vrain complained that he might have to spend the coming winter, 1825-26, in "this miserable place," as he called Fernandez de Taos. Actually, he may have intended to convey the impression of regret over the delay in not visiting his Missouri home because a combination of business and personal affairs detained him. Among the latter may have been an intention to establish a home in Taos, for at least by the following year he had acquired his first wife.[11] St. Vrain did report that already he had become able to speak Spanish well enough to dispense with an interpreter in his business dealings.

By early April 1826, St. Vrain had returned to the States and was preparing a new expedition for New Mexico.[12] This effort may have been reported in the *Missouri Intelligencer* for April 14, 1826, when it noted that a company of about 100 men, including those who had lately returned to Missouri, would be ready to start within a few weeks for

[9] Letter from C. St. Vrain to Madam F. St. Vrain, dated July 1825. Mo. Hist. Society, St. Louis.

[10] "Sketches from the Life of Pegleg Smith," *Hutching's Illustrated California Magazine* (July 1860-June 1861), v (1861), 319; and D. L. Morgan, *The West of Wm. Ashley,* 279.

[11] Reference to St. Vrain's first wife is based on probable date of conception of his first son, Vincente. Birth recorded for May 10, 1827, in "Bent Family Bible." Historical Society of New Mexico Collections, Santa Fe.

[12] L. R. Hafen, "When Was Bent's Fort Built?" in *Colorado Magazine,* XXXI (April 1954), 109; and Lavender, *Bent's Fort,* 65 and 375.

Santa Fe. Such a caravan did pull out of Franklin on June 1. Yet the not always reliable Henry Inman has declared that St. Vrain started westward with a party of forty-two men, driving twenty-six mule-drawn wagons from Ft. Osage during May 1826.[13] The caravan reached the New Mexican capital late in July.[14]

Later that year was the time of what has been called St. Vrain's Gila River expedition, but this is a misnomer, for St. Vrain was not its leader. It is true that on November 29, 1826, the governor of New Mexico, Antonio Narbona, issued passports to S. W. (W. S.?) Williams and Seran Sambrano (Ceran St. Vrain), with thirty-five followers, to travel to Sonora for purposes of private trade.[15] Similar passports were granted to other North Americans about the same time. Yet one document authorized the recipients to trap "the Gila and Colorado rivers for beaver," and since an estimated 100 American trappers headed for the Gila, it appears that all, including St. Vrain, intended to trap rather than trade. The trappers did not travel in one party, however, but in four separate groups. This fact alone suggests that St. Vrain was not the leader of the entire band.

Unfortunately, there are no details available as to the route, experiences or degree of success for the St. Vrain and Williams group. But it is known that by January 1827, St. Vrain had returned to Taos, where he joined a group of twenty-three trappers under the leadership of S. S. Pratte, which left the New Mexican settlements on a spring hunt.[16] Just where the band trapped is not recorded, although by the following June it is clear that St. Vrain was again back in Taos where he attended a wedding. One can hope that

---

[13] Henry Inman, *The Old Santa Fe Trail* (1897), 406-7.

[14] J. J. Hill, "Ewing Young in the Fur Trade of the Far Southwest, 1822-1834," reprint from the *Oregon Historical Quarterly*, XXIV, p. 1.

[15] T. M. Marshall, "St. Vrain's Expedition to the Gila in 1826," in *Southwestern Historical Quarterly*, XIX (Jan. 1916), 251 ff.

[16] Lavender, *Bent's Fort*, p. 376.

he had arrived there during the previous month, for on May 10, 1827, his first son, Vincent, was born.

St. Vrain's next trapping expedition lasted for nine months. The party was again headed by S. S. Pratte, and it included Milton Sublette and Tom Smith; St. Vrain served as clerk. The group set out hopefully from Taos in the fall of 1827 and traveled to the headwaters of the North Platte River in North Park, where it soon collected 300 beaver. While in the Park, Pratte was bitten by a dog that was infected with hydrophobia. A short and painful illness was followed by his death about October 1, 1827.[17] St. Vrain tried in every way possible to ease his leader's period of distress, and was terribly shaken when Pratte died.

After his burial the other members of the group, according to St. Vrain, confronted him with the question of what was to be done, or more particularly, who would pay them their wages. The men themselves, however, later claimed that they had unanimously requested St. Vrain to take command. In either case, Ceran accepted the role of leader and gave his companions his solemn promise that so far as he had or should have property or funds of the deceased under his control, the men would be paid their several demands. This promise was accepted as satisfactory to all concerned.

It was about this time St. Vrain undertook to caution the reckless Tom Smith not to expose himself so much to possible Indian attack.[18] But before the suggestion was completed, an Indian arrow pierced Smith's leg and necessitated its amputation. St. Vrain accorded Smith every attention and comfort. When the latter was able to be moved, the party left North Park and headed, according to Smith, southwestwardly for the Green River. There during No-

17 Letter from C. St. Vrain to B. Pratte & Co., undated but received Sept. 28, 1828; and Deposition of Twelve Trappers, dated at Taos, Sept. 1, 1829. Bent and St. Vrain Papers, Mo. Hist. Soc.

18 "Sketches from the Life of Pegleg Smith," 420-21.

vember, winter quarters were established. Shortly, a band consisting of forty lodges of Utes, friendly to Smith, encamped near them.

After surviving what St. Vrain described as "the most vigorous winter I have yet Experienced," the trappers began their spring hunt. Considerable success then caused a portion of the company, which had caught about a thousand beaver, to head eastward across the mountains for St. Louis by way of the Platte River. Yet after traveling on that course for four or five days, they "struck upon a large Indian trace which . . . [they] supposed to be the sign of a hostile party." Since the trappers were too short of ammunition to risk a fight, they decided to return to Taos, where they arrived safely by about May 23, 1828. There St. Vrain sold all that he could, to be able to pay off his men. A few months later he sent a report of his transactions, along with his available accounts, to Pratte and Co.[19] He had to confess that he could not then include "a Recappitulation of the Books, for these have been cep in such . . . [an irregular?] maner that I am at a loss in [a] grate meney accounts." He could only promise to send them later as nearly correct as possible. He added, with undoubted satisfaction, that there was a balance in his own favor of $522.26½, which he wished paid to his partner, Paul Baillio.

At the end of September, 1828, St. Vrain, Antoine Robidoux, David Waldo and Richard Campbell obtained passports from the governor of New Mexico for a trip to Chihuahua and Sonora.[20] If the evidence for David Waldo is any indication, the purpose of this expedition was trade, not trapping. Perhaps St. Vrain did embark on the venture, yet there is no certain record of just what his activities were

19 Deposition of Twelve Trappers cited in fn. 17.

20 "Mexican Passports, Aug. 14, 1828-Oct. 22, 1836. New Mexico." R.I. 108. Ritch Collection, Huntington Library.

during the winter of 1828-29. Then by the fall of 1829 he appeared to be in New Mexico.[21]

By the spring of 1830, St. Vrain had returned to Missouri. During April he signed a nine months' note in St. Louis in favor of Bernard Pratte and Co., for the sum of $2,570.63.[22] Probably the note covered the cost of goods that Ceran prepared to accompany to New Mexico. He may well have joined a caravan composed of 120 men and 60 wagons which left Franklin for Santa Fe on May 22, 1830.[23] In any case, he reached the New Mexican capital by August 4 and paid the full duty of sixty percent on the original cost of all the goods.[24] St. Vrain was the first to place his wares in the customs house, and promptly began retailing his merchandise. The market proved to be too slow to suit St. Vrain, so he decided to offer his goods at "hole sailes." He must have found a ready purchaser, or purchasers, because it was reported that he received $10,000 for the commodities that had cost him about $3,000.[25]

Instead of returning to Missouri, he signed notes in Santa Fe, for a total of $3,405.12, payable to B. Pratte and Co.[26] Then during the first week in September he went to Taos and purchased what furs were available – he confesses that he had arrived after the hunters had disposed of most of their catch.[27] A fortnight later he arranged with Andrew Carson and Savase Ruel to take charge of a wagon, eleven

21 F. X. DeLisle recalled in 1877 that in 1829 he went to New Mexico with St. Vrain and C. Bent. R.I. 2212. vol. 1, p. 79. Ritch Collection, Huntington Library.

22 Chouteau-Maffitt Collection, Mo. Hist. Soc. I am indebted to Dr. L. R. Hafen for lending me copies of this note and several other original sources cited herein.

23 Hafen, "When Was Bent's Fort Built?", 110.

24 Letter from C. St. Vrain to B. Pratte & Co., dated Taos, Sept. 14, 1830. Pierre Chouteau Collection, Mo. Hist. Soc.

25 Theodore Papin to P. M. Papin, Feb. 24, 1831. Mo. Hist. Soc.

26 Letter from C. St. Vrain to B. Pratte & Co., dated Taos, Sept. 14, 1830. P. Chouteau Collection. Also a sight-draft signed by C. St. Vrain to R. D. Shackleford at Santa Fe, August 31, 1830. Chouteau-Maffitt Collection, Mo. Hist. Soc.

27 C. St. Vrain to B. Pratte & Co., Sept. 14, 1830, cited in fn. 26.

mules, and 653 "Skeins of Bever," weighing 961 pounds, for shipment to Missouri, where they were to be credited to St. Vrain's account with Pratte and Co. A surplus wagon he lent to Charles Bent for returning to the States.

Later in the year, St. Vrain planned to head east, when Charles Bent proposed a cooperative arrangement for the two of them.[28] St. Vrain was to purchase half of Bent's goods and remain in New Mexico to sell them, along with Bent's half. Meanwhile, Bent would return to Missouri and purchase additional merchandise for the two of them. The offer appealed to Ceran, so he paid cash for his purchase from Bent, and the latter set out for the States. Bent carried with him $600 to be placed to St. Vrain's account with Pratte and Co., as well as a letter dated January 6, 1831, from St. Vrain explaining the foregoing developments.

It might seem that the cooperative effort of Bent and St. Vrain faced rather dismal prospects. St. Vrain himself had reported that money was very scarce in New Mexico, that goods sold at low prices, and that duties were high. Still he believed that prospects for trade were better in New Mexico than in Missouri. He probably planned to supplement the trade, as usual, by continuing to deal in furs.

While there are no statistics available for the value of Bent and St. Vrain's trade in 1831, the total worth of furs shipped from Santa Fe to Missouri that year was estimated at $50,000, which was nearly half the amount of the return estimated as coming directly from the Rocky Mountains to Missouri.[29] The $50,000 sum accrued to two unnamed companies fitting out in Santa Fe. Before the decade ran out, Bent and St. Vrain collected from $20,000 to $40,00 an-

28 Letter from C. St. Vrain to B. Pratte & Co., dated at Taos, Jan. 6, 1831. Chouteau-Maffitt Collection.

29 Letter from Wm. Gordon to Sec. of War Lewis Cass, Oct. 3, 1831. Quoted in A. H. Abel, ed., *Chardon's Journal at Ft. Clark, 1834-39* (1932), 347.

nually in their fur trade.[30] In short, the two men, through the company which they formed at least by 1832, were to build up what Hiram Chittenden termed "one of the most important fur trading firms" of the West, ranking next to the American Fur Company in the amount of business transacted in the period about 1840.[31]

But to return to 1831. When St. Vrain had agreed to remain in New Mexico as the merchant for his own and Bent's goods, he committed himself to a new country. On February 15, 1831, he became a naturalized Mexican citizen.[32] Actually, such a step meant a kind of dual citizenship, with benefits from both countries, though just how, if at all, it affected St. Vrain's operations as a trader is not clear. He did maintain a home in Taos and, by 1832, he and his partner operated a store there on the south side of the plaza. On the other hand, two years later he was appointed U.S. Consul at Santa Fe, although he seems never to have fulfilled the duties of his office.[33]

Meanwhile, the new company had erected a stockade fort, called Ft. William, nine miles below the mouth of Fountain Creek (near present Pueblo, Colorado), for trade with the Cheyennes and Arapahoes.[34] A year later, that is in 1834, the company erected the more famous Ft. William, also called Bent's Fort, ten miles above the mouth of the Purgatoire River.[35]

For a dozen years after its founding, St. Vrain spent

---

30 Letter from Alexander Barclay to George Barclay, dated at Ft. William, May 1, 1840. Barclay Papers. Colorado Archives and Records Service, Denver, Colo. *The Missouri Republican,* June 12, 1840, reported that Bent & St. Vrain had obtained 15,000 buffalo skins during the past season.

31 H. M. Chittenden, *American Fur Trade of the Far West* (1954 edit.), II, p. 543 fn.

32 R.I. 113. Ritch Collection, Huntington Library.

33 Lavender, *Bent's Fort,* 191.

34 J. LeCompte, "Gantt's Fort and Bent's Picket Post," in *Colorado Magazine,* XLI (Spring 1964), 115 ff.

35 Letter from C. St. Vrain to Lt. Col. Eneas Mackey, dated at St. Louis, July 21, 1847. Quoted in N. Mumey, *Old Forts and Trading Posts* (1956), I, pp. 85-88.

considerable periods at Bent's Fort, trading with Arapahoes, Cheyennes, Comanches, Kiowas, and other Indians, supervising company activities, and welcoming both casual and important visitors, including members of the United States Army. From it, he occasionally traveled to the other forts the company established, namely Ft. St. Vrain (1837) on the South Platte River, and Bent's Fort on the Canadian (1842). He also, of course, accompanied company wagons to and from Missouri and still managed to spend some time in Taos and Santa Fe, with an occasional side trip to Washington.

Many of these activities were carried on jointly by St. Vrain and Bent. The two men complemented each other very well. Bent, a small man, was the more dynamic of the two and perhaps showed more initiative; St. Vrain, a large and portly man, with a Lincoln-like beard that caused the Indians to call him Black Beard, was more reserved, less in a hurry, and less volatile.[36] There is no record of a quarrel arising between the two men.

St. Vrain was on hand when Colonel Henry Dodge reached the Fort in 1835 while on a 1,600-mile swing up the Platte River and back by the Arkansas with a force of 120 troops.[37] Charles Bent was present, too, and one officer recorded that the proprietors greeted them "in a very friendly manner and invited them to dine at the Fort." The same officer observed that Bent and St. Vrain "appear to be much of gentlemen."

A year later, St. Vrain equipped R. L. (Uncle Dick) Wootton and a dozen other men with ten wagons loaded with goods for Indian trade and sent them northward into the Sioux country.[38] This party spent the winter north of

---

36 G. B. Grinnell, *Bent's Old Fort and Its Builders* (1914), 7 fn.

37 L. Pelzer, ed., "Captain Ford's Journal of an Expedition to the Rocky Mountains," in *New Mexico Historical Review,* XII (March 1926), 566.

38 H. L. Conard, *Uncle Dick Wootton* (1950 edit.), 29, 42-43, 46-47.

Ft. Laramie and returned to Bent's Fort in the spring with robes and furs worth about $25,000.

Whether or not Wootton's trading expedition was the precipitating factor is uncertain, but in 1838, St. Vrain reached an agreement with Pierre Chouteau not to send men on the North Platte for trading with the Indians.[39] This step may have been taken as a friendly move, or as the result of rivalry – probably the former. The previous association of St. Vrain with the western agent for the American Fur Company (Pratte and Co.), and the continued close relationship of Bent, St. Vrain and Company with both the agent and the A.F.C., indicate harmonious, if not stronger, ties. For example, in May 1838, the Bent, St. Vrain firm purchased a total of $13,257.33 worth of goods and supplies from the A.F.C.[40]

In 1843, St. Vrain had also assumed charge of an experiment in shipping his firm's furs down the Arkansas River by boat.[41] Difficulties and delays developed en route, so that while the venture was described as "not altogether unsuccessful," it had to be abandoned west of Walnut Creek. St. Vrain then ordered five wagons from the fort and reloaded the peltries on them. This small caravan pushed on to Walnut Creek, which was flooded, and there it caught up with Charles Bent and his fourteen well-ladened wagons. Nearby, Captain P. St. G. Cooke and his troops, who were escorting westbound caravans, also waited for the flood waters to subside.[42] St. Vrain was able to inform Captain Cooke, "with apprehension and secrecy," that about 180 Texans under Colonel Jacob Snively were encamped near the Arkansas crossing, and they probably intended to attack

[39] Letter from F. Laboue to P. D. Papin, Dec. 15, 1838. Chouteau-Papin Collection, Mo. Hist. Soc.

[40] Ledger Z, American Fur Co., under dates of May 11-18, 1838. Mo. Hist. Soc. Photostats in possession of author.

[41] W. E. Connelley, ed., "A Journal of the Santa Fe Trail," in *Miss. Valley Hist. Rev.*, XII (June 1925), 86.

[42] *Ibid.*, 90.

the Mexican portion (32 wagons) of the westbound caravan on Mexican soil. So Captain Cooke moved to the Snively camp and disarmed its men, for he believed it to be on United States soil.

After St. Vrain reached St. Louis and was prepared to return to New Mexico, during the latter part of August 1843, he was given a contract to establish a depot of provisions at Bent's Fort for Captain Cooke's troops, for they might have to winter nearby.[43] St. Vrain hurried to the captain's camp near the Arkansas crossing, found that the provisions would be needed, and so continued on to the Mexican settlements where he purchased and sent to the fort $6,500 worth of food. Meanwhile, Captain Cooke suddenly decided to return to Missouri, but St. Vrain was not informed of the decision. Subsequently, the military authorities refused to pay for the provisions, so early in the summer of 1844, St. Vrain went to Washington in connection with this and another company claim.[44] The second claim related to remuneration for a destructive Pawnee Indian attack on a small Bent, St. Vrain and Co. wagon train in 1837.[45] This claim Congress rejected, but finally in February 1848, Congress authorized payment for the 1843 supply of food.[46]

St. Vrain spent the winter of 1844-45 at Bent's Fort. During January 1845, he warned Bent in Taos of a large, suspicious looking party of whites camped near the Arkansas crossing.[47] A month later St. Vrain reported that he had learned from the Cheyennes that the party numbered 350.[48] He described them as "texians or rather robbers . . .

[43] *Sen. Rept. 115*, 29 Cong., 1 sess. (serial 473).

[44] *H. Rept. 194*, 28 Cong., 2 sess. (serial 468), 8.

[45] *Ibid.*, 1-8.

[46] *Sen. Misc. Doc. 67*, 30 Cong., 2 sess. (serial 534), 84.

[47] Letter from C. Bent to M. Alvarez, dated Rio Ariba, Jan. 24, 1845, in *New Mexican Historical Review*, xxx (July 1955), 252.

[48] Letter from C. St. Vrain to C. Bent, dated Ft. William, Feb. 11, 1845. Alvarez Papers. B. M. Read Collection, New Mexico State Archives and Records Center, Santa Fe.

[who would] remain there [at the crossing] for the express purpose of robbing whoever they chance to meet." St. Vrain therefore advised Bent that all parties who planned a trip to the East take the Platte River route.

At the end of June, St. Vrain and his partner Charles Bent, welcomed Colonel S. W. Kearny to the comforts of the fort.[49] He and some of his officers dined heartily and well there. Just a year later, the colonel returned to the fort with his Army of the West, as subsequent comment will develop.

During February and March of 1846, St. Vrain traded with the Comanches at the company's Canadian River fort; he was reported to be doing "very well and prospects good."[50] Less than two months later he had returned to Taos, and soon took part in the effort to develop one of the several Mexican land grants in which he and Charles Bent were interested.

The story of the grants that is pertinent here concerns first the Vigil and St. Vrain, or Las Animas, grant, originating in 1843, according to the official record.[51] It was one of the large Spanish and Mexican grants lying north and east of Taos that was based on documents of such questionable validity that it is difficult to be certain just what took place. But according to the official grant papers, on Decembre 8, 1843, Ceran St. Vrain and Cornelio Vigil, an alcalde of Taos, petitioned the governor of New Mexico for a large tract of land south of the Arkansas River and opposite Bent's Fort. Governor Manuel Armijo approved the petition and soon the claimants were placed in possession of an approximately four-million-acre tract. Some effort to develop or use this land, such as herding cattle on it, according

[49] L. Pelzer, *Marches of the Dragoons in the Mississippi Valley* (1917), 137-9.

[50] Letter from C. Bent to M. Alvarez, dated Taos, Mar. 6, 1846. *N.M.H.R.*, xxx (Oct. 1955), 52.

[51] *H. Rept. 321,* 36 Cong., 1 sess., 269-78.

to later testimony, took place prior to the Mexican War. After the war, St. Vrain and his agents sold large portions of the land grant, far more in fact than Congress confirmed for it, namely 97,000 acres. The resulting conflict lies beyond the scope of this sketch, although the point should be added that Charles Bent had become a part owner of the grant in 1844.

The land grant which St. Vrain especially helped to develop in the spring of 1846 lay just south of the Las Animas grant, and was called the Beaubien and Miranda (later, the Maxwell) grant. During the latter part of May 1846, St. Vrain was delegated to select an appropriate site for a settlement on this grant, and he chose a place on the Cimarron River, across the mountains from Taos, which he called Montezuma.[52] Yet before there could be much of a follow-up on this beginning, the clouds of the Mexican War arose and Bent and St. Vrain hastily set out for Missouri.

The two partners left Taos on June 3, and after stopping at Bent's Fort, effected a rapid sixteen day crossing of the prairies, reaching Ft. Leavenworth on June 28.[53] They reported to Colonel Kearny on the leaders, the activities and the attitudes of New Mexican residents, and doubtless agreed on the army's use of Bent's Fort as a place of rendezvous for the invasion of New Mexico. Afterwards they boarded a boat for St. Louis. St. Vrain appears to have busied himself in the city for two months, while Bent returned earlier to New Mexico.

On August 24, St. Vrain began his return journey with a large supply of trade goods.[54] Accompanying him was the

[52] Letter from C. Bent to M. Alvarez, dated Taos, May 30, 1846. *N.M.H.R.*, XXXI (Apr. 1956), 163.

[53] *Missouri Republican*, July 3, 1846; and J. W. Cason, "The Bent Brothers on the Frontier," M.A. thesis, Univ. of New Mexico, 1939, p. 24.

[54] L. H. Garrard, *Wah-To-Yah and the Taos Trail*, R. P. Bieber, ed. (1938), 54 fn.

youthful and perceptive Lewis H. Garrard who later wrote the following tribute:

> Mr. St. Vrain was a gentleman in the true sense of the term, his French descent imparting an exquisite, indefinable degree of politeness, . . [which] combined with the frankness of a mountain man, made him an amiable fellow traveller. His kindness and respect for me, I shall always gratefully remember.[55]

St. Vrain reached Bent's Fort before November 1, ahead of his train, and later pushed on to Santa Fe, where Charles Bent had been appointed first civil governor of New Mexico on September 22. In the capital, St. Vrain divided his time between managing the company store, furthering his rights under the new government to his land grant, consulting or advising with territorial officials, and enjoying social events such as the splendid ball Governor Bent staged in the old Governor's Palace on December 26.[56]

These activities were soon interrupted by the tragic circumstances of Governor Bent's death. Various aspects of the United States occupation of the territory provoked an attempted revolt of Mexicans and Pueblo Indians, which broke out in Taos on January 17, 1847, and led to the murder and scalping of Governor Bent, as well as several other officials and citizens.[57] Shortly after the news of the massacre reached Santa Fe, St. Vrain hurriedly organized a company of sixty-eight mounted volunteers, composed of Mexican and United States Mountain Men, traders and residents of New Mexico, and joined Colonel Sterling Price in a mid-winter march northward to suppress the spreading revolt.[58] Captain St. Vrain and his troops played a notable part in dispersing the rebel contingents, particularly in the

55 *Ibid.*, 58.

56 "Report of Lt. J. W. Abert of His Examination of New Mexico . . . 1846-'47" *H. Ex. Doc. 41,* 30 Cong., 1 sess. (serial 517), 512-13.

57 *St. Louis Republican,* Apr. 8, 1847.

58 Inman, *Old Santa Fe Trail,* 124-132.

final struggle around the Taos Pueblo church. On one occasion, Captain St. Vrain dismounted to examine a powerfully built Indian who lay prone on the ground and whom the captain recognized.[59] This figure suddenly sprang to life and a deadly struggle ensued until the Indian was slain.

St. Vrain remained at Taos for a time and served as interpreter in the trials for some of the rebels who had been captured.[60] Meanwhile, he extended the hospitality of his home to Garrard, who was nearly overwhelmed at meeting the "dark-eyed, languidly handsome" Senora St. Vrain. It was during the post-revolt period that St. Vrain was unsuccessfully recommended for appointment as the new civil governor to succeed Charles Bent.[61]

In the summer following the Taos rebellion, St. Vrain returned to St. Louis. During July, he offered to sell Bent's Fort to the United States government for $15,000.[62] The offer was refused, although the military continued to use the fort for at least a year longer, and its owners supplied Major William Gilpin with some of his necessities during his 1847 expedition along the Santa Fe Trail to suppress Indian attacks.[63]

Meanwhile, Bent, St. Vrain and Co., was reorganized as St. Vrain and Bent, with William Bent as the junior partner. The new firm established a second store in Santa Fe, but almost immediately in 1847, St. Vrain sold out the entire stock there to Judge Joab Houghton and his partner J. W. Folger.[64] He then began to diversify his areas of busi-

---

59 Conard, *"Uncle Dick" Wootton,* 183-4.

60 Garrard, *Wah-to-Yah,* 234, 239.

61 *St. Louis Reveille,* Apr. 12, 1847.

62 See fn. 35 above.

63 Letter from Wm. Bent to C. St. Vrain, dated Ft. William, Sept. 1, 1848, quoted in C. W. Hurd, "Bent's First Stockade, 1824-26," in *Denver Westerners Monthly Roundup,* Apr. 1960, p. 13; and O. L. Baskins, *History of the Arkansas Valley* (1881), 828.

64 *Santa Fe Republican,* Nov. 20, 1847; and R.I. 1915, p. 5, Ritch Collection, Huntington Library.

ness enterprise, and probably by 1850 had dropped his association with William Bent.

The diversification included selling land within the boundaries of the Vigil and St. Vrain land grant, and speculating in land at what became Canon City, Colorado, and Denver City.[65] St. Vrain appears to have erected saw mills in the Rio Grande Valley, and, among other customers, supplied lumber to the Commissioners of Public Buildings in Santa Fe.[66] In 1855 he erected the first flour mill in Mora, New Mexico, and a decade later supplied the military forces of the territory with as much as $20,000 worth of grain and flour, along with beef, during a given month.[67] In 1853, he became interested in the railroad projects that were to affect New Mexico, and a decade later he was associated with the unsuccessful effort to secure official approval for the incorporation of the first national bank in New Mexico.[68]

Yet success did attend his entry into the publishing field, for not only did he join the organization which published the *Santa Fe Gazette,* but in 1858 he was designated the public printer of the territory.[69] At one time, it was reported that because of his great wealth and his desire for a new way of life he moved to New York, but he so missed the West that he returned to his home in Mora, where he had moved from Taos in 1855.[70]

The same year, St. Vrain was appointed lieutenant colonel of Mounted Volunteers and charged with recruiting troops to subdue marauding bands of Utes and Apaches.[71] He then served under Colonel F. F. Fauntleroy in fighting from the

---

65 Mumey, "Black Beard," 12, 15.

66 R.I. 588 and 591, Ritch Collection, Huntington Library.

67 *Sen. Rept. 156,* 39 Cong., 2 sess. (serial 1279), 276-77.

68 Mumey, "Black Beard," 10; and F. S. Fierman, "The Spiegelbergs of New Mexico . . .," in *Southwestern Studies,* I, (1964), 31-32.

69 *Missouri Republican,* Jan. 29, 1858; and R.I. 1802, Ritch Collection, Huntington Library.

70 A. D. Richardson, *Beyond the Mississippi* (1867), 255.

71 R.I. 703, Ritch Collection, Huntington Library; and DeW. C. Peters, *Life and Adventures of Kit Carson* (1859), 480 ff.

headwaters of the Rio Grande to east of the Sangre de Cristo Mountains, and helped force the Indians to sue for peace in Santa Fe.

Several months after the opening of the Civil War, St. Vrain was commissioned colonel of the First New Mexican Cavalry, and promptly on August 16, 1861, he began to select his officers and recruit his men for the regiment.[72] These tasks proved to be too burdensome for him, however, so on September 30, 1861, he resigned his commission, and Lt. Colonel Christopher Carson, a scout in the 1855 expedition, took command.

St. Vrain's political activities in New Mexico readily developed from his abilities, his concerns, his prominence, and his association with men appointed to civil office by General Kearny in September 1846. By 1849 he was greatly concerned over the chaotic political situation, which was partly caused by disagreement and delay at the national level over the type of government New Mexico should have, and the slavery issue.[73] St. Vrain was chosen one of the three representatives from Taos County for the territorial convention which met in Santa Fe during the fall of 1849.[74] The convention confined itself to adopting a plan to obtain territorial status from Congress. About that time two parties or factions sprang up in New Mexico, and St. Vrain favored the territorial group, while Manuel Alvarez headed the state group. Despite this alignment, in 1850 St. Vrain was a candidate for lieutenant governor against Alvarez on a statehood ticket. Alvarez won by a vote of 4,586 to 3,465 and brought an end to St. Vrain's formal participation in politics, though not in public affairs.[75]

---

[72] R.I. 1059 and 2212 (vol. 2, p. 329), Ritch Collection, Huntington Library.

[73] A. H. Abel, ed., *Correspondence of James S. Calhoun* (1915), 41.

[74] H. H. Bancroft, *History of Arizona and New Mexico* (1889), 445 and fn.; and R. E. Twitchell, *Military Occupation of New Mexico, 1846-1851* (1909), 181.

[75] *Sen. Ex. Doc. 26,* 31 Cong., 2 sess. (serial 589), 16; and Bancroft, *History of Arizona and New Mexico,* 446-7.

From 1855 until his death at the age of sixty-eight, St. Vrain made Mora his home. He joined the Bent Lodge of the Masons in 1860, when it was founded in Mora. During his latter years he was married to the former Louisa Branch. This marriage was reported to have been the fourth of his career, and by each one he had had one child.[76] Three of these children were living at the time St. Vrain drew up his will in 1866.[77] His death at his home on October 28, 1870, was followed two days later by a funeral which more than 2,000 people attended, including officers and troops from Ft. Union.[78] He was buried by the Masons, with military honors, in the family plot near Mora, after a life full of accomplishments, service and honors.

76 Letter from M. E. Jenkins, New Mexico State Records Center and Archives, to author, Jan. 31, 1964, citing records of Adjutant General.

77 Reproduced in Mumey, "Black Beard," 14-15.

78 *Rocky Mountain News,* Nov. 1, 1870. St. Vrain had been a member of the Masonic lodge in Santa Fe at least since 1855.

Kit Carson

by HARVEY L. CARTER
Colorado College, Colorado Springs

Of all the hardy and adventurous trappers who roamed the western mountains, only Kit Carson became so widely known that he achieved the status of a national hero. As this is written, nearly a century after his death, his name and fame are still familiar to the general public. As Daniel Boone typified the early frontier, so Kit Carson typified the frontier of the Far West. It is a curious fact that Carson was born within a few miles of Boonesborough, Kentucky, and grew up in the Boone's Lick Country in Missouri, near which the last years of the older pioneer were spent.

Christopher Houston Carson, called Kit from a very early age, was born on his father's farm two miles northwest of Richmond, Madison County, Kentucky, on December 24, 1809, being the sixth of ten children of Lindsey Carson and his second wife, Rebecca Robinson Carson.[1] In October 1811, Lindsey Carson sold his farm, and then moved to Howard County, Missouri, probably in the summer of 1812. Lindsey Carson was killed by a falling tree in 1818 and his

[1] Lindsey Carson (1745-1818) was the eldest son of William Carson, born c. 1720 in Ireland, who emigrated to America in the 1740s and settled first in Pennsylvania and later in North Carolina, where he married Eleanor McDuff. Lindsey saw irregular service in the American Revolutionary War. By his first wife, Lucy Bradley (d. 1794) his children were William, Sarah, Andrew, Moses, and Sophia. The family moved to Kentucky about 1792. After the death of his first wife, Lindsey married Rebecca Robinson. Their children were Elizabeth, Nancy, Robert, Matilda, Hamilton, Christopher, Hampton, Mary, Sarshall, and Lindsey. A tradition in the family was that Christopher was born while his parents were in North Carolina on a visit. Such a visit seems most unlikely in the circumstances of pioneer life and Kit Carson himself gave no credit to the story. See Quantrille D. McClung, *Carson-Bent-Boggs Genealogy* (Denver, 1962), 10-16.

widow, in 1821, married Joseph Martin by whom she had other children.[2]

At the age of fourteen, Kit was apprenticed to David Workman of Franklin, Missouri, to learn the saddle making trade. Acquiring an increasing dislike for the work, he ran away in August 1826 to Independence, where he joined a wagon train bound for Santa Fe. The advertisement of the saddler for the return of the runaway apprentice described him as a light-haired boy, who was small for his age, but thick-set. A reward of one cent was offered for his return![3]

Upon the arrival of the wagon train in Santa Fe, in November 1826, young Carson went almost immediately to Taos. There he spent the winter with Mathew Kinkead, who was fifteen years older than Kit and already a Mountain Man of two seasons' experience.[4]

In the spring of 1827, Kit started back to Missouri with a wagon train but, meeting a west bound train on the Arkansas River, he transferred to it as a teamster and went as far as El Paso. Returning to Taos for the winter, he worked as a cook for Ewing Young, in return for his board. In the spring, he repeated his experience of the previous year by changing from an east-bound to a west-bound train. This time he went all the way to Chihuahua, as interpreter for a merchant, Colonel Trammell. He then worked as a teamster for Robert McKnight at the Santa Rita copper mine.[5] Tir-

[2] *Ibid.* The names of the Martin half-brothers and a Martin half-sister of Kit Carson have not been found. Several Carson men married Boone women.

[3] M. Marion Estergren, *Kit Carson: A Portrait in Courage* (Norman, 1962), 24-25, reprints the advertisement, which originally appeared in the *Missouri Intelligencer*. It is not known who headed the wagon train. Certainly it was not Charles Bent, as many biographers have stated. Bent first went to Santa Fe in 1829.

[4] Mathew Kinkead was also born in Madison County, Kentucky, and had come to Santa Fe from Boone's Lick, Missouri. This may account for his hospitality to the sixteen year old Carson. The fine sketch of Kinkead by Mrs. Janet S. Lecompte in volume II of this Series, 189-99, rescues this Mountain Man from an undeserved obscurity.

[5] Kit Carson's *Autobiography,* edited by Milo M. Quaife (Lincoln, 1965; original edition Chicago, 1935), 6-9. Trammel was probably Richard Campbell.

ing of this, he returned to Taos in August 1828. Just a year later, he left Taos as a member of Ewing Young's first great trapping expedition to California. It was under Young, an old and capable hand at the game, that Kit learned the secrets of successful beaver trapping and the arduous art of survival under difficult conditions. Young found in Carson an apt pupil, who became a trusted lieutenant before they arrived back in Taos in April 1831. They had trapped the Arizona streams, both going out and coming back, and had penetrated as far as the Sacramento River in California.[6]

Like his fellow trappers, Carson now lived high for a few months on what he had earned during the last two years. By fall, the several hundred dollars he had earned by trapping were gone and he was glad to sign up with Thomas Fitzpatrick for a beaver hunt in the Rocky Mountains.[7] After trapping the Platte, the Sweetwater, and the Green, they wintered on the headwaters of Salmon River. In April 1832, trapping on Bear River and on Green River once more, they met the Sinclair party from Arkansas and learned that Captain John Gantt was trapping in New Park. Carson and three others left Fitzpatrick to work for Gantt, remaining in his employ about a year.

During January 1833, while they were camped on the Arkansas River, a band of fifty Crows stole nine of their horses. Carson was among a dozen men who went in pursuit, recovered the horses by stealth and then attacked the Crow camp for the pure excitement of doing it. During their spring hunt on the Laramie, two deserters made off with 400 pounds of beaver. Gantt sent Carson and another man after them but they were unsuccessful in catching the thieves.

---

[6] *Ibid.*, 9-21. Carson's *Autobiography* is the most reliable source available and is cited in preference to other sources, as a rule. For details of Young's expedition, which are not given here, see my sketch of Ewing Young in volume II of this Series, 385-87.

[7] Fitzpatrick was in Santa Fe because he had accompanied Smith, Jackson, and Sublette on the trading expedition in which Jedediah Smith lost his life.

However, they spent some time in one of Gantt's cabins on the Arkansas River.[8] From this base, Carson, Mitchell, Meek, and three Delawares, Tom Hill, Manhead, and Jonas, made an excursion into the Comanche country where they had quite an adventure. Attacked by a band of 200 Comanches, they cut the throats of their mules and forted up behind the bodies of the animals. With three firing, while the other three reloaded, they held off a dozen attacks, killing 42 Comanches. The horses of the attackers shied at the scent of fresh blood from the dead mules and would not approach very near. When night came, the six defenders headed back for the Arkansas on foot, abandoning their beaver.[9]

Upon their arrival, some of Gantt's men found them and told them that the rest were trapping in the Bayou Salade, or South Park. There they had trouble with horse-stealing Indians but Carson and three others recovered the animals. Flushed with success, Carson proposed to charge four Indians that were sighted at some distance, only to find that they belonged to a band of sixty. The charge turned into a headlong retreat until they reached the safety of their own camp. Soon after this, Carson and two others left Gantt and trapped the high mountain streams on their own. They had good luck and disposed of their beaver in Taos, in October 1833.[10]

8 Carson's *Autobiography,* 22-29.

9 Carson did not mention this incident in his *Autobiography.* Joe Meek described it fully but gave the date as May, 1834. This is obviously an impossible date insofar as Carson is concerned. It has caused some to reject the incident as one of Meek's more imaginary flights. However, it fits in perfectly, if dated a year earlier, when Carson was on the Arkansas River. Both Meek and Carson agree in saying that they afterward trapped in the Bayou Salade and Meek recounts the death of Guthrie by a stroke of lightning, while standing in Fraeb's tent. Thomas Fitzpatrick reports the death of Guthrie in his letter of Nov. 13, 1833, Sublette Papers, Mo. Hist. Soc. See Frances Fuller Victor, *River of the West* (Hartford, 1870), 154-58. Contrary to some opinion, I see nothing improbable about the story when the matter of the date is satisfactorily settled.

10 Carson's *Autobiography,* 29-33.

Before the month ended, Kit joined Richard Bland Lee, who had a stock of trade goods to barter with the trappers in the mountain. They took the Old Spanish Trail and found Antoine Robidoux, with twenty men, on the Uinta River. While Lee traded with Robidoux, Kit pursued an Indian horse thief for 130 miles, killed him, and recovered the horses. Word was brought in that Bridger and Fitzpatrick were on the Little Snake River so, in March 1834, Lee and Carson went there. Lee sold the rest of his goods to Fitzpatrick but, after a month, he and three others left to become free trappers on the Laramie.[11]

After their hunt, on the way to join Jim Bridger's party and attend the summer rendezvous on Green River, Kit had what he described as his "worst difficult" experience. He had just fired at an elk, when he was rushed by two large grizzly bears. He managed to climb a tree, but lost his gun in the process, and had to remain there several hours until the bears finally decided they could not shake him out of the tree.[12]

At the rendezvous, Carson sold his beaver and bought supplies at high prices. When the rendezvous broke up in September, Carson joined a party of fifty under Bridger, which was headed for the Three Forks of the Missouri. The Blackfeet were so troublesome that they returned to the Snake River and camped there till February 1835. About thirty Blackfeet ran off eighteen of their horses and Carson was one of a dozen men who pursued them. In the ensuing fight, Kit saved the life of Mark Head but was painfully

---

[11] *Ibid.*, 33-37. I believe Carson to have been mistaken in referring to Lee as a partner of Bent Brothers and St. Vrain, although there may have been some temporary business association. The *Missouri Republican,* October 14, 1834, reported the return of "Capt. R. B. Lee, U.S. Army," from Santa Fe with eleven Bent and St. Vrain wagons. Carson stated that his employer was "Capt. Lee, U.S.A.," so it was not Stephen Louis Lee, as often has been assumed, for he was never an army officer.

[12] It was Carson's niece, Teresina Bent Scheurich, who supplied the "worst difficult" phrase. It is doubtless a fair sample of Carson's language.

wounded in the shoulder himself. He recovered in time to participate in the spring hunt, after which Bridger's party attended the rendezvous on Green River in the summer of 1835.[13]

It was at this rendezvous that Kit had his celebrated duel with a big Frenchman, whom he called "Shunar," who was attached to the party of Captain Drips. This man was a braggart and bully, who had beaten up several French trappers, which emboldened him to challenge the Americans. There is also some reason to believe that he and Kit Carson were both interested in the Arapaho girl that Carson married some time afterward. At any rate, Carson told him to shut up "or he would rip his guts." Both men went for a gun, mounted horses, and defied each other. Shunar's rifle bullet grazed Carson's head and neck, singeing his hair. Kit, at the same time, shot his antagonist in the forearm with a pistol. Carson started to get another pistol but Shunar begged for his life. Carson displayed marked resentment toward Shunar when he recounted the story in later years.[14]

Carson remained with Bridger's brigade for the fall hunt. On September 7, 1835, with Joe Meek and a dozen others, he encountered the remnant of Joseph Gale's party on the Madison River and the following day they combined to

[13] *Ibid.*, 39-42.

[14] *Ibid.*, 42-44. "Shunar's" name was probably Chouinard, Chinard, or something of the sort, since he was French. The earliest account is found in Samuel Parker, *Journal of an Exploring Tour beyond the Rocky Mountains* (Ithaca, 1838), 79-80. The Reverend Mr. Parker, a missionary, was present at the rendezvous, although he does not specifically say that he was an eyewitness. Neither he, nor Carson in his *Autobiography,* says that Shunar was killed. Dr. De Witt C. Peters, *Story of Kit Carson's Life and Adventures* (Hartford, 1874; original edition, 1858) relates the incident, 110-16. Dr. Peters contends that Kit did not intend to kill Shunar (whom he calls "Captain Shunan") but his argument is unconvincing. Stanley Vestal (pseud.), *Kit Carson: Happy Warrior of the Old West* (Boston, 1928), 117-27, relates upon flimsy authority, that Carson got another pistol and killed Shunar; this would have been plain murder. Vestal characterized Dr. Peters as "an ass," which may be so; but the braying of Peters is somewhat preferable to that of Vestal, both with reference to this incident and to the comparative value of their books.

stand off an attack by eighty Blackfeet. When winter set in, they retired to the vicinity of Fort Hall. In the spring of 1836, Carson, with Alexis Godey and four others, went over to Thomas McKay and his Hudson's Bay Company outfit. They trapped the entire length of the Humboldt (then called Mary's River) but did poorly. McKay then went to Fort Walla Walla and the Americans made a nearly starving return to Fort Hall. When McKay returned with plenty of horses, Carson accompanied him to the rendezvous of 1836, at the confluence of Horse Creek and Green River.[15]

Carson now cut loose from McKay and rejoined Bridger, who trapped the tributaries of the Yellowstone with a large number of men. In February 1837, while encamped on the Yellowstone opposite the mouth of Clark's Fork, a skirmish with some Blackfeet occurred. Bridger predicted they would be back in greater force and his men built a strong fort of cottonwood and brush. On February 22, the Blackfeet returned, eleven hundred strong. They built small conical forts suitable to cover ten men each and some skirmishing took place. However, the big fight which everyone anticipated failed to develop because the Blackfeet withdrew, alarmed by an appearance of aurora borealis. The spring hunt was made in the Crow country. At the rendezvous in July 1837, held on Horse Creek for the third consecutive year, Carson met Sir William Drummond Stewart.[16]

---

[15] For the period 1835-1839, Carson's recollection of events, as set forth in his *Autobiography*, 45-62, is somewhat confused and his chronology is demonstrably in error at several points. His dating of his service with McKay (whom he calls McCoy) is correct. His dating of the meeting with Joseph Gale's men as 1839 is four years off. See Osborne Russell, *Journal of A Trapper*, edited by Aubrey L. Haines (Portland, 1955), 30-31; also Victor, *op. cit.*, 167-69.

[16] The year 1836-1837 Carson characterized as uneventful due to smallpox among the Blackfeet. This is obviously wrong. He also placed the fort building episode in 1839, which is two years off. Russell, *op. cit.*, 53-4, gave the date correctly and Meek in Victor, *op. cit.*, 196-7, gave it within a month of the actual time. A comparison of the three accounts is interesting. All mention the small conical forts by means of which the number of Indians was estimated at 1100.

For the fall hunt, Lucien Fontenelle took charge of more than a hundred trappers, of whom Carson was one. Bridger acted as guide or pilot for the party. They moved farther east this year and winter quarters were established on Powder River. Carson said it was the coldest winter of his recollection and they did not move out of camp till April 1, 1838. They passed quickly to the Yellowstone and thence to the Gallatin and finally to the Madison. Because of the great smallpox epidemic of 1837, there was no trouble with Blackfeet. However, on June 3, while scouting ahead up the Madison, Kit and a half dozen others came upon a large camp of Blackfeet. After reporting this, Kit went with forty men to attack the village. The trappers maintained the offensive for three hours, when their ammunition ran low, which enabled the Indians to counter attack. During the ensuing retreat to camp, Kit saved the life of Cotton Mansfield and, in his turn, was helped out of danger by David White. With ammunition replenished and with reinforcements from their camp, the trappers routed the enemy at last. This battle Kit described as "the prettiest fight I ever saw."[17]

After attending the rendezvous in the summer of 1838 on the Popo Agie and renewing his acquaintance with Stewart, Carson and seven others decided to go to Brown's Hole. There he joined two of the proprietors of Fort Davy Crockett, Philip Thompson and Prewitt Sinclair, who made a trading expedition that fall to the Navajo country.

[17] Russell, *op. cit.*, 81, 86-88; Victor, *op. cit.*, 230-32. *Robert Newell's Memoranda* edited by Dorothy Johansen (Portland, 1959), 35-36. Carson's recollection was that he spent the fall and winter of 1837-1838 at Fort Davy Crockett but this is one year too early. He definitely described the camp on Powder River and said he was there. Russell, Meek, and Newell all agree in saying that the Powder River camp was during the winter of 1837-1838. Russell said they broke camp March 25; Meek said March 1, Newell said March 29, and Carson said April 1. It is possible that small parties moved out for the spring hunt at slightly different times. Russell's description of the fight with the Blackfeet on June 3, 1838 does not agree too well with Carson's recollection, but both Russell and Meek mention Cotton Mansfield. Carson is two years off in his date for Powder River camp.

On his return, he spent the winter of 1838-1839 as a hunter for the fort. In the spring of 1839, he rejoined Bridger's party but soon teamed up with Dick Owens and three Canadians for a hunt of three months duration in the Black Hills. They had a good catch of beaver and returned to the rendezvous on Horse Creek in July, 1839.[18]

When it broke up, he and Owens went for a short time to Fort Hall, but soon returned to Brown's Hole, falling in with Doc Newell's small party on Black's Fork on August 23. They all arrived at Fort Davy Crockett on September 1, 1839. Later that month Carson participated in a fight against a band of Sioux that passed that way. In the horse stealing episodes that occurred later that fall, Owens was among the horse thieves and Carson was among those who disapproved of the thievery and tried to recover the horses for the purpose of returning them to the Shoshones from whom they had been stolen.[19]

In the spring of 1840, Carson went with Jack Robertson to Fort Uintah and sold such peltry as he had to Antoine Robidoux. That fall he trapped with six others on Grand River and spent the winter at Fort Davy Crockett in Brown's Hole. In the spring of 1841, he made a hunt in Utah and in New Park and sold his catch at Fort Uintah, remaining there till September 1841[20]

---

18 My reconstruction of Carson's chronology puts him in Brown's Hole during two consecutive years, 1838-1839 and 1839-40, broken only by his hunt with Owens during the spring of 1839, which Carson placed one year too early. The Black Hills where they hunted are the Laramie Mountains, always so called by the trappers. There is no indication that the Black Hills of South Dakota were meant. Suppositions to this effect are based on the erroneous assumption that this hunt used the Powder River camp as its point of origin. Bearing these corrections in mind, see Carson's *Autobiography*, 54-56.

19 *Newell's Memoranda, op. cit.*, 38-39; Victor, *op. cit.*, 259-260; see also LeRoy R. and Ann W. Hafen, *To the Rockies and Oregon* (Glendale, 1955), in *Far West and the Rockies Series*, vol. III, pp. 174-177, where E. W. Smith's Diary confirms Carson's presence at Fort Davy Crockett. It is probable that Carson's Indian wife died about this time. My thanks are due to the editor, Dr. Hafen, for advice and encouragement in making the revision of Carson's chronology that has been presented here.

20 Carson's *Autobiography*, 62.

Beaver had been getting very scarce for the past few years and the price had also declined. Mountain Men were being forced to leave the mountains or face starvation. Carson was no exception. His wife had died and he had two children to support. In company with Old Bill Williams, Bill New, Colorado Mitchell, and a trapper named Frederick, they started for Bent's Old Fort on the Arkansas, where Carson took a job as hunter at a dollar a day. About this time, if not before, he took another squaw as wife.[21] In April 1842, he decided to return to Missouri with one of Bent's wagon trains. He visited friends and relatives, put his daughter Adaline in school, and went on to St. Louis. Feeling out of place after so long an absence, he boarded a steamer ascending the Missouri. On the boat he met John C. Frémont, of the Topographical Engineers of the U.S. Army, who was hoping to employ Captain Andrew Drips as guide for a government expedition to the Rocky Mountains. Carson told him he could do the job. Frémont liked him and, after checking on his reliability, offered him $100 a month.[22]

It should be noted that Carson was employed as a hunter at Bent's Fort only from September 1841 to April 1842. He could not have been, in that time, the leader of an independent band of trappers and Indian fighters as so many writers have depicted him. All such statements are traceable to the

21 Carson does not mention his Indian wife, Waanibe, or his daughter by her in his *Autobiography*. It is not possible to say when they were married (by Indian custom) but Adaline, the first child, was probably born in 1837. Several sources mention a second daughter, who died at about the age of three by falling into a kettle of boiling soap in Taos. F. W. Cragin Papers, The Pioneer's Museum, Colorado Springs, Colorado, Notebook XII, p. 21. Cragin's informant was Carson's eldest daughter by his last marriage, Teresina (Mrs. DeWitt Fulton Allen), in an interview of March 18, 1908, at her home in Raton, New Mexico. On the question of his second squaw, see note 26 below. It must also be noted, at this point, that Carson's residence at Bent's Old Fort, in September 1841, was his first connection with that famous place. He could not have helped to build it, as many writers have stated, because it was not built until 1834 and Carson was last on the Arkansas, prior to 1841, in May 1833, at which time he was employed by John Gantt not by William Bent. In addition, he was a hunter and trapper not a bricklayer.

22 Carson's *Autobiography*, 65-66.

stories of Oliver P. Wiggins and it is highly doubtful if any credence can be placed in any of the statements made by Wiggins insofar as Kit Carson is concerned. It may be well to state here that Kit Carson was a free trapper for a good many different employers, as has been shown; that he was a hunter for Fort Davy Crockett and Bent's Fort, but that he never commanded any body of men engaged in the fur trade, or in buffalo hunting, nor was he in command during any of the Indian fights in which he took part over the years.[23]

Carson's meeting with Frémont occurred when he was thirty-two years old and Frémont was twenty-eight. Frémont was just launching his career of western exploration. For Carson, this was the turning point of his life. He now had the chance to continue his life in the west on a different basis. His knowledge of the country and how to survive as he traveled over it must now be employed in directing and serving a new sort of enterprise. Carson took his duties seriously and measured up well.

Frémont's first expedition surveyed South Pass and climbed Fremont Peak in the Wind River Range, which he erroneously believed to be the highest elevation in the Rocky Mountains. Carson climbed with the rest; if the

[23] The life story of Oliver P. Wiggins was dictated by Wiggins to Dr. F. W. Cragin and occupies considerable space in his notebooks. Cragin himself had doubts of the veracity of Wiggins. I have gone over the material carefully and it is my belief that nothing said by Wiggins regarding Carson can be accepted. See Lorene and Kenny Englert, "Oliver Perry Wiggins: Fantastic Bombastic Frontiersman" in *The Denver Westerners Monthly Roundup* (February, 1964) xx, pp. 3-14, which reaches the same conclusion. Another writer on Carson, William F. Drannan, *Thirty-One Years on the Plains and in the Mountains* (1900) has been exposed as a fraud in W. N. Bate, *Frontier Legend* (1954). Wiggins has been accepted by Charles Coutant, E. L. Sabin, Stanley Vestal, David Lavender, Bernice Blackwelder, and M. Morgan Estergren, among writers on Kit Carson. Sabin and Vestal have been widely quoted by other writers. All have been deceived by Oliver P. Wiggins, who may have seen Carson but was certainly never acquainted with him in the intimate way he claimed and probably not at all. LeRoy Hafen has informed me that he knew another similar fraudulent character, Col. Dick Rutledge, who paraded in long hair and buckskin suit in Denver in the 1920s.

government wanted to pay him for climbing mountains, he would do it. He educated Frémont with respect to Indians; occasionally he and Frémont squabbled but it was soon forgotten and neither ever said a harsh word about the other that would be made public. Charles Preuss, Frémont's German-born cartographer, felt that Carson insisted on warning them about Indians in order to make himself more important. Preuss enjoyed good eating, however, and he appreciated the fact that Carson would take the trouble to get the fattest buffalo cow even though it meant more work.[24] Carson was with the first expedition from June 10, 1842, to August 31, 1842, leaving it when Fort Laramie was reached.[25] Where he spent the next four months is not recorded. He says that he went to Bent's Fort in January 1843, and from there to Taos where he was married to Marie Josefa Jaramillo, younger sister of the wife of Charles Bent, on February 6, 1843.[26] Carson was thirty-three and

24 Charles Preuss, *Exploring With Fremont,* translated and edited by Erwin G. Gudde and Elizabeth K. Gudde (Norman, 1958), 47, 70. Preuss referred to Carson as "Kid Karsten." This was not in levity, as his translators believe, but in ignorance, for he writes of the young of the beaver as "kids" not as kits.

25 John C. Frémont, *Narrative of the Exploring Expedition to the Rocky Mountains in the Year 1842 and to Oregon and California in the Years 1843 and 1844.* (New York, 1846), 5-51.

26 Quantrille D. McClung, *Carson-Bent-Boggs Geneology* (Denver, 1962), 72-73, reproduces the Baptismal Certificate of Carson as well as the Marriage Certificate. Carson had become a Catholic and had been baptized on January 28, 1842, in Taos. This was while he was hunter at Bent's Fort and it may be surmised that he was contemplating marriage to Josefa at this time. Concerning the question of whether Carson had a second Indian wife, a Cheyenne squaw, called Making Out Road, I am inclined to think that he did for a short time, until she left him. This has been denied, on the authority of Teresina Bent Scheurich, by recent Carson biographers such as M. Morgan Estergren and Bernice Blackwelder. However, Jesse Nelson, husband of Susan Carson, Kit's niece, told F. W. Cragin in an interview dated July 9, 1908, that this was true and also that he lived for a time with Antonina Luna who later married Bill Tharp. My belief is that Carson habitually concealed these connections from the women of his family, in accordance with the standards of the time, but did not attempt to conceal them from the men. Adaline was tangible proof of his first marriage, so that could not be concealed, but he did not mention her in his *Autobiography.* For Jesse Nelson's statement, see F. W. Cragin Papers, Notebook VIII, p. 83.

his bride was fifteen. L. H. Garrard, who saw her four years later, credited her with a rather haughty kind of beauty.[27]

In April 1843, Kit left Taos to accompany an east-bound wagon train of Bent Brothers and St. Vrain as a hunter. They encountered Captain Philip St. George Cooke endeavoring to protect some Mexican traders from attack by Jacob Snively and other Texans. Cooke could only police the Santa Fe Trail within American territory. Carson was offered $300 to carry word to Governor Armijo of New Mexico, so that he could provide protection for the American traders. Dick Owens accompanied Carson as far as Bent's Fort, and Carson went on to Taos where he asked the alcalde to forward the information to the governor. He then carried messages for Armijo to the traders with a Mexican companion. They were beset by Indians. The Mexican offered to be captured and let Carson escape. Carson, admiring his bravery, stayed with him and they bluffed the Indians out of their hostile intentions. When Carson reached Bent's Fort, he learned that Cooke had disarmed the Texans and that Frémont had just passed by on his second expedition and wanted Carson to accompany him.[28]

Carson caught up with Frémont, who sent him back to get mules at Bent's Fort. He rejoined Frémont at Fort St. Vrain a few days later. Frémont reached Fort St. Vrain on July 4, 1843, and it was a full year later, on July 2, 1844, that the expedition returned to Bent's Fort. During that time they had explored the Great Salt Lake, traversed the Oregon Trail to Fort Vancouver, explored southeastern Oregon and northwestern Nevada, crossed the Sierras in winter to Sutter's Fort, visited the California towns, re-

[27] Lewis Hector Garrard, *Wah-to-Yah and the Taos Trail* (Norman, 1955; original edition, 1850), 181.

[28] Carson's *Autobiography,* 69-73. Cooke's journal covering this affair may be found in *Mississippi Valley Historical Review* (1925-6), XII, pp. 72-98, 227-55.

crossed by Oak Creek Pass to the Mojave River, and followed a difficult desert route back to the Rocky Mountains of Colorado, which they crossed by an unusual path.[29] The crossing of the Sierras in winter was rather foolhardy and the party was lucky to come through as well as it did. Thomas Fitzpatrick, as well as Carson, guided this expedition but Frémont never became friendly with him as he did with Kit. Alexis Godey received a share of the admiration Frémont expressed for Carson, particularly in the well-known incident in which the two pursued some Indian thieves on behalf of a Mexican and came back with two scalps.[30] Joseph R. Walker, a famous Mountain Man, joined them in the desert on the way back and his knowledge was useful to the expedition. But no one displaced Carson as Frémont's ideal frontiersman and so he gained his hold on the public imagination when Frémont's reports were published.

Carson now spent several months at his home in Taos. In March 1845, he and Dick Owens decided to try farming on the Little Cimarron, about 50 miles east of Taos and Josefa joined him there after he had a cabin built. But in August word came that Frémont was at Bent's Fort on his way to California and wanted his services again. Carson and Owens sold out quickly and joined Frémont, while Josefa went back to Taos.[31] They crossed the Nevada desert south of the Humboldt, split into two groups, one headed by Frémont, the other by Theodore Talbot and Joseph R. Walker. Carson remained with Frémont, crossing to Sutter's Fort. Through some misunderstanding, Walker was not on the Tulare Lake Fork where they had expected to meet him.

---

[29] Frémont, *op. cit., passim.*

[30] Preuss, *op. cit.*, 127, expressed disgust at the Carson-Godey exploit, so highly praised by Frémont. He also stated that Carson was disgruntled because Godey was entitled to both scalps. However, after Tabeau's death at the hands of Indians, Preuss modified his attitude to some extent; *ibid.*, 130.

[31] Carson's *Autobiography*, 87-88.

Carson and Owens were sent to look for him and found him on the San Joaquin.[32]

After Frémont had second thoughts about defying General Castro at Gavilan Peak, he led his party northward into the Klamath Indian country. Here Lieutenant Gillespie reached him with news that war with Mexico had been declared. The Klamaths were hostile, however, and it was Carson's vigilance that enabled a night attack to be repelled. Carson, on this occasion, referred to Godey as a fool for exposing himself in the firelight to the arrows of the Indians. Two good men, Basil Lajeunesse and a Delaware named Crane, were killed. Punitive measures were taken and the Delawares felt better. But Carson felt that the Klamaths were even tougher warriors than the Blackfeet.[33]

When they got back to Sutter's Fort, events began to move swiftly. The Bear Flag party was organized and, with help from Frémont's men, fought the Californians in Petaluma Valley and drove them back to San Rafael. Frémont stopped to rest here and sent Carson, with Granville P. Swift and Jack Neil, ahead to scout. They captured Francisco and Ramon de Haro and their uncle, Jose de los Berreyesa, who had landed from a boat at the Embarcadero. Carson rode back and reported this to Frémont and asked what should be done with the prisoners. Frémont said, "Mr. Carson, I have no use for prisoners – do your duty." Carson returned, conferred with Swift and Neil, and they had the prisoners shot. They were influenced by the killing of two young Americans, Cowey and Fowler, by Californians, and by the rumor that this had been done in a barbarous manner. Thus, it was considered to be retaliation.[34]

---

[32] *Ibid.*, 89-93; John C. Frémont, *Memoirs of My Life* (Chicago and New York, 1887), 432-55.

[33] Frémont, *Memoirs*, 487-96. Carson's life was saved by Sagundai, one of the Delaware chiefs, a few days after the night attack.

[34] The account of this controversial episode is taken from William M. Boggs, "Manuscript about Bents' Fort, Kit Carson, the Far West and Life Among the

When the California Battalion of mounted riflemen was formed, Carson became a private in one of the companies and served until he was detached on September 5, 1846, by Frémont to carry dispatches to Washington, D.C., with an escort of 15 men. One month later, he met General Stephen Watts Kearny at Socorro, New Mexico, and was ordered by him to exchange places with Thomas Fitzpatrick. It now became Fitzpatrick's task to deliver the messages to Washington and Carson's task to guide Kearny's small force to California. Carson accepted his fate most reluctantly but brought Kearny safely to Warner's Ranch by December 2, 1846. However, a force of Californians had gathered at the Indian village of San Pasqual in a belated effort to oppose American occupation. This force Kearny attacked on December 5, at the same time sending Alexis Godey and two companions to get help from Commodore Stockton at San Diego, thirty miles away. When Godey and his men returned, they were captured by the Californians, who now had Kearny surrounded. Burgess, one of Godey's men, was exchanged but was unable to say what measures were being taken by Stockton. It was in this situation, that Kit Carson and the naval lieutenant, Edward Fitzgerald Beale, volunteered to go through the enemy lines for reinforcements. A young Delaware Indian, a servant of Beale, also went and was actually the first to get through. Beale and Carson also made it, so much exhausted that it took Carson several days and Beale much longer to recover.[35] Stockton had already sent the required aid, so the heroic journey had been unnecessary. Carson participated in the battle of San Gabriel and when Frémont arrived in mid-January, rejoined him.

On February 25, 1847, Frémont again sent Carson with

Indians," edited by LeRoy R. Hafen in *Colorado Magazine* (March, 1930), VII, pp. 62-63. Boggs had it directly from Carson, whom he questioned about it. More blame attaches to Frémont than to Carson for the shooting. Frémont, in his *Memoirs*, 525, placed the blame on his Delaware Indians!

[35] Carson's *Autobiography*, 108-117.

dispatches to the war department in Washington. Beale accompanied him and they reached Washington in June 1847. Carson returned to California, bearing dispatches from President Polk, arriving in Los Angeles in October 1847.[36] During the winter he was assigned to scouting duty and, on May 4, 1848, he left once more as a courier to Washington. This transcontinental trip is the one made famous by the detailed description written by Lieutenant George D. Brewerton and published in *Harper's Magagine*.[37]

Carson and Brewerton parted company in Taos. Carson picked up ten men in Taos and went first to Fort Leavenworth. From there, he went on to Washington alone and was back in Taos by October 1848, having stopped to visit briefly in St. Louis.[38] During the winter, Kit acted as a guide for two expeditions under Major Benjamin Beall, policing the Indians north and east of Taos.[39] He was at home when Frémont came to Taos, in January 1849, from his disastrous attempt to make a winter crossing of the San Juan Mountains. Frémont stayed at Carson's house for several days.

In April 1849, Carson and Maxwell started farming and ranching operations at Rayado, on land to which Maxwell had a claim which was eventually made good. But Carson

---

36 *Ibid.*, 117-122. Carson called on President Polk, on June 7 and again on June 14, 1847, presenting Frémont's side of his controversy with General Kearny. Carson was in California when the court marital decided, January 31, 1848, in Washington, to uphold Kearny's charges.

37 George D. Brewerton, "A Ride with Kit Carson" in *Harper's Magazine*, (August, 1853) VII, pp. 306-334. The article added substantially to Carson's fame. It seems probable, although it is not certain, that Carson carried the letter which first acquainted the rest of the country with the discovery of gold in California.

38 F. W. Cragin Papers, Notebook VIII, pp. 51, 75, 77. Jesse Nelson (1827-1923) was Cragin's informant. He mentioned Jim Dawzle, George Simpson, Louis Simmons, Auguste Archambeau, and another Frenchman, Lawrence, as among the ten, in addition to himself, who went to Fort Leavenworth. He said that Carson resigned as lieutenant in the regular army at Fort Leavenworth. However, Carson's commission had never been approved by the Senate.

39 Carson's *Autobiography*, 127-29.

was in demand as a guide for military units and was often absent from the ranch.[40]

In November 1849, when Major Grier endeavored to rescue Mrs. White and her child from the Jicarilla Apaches, Carson was added as a guide, although Antoine Leroux and Robert Fisher were already so employed. The failure of Major Grier to order an immediate attack, when the Apache camp was found, gave the Indians time to kill Mrs. White before making off. In the Apache camp was found a yellow back novel, possibly the property of Mrs. White, which represented Carson as a great Indian fighter, and it saddened him to think he had failed to save her life. Returning, they encountered the worst snow storm Carson was ever in, and did not reach Barclay's Fort until November 25, although Fisher and a few others came in on November 23.[41]

In March 1850, Kit led a pursuit of nine Indians, who had stolen horses from his ranch, and killed five of them. Two months later, he and Tim Goodale drove about fifty horses and mules to Fort Laramie to trade with the emigrants. Goodale went to California and Carson, on his way home, learned at the Greenhorn settlement of an Apache ambush. Charles Kinney, a Mountain Man living at Greenhorn, was the only one he could get to accompany him. They evaded the Indians and got through to Taos. That fall, Kit

---

[40] *Ibid.*, 130-131; also F. W. Cragin Papers, Notebook VIII, pp. 49, 83. Jesse Nelson, husband of Carson's niece, Susan, settled at Rayado in 1851. He said that Carson bought the old Army hospital at Rayado, when the soldiers moved to Fort Union in 1851, and the Nelsons lived in it with the Carsons. When Kit was away, Josefa would leave Rayado for a visit with her relatives in Taos.

[41] Carson's *Autobiography,* 131-36. Alexander Barclay's Diary gives details of the storm under the dates mentioned. Carson said he had heard that Leroux advised a delay and a parley with the Indians. Dick Wootton, who was present, and who had no great love for Leroux, blamed Grier for the decision. See also Forbes Parkhill, *Blazed Trail of Antoine Leroux* (Los Angeles, 1965), 134-42. The dime novel found was probably Charles Averill, *Kit Carson, Prince of the Gold Hunters,* which was published in 1849, and is thought to have been the first of many thrillers exploiting the real and imaginary adventures of Carson. Carson did not participate in the California gold rush.

arrested a man named Fox, who was charged with planning to murder Samuel Weatherhead and Elias Brevoort, in order to rob a wagon train of theirs. The arrest was made at the request of Lieutenant Oliver Taylor of the Dragoons, to whom the plot had been divulged but nothing could afterward be proved in court.[42]

In March 1851, Kit took a dozen wagons and went to St. Louis to get goods for Lucien Maxwell. On the way back he decided to follow the Arkansas to Bent's Fort and fell afoul of a Cheyenne band that was seeking revenge for the flogging of one of their chiefs by order of an officer of Colonel Edwin V. Sumner's command. Kit had only fifteen men, of whom thirteen were Mexicans. He talked the Indians out of the notion of immediate revenge and sent off a rider to Rayado for help. The rider first met Colonel Sumner, who refused help, but Major Grier at Rayado sent aid. As Jesse Nelson described the incident, twenty Cheyennes, with a whole village nearby, made the threat. A big Indian had a hatchet over Kit's head, Nelson had a gun on this Indian and another Indian had a bow, with the arrow pulled back to the head, on Nelson. Ah-mah-nah-ko, the son of Old Bark, a Cheyenne Chief, recognized Kit and averted the crisis. He also warned Kit that the Cheyennes would try to ambush him and Nelson felt that this friendly act saved their lives.[43]

In March 1852, Maxwell and Carson got together eighteen men to go trapping, with Carson in charge. They trapped South Park, followed the South Platte to the plains, then on to the Laramie River, then into New Park and Old Park in turn, finally crossing to the headwaters of the

[42] Carson's *Autobiography*, 138-41. The Elias Brevoort Manuscript, in the Bancroft Library, Berkeley, California, substantiates Carson's account.

[43] Carson's *Autobiography*, 141-46. Nelson's account is in F. W. Cragin Papers, Notebook VIII, pp. 61, 65, 69. There is a drawing of Ah-mah-nah-ko and his wife in Lieutenant J. W. Abert's Report, *House Exec. Doc. no. 41, 30 Cong., 1 sess.* (Serial 517.).

Arkansas and trapping it till it emerged from the mountains. This was more of a pleasure trip, organized as a final farewell to the old life that Carson loved so well, though they were quite successful in catching beaver.[44]

The next year, 1853, Carson and Maxwell made their famous sheep drive to California. Carson left in February and arrived over the California Trail in August. Maxwell arrived a little later; John Hatcher had been the first to set out and the first to reach California. The sheep cost not more than fifty cents each and were sold at $5.50 per head. Carson and Maxwell returned from Los Angeles across Arizona, arriving back in Taos on Christmas day, 1853.[45]

Carson now learned that he had been appointed Indian agent and entered upon the duties connected with that difficult assignment, which were to occupy his time and provide his living until 1861. During this time he made his residence at Taos, whither the Indian delegations came to transact their business. During the earlier years, the Indians were very restless and often hostile. Carson accompanied a number of military expeditions against them under various army officers.[46] He was also a very good agent, doing his best to carry out the orders of the government but retaining always a sympathetic understanding of the Indians and

[44] Carson's *Autobiography,* 146. It would be interesting to know the names of the men who made this hunt. It seems probable that it included a number of the old Mountain Men who took the sheep to California in 1853. The expedition resembled Sir William Drummond Stewart's farewell trip of 1843 in its conception and purpose. No other reference of any value has come to my attention on this matter.

[45] *Ibid.,* 146-48. Carson's achievement in respect to the sheep drive has been overrated. Dick Wooton had made such a drive a year earlier. Also, while Carson mentions only Maxwell and himself and two other men as participating, there were 33 men in all, and the sheep were in several herds. Louis Simmons, and his wife, Carson's daughter Adaline, went on this drive and remained in California as did John L. Hatcher. See F. W. Cragin Papers, Notebook 1, p. 24. Cragin's informant was Jake Beard, interviewed at Trinidad, Colorado, October 31, 1904. Beard was one of those who made the trip.

[46] Carson's *Autobiography,* 149-70, contains details of these various expeditions which will not be given here.

their problems. He did what he could to improve their situation and the Indians had much respect for him. He was handicapped by his illiteracy and by his inability to keep his accounts in a satisfactory way. He was forced to pay some one to help him in these matters, for the government would make him no allowance for such expenses.[47]

In the fall of 1856 occurred an altercation between David Meriwether, Territorial Governor of New Mexico and Superintendent of Indian affairs, and Carson, as Indian Agent, which led to Meriwether's suspension of Carson and to his lodging charges of disobedience, insubordination, and cowardice against him. Carson acknowledged his misconduct and was re-instated. An examination of Meriwether's account of the incident, dictated in his old age, leads to the conclusion that Carson merited censure on the first two charges. He was not guilty of cowardice, although a faulty judgment of Indian demonstrations led him to be over cautious on this occasion. It speaks well for him that he acknowledged his error.[48]

It was in 1856 that Kit Carson, prompted by the desire to capitalize in a financial way upon the tremendous and far-flung reputation he had achieved, dictated his autobiography and turned it over to Jesse B. Turley, to be used as Turley thought proper for their joint benefit. The actual writer of Carson's memoirs was neither Turley nor Dr. Peters nor Mrs. Peters. It was John Mostin, Carson's secretary. However, Turley undoubtedly transferred the manuscript to Peters, who used it in writing a biography of Carson

---

47 A fair evaluation is that of Marshall D. Moody, "Kit Carson, Agent to the Indians of New Mexico, 1853-1861," in *New Mexico Historical Review* (January, 1953), XXVIII, pp. 1-20. Concerning Carson's illiteracy, it should be said that there is ample evidence to indicate that he could neither read nor write, except for the ability to sign his name, C. Carson. Two recent biographers, M. Marion Estergren and Bernice Blackwelder, contend that he was literate but the evidence presented is unconvincing.

48 David Meriwether, *My Life in the Mountains and on the Plains,* edited by Robert A. Griffin (Norman, Okla., 1965), 226-33.

which he published in 1858. Peters was able to supply quite a few details from having heard some of Carson's stories during his two years as an army surgeon stationed in New Mexico, 1854-1856. In addition, there was much padding of a rather unrealistic nature, which caused Carson to remark on having it read to him that he thought Dr. Peters "had laid it on a leetle too thick"[49]

In 1860, while hunting in the San Juan Mountains, Kit had an accident. He was leading his horse, when the animal fell and rolled down a steep slope, dragging Carson after him entangled in the reins. He never fully recovered from the injury to his chest that he incurred at this time.

In 1861 he resigned as Indian Agent and entered the United States Army as colonel of the First New Mexico Volunteer Infantry. He participated in the battle of Valverde, under General Canby, and was brevetted brigadier general for his services in that battle. There followed, in 1863-1864, a long and arduous campaign against the Navajos, planned and directed by General Carleton and ably executed by Carson, who destroyed their crops and penetrated their stronghold in the Cañon de Chelly. Although Carson had carried out a "scorched earth" policy, he was as generous as possible in all his recommendations for government policy toward the conquered Indians.[50]

In November 1864, he was ordered by General Carleton to invade the Kiowa and Comanche country, having under

49 For a discussion of the recovery of this manuscript and of Turley's connection with it, see Milo M. Quaife's introduction in his edition of the *Autobiography,* so frequently cited heretofore. Information regarding Jesse B. Turley is to be found in Jesse Nelson's statement in F. W. Cragin Papers, Notebook VII, p. 59. The identity of Carson's scribe has been established by comparing the handwriting of the manuscript in the Newberry Library, Chicago, with that of a holograph letter of John Mostin, Taos, New Mexico, September 22, 1856, a copy of which was kindly furnished to me by Mr. Dale L. Morgan.

50 See Estergren, *op. cit.,* 231-33; 238-50. Also Raymond E. Lundgren, ed., "A Diary of Kit Carson's Navajo Campaign, 1863-1864," in *New Mexico Historical Review* (July, 1946), XXI, pp. 226-46.

his command 335 men and 75 scouts. With this force he penetrated to the old Bent trading post of Adobe Walls, on the Canadian River, and gave battle to about 3,000 Indians, chiefly Kiowas but with some Comanches, Apaches, and a few Arapahoes as well. Fortunately, Carson had two small howitzers, which Lieutenant Pettis employed to good effect. Carson lost two men, estimated the Indian loss at 60 (others placed it higher), and withdrew in good order. It was his opinion that, but for the howitzers, the Indians would have wiped them out. He prudently resisted sentiment on the part of some to engage the Indians again, judging correctly that they had been taught a good lesson.[51]

This battle occurred almost simulanteously with Colonel Chivington's massacre of the Cheyennes on their Sand Creek reservation. When Carson heard of what had happened there, he was extremely indignant, especially at the killing of Indian women and children.[52]

After this, Carson commanded briefly at Camp Nichols and then made a trip east, stopping at Fort Leavenworth, St. Louis, Washington, and New York. In July 1866, he was assigned to the command of Fort Garland, north of Taos in Colorado territory, where General W. T. Sherman visited him in September of that year.[53] Carson was mustered out of the army on November 22, 1867. He had already decided to settle at Boggsville, Colorado (near present Las Animas) where William Bent had made some land available to him and Tom Boggs. His family was already established there.

In February 1868, however, he made another trip to Washington on behalf of the Ute Indians, always his favorite tribe. He also went to New York and Boston to see if medical men could help his chest and neck pains. He arrived back in mid-April, much exhausted by constant

[51] Estergren, *op. cit.*, 253-61.

[52] James F. Rusling, *Across America* (New York, 1874), 138.

[53] *Ibid.*, 139-40.

coughing, caused by an aneurysm which had developed and caused spasms in the bronchial tubes. On April 13, 1868, two days after his return, Josefa gave birth to a girl, her seventh living child, and died ten days later.[54] Kit died exactly one month later, May 23, 1868, at Fort Lyon, where he had been taken about a week earlier at the suggestion of Dr. Tilton, the army surgeon at the fort. Kit knew that his end was near and asked Aloys Scheurich to prepare him a buffalo steak and some coffee. After eating, he smoked his clay pipe until the final hemorrhage that produced his death. His will, dated May 15, 1868, named Tom Boggs as guardian of his children, a duty which Boggs carried out as best he could. The remains of Carson and his wife were removed to Taos in January 1869, where their graves are still to be seen.[55]

Kit Carson was not very impressive to look at. The Carson men were usually large. Kit was the runt of the family. Numerous people have described their surprise and disappointment on first seeing him. William Tecumseh Sherman described him as "a small stoop-shouldered man, with reddish hair, freckled face, soft blue eyes, and nothing to indicate extraordinary courage or daring."[56] He was long in the body and short in the legs, which helps to account for Frémont's great admiration for Kit as "one of the finest horsemen I have ever seen."[57]

Carson was catapulted into fame by Frémont's *Reports.*

---

[54] The children of Christopher and Josepha Jaramillo Carson were as follows: Charles, b. 1849, d. 1851; William (Julian), b. October 1, 1852; Teresina, b. June 23, 1855; Christopher, b. June 13, 1858; Charles, b. August 2, 1861; Rebecca, b. April 13, 1864; Estafanita, b. December 23, 1866; Josefita, b. April 13, 1868. There are numerous descendants of several of these children. See Quantrille D. McClung, *Carson-Bent-Boggs Genealogy* (Denver, 1962), 74-75 ff.

[55] Albert W. Thompson "Thomas O. Boggs, Early Scout," in *Colorado Magazine* (July, 1930), VII, p. 159.

[56] William T. Sherman, *Memoirs* (New York, 1875), I, pp. 46-47.

A portrait of Carson appears herein at page 14.

[57] Frémont, *Narrative,* 9.

It is doubtful if government documents ever achieved such popularity before or ever will again. The question arises as to how Carson came to be the sole beneficiary of Frémont's hero worship. Basil Lajeunesse was his favorite. He spoke of Dick Owens and Alexis Godey with the same praise that he lavished on Carson, declaring that under Napoleon, all three would have become marshals.[58] Both Godey and Lajeunesse were French, as were most of Frémont's men, and the American public was not looking for a French hero. Jesse Benton Frémont described Carson as "perfectly Saxon . . . clear and fair." Carson was the type that the American public could take to its heart. Owens was with Frémont only on the third expedition; Fitzpatrick and Walker were older men, whose reputations were already established within their limited world. Carson alone seemed to fill the popular conception of the all-American boy-hero.

By a similar process, an earlier generation had made an idol of Daniel Boone. Despite the ease with which it has been demonstrated that many others had the same qualifications or even better ones for being frontier heroes, both Boone and Carson have retained their place in the public affection with remarkable success. The answer lies in their simplicity. They were not self-seeking; fame came to them, and they accepted it with becoming modesty. The very lack of those qualities of leadership, which others had in greater degree, was what enabled Boone and Carson to survive untarnished in public estimation.

Of the two, Carson had more ability than Boone, as a glance at Carson's army career will show. Carson loved the free and easy life of the trapper as well as Boone. But he also had a devotion to duty that made him a sucessful army officer. There was nothing of the self-advertising showman in Carson. His autobiography is a straightforward, un-

[58] Frémont, *Memoirs,* 427.

adorned account, which has the ring of truth for any reader. In 1866, when shown the cover of a magazine on which he was depicted with one arm around a woman he had just saved from a number of Indians shown biting the dust, Carson gazed intently at the picture for a short time. Then he said, "Gentlemen, that thar may be true, but I haint got no recollection of it."[59]

It has been pointed out that there were two ways in which Carson suffered at the hands of literary people. First, there was Dr. Peters and a long line of later biographers, who made him into a genteel, manly type, acceptable to mid-nineteenth century standards of proper behavior. There was also an avid crew of hack writers of dime novels, who made him into a blood and thunder hero who turned up to rescue emigrant parties most providentially and always in a manner that bore slight resemblance to reality. Strangely enough, these two widely different literary types were frequently combined.[60]

Yet there is less difference between the real Carson and his legend than is usually the case with frontier heroes. This is because Carson was really a man of many admirable qualities and few reprehensible traits and because he really did lead a strenuous and adventuresome life.

Bill Bent, Montana pioneer and squaw man, said, "In the light of my own experiences I can come to but one conclusion and that is my uncle Kit was an over-rated man. These same hair-breadth escapes, these same trials caused by hunger and cold have been gone through by many a man who has helped make this country and not one word has

---

59 Henry Inman, *Old Santa Fe Trail* (New York, 1898), 381.

60 The analysis presented here is that of Kent Ladd Steckmesser, *Western Hero in History and Legend* (Norman, 1965), 13-53. This is a perceptive study, marred only by the author's perpetuation of the myth that Carson was the leader of his own band of trappers, known as the "Carson Men."

been written into the story of their deeds."[61] Bent was both right and wrong. It was not that Kit was overrated (although he was, to some extent), so much as that others, who were just as deserving, were underrated or not rated at all. Yet, if history must single out one individual to receive all the credit that should be shared with others of his kind, it is difficult to find a more deserving candidate for the honor than Kit Carson.[62] He was a diamond in the rough.[63]

---

[61] A. J. Noyes, *In the Land of the Chinook* (Helena, 1917), 88-89. The Montana pioneer claimed to have been born in St. Louis in 1846, and to have been the son of William Bent, of Bent's Fort, and Sarah Sullivan. I have been unable to verify this or to fit him into the Bent family. However, his observation on Carson is of interest, regardless of his parentage.

[62] Allan Nevins, "Kit Carson, Bayard of the Plains," in *American Scholar,* (Summer, 1939), VIII, pp. 333-49, concludes that Carson was not greater than others of his kind but more typical. The comparison with Bayard was originally made by Frémont; perhaps Crillon would have been a more accurate choice from French history. Dixon Wecter, *Hero in America* (New York, 1941), makes no mention of Kit Carson, as unaccountable omission in such a book.

[63] My former colleague of many years, Dr. Elizabeth B. White, a scholar of rigorous historical standards, on learning that I was engaged in preparing a sketch of Carson admonished me, "Don't be too hard on Kit; we need a few legends." For a much fuller treatment of Carson, see my new edition of his memoirs, published under the title *"Dear Old Kit": The Historical Christopher Carson* (Norman, 1968).

William Sherley (Old Bill) Williams

by Frederic E. Voelker
St. Louis Westerners

William Sherley Williams, fourth of the nine children of Joseph and Sarah (Musick) Williams, was born June 3, 1787, in a cabin on Horse Creek, old Rutherford County, North Carolina. Both parents, of predominantly Welsh ancestry, were natives of Virginia. During the Revolution, Joseph served against both the British and their Cherokee allies until incapacitated by a bad leg wound.[1]

In the remote area of the Williams farm, under the east front of the Blue Ridge, where "educational facilities were . . . meagre and insufficient," the Williams children were taught the fundamentals, some Latin, and the Baptist precepts by a knowledgeable mother. One of the boys, Lewis, became a famous Missouri preacher.[2]

About 1793, encouraged by "a kind of proclamation issued by the Governor of the Spanish posts at the Illinois" (Upper Louisiana Territory) inviting settlers, many members of the Musick-Williams clan of North Carolina decided to move west. In July 1794, Joseph Williams disposed of his 650 acres in Rutherford County, packed up his family and goods and joined the exodus.[3]

---

1 William Terrell Lewis, *Genealogy of the Lewis Family in America* (Louisville, 1893), 57, 187, 191-92; William R. Vaughan's copy of Sarah Williams' family *Bible* record (ms.); Record of Deeds, Book E-1 (ms.), 413-14, Rutherford Co. Reg. of Deeds, Rutherfordton, N.C.; writer's notes of an interview with C. E. Vaughan, Owensville, Mo., grandson of the subject's sister Arabella, May 28-29, 1936. The Williams farm lay in that part of old Rutherford Co. now within Polk Co.

2 Clarence W. Griffin, *History of Old Tryon and Rutherford Counties, North Carolina* (Asheville, 1937), 122; R. S. Duncan, *A History of the Baptists in Missouri* (St. Louis, 1882), 79; writer's field notes, Aug., 1937; C. E. Vaughan interview, *loc. cit.*

3 *Debates and Proceedings in the Congress of the U.S.* (Washington, 1834), 624; Record of Deeds, *loc. cit.*, Book M-Q, 237-38.

The only regularly traveled route northwest, a rough horse-trail, crossed the Great Smoky Mountains near Warm Springs, on the French Broad River, some fifty-five miles from the Williams farm, went northwest across Tennessee and into Kentucky at Cumberland Gap, thence by the Wilderness Trail to Crab Orchard, and farther northwest to the Falls of the Ohio (Louisville). The clan crossed the Ohio there or at some point downstream, and ultimately reached Whiteside Station, Northwest Territory, fifteen miles south of St. Louis.[4]

In the summer of 1795 Joseph Williams and his family crossed the Mississippi into Spanish Louisiana Territory and halted at a fortified settlement called Owen's Station, or Village à Robert, sixteen miles northwest of St. Louis and five miles from the Missouri River. On August 26, 1796, the Spanish government granted Joseph eight hundred arpens of land (about 680 acres) on the south bank of the Missouri, four miles west of Owen's Station.[5]

From the new farm the Williams boys ranged widely, hunting, trapping, perfecting woodland skills. Will, as his family called him, gradually expanded his trapping radius, and one day, after a long hunt, arrived at a village of the Osage Indians, on the waters of the Osage River, two hundred miles from home. There he decided to stay. He was about sixteen when one day he suddenly appeared at home and announced that thenceforward he would live as an Osage.[6]

---

4 Thomas Perkins Abernathy, *From Frontier to Plantation in Tennessee* (Chapel Hill, 1932), 154-55, 157 (map); William Allen Pusey, *The Wilderness Road to Kentucky* (N.Y., n.d.), 1, 15, 50 (map), 55, 62, 65-66, 113-29; Col. David R. Musick, autobiographical note (typescript copy), Etta Musick Nason papers (private), St. Louis. Warm Springs is now Hot Springs, Madison Co., N.C.; and Whiteside Station is now Columbia, Monroe Co., Ill.

5 Hunt's Minutes, vol. 1 (typescript copy), 208, Mo. Hist. Soc., St. Louis; *American State Papers, Public Lands* (Washington, 1861), VIII, pp. 852-53; Field Notes, U.S. Surveys, St. Louis County, Mo. (ms.), II, p. 169, Surveyor's Office, Clayton, Mo. Owen's Station is now Bridgeton, St. Louis Co., Mo. The Williams farm was confirmed as U.S. Survey 282.

6 Duncan, *op. cit.*, 79-80; Draper's Notes, vol. 22, Trip 1868, 1 s (ms.), 167-68;

Will settled with the Big Hill band of the Great Osages who liked and respected him. He learned their language, hunted with them, counseled them in their dealings with the whites, acquired considerable influence among them, undoubtedly was adopted by the Big Hills, married, in native manner, one of their girls by whom he had two daughters, Sarah and Mary, and remained with them nearly a quarter of a century.[7]

While pursuing the indispensable, westward-ranging buffalo, Will learned much about the immense area between the Osage country (along the waters of the lower Missouri and the middle Arkansas) and the Rocky Mountains, and there are indications he may have reached some northwestern beaver streams and the settlements of the Spanish Southwest long before the organized brigades of beaver hunters.[8]

Vaughan interview, *loc. cit.;* writer's notes of an interview with Perry and Josie Williams, Brinktown, Mo., grandchildren of the subject's brother John W., June 2, 1936.

[7] John Joseph Mathews, *The Osages* (Norman, 1961), ix, x; *American Missionary Register* (cited below as *A.M.R.*), vol. II, no. 10 (Apr. 1822), 402; writer's notes of a conference with members of the William S. Mathews family, Pawhuska, Okla., Aug. 30, 1933. John Joseph Mathews is the grandson of Sarah (Williams) Mathews, daughter of the subject.

[8] George Champlin Sibley, in *The Road to Santa Fe,* ed. Kate L. Gregg (Albuquerque, 1952), 253; John D. Hunter, *Memoirs of a Captivity Among the Indians of North America* (London, 1824), 455; George Frederick Ruxton, *Life in the Far West* (N.Y., 1849), 123; *Denver Republican,* Oct. 5, 1897, interview with Philander Simmons; [M. C. Field], "The Old Man of the Mountains," New Orleans *Daily Picayune,* Jan. 4, 1844; statement of Anson Rudd, Aug. 2, 1901 (typescript), Pioneer Envelope, F. W. Cragin Papers, Pioneers' Museum, Colorado Springs, Colo.

Operating independently, frequently alone, and keeping no written record, so far as known, the precise date of Williams advent in the Rocky Mountains is problematical. He appears to have known his way around the mountains before his first recorded trip. There is a living tradition among the Osages that some of their people had reached not only the Ute country, but the land of living "Cliff Dwellers" still farther southwest, at least seventy-five years before Williams first met the Osages. Mathews, *op. cit.,* 149-53. That Williams made excursions with the Osages far to the west, *ca.* 1803-1825, can hardly be doubted.

Ruxton indicated Williams first went to the mountains about 1807; Simmons said Williams went to what is now Colorado in 1808; Field indicated Williams had been in the mountains since 1815; and Rudd indicated Williams went to the mountains in 1807. All these men were personally acquainted with Williams.

When, in the spring of 1812, war broke out on the Missouri frontier, and Britain's Indian allies north of the Missouri River began their murderous raids, Will volunteered for service with Captain James Callaway's Company C, Mounted Rangers, assigned as scouts and spies in the area "northeast of St. Charles," in the Missouri Point-Piasa country along the Mississippi. He appears on the company roster as "fourth sergeant." His length of service is problematical, but he was back at the Osage village by December 1813. On September 15, 1814, his daughter Mary was born.[9]

Williams is recorded as official interpreter for George C. Sibley, United States Indian Agent and factor at Fort Osage on the Missouri River, from May 13, 1817, to June 30, 1818, and probably served in that capacity for a longer period; and he also pressed and packed furs at the fort. His daughter was baptised in the Catholic faith in July 1819; and on April 28, 1820, he sold to a kinsman the forty acres of the home farm willed him by his father, who had died the preceding January.[10]

In July 1821, a sub-station of the United States factory was established on the Marias des Cygnes River, about five miles from its mouth, near the Osage villages, with Paul Baillio as sub-factor and Williams as official interpreter. Next month a band of New England missionaries, sent by the United Foreign Missionary Society with the blessing of the government, arrived in the Osage country.[11]

---

[9] John R. Callaway papers (mss.), Joseph Maher Coll., Mo. Hist. Soc., St. Louis; Edgar B. Wesley, "James Callaway in the War of 1812," *Missouri Historical Society Collections,* vol. v, no. 1 (Oct. 1927), 77; Register Baptismalis Nationis Osagaiae (ms.), [7], Monastery of St. Francis de Hieronymus, St. Paul, Kan.

[10] Receipts from Wm. S. Williams to G. C. Sibley, June 30, 1817 (mss.), Fort Osage papers, Ret. Files, Ind. Trade, Off. of Ind. Affrs., Washington; Geo. C. Sibley Memo. Book, 1812-1818 (ms.), Sibley papers, Lindenwood Coll., St. Charles, Mo.; Register Baptismalis, *loc. cit.;* General Records, Book I-J (ms.), 283, Off. Recorder of Deeds, City Hall, St. Louis, Mo. A military post, Indian agency and factory, Fort Osage was established in 1808, on the south bank of the Missouri, some fifty river miles east of present Kansas City, Mo.

[11] *A.M.R., loc. cit.,* vol. I, no. 12 (June 1821), 485; vol. II, no. 7 (Jan. 1822), 275; vol. II, no. 9 (Mar. 1822), 351; vol. II, no. 10 (Apr. 1822), 405.

This was an important event in Williams' life because it revealed his intellectual capacity, and his impatience with the white man's civilization and Christianity as he saw them practiced; it led to many a widely spread humorous tale about "Parson Williams"; and, it appears, contributed to his domestic infelicity and his leaving the Osages, who were being crowded by whites and "removed" Indians.

To the missionaries Williams immediately became a benefactor by furnishing practical information about the Osages, and volunteering his services as interpreter and translator. By the end of 1821 he had produced a two-thousand-word Osage-English dictionary, had a grammar well under way, and was constructing sentences.[12] Subsequently completed, the material was made into a book.[13]

In the late summer of 1822 Williams served as guide and interpreter in the Osage country for generals Henry Atkinson and Edmund P. Gaines and other army officers on tours of military inspection and of conciliation between the Osages and their enemies, the Cherokees and their allies.[14]

By this time relations between Williams and the missionaries had cooled, due to Williams' reluctance to interpret sermons orally, and the missionaries' uncertainty about the "accuracy" of his translations; and because of his great influence with the Osages, they dared not preach without his approval. By this time, too, Williams had acquired, in the

12 *Ibid.*, vol. II, no. 8 (Feb. 1822), 329; vol. II, no. 10 (Apr. 1822), 402, 406; vol. II, no. 12 (June 1822), 489.

13 *Washashe Wageressa Pahugreh Tse: The Osage First Book* (Boston, 1834). The volume nowhere names the compiler. The title literally translates: Osage First Lines of Writing. James Constantine Pilling, *Bibliography of the Siouan Language* in Bulletin [5], Bureau of Ethnology (Washington, 1887) names as compilers: William B. Montgomery and W. C. Requa, two of the missionaries instructed by Williams. It is a small book of 126 pages with "familiar sentences in Osage and English interlinear," and selections from the Old and New Testaments, and spelling lessons in the Osage. Only five hundred copies were issued and the work is now very scarce.

14 Journal of Union Mission, Aug. 29 and Sept. 2, 1822 (ms.), Okla. Hist. Soc.; *A.M.R., loc. cit.*, vol. III, no. 5 (Nov. 1822), 186; vol. IV, no. 2 (Feb. 1823), 41, 43; vol. IV, no. 3 (Mar. 1823), 75.

accepted Osage manner, two more wives. His thoughts and his manner of life distressed the missionaries and they fervently prayed for his redemption, while Williams continued to interpret for them.[15]

When the act of Congress abolishing the Indian factory system became effective among the Osages in the late summer of 1822, the sub-factory on the Marias des Cygnes was closed and Williams lost his job as its interpreter. He became an independent trader among the Indians of the middle Arkansas River area, and appears to have prospered. About this time he moved with his enlarged family to a new Osage village not far from his trading post on the Neosho (Grand) River. On May 30, 1824, he was granted a one-year license to trade with the Osages and immigrant Kickapoos at the "Fork of Grand River."[16]

During the summer and early fall of 1824 Williams devoted considerable time, as interpreter, to the case of Bad Tempered Buffalo, Little Eagle, and three other Arkansas Osages charged with the murder of Major Curtis Welborn; all parties being poachers on Choctaw land in Arkansas Territory. This included trips to Cantonment Gibson and the Arkansas Osage village to arrange the surrender of the Indians, and to Little Rock for the trial. Only Bad Tempered Buffalo and Little Eagle were convicted, and five months later pardoned by President John Quincy Adams.[17]

[15] *A.M.R., loc. cit.*, vol. III, no. 3 (Sept. 1822), 92; vol. III, no. 5 (Nov. 1822), 185-86; vol. III, no. 6 (Dec. 1822), 212; vol. V, no. 9 (Sept. 1824), 272-73, 275; vol. VI, no. 7 (July 1825), 217.

[16] *Ibid.*, vol. III, no. 5 (Nov. 1822), 188; vol. IV, no. 2 (Feb. 1823), 44-45; vol. IV, no. 3 (Mar. 1823), 75; vol. VI, no. 7 (July 1825), 217; Boat Account, Fort Osage, 1823-24, and Blotter, 1823 (mss.), Sibley papers, *loc. cit.;* License no. 16, 1824, Indian Trade (ms.), Mss. Div., Wisc. Hist. Soc. The "Fork of Grand River" was the area on the Neosho (Grand) River where several feeder streams reached the river, in the extreme southeast corner of present Kansas. Deliberate vagueness was characteristic of many early Indian trading licenses.

[17] *A.M.R., loc. cit.*, vol. V, no. 5 (May 1824), 138-40; vol. V, no. 6 (June 1824), 178-79; vol. V, no. 10 (Oct. 1824), 301-04; vol. VI, no. 1 (Jan. 1825), 22; Journal of Union Mission, *loc. cit.*, Dec. 4, 1823, June 10 and Aug. 27, 1824; President Adams pardon (ms. copy), Osages, Ret. Files, Off. Ind. Affrs., Washington.

Later that fall, perhaps by pre-arrangement, Williams headed for the Rocky Mountains. He probably had little time for trapping on his long trans-mountain trip to a camp near Flathead (Salish) House, a Hudson's Bay Company post on Clark's Fork of the Columbia River. There, as a free trapper during the early winter of 1824-1825 he worked closely with a brigade of William H. Ashley's trappers under Jedediah S. Smith; and they encountered plenty of Indian hostility.

According to Thomas Eddie, one of Smith's men, Williams, hunting afoot up the fork for meat, ran into a hostile party of Blackfeet, wandering far from their home grounds east of the mountains, killed four of them and escaped by slithering into a side canyon, where he hid for two days while the Indians hunted for him. On the third day he sneaked to the top of a crag in time to watch his frustrated enemies leave the vicinity. Fearing the presence of more Blackfeet on the banks of the fork, Williams fashioned a rude raft and quietly floated down Clark's Fork to the trappers' camp.[18]

It appears that about this time, Williams, at thirty-seven, prematurely acquired the cognomen "Old Bill" by which he was known the rest of his life.

By the end of May 1825, Bill had arrived back at the Osage village. When the land cession treaty between United States Commissioner William Clark and the Osages was signed on June 2, 1825, in St. Louis, one section of land was reserved for each of Williams' daughters; and Williams, at the request of the Osages, was awarded $250 for "credits given" them. During the next two months Bill put his business affairs in order and prepared for a long absence.[19]

---

18 Boat Account, Fort Osage, 1823-1824 (ms.), Sibley papers, *loc. cit.;* Frank Triplett, *Conquering the Wilderness* (St. Louis, 1883), 431-32, 454-55. See also the writer's "Thomas Eddie," in this *Series,* I, p. 276, and the sources there cited.

19 Journal B, 1825-1826, Bernard Pratte & Co. (ms.), 170, Mo. Hist. Soc., St. Louis; Power of attorney, June 13, 1825, Williams to his brother James, Gray Twp., Gasconade Co., Mo. (ms.), Cons. Files, U.S. Gen. Acctg. Off., Washington.

By August 1 he had joined the government expedition under George C. Sibley, Thomas Mather and Benjamin H. Reeves, commissioners, to survey and mark the trade road from Fort Osage to Santa Fe, New Mexico, and negotiate its rights-of-way through the Indian country. Bill was engaged as "Interpreter, Runner, Hunter, etc." Because of his wide acquaintance and high reputation among the Osages his initial duty was to call their leaders to a treaty council on the Neosho River at the place Sibley named "Council Grove." The signature of William S. Williams, interpreter, was among those affixed to the pact on August 10.[20]

From Council Grove, Bill rode to summon the headmen of the Kansa village, some forty-five miles northwest. The treaty with the Kansas was signed August 16 at Sora Kansa Creek, and again Bill was signatory.[21] Sibley consistently minimized Bill's services as diplomat and interpreter.[22]

The expedition headed west, crossed the Little Arkansas and struck the Arkansas about 270 miles west of Fort Osage. They followed the north bank of the river about 190 miles, crossed to the south bank and traveled south forty miles across the "Cimarron Desert" to the Cimarron River, which they followed to Upper Cimarron Spring, rode south and crossed the North Canadian River, passed Rabbit Ears Mountain, and continued west to a point about seventy miles directly east of Taos, New Mexico. From there they were guided a hundred devious miles through the Sangre de Cristo mountain mass by "Francisco Largo (a civilized Comanche Indian)" to Taos, where they arrived October 30, 1825.[23]

---

20 Voucher 8, Settlement 452, Mexican Road Commrs., 1836 (ms.), G.A.O.; Sibley, *op. cit.*, 7, 34, 57, 59, 253; *Indian Treaties*, comp. S. S. Hamilton (Washington, 1826), 419. Council Grove is now a municipality in present central Morris Co., Kan.

21 Sibley, *op. cit.*, 59, 61-63, 252-53; *Indian Treaties*, *op. cit.*, 421. Sora Kansa Creek is a small branch of Turkey Creek, flowing near present Elyria, McPherson Co., Kan.

22 The late Dr. Kate L. Gregg, editor of the Sibley journals *(sup.)*, expressed to the writer a concurring opinion.

On November 14 Bill was granted a leave of absence to go trapping, and started "down the Rio del Norte" (Rio Grande). The record is silent as to his destination, but the lower Rio Grande waters as well as the Gila headwaters toward the southwest were acknowledged beaver waters. Bill returned to Taos on February 24, 1826, reported "good success," and began gambling. On March 9 he was still gambling and had "not yet joined the Service"; and that ended his tenure with the road commissioners.[24]

Soon after that Bill started back to the Northwest and, losing no time, joined his companions of the 1824-1825 season at or near Great Salt Lake. They set out for the Yellowstone by way of Bear River, turned east, and between Bear River Divide and Commissary Ridge picked up the Sublette Cut-off, followed it and crossed Green River in the vicinity of Names Hill. As they approached the Wind River Mountains they had daily skirmishes with the pugnacious Blackfeet. When they arrived at a point about twenty miles east of Sublette's Spring, Bill and three others started north into the mountains on a short hunt, with the intention of crossing the mountains and rejoining the main party east of the mountains.[25]

In the southern end of the Wind River Mountains Bill's trappers were thrice attacked by Blackfeet, but came off with Williams, Bill Gordon and Joe Lajeunesse only superficially wounded. They fled along the route laid out, probably over Sioux Pass, onto the Little Popo Agie and the

---

23 Sibley, *op. cit.*, 63-66, 68, 70-80, 82, 84-111, 254-60. The point 270 miles from Fort Osage would be the vicinity of present Sterling, Rice Co., Kan.; and 190 miles farther west would be at about present Deerfield, Kearny Co., Kan.

It appears that from present Mt. Dora, just west of Rabbit Ears Mountain, both in present Union Co., N.M., they followed a fairly easy road to the neighborhood of present Springer, Colfax Co., N.M. Some earlier road maps (*e.g.* Conoco) show a dirt road following this identical route.

24 Sibley, *op. cit.*, 132, 152, 155.

25 Triplett, *op. cit.*, 415, 432-33. Triplett had the details from Thomas Eddie, one of the main party. Names Hill is in present northeast Lincoln Co., Wyo. Sublette's Spring is in present south central Sublette Co., Wyo.

Popo Agie, which they followed to its junction with Wind River, which presently becomes the Bighorn. There they joined the main party and continued down the Bighorn. They eluded a Blackfeet ambush, but not without serious wounds, and arrived at their semi-permanent camp on the Yellowstone near the mouth of the Bighorn.[26]

Late in the summer of 1826 Bill returned to New Mexico where, on August 29, at Santa Fe, he and Ceran St. Vrain and their thirty-five "servants" were given a "passport" by Governor Antonio Norbona "to pass to the State of Sonora [Arizona] for private trade." Although Norbona suspected that the trappers' real purpose was to hunt beaver his official records protested that the "passport" did not include the privilege of "lingering" to trap beavers on the rivers of Sonora. Undeterred, that fall the trappers penetrated deep into the Apache country north of the Gila, working it and its upper affluents.[27]

One day, as Bill worked alone, he was surprised by the Apaches, captured, "stripped of everything, clothes, arms, traps and mule and turned loose in the desert." Stark naked, afoot, and without a weapon, he headed northeast toward Taos. After a 160-mile travail through the White Mountains, the arid valley of the Little Colorado, and the desert country of the Zunis, Bill was picked up among the mesas by the Zunis, taken to their pueblo, ceremoniously welcomed, provided with a blanket and moccasins, and "treated with great veneration and almost worship." After he left the Zunis he appears to have spent some time during the sum-

---

26 Triplett, *op. cit.*, 416-18, 433-39. Sioux Pass is in present southwest Fremont Co., Wyo. Their semi-permanent camp was near present Bighorn, southwest Treasure Co., Mont.

27 Thomas Maitland Marshall, "St. Vrain's Expedition to the Gila in 1826," in *Southwest Historical Quarterly*, vol. XIX, no. 3 (Jan. 1916), 253, 255, 257-58. There is much more to the story, involving politics, Mexican-Indian relations, bribery, personalities, etc. The entire subject of Mexican-trapper relations invites scholarly exploration. See Thomas J. Farnham, *Travels in the Californias* (N.Y., 1846), 84-86.

mer of 1827 among the Navahos. Ultimately he made it back to Taos, some two hundred miles.[28]

Bill left Taos early in the fall of 1827 with a trapping party led by Sylvestre S. Pratte, with Ceran St. Vrain as clerk, bound for Green River. On their way north they camped in Park Kyack, a lush basin full of game, girt on the west and south by the snowy Park Range (Continental Divide), on the east by the Medicine Bow Mountains. The North Platte River rises in the park and emerges northward between spurs of the Sierra Madre and Medicine Bows. There, on October 1, Pratte sickened and died, and was succeeded by St. Vrain. They went on to Green River waters, where they wintered. In April 1828, the party broke up, and most of the men, probably including Bill Williams, reached Taos about May 23.[29]

From the spring of 1828 to the spring of 1830 Bill apparently became better acquainted with the Utes, their country, and other recesses of the Rocky Mountains theretofore known only to the natives; and acquired wide repute for an accurate knowledge of his range. At Taos, in the spring of 1830, he met young Jesús Archuleta, who began a tenure as Bill's loyal retainer by accompanying him on a trip to South Park and the valley of the South Platte.

They went north over Raton Pass and, keeping east of the mountains, arrived at a point near Manitou Springs where they swung around Pike's Peak and crossed the mountains into a splendid hunting ground, South Park, headwaters

28 James J. Webb's signed statement (ms.), Webb papers (private), St. Louis, Mo.; William Ingraham Kip, "The Last of the Leatherstockings," in *The Overland Monthly,* vol. II, no. 5 (May, 1869), 409; *St. Louis Globe-Democrat,* Dec. 24, 1911; W. T. Hamilton, *My Sixty Years on the Plains* (N.Y., 1905), 102.

29 Ceran St. Vrain to B. Pratte & Co., enclosing undated memo. of acct., cert. of services, etc., dated Sept. 1, 1829 (mss.), Bent-St. Vrain Papers, P. Chouteau Maffitt Coll., Mo. Hist. Soc., St. Louis. The letter, probably sent from Taos, is undated and was received in St. Louis Sept. 28, 1828. Park Kyack, also known to the mountain men as The Bull Pen, The Buffalo Pasture, New Park, and North Park (its present name), occupies most of Jackson Co., Colo.

country of the South Platte. Though their route north out of the park is uncertain, it seems likely they went as far northwest as Williams Fork of the upper Colorado River, then circled southward to the South Platte, followed it to about its junction with Cherry Creek, and went south by an unknown route to the Arkansas, which they followed to Bent's Fort.[30]

On September 4, 1832, at the bid of John Harris, a motley crew of some seventy-five trappers and adventurers from the New Mexico settlements, including Bill Williams and another seasoned trapper, Aaron B. Lewis, and Albert Pike, a young Easterner of literary proclivity, rendezvoused in the valley of the Rio Pueblo de Picuris, on the western slope of the Sangre de Cristo Mountains, about twenty-seven miles south of Taos. The announced intention was to trap "the Cumanche country, upon the heads of the Red river and Fausse Washita." They left on the sixth, and the entire course trended southeast.[31]

They crossed the mountains near Tres Ritos into Mora Valley, continued to the junction of the Mora River and Sapello Creek, where they struck the Santa Fe Trail and followed it to a point six miles beyond the Gallinas River crossing. There they left it and crossed to the Pecos River at Anton Chico. Eleven days and nearly ninety miles of following the Pecos brought them to Bosque Redondo, where they left the river and headed toward the western escarpment of the Llano Estacado (Staked Plain), up which they wound to a Comanche trail.[32]

The trail led them down the Double Mountain Fork of the Brazos River, a succession of depressions holding more

---

30 *St. Louis Globe-Democrat,* Dec. 24, 1911. See note 37.

31 Albert Pike, "Narrative of a Journey in the Prairie," in *Publications of the Arkansas Historical Association* (Conway, Ark., 1917), IV, pp. 94-96; Writers' Program, W.P.A., *New Mexico* (N.Y., 1940), 377. Originally included in Pike's *Prose Sketches and Poems* (Boston, 1834), his "Narrative" was reprinted in 1835 with emended text in Pike's newspaper, *The Arkansas Advocate.* The 1917 printing copies the 1835 text.

32 Pike, *op. cit.,* 95-96, 98-101; Writers' Program, *New Mexico,* 355, 370, 377.

or less water. For eighteen days and well over two hundred miles they followed the fork across the arid *llano,* met nominally friendly Comanches, lost and recovered the trail, lost men by desertion, and hunted with little success. Near the junction of the Double Mountain Fork and its South Branch the outfit got lost in the sand hills and broke up.[33]

Ill-conceived, misdirected, with overtones of deceit and fraud, and with constantly impending Mexican and Comanche treachery, the expedition never reached the waters of either the Red or the Washita; and beavers, like the buffalo, were always "just ahead" and not one beaver was taken. Bill Williams returned to Taos in time to outfit for the 1832-1833 trapping season.[34]

In middle November 1833, Bill, as guide, left a trappers' camp on Ham's Fork, a tributary of Black's Fork of Green River, with a Rocky Mountain Fur Company outfit under Henry Fraeb. They headed for Green River and, as the signs indicated a good season, expected to remain out until about March 1, 1834, and appear to have done so. Bill was back in Taos before April 1.[35]

Some time before this Bill had taken up residence in a Taos adobe with a Mexican widow with three children. It is known that her maiden name was Antonia Baca, and she came of a good family. One son, Jose, was born about 1834 to Antonia and Bill, who probably lived together for some years after that.[36]

Bill now sought wider knowledge of the Far West. According to the narrative of Jesús Ruperto Valdez (Pepe) Archuleta, his camp keeper, Bill arranged a two-man "ex-

---

33 Pike, *op. cit.,* 102-15; William Curry Holden, "Comanche Trail," in *The Handbook of Texas,* ed. Walter Prescott Webb (Austin, 1952), I, p. 386; *Id.,* Anon., "Double Mountain Fork of the Brazos River," 515.

34 Pike, *op. cit.,* 94-115.

35 Thomas Fitzpatrick to William Sublette, Nov. 13, 1833 (ms.), Sublette Papers, Mo. Hist. Soc., St. Louis; Hiram Martin Chittenden, *The American Fur Trade of the Far West* (Stanford, 1954), I, pp. 260, 476.

36 Statements at Taos of Juan Santistevan, Apr. 24 and 27, 1908, and Teresina (Bent) Scheurich, Apr. 29, 1908, Early Far West Notebook XII (ms.), 47-49, 53-55, 58-59, F. W. Cragin Papers, *loc. cit.;* Lewis, *op. cit.,* 192.

ploring expedition" into the vast Mexican land between the middle Rio Grande settlements and the Pacific, finding "his own trail" from near Zuni Pueblo "clear through to the missions" in California, to test stories he had heard from "Indians and priests . . . of some very wonderful things" farther west. It was to be a leisurely reconnaissance, spiced with hunts and visits with strange people.[37]

Bill gathered Pepe and "two fine saddle horses," three pack mules, ammunition, only four traps, and left Taos on April 1, 1834, for Santa Fe, where he bought food staples and medicines, and followed the old Chihuahua Trail to Albuquerque. There, says Archuleta, they visited the "mission" (San Felipe Neri Church), where Bill assisted "the padres in translating some Bible lessons into Navajo lingo."[38]

They continued down the old trail to Isleta Pueblo, left it to cross westward to Laguna Pueblo, turned southwest into "a maze of canyons and *cul de sacs,*" skirted the Malpais (lava beds), headed south into the San Augustine Plains, and watered at Horse Springs. They worked west and north around the Datil Range into very rough country, and discovered that a volcanic hill they climbed to spot a better trail contained within its crater the fabled Zuni Salt Lake.[39]

---

[37] Archuleta's narrative was first published in the *St. Louis Globe-Democrat,* Dec. 24, 1911, partially subtitled: "The Story of Bill Williams, . . . told here for the first time," and with the narrator's portrait. Its authenticity has been questioned; however, the results of certain tests and investigations (too numerous and lengthy to recount here), applied to the story, are sufficient to convince us that, despite occasional anachromisms and other lapses, the narrative is essentially true in all matters of which the narrator could have had personal knowledge; and that part has been accepted as substantially correct. One important change has been made – in order to harmonize with an established chronology, and in the absence of reliable conflicting testimony, the events have been shifted from the years 1832-1835 to 1834-1837.

[38] Hamilton, *op. cit.,* 102.

[39] Isleta is fifteen miles south of Albuquerque, Laguna fifty miles west of Isleta. The Malpais, in present Valencia Co., N.M., is twenty-five miles southwest of Laguna. Horse Springs, in the west central part of the San Augustine Plains, in present Catron Co., N.M., is about fifty miles directly south of The Malpais. The Datil Range is in present western Catron Co., N.M., and the Salt Lake in the northwest corner of the county.

By a devious trail they arrived at the "extreme border house where a civilized man lived," the Cienega Amarilla rancho of Pedro Sanchez, whom Bill had met at Zuni Pueblo in 1827. Continuing west, they crossed the Little Colorado River, and one day met a hunting party of Hopis who directed them to the Petrified Forest. Fascinated, they rode through it to a Hopi village where they learned enough about the Grand Canyon to urge them toward its rim, and after a zig-zag trip they camped above Marble Canyon, where they sat in enchanted stupor.[40]

Next morning they started south, ran into the formidable canyon of the Little Colorado, retreated eastward to a river crossing, and rode south and west to the neighborhood of what became known as Bill Williams Mountain, where they spent the winter of 1834-1835 in a Walapai village. In the spring they rode west to the Colorado River where, at another Walapai village they met Padre Gonzales, a wandering Franciscan who, since they were seeking enjoyment, not hardship, dissuaded them from crossing the inhospitable Mohave Desert.[41]

They crossed the Colorado, Bill and Pepe in a canoe, the animals swimming, headed upriver and generally followed the north bank to a low mountain, probably in the Muddy Range, from which they descried the cottonwood fringe along the Virgin River. From that point their northward course is undefined; but thirty-five days later they were at Great Salt Lake, and finally, after many summer days and

40 Cienega Amarilla (Yellow Meadow) lies in present western McKinley Co., N.M., and eastern Apache Co., Ariz., centering near St. Michaels, Ariz. Marble Canyon is the northern arm of the Grand Canyon, above the mouth of the Little Colorado.

41 Bill Williams Mountain, in present southwestern Coconino Co., Ariz., is believed to have been named by Bill's friend Antoine Leroux. In both instances Archuleta called the Indians "Maricopas," but it is believed that he referred to the Mata' va-kapai (north people), a subdivision of the Walapai. See John R. Swanton, *The Indian Tribes of North America* in Bulletin 145, Bur. of Am. Ethnol. (Washington, 1952), 366. The *padre* could well have been Rubio Gonzales, "the Zacatecan," exiled from a California mission during secularization, just prior to this time.

hundreds of mountain miles, they found a Hudson's Bay Company camp on Lake Coeur d'Alene, where Bill outfitted for the trapping season and Pepe went to cook for a camp at Lake Pend d'Oreille.[42]

Bill called for Pepe in the spring of 1836 and they rode southeast up Clark's Fork, Hell Gate and Bitterroot rivers, and east across the main Rockies to Bozeman Pass, where they descended to the Yellowstone. The next season, 1836-1837, with a fifty-trap line, they worked the Yellowstone waters, took six hundred skins and headed for the summer rendezvous on Green River near the mouth of Horse Creek, where they sold out and headed for Bent's Fort, where Bill took charge of a Bent-St. Vrain wagon train going to Santa Fe.[43]

Later in 1837 Bill again went out to the Colorado River. He appears to have traveled from the Bill Williams Mountain neighborhood through the Santa Maria country and down that stream to Bill Williams Fork of the Colorado which he followed to its mouth. There he met Antoine Leroux who reported Bill had "found water all along in holes & some beaver." The next summer, 1838, Bill was at the rendezvous on the Popo Agie, near its junction with Wind River.[44]

Bill's trapping now became sporadic. The steady decline of the fur trade, as the Mountain Men knew it, was making trapping unprofitable, and many trappers sought other fields: they hunted meat for the trading posts, guided trading, missionary, and immigrant parties, loafed around the Indian villages, lived off the country on long pleasure hunts, served as interpreters, and "collected" California horses. It

---

42 The Muddy Range is in present central Clark Co., Nev. The shores of lakes Coeur d'Alene and Pend d'Oreille, respectively in present Kootenai and Bonner cos., Idaho, were well-known fur trade camp grounds.

43 Here ends Archuleta's story of the "exploring expedition."

44 Richard H. Kern diary, Oct. 23, 1851 (ms.), Huntington Library, San Marino, Cal.; James B. Marsh, *Four Years in the Rockies* (New Castle, 1884; reprinted Columbus, n.d.), 225-26; Edwin L. Sabin, *Kit Carson Days* (N.Y., 1935), I, p. 277.

probably was during the years 1838-1841 that Bill pursued his comfortable relationship with the Utes, and he was reliably reported to have had a succession of Ute consorts.[45]

In the spring of 1840, after careful planning and local "arrangements" by scouts, a band of "Chaguanosos" descended upon Southern California in a sweeping raid on its horse herds. In this well-organized enterprise, which included American trappers, New Mexicans, French-Canadians and Indians, including mission apostates, Bill Williams had a directing hand. Its main objectives were the horses, once mission property but, since secularization of the missions in 1834, largely abandoned, with ownership in controversy.[46]

Late in April the Chaguanosos ran off about twelve hundred horses from the San Luis Obispo Mission herd and, by mid-May had collected about 1800 more, mostly from San Gabriel Mission and the *ranchos* between it and the abandoned San Bernardino *assistencia* (mission station), on the road to their main rendezvous in Summit Valley, just south of the climb to Cajon Pass. The three thousand animals were grazed in the lush valley, and driven up the pass onto the Mohave Desert, on the way to the Bent's Fort horse market on the Arkansas River, a hard journey of about a thousand miles.[47]

The scarcity of grass and water, and the relentless pace to elude pursuing Californios and predatory Indians, cost

[45] Micajah McGehee, "Narrative," in *Fremont's Fourth Expedition*, ed. LeRoy R. and Ann W. Hafen (Glendale, 1960), 144; Thomas E. Breckenridge, autobiographical notes dictated to C. W. Watson about 1894 (typescript), 44, 46, Harriet (Breckenridge) Knott papers (private), Hannibal, Mo.

[46] George William and Helen Pruitt Beattie, *Heritage of the Valley* (Pasadena, 1939), 37-38, 140; George D. Brewerton, "A Ride with Kit Carson," in *Harper's New Monthly Magazine*, VII (Aug. 1853), 316; Eleanor Frances Lawrence, "The Old Spanish Trail from Santa Fe to California," 1930 (typescript), 68, Bancroft Library, Berkeley, Cal.

[47] [California] Departmental State Papers: Prefectures & Juzgados, Angeles (ms.), IV, pp. 72, 88, 100, 105-06, Bancroft Lib.; Beattie, *op. cit.*, 140-43, where the affair is well summarized; G. W. Beattie to the writer, April 23, 1940.

the Chaguanosos some 1500 animals before they had cleared the desert. They probably lost many more along the Old Spanish Trail before reaching Bent's Fort; and there is a story that Bill turned his surviving share into Bent's corral and settled for a barrel of whiskey.[48]

About this time Bill took a notion to visit the folks back in Missouri. Late in 1840 he started from Taos for his old home and apparently was beyond Bent's Fort when he changed his mind, turned back and spent some time at the fort. However, in the summer of 1841 he went all the way, probably visited the Osage villages, went to see his little granddaughter, Mary's child Susan, who was living with an uncle in Neosho, Missouri, and remained to spend the winter of 1841-1842 with his aged mother and his brothers and sisters in Gasconade and Franklin counties; and many are the tales in the Ozark foothills of Bill's memorable return to Missouri.[49]

Early in 1842 Bill went to St. Louis to outfit a trading expedition. His partner was George Perkins, an experienced free trapper, and they recruited six others, including a young greenhorn, William T. Hamilton. Well armed, equipped and mounted, with wagons and pack horses loaded with merchandise and supplies, they left St. Louis early in March and followed the Missouri River to Independence, where they sold the wagons, and with an augmented pack train headed west. They probably followed the Kansas, Smoky Hill and Saline rivers. They crossed to the South Platte near the mouth of Cherry Creek where they traded with a Cheyenne village.[50]

---

48 Dept. State Papers, *loc. cit.*, 105-06; Micajah McGehee, "Rough Notes of Rough Times in Rough Places" (typescript), 53-54, Private Papers of James Stewart McGehee, St. Louis, Mo. (transcript in writer's collection).

49 Simeon Turley to Jesse B. Turley, Apr. 18 and Aug. 3, 1841, Turley Papers, Mo. Hist. Soc., St. Louis; interviews with C. E. Vaughan, Perry and Josie Williams, and conference with the William S. Mathews family, *loc. cit.;* writer's notes of an interview with Walter Williams, Brinktown, Mo., June 2, 1936.

50 Hamilton, *op. cit.*, 18-25.

They rode north to trade for furs and buffalo robes at the Sioux villages east of Fort Laramie, and sold their purchases to another trader for cash, thus setting a pattern for the trip – buying and selling promptly for an immediate cash profit. They moved west along the North Platte and the Sweetwater to the Oregon Trail Crossing and northwest to nominally Shoshoni country east of the Wind River Mountains where, on Little Wind River, they had a battle with a band of Blackfeet, all of whom, according to Hamilton, were killed.[51]

On Wind River they met Bill's "old friend" Washakie and his Eastern Shoshonis, and learned that Blackfeet war parties hovered nearby. The recent deaths of two strange trappers and the theft of Shoshoni horses called for war. Bill Williams led in planning a three-pronged campaign by combined Mountain Man-Shoshoni forces, which resulted in a series of skirmishes and battles in the area east of the mountains, between the Owl Creek Mountains and the Bull Lake Creek-Wind River timber belt, in which the enemy lost twenty-one men, many horses and much property, and the allies one Shoshoni warrior. Both the victory and the celebration which followed were still being recalled by the Shoshonis nearly a century later.[52]

Bill's party traded with the Shoshonis, induced Washakie to take the accumulated skins to Jim Bridger's camp on Black's Fork of Green River, trapped Bull Lake, crossed Wind River Mountains to the head of the Green, worked down river, and crossed to Bridger's where they found Washakie and his Shoshonis with the skins, which they sold on the spot. They moved southeast to Brown's Hole near the junction of the Green and the Yampa, from which they made excursions into the Uinta Mountains. About September 1, after promising to return to Brown's Hole the fol-

[51] *Ibid.*, 35, 42, 44-49, 51-58.
[52] *Ibid.*, 60-80; A. F. C. Greene to the writer, July 10, 1937.

lowing spring to lead a trapping and trading expedition toward the farther West, Bill left for Taos.[53]

Next March 1843, Bill got some traps at Bent's, and went to Brown's Hole from which he and Perkins led about forty Mountain Men, with a pack train of trade goods, northwest on a trip of several thousand miles and two years' duration. They preferred to associate and trade with peaceful Indians, but if they encountered some with opposite inclinations they were prepared to take care of them in Mountain Man style. They did both and lost few men.[54]

They crossed the Uinta Mountains, went north to the Snake River and down it to work the Blackfoot, then returned to follow the Snake west to Fort Boise, a Hudson's Bay Company post near the mouth of the Boise; and crossed the Blue Mountains to the Umatilla River, and continued west to the John Day and the Deschutes, pausing to visit a Hudson's Bay camp on the Columbia near the mouth of the Deschutes (perhaps near The Dalles). They went south beyond the head of the Deschutes to Upper Klamath Lake, near which they went into winter quarters. It was from this camp apparently that Bill Williams, accomplished long-distance traveler, returned to Taos.[55]

In the spring of 1844 Bill left Taos, stopped to visit The Pueblo on the Arkansas, set out "for to'ther side of the 'big hills,'" and in due time arrived at the Klamath Lake camp. Soon after this the trappers broke camp and went to explore Lost River to its head. On the way back down river, to Tule Lake, the sink of Lost River, they were attacked by Modoc Indians and in the ensuing battle, according to Hamilton, the trappers lost three men, the Modocs about thirty.[56]

---

53 *Ibid.*, 81, 83-84, 86, 88, 92-93, 97, 99, 101.

54 Charles W. Bowman, "History of Bent County," in *History of the Arkansas Valley, Colorado* (Chicago, 1881), 829; Hamilton, *op. cit.*, 123-24.

55 *Ibid.*, 124, 126, 133, 138-46.

56 George S. Simpson to George C. Sibley, Apr. 10, 1844, Sibley Mss., vol. II, [1-3], Mo. Hist. Soc., St. Louis; Hamilton, *op. cit.*, 146-47, 153.

The trappers rode east to Clear Lake, and on to a branch of Pit River, thence almost directly south to Honey Lake where they set up a temporary camp. Three months later they rode east to skirt Pyramid Lake, on to the Truckee River, and across to Carson River, where they turned north to Humboldt Lake and went up the Humboldt River northeast to Thousand Springs Creek and the waters of Goose Creek. Then, in big jumps, they crossed to Raft River, to the Bear, to the Green, and probably used South Pass to get on to Wind River and follow it north to the Hot Springs where they rested. They resumed the journey by crossing the country southeast to the North Platte and following it east to Fort Laramie. There, in the summer of 1845 the party disbanded, and Bill returned briefly to Taos.[57]

Bill went up to visit the Mountain Men living at The Pueblo, and was there in August 1845, when Captain John C. Frémont, of the United States Topographical Engineers, induced him and Kit Carson to serve as guides on a journey officially indicated to be an examination of "unexplored" western regions, preparatory to the publication of a reliable map of the West. The party, nearly sixty strong, went up the Arkansas, detouring the Royal Gorge, past Williams Fishery (Twin Lakes), crossed the Sawatch Range over Tennessee Pass onto the head of Eagle River, followed the Eagle to the Colorado, and crossed over to White River which they followed to its junction with the Green, where they were joined by Joseph R. Walker, then crossed the Wasatch Mountains to Utah Lake, and went down the Jordan to Great Salt Lake. At a camp somewhere between the Cedar Mountains and the lake there was a serious disagreement between Frémont and the guides about the route across the Salt Desert, as the result of which, on October 27,

[57] *Ibid.*, 158-59, 161, 165, 167, 172, 174-77.

the day before the party started across the desert, Bill left the party.[58]

Bill is recorded at Bridger's Fort in July 1846; and about mid-June 1847, during the war with Mexico, he was one of the Mountain Men engaged to guide and guard the wagon train being taken from Fort Leavenworth across the plains to Santa Fe with Colonel Alton R. Easton's volunteer infantry battalion of St. Louisans. There was trouble with the Comanches, but the troops arrived practically intact at Santa Fe late in August. Some time between the fall of 1847 and the spring of 1848 Bill drifted up to the American Fur Company's Fort Union on the Yellowstone, and later in 1848 returned south.[59]

Bill arranged a sort of loose partnership with Josiah J. Webb of Webb & Doan in the spring of 1848 to trade with travelers along the Santa Fe Trail, and apparently was engaged in that enterprise when he was called to serve, with other Mountain Men, as scout and guide for Major W. W. Reynolds in a military campaign, starting from Taos, against a large band of Ute and Apache raiders who had been harassing the northern New Mexico settlements. The Indians were followed to Cumbres Pass in the southern extremity of the San Juan Mountains, where a fierce battle resulted in the rout of the Indians, after thirty-six of them and two soldiers were killed and many on both sides wounded, including Bill Williams, "who behaved himself

58 Frederick S. Dellenbaugh, *Fremont and '49* (N.Y., 1914), 289-93; U.S. 28 Cong., 2 sess., *Sen. Ex. Doc.* no. 1, pp. 221-22; John Charles Frémont, *Narratives of Exploration and Adventure* (N.Y., 1957), 440-42; W. J. Ghent, *The Early Far West* (N.Y., 1936), 344; Thomas S. Martin, "Narrative of John C. Fremont's Expedn. to California in 1845-6," dictated to E. F. Murray, Sept. 5, 1878 (ms.), 9-10, Bancroft Library; Breckenridge notes, *loc. cit.*, 42-43; Abstract of expenses and supporting vouchers, Fremont's third expedition, Settlement 7634, Mar. 9, 1849, Cons. Files, Gen. Acctg. Off., Washington.

59 Edwin Bryant, *What I Saw in California* (N.Y., 1848), 145. Bryant, who recorded the Bridger's Fort visit, disguises Bill Williams under the name "Bill Smith." *Daily Missouri Republican,* July 10, Aug. 12, Sept. 6, Oct. 23, 1847; *St. Louis Daily New Era,* Aug. 27, 1847; John Palliser, *The Solitary Hunter* (London, 1860), 87-88.

gallantly" and "was shot in the arm, shattering it most horrible." [60]

Bill was at The Pueblo on the Arkansas River on November 21, 1848, when Captain Frémont arrived with his fourth exploring expedition seeking a guide. Despite his conviction, based on unfailing signs of extremely severe weather ahead, that it was far too late in the season for the successful mountain crossing Frémont anticipated in his search for a practicable railroad route to California, Bill yielded to Frémont's pleas and agreed to guide the expedition. They left The Pueblo next day.

They went up the Arkansas and crossed over to the Mountain Men's Hardscrabble settlement, near the east foot of the Wet Mountains, where they packed the 120 mules with an additional supply of corn and, thirty-three strong, went southwest across the Wet Mountains and the Wet Mountain Valley to Robidoux (Mosca) Pass across the Sangre de Cristos. At the west end of the pass they veered north to round the sand hills in San Luis Valley and head northwest toward Saguache Creek on the west side of the valley; and there the trouble began.

According to Thomas Fitzpatrick's understanding (not to be discounted), after a discussion of the route with Frémont, it was the latter's intention, after crossing San Luis Valley, to "steer directly for California, leaving the two hitherto traveled routes, one north [the old trail up Saguache Creek to Cochetopa Pass] and the other south [the old Spanish Trail through Abiquiu] of him and passing midway between the two" [up the Rio Grande to its head]. Fitzpatrick was by no means sure that Frémont could "find a practicable route."

---

60 Account books, 1848-1850: Ledger, 27, Day Book, 10-12, Cash Book, 1, Webb papers, *loc. cit.;* W. W. Reynolds to Sterling Price, Aug. 6, 1848, Old Files Sec., Exec. Div., Adj. Gen. Off., War Dept., Washington; Betty Woods, *101 Trips in the Land of Enchantment* (Santa Fe, 1956), 46. Cumbres Pass lies about athwart the Colo.-New Mex. line, some forty miles southeast of Pagosa Springs, Colo.

Bill Williams well knew the extreme difficulty, if not the impossibility of crossing the main middle ranges of the Rocky Mountains in winter; and as the winter settled into dangerous severity, with snow storms, deepening drifts, fierce winds and killing drops in temperature, he tried to lead the expedition from the sand hills toward what he considered the least formidable crossing – the Saguache Creek route, a course Frémont, according to Fitzpatrick, had already rejected. Consequently, even before they had left the sand hills, Williams was halted and the expedition turned southwest toward the Rio Grande. From then on Williams ceased to function as "the" guide; others, such as Henry King and Alexis Godey, veterans of former Frémont expeditions, but unacquainted with the Rio Grande country, occasionally essayed to find a trail; and while Frémont continued to seek information from Williams and argue with him about the route, generally he disregarded Bill's few words of counsel, and Bill's responses were mainly to questions from other members of the party.

Accordingly, Frémont's course was followed up the Rio Grande to the mouth of Alder Creek, where he decided to leave the river and head north into the mountains. Whether or not Williams advised this move is unclear. All accounts indicate that no trail up Alder Creek was thought to exist, yet, incredibly, according to Richard H. Kern, one of the party, King "reported to the Colonel [Frémont] that he had found a wagon road," and thereupon "undertook the pilotage," and soon after that they "found a tolerable level road," which later seems to have disappeared in the deep drifts.

They followed the canyon of Alder Creek north to the junction of its East and West forks, then struggled up the West Fork. Bucking strangling icy winds, watching frozen mules drop dead in their tracks, beating out a path for the surviving animals, almost inch by inch they pushed and twisted up the snow-choked canyons and slippery mountain sides, a little west of north, to a point near the mouth of Long Gulch, then wound irregularly northeast to a camp near the sources of Embargo Creek, just below the summit ridge of La Garita Mountains.

Storms beat back their first attempt to surmount the ridge; at the second try they scaled it and camped just beyond on a head stream of Wanamaker Creek, where the fury of the storms isolated them for five days. Men became snow-blind and badly frostbitten, food for men and animals had about vanished, and one by one the mules died. Bill Williams sagged down upon his mule in a frozen stupor, but soon revived. In this desperate situation a lull in the storm permitted them to move from their exposed position back to the Embargo Creek camp, from which, on December 26, Frémont dispatched Henry King, as leader, Bill Williams, Tom Breckenridge and Frederick Creutzfeldt to the New Mexico settlements for help, allowing them sixteen days for the round trip of about 350 miles, or nearly twenty-two miles a day through snow covered country on foot.

Because they had to break through the drifts, and because of dwindled supplies, they carried, besides their rifles and knives, a minimum of food and equipment. It took them three days in bitter weather to descend Embargo Creek twenty miles to the Rio Grande, arriving with their food exhausted, and desperately weary. On the ensuing eight-day struggle down river to the point where it turns southeast, they subsisted on a hawk, an otter, parched boots (replaced by strips of blanket), belts and knife scabbards.

Near the bend they discerned, farther toward the east, the smoke of a Ute camp, which gave hope to all but Bill Williams. He explained why he could not approach the Indian camp. He confessed that some years before he had absconded with a consignment of tribal furs, and besides, had "led the soldiers against" the Utes (a reference to the 1848 campaign), and could not blame them for seeking his scalp.

He suggested the party leave the Rio Grande, cut across country and avoid a big river bend.

Bill's plan was adopted and, weak and starving, desperate, and chewing charred leather, they crept along until within a quarter mile of the river, where King lay down to rest, and soon died. They crawled to the river, where Breckenridge happily managed to kill a deer. Revived, they were preparing to travel when they saw four horsemen. Williams shouted and waved his rifle, and soon Frémont, Godey and two others rode into the desolate camp on horses somehow acquired from the Utes.

Accounts differ as to how Williams and his two companions reached the Red River settlement (Questa). According to Tom Breckenridge, Frémont's party rode on, leaving them to make the fifty mile trip as best they could; but, according to Frémont, taken to Questa by his party. Meantime, in the mountains, men froze and starved to death.

Thus ended Frémont's disastrous fourth expedition, its toll ten men and 120 mules dead, twenty-three men crippled and ill (some never completely recovered), nearly all the equipment and personal possessions lost, and an acrimonious, continuing controversy over responsibility for the disaster that has never been resolved to the satisfaction of reasonable men. For persisting in an apparently impossible "central" course during a deadly combination of winter elements; for his failure to designate Williams as the permanent, responsible guide, and permitting or even encouraging "amateur" pilots to try to find the trails, Frémont is to blame. For consenting to guide the outfit in the face of overwhelming indications of failure for a leader with whom, three years before, he had had a serious disagreement; and for his failure to get the "rescue" party (of which he was not the leader) to the settlements after the death of King, and deliver relief to the main party within the allotted time (all of which must be considered in the light of the very difficult circumstances under which the party attempted to operate), Bill Williams is responsible. And if it was he who actually led the party up Alder Creek, whether by accident or design, he must be held accountable for that.[61]

By the middle of February 1849, Williams and his companions were in Taos, where they rapidly recuperated; and about the middle of March, Williams and Dr. Benjamin J. Kern, the expedition's physician, left Taos with a few Mexican attendants for the scene of the debacle to recover the doctor's medical equipment and supplies, his brothers' (both Edward M. and Richard H. Kern, members of the expedition, were trained artists) art materials and personal papers, and whatever expedition property and personal effects could be salvaged. Almost as soon as they were out of sight, rumors began to circulate that they had been murdered.

Bill and the doctor reached the disaster area, gathered what they could and headed for Taos. On March 21, 1849,

[61] No attempt has been made to document specific points in the account of Frémont's fourth expedition. About two hundred published and unpublished sources on it exist and have been consulted, from brief contemporary newspaper items to good-sized volumes, the most useful and impartial of which is *Frémont's Fourth Expedition, op. cit.,* a compilation and digest of the most important documents on the subject. Other sources: Richard H. Kern to J. H. Simpson, Aug. 27, 1850, *Daily Missouri Republican,* Aug. 14, 1856; E. S. Erickson to the writer, June 23, 1942, with a sketch map of the camp sites, which Erickson first visited in 1928, and Dec. 13, 1942, with an annotated Forest Service map of the Alder Dist., Rio Grande N.F., Rio Grande and Saguache cos., Colo., within which the main disaster scene is located; Dellenbaugh, *op. cit.,* 390-403; Allan Nevins, *Frémont, Pathmarker of the West* (N.Y., 1939), 348-69; J. Loughborough, *The Pacific Telegraph and Railway* (St. Louis, 1849), iv-xi, 77, 79, which tackles the problem of where to lay the rails, and criticizes in detail Frémont's choice of route; Francis Grierson [Benjamin H. J. F. Shepard], *The Valley of Shadows* (Boston, 1948), 234-61, gives a most interesting retrospective account, touched with mysticism, of the expedition from the Missouri to Taos; William Brandon, *The Men and the Mountain* (N.Y., 1955), a dramatic account of the expedition which uses a number of the sources but is far from exhaustive.

Despite the rumors, which originated with Frémont and his family, there is no reliable evidence that the three survivors of the "rescue" party subsisted for a time on the body of King. For an important contribution to the question see Will C. Ferril, "The Sole Survivor," in *Rocky Mountain News,* Aug. 30, 1891, with Tom Breckenridge's fully detailed account of the movements of the "rescue" party, and his forthright written reply to Ferril's direct question concerning the alleged cannibalism.

probably not far east of the Rio Grande, and southwest of Mount Blanca, they were shot and killed. The preponderance of evidence seems to indicate that they were murdered by Utes, with the connivance of their own Mexican retainers. Despite rumors that their bodies were recovered, no reliable record has been found to support them.[62]

Bill Williams, lean and sinewy, stood six feet one in his moccasins, and possessed unusual strength. His facial features were small, his eyes steely blue, his face darkly weather-bronzed; his head was covered with a tangle of red hair, and he was usually well bearded.

He so excelled in the skills demanded by the trapping business that he became a legend in his own time. He was an excellent horseman, a tireless walker, an expert trailer, indefatigable in the pursuit of the beaver, and a tricky, unorthodox, effective fighter. His ability to snake himself, his animals, and his fur packs through dangerous Indian country commanded the admiration of his fellow Mountain Men. His way with Indians was uncanny. Despite the "double wabble" with which he handled his battered old Hawken rifle, he shot "plumb center." Under the prod of necessity his mental-physical co-ordination was extraordinary.

Bill Williams tagged his furs: "William S. Williams, M.T." (Master Trapper), and no one in the mountains could better claim the "degree." His traps and a sound business sense (he was a notoriously sharp trader when dealing with "company men") brought him handsome profits which he spent gambling, drinking, buying "fofarraw" for his wives and fair companions, and helping others.

Despite his high-pitched, cracked voice Williams was an impressive speaker, an able *raconteur,* and could be a superb

[62] B. L. Beal to I. H. Dickerson, Mar. 26 and May 1, 1849, Old Files Sec., Org. Div., Adj. Gen. Off., War Dept., Washington; *Daily Missouri Republican,* July 7, 1849; *Frémont's Fourth Expedition, op. cit.,* 171, 229-30; Louis B. Sporleder, Sr., The County of Huerfano (typescript), 306, Hist. Colls., Univ. of Colo., Boulder, Colo.

actor, sometimes playing the "typical" Mountain Man. Of a superior intelligence, with intellectual attainments, he did not fit the public image of a trapper. "An educated man with a critical knowledge of Greek and Latin," and an appreciation of good literature, an understanding of history, politics and comparative religion (he was, in fact, an experimenter with religions), he transcended the image. Also, he had a sound sense of humor, and was something of a practical joker.

The impression Williams allowed or even led others to gain of his apparent profound belief in Indian religious precepts and mythology, including atavism involving the bear and metempsychosis involving the elk, caused them to regard him as a congenital eccentric. How much of his "belief" was conviction and how much mere mental pose remains undetermined; however, the common idea that he was a superstitious ignoramus has been exploded.

Williams prepared a series of sketch maps of the mountain country he knew best, one of which was used as the basis for a section of an excellent official map. Besides his Osage primer and his rendering of scriptural English into the Navaho, he prepared an account of his experiences among the Apaches, Zunis, and Navahos. He sometimes kept a notebook; and he tried his hand at watercolor sketching. (All but the primer are lost.) Williams spoke frontier North Carolina-Missouri English, the Mountain Man's mixed idiom (which he helped construct), French, Spanish, and many Indian languages and dialects besides those mentioned.

Despite his tough, uncouth exterior, Williams' fondness for children, interest in young apprentice trappers, charity toward the less fortunate and, except when doubted, helpfulness to those seeking geographical information about the West, reveal his redeeming traits. Generally he was considered an honest man and a brave one, and rated a good man to have around in a tight spot. He was not a vicious man, as some later writers, without apparent reason, have averred, but an implacable, formidable foe when confronted by overt enmity.

Two portraits of Williams, an oil and a watercolor, were made by Edward M. Kern, neither of which has been found.[63]

---

[63] Documentation for the above statements is scattered through many fur trade sources, and a complete listing would extend far beyond our space. See particularly *Frémont's Fourth Expedition, op. cit.,* 143-46; Field, *loc. cit.; St. Louis Globe-Democrat, loc. cit.;* Ruxton, *op. cit.,* viii, 123-27.

William Lewis Sublette

by JOHN E. SUNDER
University of Texas

William Lewis Sublette, fur trader, explorer, businessman, banker, investor, politician, and progressive farmer, was born on September 21, 1799, probably in a large bedchamber on the second floor of his maternal grandparents' home a short distance from the Wilderness Road just south of Stanford, Kentucky.[1] William's mother, Isabella Whitley Sublette, was the daughter of Colonel William Whitley and Esther Fullen Whitley of Virginia. The Whitleys moved to Kentucky when Isabella was a small child, carved out a large frontier estate in Lincoln County, built a brick manor-house, and filled their household with children.

William's father, Phillip Allen Sublette, probably the son of Littleberry and Sarah Burton Sublette, was an ambitious Virginian from Chesterfield County, who sought his fortune in Kentucky and married into the prominent Whitley family. In the spring of 1801, Phillip and Isabella Sublette bundled up little William and moved south from Lincoln County to the tiny settlement of Somerset, Pulaski County, Kentucky, where Phillip opened an "ordinary" at "his dwelling house," speculated in land, held several county offices, and, as a loyal Jeffersonian Republican, served as postmaster between 1807 and 1810.[2] After ten years spent in Pulaski County, however, Phillip, Isabella, and the children – two sons, Milton and Andrew, and two daughters, Sophronia and Mary, were born in Somerset –

[1] For a fully annotated, book-length biography see John E. Sunder, *Bill Sublette Mountain Man,* published in 1959 by the University of Oklahoma Press.

[2] Orders No. 1, 1799-1803, p. 298, Pulaski County Court, Somerset, Kentucky.

returned to Lincoln County. Phillip farmed and opened a tavern at the Crab Orchard near the Whitley estate, and Isabella added three children, Sally, Pinckney and Solomon, to the Sublette brood.

In 1817 the Sublettes joined the heavy postwar migration west to Missouri and settled at the old French town of St. Charles near the junction of the Missouri and Mississippi rivers. Business was booming in Missouri, and Phillip, never a man to miss a business opportunity, plunged once again into tavern-keeping, was appointed a justice of the peace, dabbled in land, and provided his family a comfortable, although not lavish, home. In Missouri the Sublette boys grew into "large, fine looking men, of great strength and agility."[3] William was six feet two inches tall with sandy hair, fair skin and blue eyes. In St. Charles he followed in his father's footsteps by taking an interest in business, land and politics. He leased timberland which he improved by cutting trees into saleable rails and, in the spring of 1820, was appointed deputy constable of the township. Later he was appointed constable, and defended the job successfully by defeating two opponents in the election of August 1822.

Phillip Sublette died in 1820; Isabella two years later. William, unmarried and nearly penniless, his younger brothers and sisters placed in the care of relatives, completed the administration of his parents' estates and looked for a new job. The Missouri River, flowing below St. Charles, carried a steady stream of fur trappers and traders to Indian country, and any intelligent, enterprising young man who watched the river and read the local newspaper accounts of money made in furs saw good reason to follow the river west. William had spent his life close to the woods of Kentucky and Missouri where he learned to hunt, fish,

[3] LeRoy R. Hafen, "Mountain Men – Andrew W. Sublette," in *Colorado Magazine,* x (1933), 179-180.

ride, and make camp and, although he had little if any formal education, he was literate and equipped to take a job either as a trapper or a clerk in a likely looking fur venture.

In 1823, William Henry Ashley, Lieutenant Governor of Missouri, and Andrew Henry his business partner, were hiring trappers to go to the upper Missouri-Yellowstone country. Sublette resigned as constable, sold his bedstead for a dollar, and joined the unruly lot of men who comprised Ashley's keelboat party bound up the Missouri. Early in June, as the expedition pushed upriver, it was assaulted by Arikara Indians near the Arikara villages in South Dakota. Sublette saved his life by swimming from a sand beach below the villages to the boats in a barrage of arrows and shot. Two months later Ashley's party, reinforced by six companies of the United States Army, attacked the villages – Sublette served as sergeant major (a temporary rank) in the engagement – and routed the Indians.

Immediately after the battle, Ashley sent a small party under Jedediah Smith to blaze a new trappers' trail overland along the White River Valley and through the Black Hills to the Crow Indian country in Wyoming. Sublette accompanied Smith's party on the difficult late autumn journey and passed part of the winter encamped near the Crows in the Wind River Valley. In February 1824, Smith's party struck out to cross the Wind River Mountains, but the heavy snow forced them south to the Popo Agie. Sublette, for the second time within nine months, narrowly missed losing his life, this time in a blizzard, before he found shelter on the Sweetwater. In early March the small party divided for the spring hunt, and Sublette probably accompanied Smith's tiny group to Black's Fork of the Green. By mid-June the parties had reunited on the Sweetwater and sent their furs downstream to market.

For the next two years Sublette trapped the mountain

country. Following the June meeting on the Sweetwater, he, Smith, and five others crossed west over South Pass and swung through southwestern Wyoming and southeastern Idaho to the headwaters of the Blackfoot and, eventually, in November, reached Flathead Post, the Hudson's Bay Company station in northwestern Montana. They enjoyed British hospitality for the winter of 1824-1825, and in mid-March set out to struggle south through the snow drifts. By late May the snow had cleared and Smith's party joined another American group, under John H. Weber, encamped on Bear River. Deserters from a nearby camp of Peter Skene Ogden, the renowned Hudson's Bay Company brigade leader, turned over approximately 700 skins to the Americans, after which the Smith and Weber parties hunted the Bear River Valley through June and then headed for Henry's Fork of Green River where Ashley's parties were scheduled to meet (rendezvous) in July to exchange furs for supplies from the east.

The early July rendezvous brought Ashley nearly $50,000 in skins. He and fifty men, one of whom was probably Sublette, conveyed the furs to the Big Horn where water transportation was available. On the way a Blackfoot war party attacked a portion of Ashley's caravan and may have wounded Sublette slightly in the encounter. When Ashley transferred his fur to boats on the Big Horn, Sublette, with the pack horses and a few men, started back to the trapping country near the Green and Bear rivers. That winter he and other trappers gathered first in Cache Valley, then in more comfortable quarters near Salt Lake. In the spring they scattered to hunt the mountain streams before meeting Ashley – he left St. Louis in March, 1826, with the supply train – in rendezvous in Cache Valley.

While most of the trappers drank and gambled at the rendezvous, Ashley negotiated the transfer of his business to Smith, David E. Jackson, and Sublette. By written agreement of July 18, Ashley transferred his supplies in the mountains to the three partners, and they promised to market their fur with Ashley until the debt was paid. He agreed, if notified by March 1, 1827, to supply them at the next rendezvous. When the arrangements were completed he returned to Missouri with the fur catch, and the new partners returned to the fur grounds. Smith and fifteen men headed southwest and eventually reached California. Jackson and Sublette traded with the Indians in western Wyoming as far north as Yellowstone Lake and then went into winter camp in Cache Valley.

Sublette and Black Harris, a tough, experienced mountain man, left the camp on New Year's Day, 1827, and hiked east cross country to St. Louis to guarantee that Ashley would supply Smith, Jackson and Sublette at the 1827 rendezvous. Sublette reached St. Louis early in March and within three weeks was again on his way west, accompanied by his younger brother Pinckney (who was killed by Indians less than a year later), leading the supply train to the 1827 rendezvous.

Late in June the trappers met at Bear Lake, bringing furs valued at $60,000-70,000 on the eastern market. After the rendezvous, where, according to Jim Beckwourth, Sublette fought a battle with a large Blackfoot war party, Smith returned to California and Sublette trapped the Snake-Salmon River country. The following year, after the summer rendezvous of 1828 probably near Bear Lake, William took the year's fur returns to St. Louis and spent six busy months there before starting west with the annual supply caravan in March 1829.

The early July rendezvous on the Popo Agie was only a small gathering. Sublette sent the company clerk, Robert Campbell, to St. Louis with forty-five packs of fur and dashed to Pierre's Hole, below the west face of the Tetons, to meet Smith and Jackson in a second rendezvous. In the fall Sublette led a hunting party along Henrys Fork of the Snake through dangerous Blackfoot country to Missouri Lake. They crossed the Madison and Gallatin ranges to the east, moved south along the Big Horn, and made winter camp, with Smith's and Jackson's parties, on Wind River. In winter quarters the three leaders discussed the future of their barely solvent partnership and decided to outfit a hunt in 1830. Immediately, Sublette, joined once again by Black Harris, set out overland for Missouri and reached St. Louis in mid-February.

He organized quickly a supply caravan, including ten mule-drawn wagons and two dearborns, and by June was well on his way west along the Blue and Platte rivers. Although each wagon weighed 1800 pounds and at times had to be hoisted over embankments, the caravan safely reached the mid-July rendezvous near the junction of the Wind and Popo Agie and created quite a sensation among the trappers, most of whom never expected to see wagons in the mountains. At the rendezvous Smith, Jackson and Sublette sold out to five hardy mountaineers, Thomas Fitzpatrick, Jim Bridger, Milton Sublette, Henry Fraeb, and Jean Baptiste Gervais, for approximately $16,000. Sublette, anxious to escape the financial uncertainties of the mountain trade and to return to civilization, left the rendezvous with the wagon train on August 4 and reached St. Louis two months later.

During the fall he settled his outstanding accounts and, in cooperation with Smith and Jackson, wrote a long, historically important letter to the Secretary of War emphasizing the possibility of wagon transportation to the Oregon country. Then, he settled down to a winter of relaxation in St. Louis. Early in the spring, however, he bought 779 acres of excellent land a few miles west of St. Louis and, together with Smith, Jackson and several small investors, gathered twenty-three wagon loads of goods to carry to Santa Fe.

Sublette, however, was disappointed by the southwestern overland trade. The trail to and from Santa Fe was long, dry and dangerous. Hostile Indians threatened the caravan frequently, Smith was killed by Comanches on the Cimarron, and in Santa Fe Jackson left the party for California. When Sublette returned to St. Louis in October, he took rooms at the City Hotel and spent the fall and winter discussing business with Ashley and others, caring for his new farm, and preparing the supply train he had promised the Rocky Mountain Fur Company (Fitzpatrick, Bridger, Sublette, Fraeb, and Gervais) he would lead to the 1832 rendezvous.

On May 13, 1832, Sublette's party left Independence bound for the Teton country, accompanied by a party of adventurers led by Nathaniel Wyeth. The expedition made good time along the Platte and Sweetwater, lost a few horses in an Indian skirmish in the foothills of the Wind River range, and encamped briefly below the Three Tetons early in July before crossing the mountains to a ten day rendezvous in Pierre's Hole. Shortly after Wyeth and Milton Sublette broke camp to leave the rendezvous they stumbled upon a large band of Blackfeet Indians. William and the other trappers remaining in Pierre's Hole rushed to assist Wyeth and Milton Sublette and engaged the Indians in battle in a willow swamp. William was shot in the left arm. The Blackfeet fled the battleground under cover of darkness, and William, his arm in a sling, returned to St. Louis with his old friend and companion in battle, Robert Campbell, and 169 packs of beaver.

At his farm (Sulphur Springs) near St. Louis he and Campbell worked out the details of a business partnership and in December 1832, left for the East to arrange credit and goods needed to enter the Upper Missouri River fur trade. In April they returned to St. Louis and took out a federal license permitting them to participate in the Indian country trade. They planned to build fur trading posts at several locations on the Upper Missouri to compete with John Jacob Astor's colossal American Fur Company. Campbell proceeded to the summer rendezvous to undersell the American Fur Company suppliers while Sublette took a keelboat up the Missouri to the mouth of the Yellowstone where Campbell met him late in August with proceeds from the mountain meeting. Sublette returned to St. Louis with the keelboat loaded with fur, leaving Campbell to complete construction of a trading post, Ft. William, near the junction of the Missouri and Yellowstone rivers.[4]

After a few weeks' rest at Sulphur Springs, Sublette traveled east and early in the year 1834, drew up an agreement with the American Fur Company whereby Sublette and Campbell relinquished their Upper Missouri trade and the American Fur Company agreed to leave the mountain fur trade for one year. Evidently, Sublette and Campbell had decided, before they parted on the Yellowstone late in the summer of 1833, to work diligently during the winter to force the opposition to conclude an agreement. Campbell kept up a strong winter competition with Astor's upriver posts while Sublette, having convinced Astor's representatives that he had won unlimited credit and might continue indefinitely to oppose them on the Missouri, frightened them into partitioning the fur country.

When he returned to St. Louis early in 1834, he organized immediately a supply train for the next mountain rendezvous and by April was headed west. At the mouth of Laramie Fork of the North Platte he laid the foundation of a new trading post, Fort William, and pushed on over South Pass to the rendezvous on Ham's Fork of the Green. The Rocky Mountain Fur Company repudiated its contract to

[4] George R. Brooks (ed.), "The Private Journal of Robert Campbell," in *Bulletin of the Missouri Historical Society,* XX, no. 1 (October 1963), 1-24, and XX, no. 2 (January 1964), 107-118.

buy supplies from Wyeth, who was also at the rendezvous, and, instead, purchased them of Sublette. Before the end of July, Sublette was in St. Louis again with approximately seventy packs of beaver from the rendezvous. Campbell was waiting for him, and during the fall, while Sublette oversaw construction of a large home at Sulphur Springs, they examined the future prospects of their business partnership.

Sublette spent most of the year 1835 in St. Louis. In the spring Campbell led a small party to Ft. William on the Laramie where he transferred the post to Fitzpatrick, Bridger and Milton Sublette and then returned to St. Louis with several packs of buffalo robes to supply the growing robe market. Sublette remained at his farm, while Campbell was in the West, and nursed his brother Milton who was suffering from a "bone tumor of lowgrade malignancy."[5] Later in the year Campbell traveled to Philadelphia to visit his relatives for the winter; Sublette made a business trip to western Missouri and prepared his younger brother Solomon for a mercantile career.

National prosperity continued into the year of 1836. Campbell returned from the east and renewed his business partnership with Sublette. They purchased a brick store, opposite the St. Louis branch of the United States Bank, and advertised a large stock of dry goods and other items for sale, wholesale and retail. During the next few years they increased the variety of stock; sold to many buyers in towns along the Ohio, Mississippi, and Lower Missouri rivers; and, generally, although new in the mercantile trade, prospered from the business. At least until 1840 they continued to invest in the fur trade, sold fur received from the West, and speculated in land.

[5] R. W. Gaul, "Death of the Thunderbolt: Some Notes on the Final Illness of Milton Sublette," in *Bulletin of the Missouri Historical Society,* XVIII, no. 1 (October 1961), 36.

A few months after they extended their partnership for a second time, in 1839, the depression, set off by the Panic of 1837, struck the St. Louis area. Trade declined alarmingly at the Sublette and Campbell store, credit was tight, and the partners were forced by the economic pinch to bring suit in at least fifteen counties against former customers indebted to them. Finally, on January 15, 1842, they dissolved their partnership, and Campbell purchased the goods and furnishings remaining in the store.

Sublette now gave more and more attention to Sulphur Springs and to politics. He was a strong supporter of Senator Thomas Hart Benton and the Jackson-Van Buren administrations, and in 1837 had been selected by the Legislature of Missouri to serve on the board of directors of the new Bank of the State of Missouri. In 1840, however, he was dropped from the board, possibly because of his hard money views. Campbell was placed on the board when Sublette was removed, was re-elected in December, 1842 – Sublette was returned to the board at that time – and became president of the board in 1846, seventeen months after Sublette's death.

In addition to his service on the bank board and his mercantile activity, Sublette participated as an investor in the organiaztion of the St. Louis Insurance Company, the Marine Insurance Company, and the St. Louis Hotel Company, all chartered by the Legislature of Missouri in 1837. He was seen frequently at political gatherings and dinners in St. Louis, at meetings of the Central Fire Company, and in torchlight processions. In 1838 he fought hard for a seat in the Missouri State Senate, but was defeated by the Whig candidate, John F. Darby. Although Sublette worked for the Democratic Party in 1839 and 1840, he refused to run again for any office.

His friends enjoyed the hospitality of his attractive, expensively furnished home overlooking the tiny River des

Peres at Sulphur Springs.[6] Slaves and hired farm laborers tilled the fields of grain and vegetables and worked in the large orchard. Sublette purchased the best varieties of seed and plants available and was one of the most progressive farmers in the St. Louis area. He raised pedigreed shorthorn cattle, from stock imported directly from England, and collected a menagerie of buffalo, deer, antelope, bear, and wild birds. His sister, Sophronia Sublette Cook, was in charge of housekeeping at Sulphur Springs after she divorced Grove Cook in 1840, and William's brother, Andrew Sublette, also lived at the farm for several years.

In addition to grain and vegetables, fruit and livestock, the farm produced coal, ice and lumber. Between 1835 and 1840 Sublette opened three coal deposits and contracted with various miners to extract the coal for shipment from Sulphur Springs to St. Louis. He also marketed cordwood and lumber, and in the winter cut and stored ice for his own use in the warmer months and for sale to neighbors. Since the roads linking Sulphur Springs to St. Louis were his lifeline to his downtown store, to market, and to "divrs & Sunday Balls & parties," he supported local road improvement projects and advised the county on road conditions.[7]

To profit from the spring water at the farm which was believed to be therapeutic, he built a hotel and several guest cottages to accommodate visitors, leased the improvements to business managers, and laid out a race track near the spa. Unfortunately, the resort managers were poor, and Sublette could not rely on any one of them until Dr. Thomas Hereford, an Alabama physician, leased the business in 1842 and settled his large family at the farm. Two years later, in

6 The only known illustration of Sublette's home at Sulphur Springs appears in a watercolor painting made by the artist Albert J. F. Muegge. The painting has been reproduced as Plate IV in George R. Brooks, "Some New Views of Old Cheltenham," in *Bulletin of the Missouri Historical Society,* XXII, no. 1 (October 1965).

7 William L. Sublette to Robert Campbell, January 30, 1836, Campbell Papers, Missouri Historical Society, St. Louis.

March 1844, his eldest daughter, dark, attractive Frances Hereford, married Sublette at the farm in an evening service conducted by Rev. William S. Potts, a prominent Presbyterian minister. Sublette was not a member of the Presbyterian church, although he believed in predestination.

A few months before his marriage he and his old friend Sir William Drummond Stewart shared command of a pleasure party that visited Wyoming to savor once again the rendezvous-land of the fur trade. The expedition was large, well-supplied, and included men of many occupations, talents, and temperaments. They followed the Platte-Sweetwater route to the Green River Valley where a few trappers and numerous Indians met them for several days of carousing and trade. The rendezvous broke up in mid-August, and the Stewart-Sublette party headed home. At Ash Hollow on the Platte, Sublette filled his traveling companions with apple brandy in honor of his birthday on September 21. By early November he was at Sulphur Springs where the eminent physician, Dr. William Beaumont, examined him and told him that his health was poor.

Despite Dr. Beaumont's warning, Sublette returned to his political battles – this time for unity within the Missouri Democratic Party. The Hard and Soft (money) factions of the party disagreed violently over the ticket to be presented in 1844. In April Sublette served as a Hard delegate from St. Louis County to the tumultuous state convention and, since unity had failed, threw his support to the faction supporting Senator Benton. In the summer, shortly after the Democratic National Convention nominated Polk and Dallas as principal standardbearers of the party, one of the Democratic electors in Missouri denounced the national ticket. The state party leaders asked Sublette to serve as elector for the seventh district. He accepted and, a few weeks after Polk and Dallas carried Missouri in the fall election, cast his electoral ballot at Jefferson City.

His health remained precarious throughout 1844 while he devoted much of his time to his real estate, particularly to a large tract of land he and friends held on the site of Kansas City. Scores of business and political associates petitioned the President and the War Department to appoint him Superintendent of Indian Affairs at St. Louis. He waited at Sulphur Springs until July 1845 – waited to receive the appointment which never came – and then decided to take his wife to Cape May, New Jersey, for the remainder of the summer. On the way east he became seriously ill, and on July 23 died of tuberculosis at the Exchange Hotel in downtown Pittsburgh. His remains were returned by steamboat to St. Louis for burial at the farm on August 8, and several years later were reinterred beneath a tall granite shaft in Bellefontaine Cemetery, St. Louis.

Thomas Fitzpatrick

by LEROY R. and ANN W. HAFEN
Provo, Utah

The Irish-American Thomas Fitzpatrick was a native of County Cavan, born in 1799. Of his early years we know little, except that he was of a Catholic family and that he had the fundamentals of a good education, as his later well-written prose testifies.[1] He was destined to be a leader in the fur trade of the West, and as that business declined he carved out two other successive careers – as a guide and then as Indian Agent – being outstanding in both.

Before he was seventeen Fitzpatrick came to America,

---

1 For an account of his life see LeRoy R. Hafen and W. J. Ghent, *Broken Hand; the Life Story of Thomas Fitzpatrick, Chief of the Mountain Men* (Denver, 1931). Much new material has come to light since the publication of this first work on Fitzpatrick, and an amplified biography is being undertaken by the writer of this sketch.

"Broken Hand" was the name by which he was known among the Indians, according to John C. Frémont, who says "one of his hands having been shattered by the bursting of his gun." – Frémont's *Report of the Exploring Expedition to the Rocky Mountains, etc.* (Washington, 1845), 41. Another account of the incident was published in the *St. Louis News-Letter* and reprinted in the *Jefferson* (Mo.) *Inquirer* of Dec. 25, 1847. The fantastic story comes from a Mr. Sarpy, alleged companion of Fitzpatrick in an adventure that is said to have occurred in 1835.

Fitzpatrick was pursued by Blackfeet Indians, says Sarpy, and on coming suddenly to the Yellowstone River, Fitzpatrick and his horse took a leap from a 40-foot cliff into the river and swam across. The Indians continued pursuit and Fitzpatrick "in his haste to pull off the cover [from his rifle] by some mismanagement received the contents of his piece in his left wrist, which was frightfully shattered from the discharge. Nothing daunted by the accident, he reloaded and fired, killing two of his pursuers before he left the spot. He then made for the woods, and dodged his enemies for some days." No account is given of the treatment of the wound. "Thirty days after this adventure, he got up with Mr. Sarpy, and gave him the details of this extraordinary escape." No other substantiation of this story has been found.

The early family data on Fitzpatrick – distressingly scant – came in letters to LeRoy R. Hafen from Fitzpatrick's daughter Virginia, dated June 7 and September 24, 1928, from El Reno, Oklahoma; and from his grand niece, Mrs. M. C. McCarthy of Washingon, D.C., Mar. 14, 1929.

and was soon in the Middle West, apparently engaged in the Indian trade. He accompanied the Ashley expedition of 1823 up the Missouri River and was involved in the Arikara fight and the subsequent Leavenworth fiasco. Following the collapse of the Ashley-Henry trade venture on the upper Missouri, Fitzpatrick and Jedediah Smith led a small detachment overland to present Wyoming and wintered near the Crows in Wind River Valley.[2] Learning from the Indians of good beaver country in Green River Valley, and of a feasible route leading thereto, the party crossed South Pass and began profitable trapping in the virgin territory. Upon division of the company, Fitzpatrick led one group up Green River. They fared well, soon accumulating packs of prime pelts. Supposedly friendly Shoshones ran off with their horses, which the white men subsequently recovered, and loading the animals with their packs recrossed South Pass. At the appointed meeting with Jedediah Smith it was agreed that Fitzpatrick carry the furs back to Missouri, while Smith with most of the men continue trapping.

Encouraged by a rise in the Sweetwater, Fitzpatrick and his two companions built a bullboat, loaded their furs in it, and commenced their voyage. Rapids and other difficulties induced them to abandon boat, cache their furs, and make their way eastward on foot. After a difficult journey they finally reached Fort Atkinson on the Missouri. Fitzpatrick wrote to Ashley at St. Louis, telling of the wonderful trapping grounds in Green River Valley and urging him to come with a large party to reap the harvest. Then Fitzpatrick hired pack horses, returned up the Platte, uncached his furs and brought them back to the Missouri.

Meanwhile Ashley responded in the fall of 1824 and came out with ample supplies and trade goods. Guided by Fitzpatrick, the party reached Green River in April. Ash-

2 The story of these general events is told and documented in the "Brief History of the Fur Trade of the Far West" in this *Series*, I, pp. 77-88.

ley divided his party into trapping groups, appointed a site where all were to rendezvous in early July, and himself floated down Green River in a bullboat to search out beaver country.

Fitzpatrick led a small party up Rendezvous Creek (Henry's Fork of Green River) and trapped the streams running north from the Uinta Mountains. They joined Ashley and the other groups at the fur trade rendezvous, the first of the sixteen annual gatherings now famous in fur trade history. The Ashley account books recording trade have this item: "140 Fitzpatrick." Whether this was Fitzpatrick's personal catch or that of his party is not clear.

Fitzpatrick's activity during the next year or two cannot be traced in detail. Jim Beckwourth, in Fitzpatrick's party, tells of a theft of horses from the white men encamped near Great Salt Lake. After a pursuit of several days the trappers came upon the Indian camp. Says Beckwourth:

> We then divided our forces, Fitzpatrick taking command of one party and James Bridger the other. The plan resolved upon was as follows: Fitzpatrick was to charge the Indians, and cover Bridger's party while they stampeded all the horses they could get away with . . . we rushed in upon the horses and stampeded from two to three hundred, Fitzpatrick at the same time engaging the Indians . . . we succeeded in getting off with the number of our own missing, and forty head besides. In the engagement, six of the enemy were killed and scalped, while not one of our party received a scratch.[3]

Fitzpatrick appears to have been with William Sublette in 1826-27 and was at the rendezvous of 1827 and 1828 at the south end of Bear Lake. After the latter gathering he accompanied David E. Jackson to the Flathead country and served him as clerk. Joshua Pilcher was there too, but neither of the American parties made much headway against the veteran Hudson's Bay Company, already well

[3] T. D. Bonner, *The Life and Adventures of James P. Beckwourth* (New York, 1931), 60-61.

entrenched with the Flatheads. Governor George Simpson reported at Fort Vancouver on March 1, 1829:

> Jackson, accompanied by Clerk Fitzpatrick, and a Major Pilcher with a Clerk Gardner and 40 trappers . . . visited the Flathead Post last Winter; they had very few Skins, and of those few, about half fell into our hands in exchange for necessary supplies. . . "The Major" and Smith Jackson and Siblit, are in hot opposition to each other, and both court our protection and countenance, while we contrive to profit by their strife.[4]

While Fitzpatrick and Jackson were with the Flatheads in the spring of 1829 they were delighted to welcome at their camp Jedediah Smith after his hazardous experiences in California and Oregon. Together they worked their way southward. Then Fitzpatrick rode to meet William Sublette, bringing out the supply caravan of 1829. They met on the Popo Agie branch of Wind River, where a July rendezvous was held with some of the trappers. Then Fitzpatrick guided Sublette westward to a meeting with partners Jackson and Smith at Pierre's Hole, where a second rendezvous of 1829 was held.

For the fall hunt Fitzpatrick accompanied Sublette on a trapping tour northward to the headwaters of the Missouri. En route they ran into hostile Blackfeet who tried to stampede the trappers' horse herd. But as Joe Meek relates it, the Indians were

> too hasty by a few minutes . . . only a few of the animals had been turned out, and they had not yet got far off. The noise of the charge only turned them back to camp.
>
> In an instant's time, Fitzpatrick was mounted, and commanding the men to follow, he galloped at headlong speed round and round the camp, to drive back such of the horses as were straying, or had been frightened from their pickets. In this race, two horses were shot under him; but he escaped and the camp-horses were saved.[5]

---

[4] Simpson's report quoted in Maurice S. Sullivan, *The Travels of Jedediah Smith* (Santa Ana, Calif., 1934), 26.

[5] F. F. Victor, *The River of the West* (Hartford, Conn. 1870), 70.

On Christmas Day 1829, Sublette and Moses Harris set out with a train of pack dogs and snowshoes for St. Louis to obtain supplies. Fitzpatrick presumably continued with Jackson, who went to Powder River and later moved south to the summer rendezvous at the junction of the Popo Agie and Wind River. Here they met William Sublette with his train of provisions and trade goods, this time hauled in ten wagons.

At this rendezvous of 1830 Smith, Jackson and Sublette sold their mountain fur interests to five of their most competent brigade leaders – Fitzpatrick, James Bridger, Milton Sublette, Henry Fraeb and Jean B. Gervais. These were to operate under the firm name Rocky Mountain Fur Company, of which Fitzpatrick was the acknowledged head. The five men were capable trappers and brigade leaders, but were inexperienced business men who would encounter difficulties in meeting the competition of Astor and his great financial assets.

While Fraeb and Gervais led thirty-three men into the Snake River area, Fitzpatrick and the other two partners with a strong band of eighty men ventured into the fur-rich Blackfeet country. They trapped the Three Forks region, wintered on the Yellowstone, and worked the Powder River area.

In early March 1831, Fitzpatrick took one man and headed for St. Louis to obtain the annual goods. When he reached Missouri in May the expected suppliers, Smith, Jackson, and Sublette, having decided to enter the caravan trade to Santa Fe, were already en route to New Mexico. Fitzpatrick had little choice but to accompany the partners to Santa Fe and there receive the wanted supplies. This round-about route caused a costly delay, for Fitzpatrick was not able to pack his goods until early July – at a time when he should have been unpacking them at rendezvous. Finally he pointed his forty-man pack train northward along the front range of the Rockies.

In the meantime, Fitzpatrick's partners had completed their spring hunt and were waiting restively for the expected supplies. Finally Fraeb, after consulting a Crow medicine man and being told that the bourgeois was on the wrong road, set out to find his delayed partner. After the two met on the North Platte, Fitzpatrick turned over the goods to Fraeb and then headed back to Missouri to be certain that next year's supplies would arrive at rendezvous on time.

Back in St. Louis for the winter of 1831-32, Fitzpatrick was in a difficult position. His Rocky Mountain Fur Company had been unable to get its furs to market in 1831, and the credit of the company was low. The best Fitzpatrick could do was to make a deal with William Sublette on the latter's terms. Sublette would bring a train of goods out to rendezvous and advance Fitzpatrick some cash and credit.[6] During the winter Fitzpatrick's partners carried on trapping operations, but found themselves harrassed and pursued by American Fur Company men, now aggressively competing in the field.

When the supply train of 1832 reached the upper North Platte, Fitzpatrick raced ahead to carry to rendezvous news of the approach of supplies. With two fleet horses, which he rode alternately, he pushed confidently forward. But beyond South Pass he was pursued by Gros Ventres. Abandoning his horses on a steep hill and hiding in a hole in the rocks, he escaped immediate capture. But his sufferings had only begun. In crossing a flooded stream he lost his gun and equipment. Hungry days and sleepless nights wore away his strength until he finally collapsed. In this helpless condition he was found and rescued by two men sent out from the rendezvous to search for him. In his emaciated condition he was hardly recognizable. The experience seems to have grayed his hair and he was later referred to as "White

6 Letter of William Sublette to W. H. Ashley from Independence, Mo., May 12, 1832, Campbell Papers, Missouri Hist. Soc., St. Louis.

Hair."[7] With food and safety Fitzpatrick rapidly recovered.

Sublette and the supplies had already arrived and with the Rocky Mountain Fur men, several independent parties, and Indian allies the rendezvous was one of the largest held in the mountains. Before the breakup it was further distinguished by the notable Battle of Pierre's Hole. After the beginning of the conflict the Indians withdrew behind breastworks in a jungle of willows. Fitzpatrick, recovered from his late ordeal, was, according to Leonard, commander-in-chief of the attacking force; but the undisciplined trappers mainly followed their own inclinations. In the late afternoon a false report drew the men back to their undefended main camp, and when they returned to the fray, darkness had settled down. During the night the Indians escaped, leaving their dead and some equipment. Among the abandoned horses Fitzpatrick was happy to find the two he had lost to these Indians on his perilous ride.

For the fall trapping, 1832, Fitzpatrick and Bridger led their men to the upper branches of Clark's Fork and the Missouri River, being dogged by American Fur Company men. When the two companies got into Blackfoot country both were attacked. Bridger was wounded with two arrows and W. H. Vanderburgh, leader of the opposition forces, was killed.

After wintering on Salmon River, Fitzpatrick and his men did well in spring trapping. He wrote to Robert Campbell on June 4th from the North Platte that he had a party of sixty men under his command, and had "done very well so far this hunt I put in cache a few days ago 40 packs of good fur."[8]

---

[7] The fullest account of the ordeal is given, presumably in Fitzpatrick's own words, in *Adventures of Zenas Leonard, Fur Trader,* edited by J. C. Ewers (Norman, 1959), 36-40.

[8] Letter of Fitzpatrick to Robert Campbell, in the Campbell Papers, Missouri Hist. Soc. A copy was supplied to me by Mr. Dale L. Morgan. In the letter Fitzpatrick asks Campbell to send a book or two, "such as you know would suit me."

Robert Campbell brought out the supply train for the summer rendezvous, held this year in the lush Green River Valley near present Daniel, Wyoming.[9] After the breakup of the summer trade fair, Fitzpatrick and Milton Sublette helped Campbell take the furs to the Bighorn River, whence Campbell and Milton boated the skins to St. Louis. Nathaniel Wyeth also accompanied the boats.

Fitzpatrick and Milton Sublette made a contract with Wyeth to bring out their goods to the rendezvous by July 1, 1834. Neither party was certain of its ability to fulfill the agreement, but in case of inability each was to notify the other and the party that defaulted was to forfeit $500.[10]

With the furs safely embarked on Bighorn River, Fitzpatrick with his band of twenty or thirty trappers and over one hundred horses moved eastward to work the Powder and Tongue rivers. Here they were robbed by the Crows, apparently encouraged by agents of the American Fur Company.[11] Fitzpatrick fled this country and crossed over to Green River Valley.

Wyeth carried supplies to the rendezvous of 1834, but William Sublette, learning of the agreement with Wyeth, hurried a pack horse train westward and reached the rendezvous first. There Sublette, as principal creditor, pressured the Rocky Mountain Fur men into accepting his goods and dissolving the company. They refused to accept the goods Wyeth had brought out, but they did pay the $500 forfeit.[12] Disappointed, Wyeth thereupon took his trade

9 Elliott Coues, ed., *Forty Years a Fur Trader on the Upper Missouri, the Personal Narrative of Charles Larpenteur, 1838-1872* (New York, 1899), 15-16.

10 The agreement is in the Sublette Papers, Missouri Hist. Soc.

11 Washington Irving, *The Adventures of Captain Bonneville,* ed. by E. W. Todd (Norman, 1961), 178, 207. Fitzpatrick's letter to W. H. Ashley, now congressman from Missouri, and also his letter of Nov. 13, 1833, to Milton Sublette, both found in the Sublette Papers, Missouri Hist. Soc.

12 The original papers are in the Sublete Collection, Missouri Hist. Soc. See also Wyeth's letter of July 1, 1834, in "The Correspondence and Journals of Captain Nathaniel J. Wyeth," in *Sources of the History of Oregon* (Eugene, 1899), 138.

goods on to the Snake River and there established Fort Hall. On August 3rd Fitzpatrick, Bridger and Milton Sublette joined Fontenelle and Drips to form Fontenelle, Fitzpatrick, and Company, which later obtained a trading license.[13] While Bridger and Drips conducted operations in the mountains, Fitzpatrick and Fontenelle took the furs to the States.

During the winter, which Fitzpatrick must have spent in Missouri, he and his partners bought from William Sublette and Robert Campbell their Fort William on the Laramie River. Campbell, and apparently Fitzpatrick, went out in the spring of 1835 and effected the transfer of the fort. Fitzpatrick was still at the post when the supply caravan of fifty or sixty men, six wagons, and two hundred horses, led by Fontenelle and accompanied by missionaries Marcus Whitman and Samuel Parker, arrived on July 26.[14] Fontenelle remained at the fort while Fitzpatrick conducted the train to rendezvous and back again to Fort William. The two leaders again exchanged positions, Fontenelle hauling the furs eastward.

Fitzpatrick remained at the fort trading with the Sioux until January 3, 1836, when he made a mid-winter trip to St. Louis[15] and obtained backing from Pierre Chouteau, Jr., for another venture in the mountains.[16] He conducted the trade caravan up the Platte River Road, reluctantly escorting the Whitman-Spaulding missionary party toward Oregon. Joshua Pilcher, representing the American Fur Company, joined the caravan and accompanied it to rendezvous. There he purchased for his company the assets of Fontenelle,

[13] Letter of William Clark listing licenses he issued, Indian Archives, Washington, D.C.

[14] "Journal and Report of Dr. Marcus Whitman," etc., in *Oregon Historical Quarterly*, XXVIII, pp. 239-57. A good account of the journey is also given by Parker in his *Journal of an Exploring Tour, etc.* (Ithaca, N.Y., 1844).

[15] Sublette's letter to Campbell, Feb. 27 and 29, 1836, Missouri Hist. Soc.

[16] See Fitzpatrick's letter of March 18, 1836, to Pierre Chouteau, Jr. in the Chouteau-Papin Collection, Missouri Hist. Soc.

Fitzpatrick and Co., including their fort on the Laramie[17] and hired on an annual basis Fitzpatrick and the other leaders.

Fitzpatrick and Milton Sublette returned with the furs from rendezvous to the fort on the Laramie,[18] where Milton remained as major domo, while Fitzpatrick continued on to the Missouri River with the furs. He was back to the mountains again by March[19] and was apparently at Fort Laramie when his partner Milton Sublette died there on April 5, 1837. Fitzpatrick led the supply caravan consisting of forty-five men and twenty carts to the summer rendezvous of 1837.[20] Sir William Drummond Stewart and his artist Alfred Jacob Miller accompanied the train. W. H. Gray, Oregon missionary who was at the rendezvous, tells of the arrival of the goods on July 18th and gives a jaundiced account of the celebration.[21]

It is well nigh impossible, from available records, to follow Fitzpatrick through the next year or two. He appears to have taken the train with the furs back to the States following rendezvous 1837; he was probably with traders on the South Platte in 1838 and 1839. Jim Beckwourth says that Fitzpatrick and Andrew Sublette took furs from Fort Vasquez on the South Platte to St. Louis.[22]

When Dr. F. A. Wislizenus visited Fort Vasquez on September 3, 1839, he wrote: "I met the well-known Fitzpatrick, who has passed through many an adventure during his life in the mountains. He has a spare, bony figure, a face full of expression, and white hair; his whole demeanor

17 A. B. and D. P. Hulbert, *Marcus Whitman, Crusader* (Denver, 1936), 230-31.

18 Here Fitzpatrick signed drafts on August 15 paying off some of the men.—Papers in the Chouteau-Papin Collection, Missouri Hist. Soc.

19 *Robert Newell's Memoranda,* ed. by Dorothy O. Johansen (Portland, 1959), 67.

20 A. L. Haines, ed., *Osborne Russell's Journal of a Trapper* (Portland, 1955), 60.

21 "Journal of W. H. Gray," in *Whitman College Quarterly* (June 1913), 55, 59-61.

22 T. D. Bonner, *op. cit.,* 300.

reveals strong passions."[23] Then Fitzpatrick drops from the records again, to appear next in a new role.

The small rendezvous of 1840 was the last of the picturesque gatherings of trappers in the central Rockies. The beaver trade had faded out, and Thomas Fitzpatrick had seen it come and go. He had also escorted the early missionaries to the Rockies and Oregon. Now he was to witness the natural consequence of the fur trader and missionary penetration. The first covered wagon company of west-bound homeseekers was forming on the border of Missouri. These enthusiastic but green emigrants needed a seasoned Mountain Man and trusted leader to pilot them to a new land. Thomas Fitzpatrick was their man.

That first emigrant party to trek the trail to Oregon and California joined the first Catholic missionary band headed in the same direction in 1841. Thomas Fitzpatrick served as guide for both. "And it was well that we [he] did [writes John Bidwell], for otherwise probably not one of us would ever have reached California."[24] As the caravan moved along, the guide rode ahead selecting the route, choosing camping places, and managing generally. "Every day I learned to appreciate him more," wrote Father DeSmet.[25] Fitzpatrick safeguarded the party during a buffalo stampede and helped them across the North Platte River.

After escorting the missionaries to their destination in northern Idaho, Fitzpatrick returned to the central Rockies. Here, near Fort Laramie he joined the second Oregon-bound emigrant train. "I am now in an Indian country," wrote Dr. Elijah White, the leader of the party, "with foes on every hand, subtle as the devil himself; but our party is large and strong, and I have been able to obtain the services

---

[23] Adolphus Wislizenus, *A Journey to the Rocky Mountains in the Year 1839*, translated from the German (St. Louis, 1912), 137.

[24] John Bidwell, *Echoes of the Past about California* (Chicago, 1928), 6.

[25] H. M. Chittenden and A. T. Richardson, *Life, Letters, and Travels of Father Pierre-Jean DeSmet, S.J.* (New York, 1905), 1465.

of Mr. Fitz Patrick, one of the ablest and most suitable men in the country in conducting us to Fort Hall, beyond the point of danger from savages."[26]

Fitzpatrick proved his ability as a diplomat in dealing with the Indians. J. C. Fremont in recounting the experience, wrote: "I have no doubt that the emigrants owe their lives to Mr. Fitzpatric."[27] After getting the party safely to Fort Hall, Fitzpatrick returned to the States, but had a dangerous brush with the Pawnees en route.

In the spring of 1843 Fitzpatrick was employed by J. C. Fremont as guide for his second and longest expedition. They set out from Kansas Landing in late May, taking a course south of the Oregon Trail. On June 16th Fremont divided his party, and himself hurried ahead to Fort St. Vrain. This was the first of several times that Fremont divided his party and went off on exploring tours while he left Fitzpatrick to lead the main group and conduct the carts and baggage. Upon reaching the South Platte forts, Fitzpatrick found that Fremont had obtained more horses and had induced Kit Carson to join the expedition.

While Fremont tried a new route up the Cache la Poudre and went on to examine Great Salt Lake, Fitzpatrick led the main force to Fort Hall. After reuniting, they pushed on to Fort Boise and then over the Blue Mountains and to The Dalles. After Fremont went down to Fort Vancouver and returned with supplies and additional horses the company moved southward in late November. From western Nevada they made a difficult crossing over the snow-covered Sierra and reached the safety of Sutter's Fort. With new supplies they rode through the San Joaquin Valley, recrossed the range, intercepted the Old Spanish Trail and followed into central Utah. They continued over the moun-

26 A. J. Allen, *Ten Years in Oregon, etc.* (Ithaca, 1848), 153.

27 J. C. Frémont, *Report of Exploring Expedition, op. cit.*, 41.

tains and to Bent's Fort and on to Missouri by the end of July 1844.[28]

In the spring of 1845 Fitzpatrick joined S. W. Kearny and the First Dragoons as guide for a tour to the mountains. The handsomely equipped cavalry was to impress the Indians and practice a march preliminary to the Mexican War, now anticipated. They rode the Oregon Trail to South Pass and turned south to Bent's Fort, where Fitzpatrick was detached for service with J. W. Abert. After reaching Fort Leavenworth, Colonel Kearny suggested to the War Department an exploring tour and wrote: "I would respectfully recommend for that purpose Mr. Thomas Fitzpatrick, who was our guide during the late expedition, an excellent woodsman – one who has been much west of the mountains, and who has a good, if not a better, knowledge of that country than any other man in existence." [29]

Fitzpatrick joined Abert and served him as guide and general manager of the train. The party of thirty-two men, with four wagons and sixty-three horses and mules, moved south from Bent's Fort and traversed the dangerous Comanche country of the Canadian River region. At the end of the tour Abert wrote this tribute to Fitzpatrick:

> Having spent many of the best years of his life exposed to the toils and vicissitudes of the mountain and the prairie, he had acquired an intimate knowledge of the Indian character, which enabled him to conduct our little party safely and successfully through a country inhabited by numerous and powerful hordes of people, long notorious for their faithlessness and treachery. . . The preservation of our party was due to his vigilance and discretion.[30]

Difficulties with Mexico resulted in war in the spring of

---

28 *Ibid.*

29 S. W. Kearny's "Report of a Summer Campaign to the Rocky Mountains," etc., in *Sen. Ex. Doc. 1,* 29 Cong., 1 sess., p. 213.

30 "Journal of Lieutenant J. W. Abert, from Bent's Fort to St. Louis, 1845," in *Sen. Ex. Doc. 438,* 29 Cong., 1 sess., p. 6.

1846. Ahead of the American troops on the Santa Fe Trail went some trader caravans, one of them suspected of carrying arms to New Mexico. Fitzpatrick was employed to guide Captain Moore and a detachment sent in pursuit of the traders. Failing to catch up with the party before it crossed the Arkansas boundary, Fitzpatrick and Moore's troops stopped at Bent's Fort to await the coming of Colonel Kearny and his Army of the West. Here Fitzpatrick learned of his imminent appointment as Indian Agent, but with permission to continue with the invading army if needed.

Again employed by Kearny as guide, Fitzpatrick accompanied the army to Santa Fe and then continued with it toward California.[31] Near Socorro they met Kit Carson with dispatches from California. Kearny ordered Kit to guide him westward and directed Fitzpatrick to take Carson's messages east to Washington. Upon arrival at the national capital Fitzpatrick received his appointment as Indian Agent for the region of the Upper Platte and Arkansas and was thus launched upon his third career.

Fitzpatrick's appointment was warmly acclaimed. "A better selection could not have been made," wrote T. P. Moor, Agent of the Upper Missouri.[32] The St. Louis *Weekly Reveille* of September 14, 1846, said,

> This appointment will give general satisfaction; for among both the whites and the Indians upon the frontier and the plains, Mr. Fitzpatrick is deservedly held in high respect – the latter indeed, reverence his person, and, from this fact, he has more power to control and restrain them than even the presence of armed force.

With army dispatches Fitzpatrick went to Fort Leavenworth, where his advice was sought regarding construction of forts on western trails. He recommended such establish-

---

31 In a letter Fitzpatrick expressed his pride in being with the advance arm that would plant the Stars and Stripes on the Pacific. – St. Louis *Weekly Reveille,* Oct. 26, 1846.

32 *Annual Report of the Commissioner of Indian Affairs for 1846,* p. 296.

ments near the fur posts of Fort Laramie and Fort Hall on the Oregon Trail, at the Big Bend of the Arkansas, and near Fort Bent on the Santa Fe Trail. His advice on all four sites was soon followed.

It was nearly summer 1847 before Fitzpatrick was able to begin the first official tour of his Indian territory. At Bent's Fort he held a council with Cheyennes. He told them that friendship would be rewarded and enemies punished and reminded them of the "continual decrease of all game, and advised them to turn their attention to agriculture . . . and pointed out . . . the many evils arising from the use of spirituous liquors."[33]

In February 1848, Fitzpatrick visited the Indians on the South Platte, confiscated some liquor from the white traders there, and continued down the Platte to Missouri. In the fall he was back among his wards on the upper Arkansas. Fremont, on his fourth expedition into the West, met his old guide at the Big Timbers and reported:

> We found our friend, Major Fitzpatrick, in the full exercise of his functions . . . surrounded by about 600 lodges of different nations – Apaches, Camanches, Kioways and Arapahoes. He is a most admirable agent, entirely educated for such a post, and possessing the ability and courage necessary to make his education available.[34]

Fitzpatrick now began to plan for a general council with the Indians of his extensive agency. It culminated in the great Fort Laramie Treaty of 1851. It was the largest council ever held in the far West – not only large delegations of Arapahoes and Cheyennes, but also of Shoshones and Sioux. During the sessions, which lasted more than a week, the lands claimed and allotted to particular tribes were described and boundaries agreed upon. White men were

[33] Fitzpatrick's first annual report, Sept. 18, 1847, in the *Annual Report of the Commissioner of Indian Affairs for 1847*.

[34] John Bigelow, *Memoir of the Life and Public Service of John Charles Fremont* (N.Y., 1856), 359.

granted permission to travel the Oregon and Santa Fe trails. For various concessions the Indians were promised annuities of $50,000 in goods for fifty years (later reduced by the United States Senate to fifteen years). Presents were distributed from the large wagon train, and at the end of the council a delegation of Indians was taken by Fitzpatrick to Washington, D.C. Two years later Agent Fitzpatrick, as sole commissioner, negotiated with the generally hostile Comanches and Kiowas a treaty providing annuities of $18,000 in goods.

While he was at the national capital discussing the treaty, he died of pneumonia in a Washington hotel on February 7, 1854. He was buried in the Congressional Cemetery.

In November 1849, Fitzpatrick had married Margaret, a daughter of John Poisal, a French-Canadian trapper, and Snake Woman, a sister of Chief Left Hand. Thomas and Margaret Fitzpatrick had two children – Andrew Jackson and Virginia Thomasine. Their father left an estate of over $10,000.[35]

Thomas Fitzpatrick was an outstanding Mountain Man and was highly regarded as a guide and an Indian Agent. The Arapahoes, said Little Raven in 1865, had "but one fair agent; that was Major Fitzpatrick." Said Chief Black Kettle of the Cheyenne on the same occasion: "Major Fitzpatrick was a good man. He told us that when he was gone we would have trouble, and it has proved true. We are sorry." Fitzpatrick was greatly esteemed by the Indians, and among the white men since he is reputed to have been the best agent these tribes ever had," wrote C. W. Bowman in 1881.[36]

A poetic tribute to the man, written by Mrs. Ann Woodbury Hafen forty years ago (1929) is reproduced herewith.

---

[35] The will is reproduced in *Broken Hand, op. cit.,* 288-91.

[36] See these and other appraisals of the man in *ibid.,* 262-66.

James Bridger

by CORNELIUS M. ISMERT
Kansas City, Missouri

James Bridger, guide, mountaineer, trapper, and Indian fighter, was born in Richmond, Virginia on March 17, 1804, to James and Chloe Bridger. James Bridger, Sr. was a surveyor as well as a farmer, and in 1812, looking for opportunity in the West, he emigrated with his wife and three children to St. Louis. They homesteaded at Six Mile Prairie along the Mississippi River. The hardships of pioneer life took a severe toll and within five years young James Bridger was the only surviving member of the family. He was then fourteen and was hired as an apprentice to Phil Creamer, a St. Louis blacksmith.[1]

During the next five years he learned many of the skills which contributed to his later success as a Mountain Man. By 1822 he had grown "tall and spare, but erect, active and energetic. His hair was brown and long and covered his head abundantly. . . His eyes were gray and keen; his habitual expression was mild, and his manners kind and agreeable."[2] He had learned to handle guns, boats, and horses, and in March, 1822, he felt himself qualified to answer an advertisement placed in the *Missouri Republican* by William H. Ashley for one hundred young men to ascend the Missouri River to its source.

Two new keelboats, each valued at thirty-five hundred

---

1 General Grenville M. Dodge, *Biographical Sketch of James Bridger* (N.Y., 1905), 5-6.

2 William S. Brackett, quoted in J. Cecil Alter, *James Bridger, Trapper, Frontiersman, Scout and Guide* (Salt Lake City, 1925; and facsimile reprint with addenda, Columbus, Ohio, 1950), 394-95.

dollars, had been purchased for the Ashley expedition. The first one, commanded by Major Andrew Henry, left St. Louis on April 3, 1822, with James Bridger aboard. The second boat, with General Ashley in charge, left a month later but met with disaster when it hit a snag and sank – its ten thousand dollar cargo being swallowed by the Missouri River a few miles downstream from the confluence of the Missouri and the Kaw rivers near Fort Osage.

The twenty-one men with Major Henry poled and pulled their way up the Missouri River and camped for the winter near Milk River. The following spring the group divided. Some of the men remained at the Musselshell River to trap while Major Henry and eleven of the men, including James Bridger, continued their ascent of the Missouri. Major Henry's group encountered hostile Blackfeet near Great Falls and in the resultant skirmish four members of the expedition were killed.[3] It seemed impossible to proceed without help from General Ashley and his men, and Major Henry sent Jedediah Smith back downriver with a request for horses and men. Smith returned, however, with the news that Ashley was having his own difficulties with the Indians – he had lost fourteen dead and ten wounded in an encounter with the Arikaras and had returned down stream.[4]

After the Colonel Leavenworth fiasco with the Arikaras in 1823, Henry returned to the Yellowstone, and en route occurred the famous Hugh Glass encounter with a grizzly bear. There are numerous accounts of this story and Bridger's participation in it. James Clyman wrote:

> amongst the party was a Mr Hugh Glass who could not be rstrand and kept under Subordination he went off of the line of march one afternoon and met with a large grissly Bear which he shot at and

[3] J. Cecil Alter, *James Bridger* (Norman, Okla., 1962), 20-24.

[4] Donald McKay Frost, *Notes on General Ashley* . . . (Worcester, Mass., 1945), 74-77.

> wounded . . . he attemptd to climb a tree but the bear caught him and hauled to the ground tearing and lacerating his body in feareful rate.[5]

Bridger and John S. Fitzgerald volunteered, or were drafted, to be caretakers to Hugh Glass. They abandoned his mutiliated body believing he could never live, but he miraculously survived and followed them three hundred and fifty miles to Fort Kiowa. Bridger was probably excused by Glass because of his youth. In the various interviews and narrations, Glass never named his caretakers.[6] The story is believed by some to be apocryphal.

James Bridger appears more creditably in the history of the West as the discoverer of the Great Salt Lake. In the autumn of 1824, while trapping with Captain John H. Weber and traveling in a southwesterly direction descending the course of the Bear River, Bridger came upon a body of extremely salty water. He believed it to be an arm of the Pacific Ocean; exploration by another group in 1826 proved it to have no outlet. It is not known whether Bridger was the sole discoverer of Salt Lake, but he was the first to give an eye-witness report after returning to the rendezvous in Willow (Cache) Valley, Utah.[7]

While Bridger was west of the Continental Divide, his employer, General William H. Ashley, had been defeated for the governorship of Missouri and was getting together another outfit to plunge back into the wilderness. At this time Ashley had little or no competition in the fur trade of the central Rockies. His first rendezvous, in 1825, was a success. Bridger was still on salary with Ashley and accompanied him to the lower Big Horn River.[8] Bridger later gave Captain W. F. Raynolds a description of "the grandeur of the scenery" and the river's passage as "rough and violent;

[5] Charles L. Camp, *James Clyman, Frontiersman* (Portland, Oreg., 1960), 15.

[6] Alter, *Bridger* (1962), 43.

[7] *Ibid.*, 57, 59, 60.

[8] *Ibid.*, 71-72.

making repeated falls, and rushing down long and furious rapids."[9]

During the winter of 1825-26, Bridger remained in the mountains. The following spring the trappers met at Cache Valley for a rendezvous. General Ashley had left St. Louis in March, 1826, with a party of twenty-five men and a large caravan. When Ashley's party arrived, there was "mirth, singing, dancing, shouting, trading, . . . all sorts of extravagances."[10] This was Ashley's second rendezvous and his last.

Bridger's next employer was the new firm of Smith, Jackson and Sublette, which in 1827 sold to W. H. Ashley & Co. beaver and otter skins worth $22,690. James Bridger, Robert Campbell, and others trapped the Wasatch Mountains and skirmished with the Blackfeet before wintering on the lower Weber River. During that winter they suffered extreme privation, primarily because of the absence of meat animals in the area.[11]

After the hardships of the winter, the rendezvous at Bear Lake in 1828 was particularly appreciated. Once again, however, there was trouble with the Blackfeet. The trappers lost four men killed and several wounded during the battle.[12]

In St. Louis, William L. Sublette signed up fifty-four crew members, including Joseph L. Meek and Robert Newell. They left St. Louis on March 17, 1829, and arrived at Oil Spring, Wyoming, on the following July 1st. The trading was so light that Sublette returned to St. Louis with only forty-five packs of beaver. The following year on August 4, 1830, Sublette and his partners sold the company to Thomas Fitzpatrick, Milton G. Sublette, Henry Fraeb,

---

9 William F. Raynolds, *Report on the Exploration of the Yellowstone River, 1859-1860* (Washington, 1868), 56.

10 T. D. Bonner, *Life and Adventures of James P. Beckwourth* (N.Y., 1856), 107.

11 Alter, *Bridger* (1962), 96.

12 *Ibid.*, 103.

Baptiste Gervais, and James Bridger. The five new partners operated as the Rocky Mountain Fur Company.[13]

Thomas Fitzpatrick, Milton G. Sublette and James Bridger, with a force of more than ninety men, set out to invade the dangerous Blackfoot country. They trapped numerous rivers, including the Smith River, and made their winter quarters on the Yellowstone in 1831. The following summer they rendezvoused at Green River, Wyoming. Thomas Fitzpatrick failed to arrive, having detoured by way of Santa Fe, New Mexico. In 1832 Bridger and his men were reported at Gray's Creek – "Their encampment was decked with hundreds of beaver skins, now drying in the sun."[14]

Pierre's Hole was the site of the rendezvous in the summer of 1832. In June, Bridger and Milton Sublette had dispatched scouts toward the Platte in search of and to assist their oncoming pack train. About a month later the cavalcade rolled in with one hundred pack mules and about fifty hustlers, packers and hunters.[15] On July 18, 1832, N. J. Wyeth observed a party of approaching Blackfeet, dressed in full war regalia. Antoine Godin and a Flathead Indian went out to parley with them. Godin's father had been killed by the Blackfeet and Godin recognized the approaching chief as the murderer of his father. Godin ordered his Indian companion to shoot the chief. He did, and they fled with the chief's robe as a trophy. That was the beginning of the Battle of Pierre's Hole.[16]

On July 31, 1832, Jim Bridger and "Broken Hand" Fitzpatrick broke camp at Pierre's Hole and took a sizeable force to trap the source of the Missouri. The fur business had become more competitive. There were more trappers,

---

[13] See this Series, I, p. 104.

[14] Warren A. Ferris, *Life in the Rocky Mountains* (Denver, 1940), 144.

[15] Alter, *Bridger* (1962), 120.

[16] Famous in fur trade history. There are many accounts; for a general one see this Series, I, pp. 123-26.

and the Rocky Mountain Fur Company had a formidable rival in Astor's American Fur Company. This led Bridger and his partners to venture into hostile Indian territory. Skirmishes were almost inevitable, and in one of these Bridger was wounded, receiving an arrowhead in his back.[17]

The next several months of 1833 resulted in "poor pickins" for almost all the fur trapping companies. Said Mrs. Orral Robidoux:

> The winter . . . wore away and there arrived at the camp (Antoine Robidoux's trading post in western Colorado) a small party of men from the upper country to the north, who reported that Fitzpatric [sic] and Bridger of the Rocky Mountain Fur Company had wintered in the Snake River valley and were preparing for the spring hunt.[18]

The following winter, in 1834, Bridger went to the Spanish Southwest.[19] Bridger had a growing reputation and his knowledge of the West was respected. Captain John W. Gunnison said of Bridger that he had

> traversed the region from the headwaters of the Missouri to the [Rio Grande] Del Norte, and along the Gila to the Gulf. . . His graphic sketches are delightful romances. With a buffalo skin and a piece of charcoal . . . he will map out any portion of this immense region, and delineate mountains, streams, and the circular valleys called "holes" with wonderful accuracy.[20]

On June 20, 1834, the Rocky Mountain Fur Company was dissolved and the new firm of Fitzpatrick, Sublette and Bridger was formed.[21] In September Bridger moved out of Ham's Fork with a gallant crew including Kit Carson, Joe Meek, Robert Newell and a band of Flathead and Nez

---

17 Washington Irving, *Adventures of Captain Bonneville* (N.Y., 1868), 235.

18 Orral Messmore Robidoux, *Memorial to the Robidoux Brothers* (Kansas City, 1924), 181, 183.

19 Bernard DeVoto, *Across the Wide Missouri* (Boston, 1947), 429.

20 Quoted in Alter, *Bridger* (1962), 142.

21 The original papers are in the Sublette Collection, Missouri Historical Society, St. Louis.

Perce Indians. The season had a bad beginning when some of Bridger's trappers deserted. Shortly thereafter, a band of Blackfeet crept through Monida Pass on snowshoes and cut out eighteen of Bridger's horses, among them his favorite, "Grohean." In the ensuing unsuccessful attempt to get the horses back, Kit Carson was wounded.[22] In spite of the season's unfortunate start, the beaver haul was fairly good and the following summer the trappers rendezvoused at Green River.

At this rendezvous of 1835, Bridger was fortunate in receiving medical attention from Dr. Marcus Whitman. Samuel Parker, who was traveling in the caravan with Whitman, wrote:

> While we continued in this place, Doct. Whitman was called to perform some very important surgical operations. He extracted an iron arrow, three inches long, from the back of Capt. Bridger, which was received in a skirmish, three years before, with the Blackfeet Indians. It was a difficult operation, because the arrow was hooked at the point by striking a large bone, and cartilaginous substance had grown around it. The Doctor pursued the operation with great self-possession and perseverance; and his patient manifested equal firmness.[23]

After recuperating at the rendezvous in 1835, Bridger married his first wife, Cora, daughter of the Flathead chief, Insala.[24] They had three children: Mary Ann was born in 1836, Felix in 1841 and Josephine in 1846. Cora died shortly after the birth of Josephine. Mary Ann Bridger and the daughter of Joseph L. Meek were taken captive and probably killed at the Whitman Mission School at Waiilatpu, Walla Walla (Washington), in 1847.

From the Green River rendezvous, Bridger and his party, which included his wife and father-in-law, headed out in a northwesterly direction, journeyed to the Yellowstone area,

---

[22] F. F. Victor, *River of the West* (Hartford, 1870), 89.

[23] Samuel Parker, *Journal of an Exploring Tour beyond the Rocky Mountains* (Ithaca, 1844), 80-81.

[24] Alter, *Bridger* (1962), 144.

and then south to the Blackfoot River for the winter. The winter of 1835-36 was a difficult one. There was little game and for some days the party was forced to subsist on roots and drink the blood of their mules.[25] In the spring they moved over to the Muddy and on to old Fort Bonneville for the summer trading fair.

After a month spent trading and seeing old friends Bridger and his group set out for Yellowstone Lake. They separated into trapping squads and planned to met again in Gardner's Hole. Near here Meek was captured by a band of hostile Crows. They wanted to know what band he belonged to and where they could be found. Because Bridger had a force adequate to deal with the Crows, Meek gave the chief all the information, but led him to believe that Bridger had only forty men, whereas he actually had two hundred and forty. The Crows traveled to Bridger's encampment. When they saw the size of the camp, the chief realized that Meek had misled them. He ordered Meek to call to the guards, asking them to come to him. Instead, Meek shouted at the guard to stay away but to ask Bridger to negotiate his release. Soon Bridger appeared on his large white horse and asked Meek to have the chief send one of his sub-chiefs to smoke with him. The sub-chief went to smoke and was trapped by some of Bridger's men. Bridger then proposed an exchange of prisoners. The chief reluctantly agreed; he said that he could not afford to give a chief for one white dog's scalp.[26]

The scenes of the 1837 rendezvous were recorded for posterity by the famous artist, Alfred J. Miller, who was there as a guest of Captain William Stewart of Scotland. Bridger was one of the outstanding characters and was the subject of a later Miller portrait. Describing the painting Miller wrote, "In the midst of them is Capt. Bridger in a

---

[25] M. Morgan Estergreen, *Kit Carson* (Norman, 1962), 70.

[26] Victor, *op. cit.*, 189-193.

full suit of steel armor. This gentleman was a famous mountain man, and we venture to say that no one has travelled here within the last 30 years without seeing or hearing of him. The suit of armor was imported from England and presented to Capt. B. by our commander."[27] Bridger was verbally portrayed by David L. Brown for the Cincinnati *Atlas* as "Tall – six feet at least – muscular, without an ounce of superflous flesh to impede its forces or exhaust its elasticity, he might have served as a model for a sculptor or painter." Bridger had a formidable reputation, Brown described him as a man whose "bravery was unquestionable, his horsemanship equally so, and as to his skill with the rifle, it will scarcely be doubted, when we mention the fact that he has been known to kill twenty buffaloes by the same number of consecutive shots."[28]

In August, 1837, Bridger headed north from Green River as pilot for Lucien B. Fontenelle and his company of seventy-five men. News came of a smallpox outbreak at Fort Van Buren. Kit Carson wrote that the epidemic was among the Blackfeet. In May 1838, Bridger passed an Indian lodge which contained the bodies of nine Indians, dead from smallpox. Later, in June, Bridger talked with Little Robe, Chief of the Piegans, who complained that the whites gave them smallpox, but Bridger convinced the chief that it was the Indians' fault for receiving infected articles from a Mackinaw boat, thus contracting the disease.[29]

On his way to the Snake River in June, 1838, Bridger proceeded by way of Pierre's Hole and Jackson's Little Hole to Horse Creek. Here he found a note directing him to the Wind River-Popo Agie junction, where his men relaxed for the forthcoming trading and celebrating. Some missionaries were traveling with one of the trains which

---

[27] Marvin C. Ross, *West of Alfred Jacob Miller* (Norman, 1951), 159. Also see frontispiece in volume 6 of this *Series*.

[28] Quoted in Alter, *Bridger* (1962), 171.

[29] Victor, *op. cit.*, 231-32.

arrived at the Wind River.[30] The wife of one of them, Mrs. Myra F. Eells, was horrified by the Independence Day celebration.

> Captain Bridger's Company comes in about ten o'clock with drums and firing – an apology for a scalp dance. After they had given Captain Drip's Company a shout, fifteen or twenty Mountain men and Indians came to our tent, with drumming, firing, and dancing.
>
> If I might make a comparison, I should say that they looked like the emissaries of the devil, worshipping their own master. They had the scalp of a Blackfoot Indian, which they carried for a color, all rejoicing in the fate of the Blackfeet, in consequence of the small pox.[31]

In the winter of 1838, Bridger formed a new affiliation with the American Fur Company. He left his family with his wife's people and went to St. Louis. There he met Father Pierre Jean De Smet, who would become his lifelong friend. The following two years Bridger, with his partner Louis Vasquez, slowly planned and constructed their new business venture, Fort Bridger. The building was timely, and the location on Black's Fork of Green River was strategic for the oncoming emigrants on the California and Oregon trails. The fort was probably made chiefly of logs and consisted of one-story buildings with a high picket fence.[32] Fort Bridger was to become one of the principal trading posts for western emigrants, an important military fort and a Pony Express station. In a letter dictated on December 10, 1843, by Bridger to E. S. Denig, at Fort Union addressed to "P. Chouteau & Co.," he states, "I have established a small fort, with a blacksmith shop and a supply of iron in the road of the emigrants on Black's Fork of Green River, which promises fairly."[33]

Neither of the partners spent the majority of their time

---

30 Alter, *Bridger* (1962), 179.

31 LeRoy R. Hafen and F. M. Young, *Fort Laramie* (Glendale, 1938), 54-56.

32 Laura Dahlquist, *Meet Jim Bridger* (Kemmerer, 1948), 17.

33 Robert S. Ellison, *Fort Bridger, Wyoming* (Casper, 1931), 11.

at the fort. Supplies had to be carried in from Missouri; furs had to be carried out. Bridger was in demand as a guide, and in 1844 organized an expedition to California.[34] James Clyman, en route east, states that Bridger left August 30 with less than thirty men under his command on an excursion through the mountains of northern and central Mexico.[35] Bridger, on his return in 1845, said there were plenty of beaver in California, but the Indians stole the traps as fast as they were set out.[36]

In 1848 Bridger married a Ute Indian, who died the following year giving birth to their daughter, Virginia Rosalie.[37] When William Kelly reached Fort Bridger in 1849, he said Bridger lived with his wife in a log hut, and Vasquez and his family in another. "We enjoyed the luxury of some regular roast joints, having been given the use of the kitchen."[38] In 1850 he took his third and last wife, a Shoshone, daughter of Chief Washakie.[39] They had two children: Mary Ann, born June 9, 1853, and William, born October 10, 1857. Later in 1850 they left Fort Bridger for Westport, Missouri, where they purchased the old Thatcher farm fifteen miles south of Westport.[40]

In 1850 Captain Howard Stansbury, U.S. topographical engineer, consulted Bridger concerning a more direct route from Fort Bridger to the South Platte. Using a burnt stick, Bridger sketched his route of the proposed road on a piece

[34] Harris Newmark, *Sixty Years in Southern California* (Boston, 1930), 171.

[35] Camp, *op. cit.*, 99.

[36] *Ibid.*, 324.

[37] Mrs. Virginia Bridger Wachsman Hahn stated in an interview in 1924: "My father's first wife was not an Indian, but a Mormon woman, whom he married about the time the Mormons went west. . . By this wife he had two sons, John and James," note 35 in Alter, *Bridger* (1925), 518. There is doubt as to the accuracy of this statement.

[38] Quoted in Alter, *Bridger* (1962), 231.

[39] Mrs. W. T. Brazzile, in a newspaper editorial by Harry Ross for the Kansas City *Journal Post* (1940s) said, "Her mother was the daughter of Bridger and his third Indian wife, Mary Washakie Bridger. Her Indian grandmother . . . was a full-blooded Shoshone, daughter of Washakie."

[40] Louis Honig, *James Bridger* (Kansas City, 1951), 128.

of parchment. The route sketched by Bridger was from Fort Bridger east over Green River, up Bitter Creek, across the North Platte and Laramie Rivers to the south end of the Black Hills and down Lodge Pole Creek to its mouth. Bridger led Stansbury and his party over it, and much of it later became the route of the Overland Stage and the Union Pacific Railroad.

Bridger also possessed an almost unbelievable ability with Indian sign language. Stansbury describes his conversation with a party of Sioux and Cheyennes:

> . . . he (Bridger) held the whole circle, for more than an hour, perfectly enchained and evidently most deeply interested in a conversation and narrative, the whole of which was carried on without the utterance of a single word . . . exclamations of surprise or interest, and the occasional laughter, showed that the whole party perfectly understood.[41]

In the fall of 1851 an Indian peace parley was held near Fort Laramie. Father Pierre Jean DeSmet went to Fort Union to influence the Sioux to attend the peace council. Bridger came in with a delegation of his friends, the Shoshones. Indian Commissioner D. D. Mitchell, and Indian Agent Thomas Fitzpatrick, managed the negotiations. Tribal boundaries were agreed upon and annuities were provided for the various tribes.[42]

Bridger was at his fort in 1852 and was described by Mrs. B. G. Ferris as the oldest trapper in the Rocky Mountains. "His language is very graphic and descriptive, and he is evidently a man of great shrewdness. . . His wife was simplicity itself."[43]

In 1853 Bridger was forced to abandon his fort. The Mormons apparently feared Bridger's influence over the Indians and there were rumors that Bridger had been pro-

---

41 Howard Stansbury, *Exploration and Survey of the Valley of the Great Salt Lake,* etc. (Washington, 1853), 254.

42 Hafen and Young, *op. cit.,* 177-96.

43 Alter, *Bridger* (1962), 248.

viding the Indians with guns and ammunition. A posse was sent to arrest Bridger, but he had been warned.[44] "He remained secreted for several days," says Captain Marcy, "and through the assistance of his Indian wife was enabled to elude the search of the Danites and make his way to Fort Laramie, leaving all his cattle and other property in possession of the Mormons."[45]

Bridger and Vasquez must have returned to Little Santa Fe, Missouri, for on December 24, 1853, Bridger and Vasquez together bought lots there. Six months later they sold them to Josiah Watts.[46] Vasquez moved his family to an eighty acre farm several miles northeast of Bridger's farm. Vasquez' adjacent neighbor to the north was D. Boone, Jr.[47]

In the spring of 1854, Bridger met Sir George Gore who hired him as a guide for his fabulous big game safari. The summer and fall of that year were spent in organizing the tremendous retinue and establishing them for the winter at Fort Laramie. Bridger acted intermittently as Sir George's guide for the next two years. The hunt was wildly successful. General Randolph B. Marcy said Sir George had trophies to confirm the killing of forty grizzly bears, twenty-five hundred buffaloes, besides numerous elk, deer, antelope and other small game.[48]

In 1857 Bridger was hired as a guide by Colonel Albert Sidney Johnston at five dollars a day to escort the new governor of Utah Territory, Alfred Cumming, his staff, and 2,500 United States troops to Utah. Governor Brigham Young thought this move incredible and on September 15 issued a "Proclamation of War" instructing his army to

---

[44] *Missouri Republican*, November 5, 1853.

[45] Randolph B. Marcy, *Thirty Years of Army Life on the Border* (N.Y., 1874), 401.

[46] Recorder of Deeds, Jackson County Court House, Kansas City, Missouri, Book UX, 190.

[47] Hickman's Property Map of Jackson County, Missouri, Town. 48, Range 33. Dean Earl Wood, *Old Santa Fe Trail from the Missouri River* (Kansas City, 1951), 241.

[48] Alter, *Bridger* (1962), 263.

prevent the invasion.[49] Bridger guided his party to Salt Lake City and then on to Camp Floyd, where his service ended and he started the long journey home to Missouri.

Sometime during 1858 Fort Bridger was sold. The litigation is still unsolved, although there is a deed, even several of them. There is evidence that Bridger's partner, Louis Vasquez, sold the fort, or his part of it, to the Mormons in 1855, with final payment in 1858; but Bridger appeared to be unaware of this.[50]

The following spring Bridger set out for the mountains again, as a guide to Captain William F. Raynolds in an exploration of the headwaters of the Yellowstone and Missouri rivers. The expedition included seven scientists, a military escort of thirty infantrymen, and a party of seven Congressional guests.[51] They left St. Louis in a heavily loaded river boat on May 28, 1859, disembarking at Fort Pierre. In an overland caravan they traveled on to the high country. The scientific reconnaissance was a gruelling experience for all concerned. Snow, mud and confusion plagued their route. The expedition returned to Omaha in the fall of 1860, and Bridger again returned to his family in Missouri.

Bridger acted as guide or scout for several expeditions during the following years and escaped the contagious gold fever. In a newspaper interview, Bridger was quoted as saying, "They found gold everywhere in this country in those days, but thought it unworthy of their notice to mine for it as beaver (then worth $8.00 per pound) was the best paying gold they wanted to mine for in the creeks and rivers."[52] In 1861 Bridger joined Captain E. L. Berthoud in the exploration of a pass through the mountains from Denver to Salt Lake City. They were seeking a shorter line

49 *Ibid.*, 266.

50 See the biographical sketch of Louis Vasquez in this Series, II, p. 335.

51 Alter, *Bridger* (1962), 282.

52 *Rocky Mountain News* (Denver), May 8, 1861.

for the overland stagecoach mail.[53] The route today is approximately U.S. Highway 40.

Bridger was hired as a guide to Colonel William O. Collins, in command of troops, who left Fort Leavenworth in May 1862. Their mission was to patrol and guard the mail routes. In connection with this service Captain J. Lee Humfreville became well acquainted with Bridger during the winter of 1862-63 at Fort Laramie. Concerning Bridger's literary enlightenment, Humfreville writes:

> Bridger became very much interested in this reading [Hiawatha, which Humfreville read to Bridger] and asked which was the best book that had ever been written. I told him that Shakespeare's was supposed to be the greatest book. Thereupon he made a journey to the main road and lay in wait for a wagon train, and sought a copy from some emigrants, paying for it with a yoke of cattle. . . He hired a German boy . . . at $40 a month to read to him. Bridger took great interest in reading, listening most attentively for hours at a time . . . it was amusing to hear Bridger quote Shakespeare. He could give quotation after quotation . . . sometimes he seasoned them with a broad oath.[54]

While wintering on his farm in January 1865, Major Bridger was personally called on by General Grenville M. Dodge who appointed him principal guide and chief of scouts for the Powder River Expedition. He was released as guide on November 30th of that year.[55]

Bridger had become known as a teller of tall tales when he related the phenomenal sights of the Yellowstone country to others. A British army captain, in 1866, travelling in the West gathering material for a book, interviewed Bridger and asked him for his most thrilling adventure. Bridger willingly responded with a story about the time he and his partner had been attacked by Indians:

---

53 LeRoy R. Hafen, *Overland Mail* (Cleveland, 1926), 220-23.

54 Captain J. Lee Humfreville, quoted in Alter, *Bridger* (1925), 402-03. Later, in his 1962 edition (p. 302), Alter questions the veracity of some details of Humfreville's account.

55 Alter, *Bridger* (1962), 296-97.

As we became hard pressed, one of us would dismount and fire, then mount and pass the other. . . We would continue this method of defense all day, and by night had killed thirty of the Indians. . . At the foot of the mountain where there was dense timber, we took shelter. . . We spent the night in great fear . . . knowing that at dawn they would be after us. . . The next day . . . we started to lead our horses out of the valley. . . We heard the Indians behind us. . . By this time, our broken horses began to give way at the knees. Observing a narrow canyon . . . three hundred feet high . . . we saw a waterfall, two hundred feet high, completely blocking our exit.

[Mr. Bridger paused. The Captain, all aglow with interest, cried, "Go on, Mr. Bridger; go on! How did you get out?"] Oh, bless your soul, Captain, we never did get out. The Indians killed us right there.[56]

On February 20, 1866, Bridger purchased a two story building in Westport, Missouri, from Cyprian and Nancy Chouteau.[57] It was located next door to and west of Colonel Albert G. Boone's trading post, which is still on the northwest corner of Westport Road and Pennsylvania Street in Kansas City, Missouri.

Bridger, in 1867, guided federal troops to Fort Laramie and Virginia City (Montana), locating a military road and posts. On May 22, 1868, he was assigned to Lieutenant P. F. Banard, moving supplies to the Platte River posts. On completion of that detail, Bridger was transferred to Colonel Darling at Fort D. A. Russell (Cheyenne) and on July 21, 1868, was paid and discharged. This ends the official record of scouting by James Bridger, although several months later he left for western Kansas to discourage General Philip H. Sheridan from a winter campaign against the Indians.[58]

Bridger's arduous pursuit of his life's work of pioneering ends with his final return to his farm. Captain Albert

56 Anson Mills, *My Story* (Washington, D.C., 1918), 107, 109.

57 Recorder of Deeds, Jackson County Court House, Kansas City, Missouri, Book 46, p. 150.

58 Alter, *Bridger* (1962), 335-36.

JAMES BRIDGER'S HOME IN KANSAS CITY, MISSOURI

A drawing by C. M. Ismert, from a description of the house by an old couple who lived adjacent to it and attended dances in it. No photograph of it is known. (See text page 100).

Fort Bridger, 1858, during use as a Camp for Troops enroute to Utah

Courtesy of Wyoming State Archives and Historical Department.

Wachsman, who had married Bridger's daughter Virginia in 1864, assisted Bridger during his final years in inquiring about a possible claim on the army lease of Fort Bridger from 1857 to 1890. Thirty years of legal proceedings finally resulted in the Bridger heirs receiving six thousand dollars. They were notified in the following letter from the United States Senate:

> My dear Sir: I take pleasure in advising you that the bill appropriating $6,000 in payment of the claim of Jas. Bridger became a law March 3d, 1899. It will take some weeks for the Treasury Officials to make payment. With best wishes, Yours sincerely,
>
> F. M. COCKRELL[59]

Only glimpses of Bridger's last years are seen and recorded. In a letter to General Dodge, Mrs. Wachsman wrote: "In 1873, Father's health began to fail him, and his eyes were very bad. . . I had to watch after him and lead him around . . . never still one moment. I got Father a good old gentle horse . . . he named his old horse 'Ruff.' . . Father . . . would say, 'I know that my time is near. I feel that my health is failing me very fast, and see, I am not the same man, I used to be.' "[60]

On July 17, 1881, James Bridger died on his farm near Little Santa Fe, Missouri. Two days later he was buried on the Stubbin Watts farm burial plot next to his two sons, William and Felix, several hundred yards north of the Watts Mill on Indian Creek in Dallas (now Kansas City), Missouri. Although most people forgot "Ol' Jim," General Grenville M. Dodge, Captain John B. Colton and the owners of Mount Washington Cemetery made possible the removal of Bridger's remains to Mount Washington Cemetery, Independence, Missouri, on December 11, 1904. An impressive seven-foot monument stands at the head of the grave of James Bridger.

---

59 Letter written to S. C. McPherrin, Kansas City, Missouri, in writer's possession.

60 Alter, *Bridger* (1925), 520-21.

In 1939 some reminiscences of Bridger's last days appeared in a Kansas City newspaper:

> Mrs. Virginia Bridger Wachsman Hahn used to relate how, in early summer her father would go on hands and knees in the growing wheat, to tell how tall it was and to feel and smell it.
>
> Edgar, who lived in the old Watts farmhouse, pointing to an old enormous walnut fireplace recalled, "Often old Jim Bridger has sat beside that fireplace spinning yarns to his friend, the fiddling miller, Stubbin Watts."[61]

Edgar Watts, son of Bridger's close friend, Stubbin Watts, who ran the Watts grist mill at Dallas, Missouri, recalled, "Old Jim had a gift for language. I can remember him talking to father, telling about the way people all said he was a liar when he told them about seeing springs of boiling water in the Yellowstone. 'Why Stubbins,' old Jim would say, 'They said I was the damnedest liar ever lived. That's what a man gets for telling the truth.' "[62]

Today, James Bridger's name is immortalized. In the state of Wyoming there are: Fort Bridger State Park, Bridger Creek, Bridger Ferry, Bridger Lake, Bridger Mountain, Bridger National Forest, Bridger Pass, Bridger Trail, and Bridger Wilderness.[63] The city of Bridger and the Bridger Mountains are in Montana.

---

[61] E. R. Schauffler, *Kansas City Star,* March 20, 1939.

[62] E. R. Schauffler, *Kansas City Times,* January 10, 1940.

[63] Katherine Halverson, Wyoming State Archives and Historical Department.

Benjamin L. E. Bonneville

by EDGELEY W. TODD
Colorado State University

Born in or near Paris, France, on April 14, 1796, Benjamin Louis Eulalie Bonneville was the son of Nicolas de Bonneville (1760-1825) and Margaret de Bonneville, née Bazier (1767-1846). Among his parents' closest friends was Thomas Paine, who, for some years after 1792, lived in France as an exile and promoted the anti-monarchical cause of the Revolution. In 1797, he took up residence in the Bonneville household; later when political unrest made more tranquil conditions necessary for his family, Nicolas Bonneville agreed to Paine's suggestion and sent his wife and three sons to the United States in 1803, one year after Paine's return to America. The elder Bonneville remained in France, where he was under political surveillance for his activities as a political journalist; not until 1807 or 1808 did he rejoin his family.

In the meantime, Paine looked after his friend's wife and children, and for a time Mme. Bonneville managed his household at his farm at New Rochelle, New York. There, at the age of eight, Benjamin found himself living under the roof of his benefactor, who affectionately called him "Bebia." Paine's death in 1809 left Mme. Bonneville a legatee as well as an executrix of his estate. His will provided bequests to both parents and left a portion of his farm in trust for the future education of the Bonneville children.[1]

[1] For Bonneville's early years, his father's involvement in the French Revolution and friendship with Paine, and Mme. Bonneville's removal to America, see Moncure D. Conway, *Life of Thomas Paine* (2 v., New York, 1893), *passim;* Conway, "Thomas Paine and Madame Bonneville," *Nation,* LIV (Jan., 1892), 8-9. Paine's will is in *Writings of Thomas Paine,* ed. Moncure Conway (4 v., New York, 1896),

On April 14, 1813, his seventeenth birthday, young Bonneville entered the United States Military Academy as a cadet from New York. Nothing is known of his previous education, but he appears to have had a knowledge not only of French but also of Latin, Greek, and mathematics. He spent a little over two and a half years at West Point, from which he graduated on December 11, 1815, as brevet second lieutenant assigned to light artillery.[2] In January, 1817, he was promoted to the full rank of second lieutenant; was assigned in March, 1819, to the Eighth Infantry; and in July, 1820, was promoted to first lieutenant. During these early years he served in New England (1815-19) and saw duty in the recruiting service. In 1820 he helped construct a military road through Mississippi. A year later, in June 1821, he was transferred to the Seventh Infantry and thus began his lifelong association with the trans-Mississippi frontier, his new assignments taking him to Fort Smith, Arkansas, and to San Antonio, Texas.[3] Later he went with the Seventh Infantry under Colonel Matthew Arbuckle to a point on Grand River, a tributary of the Arkansas, where in the spring of 1824 they built Fort Gibson as a focus of control over the Osage Indians. At this time, the new cantonment was the westernmost military outpost,[4] and it long remained an important frontier garrison with which much of Bonneville's life was associated.

When the Marquis de Lafayette visited the United States in 1824-25, his old friendship with the Bonneville family led him to assist Bonneville in obtaining leave of absence to

IV, pp. 508-509. See also Phillipe Le Harival, *Nicolas de Bonneville, Pré-Romantique et Revolutionnaire, 1760-1825* (Paris, 1923), and A. Aulard, *The French Revolution, a Political History, 1789-1804,* trans. Bernard Miall (4 v., New York, 1965).

2 Statement of the Military Service of Benjamin L. E. Bonneville, National Archives; hereinafter referred to as Service Record.

3 *Ibid.*

4 Grant Foreman, *Advancing the Frontier* (Norman, 1933), 35; Foreman, *Fort Gibson, a Brief History* (Norman, 1936), 7.

accompany him to France. In the meantime, Bonneville was promoted to a captaincy in October, 1825. After a year abroad, he reported to Fort Gibson eighteen months from the time of his departure with Lafayette.[5]

With Bonneville's return to Fort Gibson, he was occupied with Indian affairs. In the spring and summer of 1827 he visited Indians along the Red River. After spending 1828 at Jefferson Barracks near St. Louis, he returned to Fort Gibson and in February, 1830, spent some time among the Osages at Grand Saline, forty miles north of Fort Gibson. Later that year, in September, he conducted a survey of the country along the Canadian Fork of the Arkansas to ascertain the suitability of the area for the relocation of Indian tribes from eastern states.[6]

About this time he began to form plans to explore the Rocky Mountains at the head of a fur trading expedition. Of the various persons who doubtless helped kindle his enthusiasm for this project, the most important was Joseph Reddeford Walker. By the time he met Bonneville at Fort Gibson in February, 1831, while on a horse-buying venture to the Cherokees, Walker had become a thoroughly experienced frontiersman.[7] Together they crystallized plans for the expedition to the Oregon country, Walker to serve as Bonneville's principal lieutenant. On May 21, 1831, Bonneville wrote to Major General Alexander Macomb, commanding general of the Army, requesting leave of absence

[5] See Lafayette to Mme. Bonneville, April 24, 1825, in "Some Adventures of Captain Bonneville," by Anne E. Ford, *Chronicles of Oklahoma,* VI (June, 1928), 131-32. Also Grant Foreman, *Pioneer Days in the Southwest* (Cleveland, 1926), 243-44.

[6] Foreman, *Pioneer Days,* 245, 248; Foreman, *Advancing the Frontier,* 37; Foreman, "An Unpublished Report of Captain Bonneville," *Chronicles of Oklahoma,* X (Sept. 1932), 326-30. Also Service Record.

[7] Donald J. Berthrong and Odessa Davenport, eds., *Joseph Reddeford Walker and the Arizona Adventure,* by Donald Ellis Carter (Norman, 1956), xv. Douglas S. Watson, *West Wind* (Los Angeles, 1934), gives May, 1831, as the time of their meeting; but Watson's book, undocumented and fictionalized, is not always dependable.

for this purpose and saying that he would examine the topography of the country, study the locations and habits of the Indian tribes, familiarize himself with trading practices with them, "visit the American and British establishments," and study the best means of making the country available to American citizens.[8] He asked nothing of the government except U.S. and Mexican passports, plus leave of absence. Whether in addition to his stated purposes Bonneville was secretly employed as a government agent to report on British holdings in the Pacific Northwest is a tantalizing hypothesis that cannot be absolutely affirmed or denied.[9]

How Bonneville financed this private undertaking, if private it was, is shrouded in obscurity. The one person known definitely to have been an investor is Alfred Seton, who twenty years before had been one of John Jacob Astor's young clerks at Astoria and who now, in 1831, was a New York merchant and fur dealer. He rallied a group of businessmen to support the venture.[10]

---

8 Bonneville's letter is reprinted in the introduction to Washington Irving's *Adventures of Captain Bonneville,* ed. Edgeley W. Todd (Norman, 1961), xxv-xxvi. All subsequent citations will be to this edition, referred to as *Bonneville.*

9 See Donald M. Major, "Benjamin Bonneville," *Journal of Am. Hist.,* XXI (1927), 128; Isaac K. Russell and Howard R. Driggs, *Hidden Heroes of the Rockies* (Yonkers-on-Hudson, 1927), 253-55; "General B. L. E. Bonneville," *Washington Hist. Quar.,* XVIII (1927), 207; Bernard DeVoto, *Across the Wide Missouri* (Boston, 1947), 59-60; Alvin M. Josephy, Jr., *The Nez Perce Indians and the Opening of the Northwest* (New Haven, 1965), 76. Paul C. Phillips, *The Fur Trade* (2 v., Norman, 1961), states that imperialism was one of Bonneville's main objectives (II, p. 465). The most telling evidence is in a letter to General Macomb written after Bonneville had spent one year in the West collecting information. He wrote: "The information I have already obtained authorizes me to say this much; that if our Government ever intend taking possession of Oregon the sooner it shall be done the better." *Bonneville,* 381. He then went on to state the number of men required to carry out this intention plus conditions at various Hudson's Bay Company posts.

10 *Bonneville,* xxvi, li. One investor may have been Gabriel Franchère, also a former clerk at Astoria and in 1831 still associated with the American Fur Company; see R. G. Thwaites, ed., *Early Western Travels* (32 v., Cleveland, 1904), VI, p. 274. Astor may himself have been interested in furthering Bonneville's expedition, for Irving hints at this possibility by writing that one of Bonneville's "favorite"

With obvious interest in Bonneville's proposal, General Macomb granted him leave until October, 1833, and gave him instructions to carry out.[11] One clause, ordering him to collect "any information which may be useful to the Government," permitted Bonneville wide latitude in interpretation. By September, 1831, having secured financial backing, bought instruments, studied various books, and practiced taking astronomical observations at West Point, Bonneville was in St. Louis.[12] By the end of the following April he had organized an expedition of one hundred men; twenty wagons to carry trade goods and supplies; and horses, mules, oxen, and cows. On May 1, 1832, this large caravan left Fort Osage, Missouri.

The next three years of Bonneville's life, the years he spent in the fur trade, are the subject of Washington Irving's *Adventures of Captain Bonneville,* the first American edition of which bore the title *The Rocky Mountains; or, Scenes, Incidents, and Adventures in the Far West; Digested from the Journal of Capt. B. L. E. Bonneville* (Philadelphia, 1837). Nothing will ever replace Irving's classic narrative of Bonneville's life during these years, and the account which follows can be only a brief synopsis of Irving's pages, to which the reader is referred for fuller detail.

He followed the well-established route of the fur trade caravans leading to South Pass, over which, on July 24, 1832, he took the first wagons and thus proved the feasibility of this route for future emigration. Then, turning northwest, he reached a location on the Green River a few miles upstream from the junction of Horse Creek and built

projects was to build a post on the lower Columbia and "retrieve for his country some of the lost trade of Astoria." *Bonneville,* 159. It is also significant that upon returning from the frontier in 1835, Bonneville went directly to Astor in New York, even before reporting to authorities in Washington.

[11] Macomb's letter is given in *ibid.,* 379-80. Older editions give the date of the letter as Aug. 3, 1831, rather than the correct date of July 30, 1831.

[12] *Ibid.,* xxvi-xxvii.

a rough stockade. With one exception his journey had been without incident; but west of South Pass some of his men were lured from him by Lucien Fontenelle, a rival from the American Fur Company. Although he later snagged some men whom Fontenelle had counted on adding to his brigade, Bonneville thus had his first taste of the ruinous competition that eventually led to his downfall.

From his stockade he sent out at least two trapping brigades, one led by someone known only as Matthieu to trap the Bear River country and to trade with the Shoshonies, the other under David Adams, directed to go into the Crow country.[13] Within three weeks, Bonneville himself left. Following up the Green, he crossed over to the Gros Ventre River and entered Jackson Hole, which he left by way of Teton Pass, descending into Pierre's Hole a few weeks after the battle there between trappers and Gros Ventre Indians. After making his way up Birch Creek and down the Lemhi River to the Salmon River, he erected a few crude log huts on the Salmon. From here he dispatched three parties, one under Michel Cerré, a second under Walker, and a third under someone unidentified. A fourth was later sent out in order to decrease the pressing demand for game.

At this encampment Bonneville remained during October and most of November surrounded by friendly Nez Percé and Flathead Indians, with whom he traded. But the drain on the food supply caused him to move by gradual stages to a second winter camp on the North Fork of the Salmon. Walker's detachment had in the meantime returned and been sent south to winter along the Snake River, with orders to meet Bonneville on Horse Creek the following July (1833).[14] Late in December, Bonneville went in search of

[13] His written orders to Adams appear in *ibid.*, xxix-xxx. Adams' difficulties in this assignment are related in Chapter 19.

[14] For Walker's movements that winter and the following spring, see *ibid.*, 98-99n.

Matthieu, from whom he had heard nothing; after severe hardship in bitter weather, he found him and his men along the Snake, and by March 14 had returned to his caches on the Salmon River. Shortly thereafter he dispatched a party under one Hodgkiss to trade among the Indians, and Bonneville himself with twenty-eight men moved toward the Malade River for the spring hunt.

Now for the second time he ran into determined rivals. Led by Milton Sublette and J. B. Gervais of the Rocky Mountain Fur Company, they were also headed for the Malade. Bonneville was dismayed by the meeting. Having but one man who knew the country, he foresaw what he might expect from these veteran opponents. Each kept a guarded eye on the other as they waited to penetrate snow-blocked mountains to the west. That spring, as the two groups vied with each other, Bonneville had only "varying success." By mid-June he was back at his caches on the Salmon, and a month later reached the rendezvous at Horse Creek.

On the way he attempted to trade with a gathering of Nez Percé, Flathead, and Kutenai Indians. Bonneville sought to profit by the delay of a Hudson's Bay Company trader, but although he spread out every kind of tempting merchandise, he made no progress. As a demonstration of the influence of the rival faction, it should have instructed him in the tight monopoly of the Hudson's Bay Company and forewarned him of what he could expect when he later tried to invade their territory.

Traveling to Horse Creek, he also met Nathaniel J. Wyeth, who, like Bonneville, was trying unsuccessfully to break into the established trade. Plagued by bad luck since leaving Boston the previous year, he had been to Fort Vancouver and was now moving east. Wyeth was at loose ends and looking for an opening to wrest trade from the Hudson's Bay people. To Bonneville he proposed a joint operation south of the Columbia the following fall. This meant invading territory claimed by the Hudson's Bay Company, possibly as far south as California. Although Bonneville agreed, nothing came of the proposal.[15]

At the rendezvous (1833), Bonneville was reunited with many of his employees. The leader of one detachment, David Adams, who was to have met him on the Salmon River months before, had only a sequence of disasters to report. He arrived alone, beaver skins, traps, supplies, and horses lost to Indians. All of his men had either deserted or returned to civilization. His misfortunes were but one more example of the risks that Bonneville would have small success in combating. Walker had also had difficulties. He had run into strong competition from a group of Rocky Mountain Fur Company trappers under the redoubtable James Bridger, whose rivalry he had struggled to meet. He had little to show for his efforts.

Regardless of these setbacks, Bonneville resolved to remain in the mountains, although doing so jeopardized his army status because his furlough was to end in less than four months. By remaining, he believed he could better fulfill his instructions from Macomb. The mountain West was seemingly endless – too broad and complex to be known in a few months.

He had bold schemes. One ambition was to build a trading post near the Willamette River on the lower Columbia, "to endeavor," says Irving, "to retrieve . . . some of the lost trade of Astoria." Another was to send Walker, whom he fitted out with a year's supplies and forty or so men, ostensibly on an exploring mission to Great Salt Lake, around whose fringes, he thought, many beaver streams would yield rich returns. Although this was the purpose,

---

15 Wyeth's proposal is in his *Correspondence and Journals,* ed. F. G. Young (Eugene, 1899), 58-60. In Boston that fall, Wyeth proposed terms to Alfred Seton for transporting Bonneville's furs to Boston; *ibid.,* 100.

according to Irving, the evidence shows that Walker's real objective was California.[16]

Walker's party left the rendezvous on July 24, 1833. The next day Bonneville himself set out for the Big Horn River, down which he had four thousand pounds of fur to send in charge of Cerré, who would descend the Yellowstone and Missouri rivers in three bull boats constructed for the purpose. Bonneville also sent trappers down the Big Horn and later up the Wind River, while he returned to Fort Bonneville for supplies, which he carried back to these men in September. Returning to his fort in October, he then went south to Hams Fork, ran into Thomas Fitzpatrick there with a group of Shoshoni Indians, and turned west to the northern end of Bear Lake, where in November he arranged a rendezvous for the next summer. After meeting Hodgkiss north of the Snake, he set up winter camp in December on the Portneuf River.

Here Bonneville made preparations for his first venture into the tight domain of the Hudson's Bay Company along the Columbia on what Irving describes as "a reconnoitring expedition."[17] Taking only three men and light provisions, he set out with five horses and mules into formidable country in the dead of winter on an undertaking similar to the one that had ruined the Astorians under Wilson Price Hunt and Ramsay Crooks some twenty years before. On December 25, promising to return in March, he bade farewell to the men left behind.

He and his comrades followed the Snake until it led them into treacherous Hell's Canyon. Extricating themselves, they floundered through the Wallowa Mountains, where

[16] Zenas Leonard, Walker's clerk, states that Walker "was ordered to steer through an unknown country, towards the Pacific. . ." *Adventures of Zenas Leonard,* ed. John C. Ewers (Norman, 1959), 64. Additional evidence is summarized in *Bonneville,* 162-63n.

[17] *Bonneville,* 219.

men and animals were reduced to the limits of exhaustion. With the aid of friendly Nez Percés, they finally reached Fort Walla Walla on March 4, 1834, by which time they should have returned to the Portneuf. Pierre C. Pambrun, in charge of this Hudson's Bay post, received Bonneville and his bedraggled men hospitably though refusing supplies for their return trip. Bonneville remained only two days; but in that time he had seen enough, Irving remarks, "to convince him that an American trade [with the Indians] might be carried on with advantage in this quarter; and he determined soon to return with a stronger party, more completely fitted for the purpose."[18] Pambrun did what he could to discourage him, and Bonneville thus learned "the difference between being treated as a guest, or as a rival trader."[19]

By May 12, two months overdue, he was back on the Portneuf. About June 16, on the Bear River, he found Walker's party from California awaiting him. There was rejoicing as the two groups met, but Bonneville was dissatisfied with what Walker had done, especially his failure to bring back a rich load of furs. His reaction as transmitted through Irving shows that he ignored the real significance of Walker's accomplishment in blazing a trail across the Great Basin and through the Sierras, where he reputedly discovered what is now Yosemite Park. Though Walker had proved himself a front-rank explorer, Bonneville later chose to chastise him in print: ". . . this most disgraceful expedition" caused Bonneville to be ". . . so

[18] *Ibid.*, 261.

[19] Pambrun was acting on orders from Dr. John McLoughlin, chief factor at Fort Vancouver, who had a fixed policy of opposing American traders. Pambrun was to assist no one, even when the request was for food. In particular, ". . . he was to have no dealings at all with Captain Bonneville . . . who appeared to McLoughlin liable to founder for lack of goods." E. E. Rich, *Hudson's Bay Company, 1620-1870* (3 v., New York, 1961), III, p. 661. This policy helped to defeat Bonneville's second venture to the Columbia in September, 1834.

deeply grieved at the failure of his plans, and so indignant at the atrocities [against Digger Indians] related to him, that he turned, with disgust and horror, from the narrators." Bonneville's pride was deeply injured. The means which had supplied the expedition had "all been squandered at Monterey," and his purse had received an even greater blow than his pride. So great were his losses that he considered leaving the mountains.[20] Yet a review of accounts left by participants hardly justifies Bonneville's reaction except for his disappointment concerning the lack of furs. Shifting blame to Walker might, he may have reasoned, cover up his own failures. Or his fuming may simply have been a blind to conceal more important reasons why a trading venture in which the government was interested should have wanted to look into California, using the very passports with which Bonneville had been provided in Washington.[21]

Bonneville did not go that summer to the general rendezvous on Hams Fork. By prior arrangement, Cerré met him on July 28 at Bear Lake with goods and equipment from the East. He had been to Washington after delivering Bonneville's furs at St. Louis and in the capital gave Macomb a long report that Bonneville had written the previous summer on the Wind River.[22] Bonneville expected it to furnish grounds for an extension of his leave, but Cerré, though he had talked to Macomb, had brought no written orders. Yet Bonneville, believing with Cerré that his furlough had been extended, decided to remain, completely unaware that Macomb, on May 28, 1834, had already reported him absent

---

20 Irving devotes two chapters, *Bonneville,* 281-96, to a somewhat distorted account of the expedition. To exonerate him, one must remember that he had only Bonneville's version to rely upon, and this was second hand. The most reliable version is Leonard's, whose *Adventures* was not published until 1839, too late for Irving's use. For other first hand sources, see *Bonneville,* 281n.

21 "One reason why Bonneville sent an expedition to California may have been that the Secretary of War ordered him to." DeVoto, *op. cit.,* 110.

22 The complete report appears in *Bonneville,* 381-95.

without leave and that on May 30 he had been dropped from the rolls of the army.[23] Additional reports which Bonneville now wrote disappeared after Cerré carried them as far as Council Bluffs, much to Bonneville's subsequent distress when he sought reinstatement in the Army. What he reported at this time about his actions since the previous summer has been forever lost.[24]

Within five days of meeting Cerré, Bonneville departed with twenty-three men on a second attempt to penetrate Hudson's Bay country,[25] hoping to accomplish what he had failed to do the first time. This ill-conceived venture occupied him the rest of the summer and early fall. Once more Pambrun repulsed him and even tried to induce some of his men to desert. This they refused. Confronted with starvation, Bonneville attempted to trade for fish with Indians on the Columbia, but, dominated by his rivals, they, too, refused aid. Even the country offered nothing, and he was forced to kill some of his horses for food. These circumstances forced Bonneville to abandon his intention of reaching the Willamette. Three months later he was back on the Portneuf.[26]

Bonneville wintered that year (1834-35) in the valley of the Bear River, richly supplied with buffalo and other game. Nearby camped friendly Utes and Shoshonies. With the coming of spring, he started for a previously-appointed rendezvous with his men on the Wind River, which he

---

23 See *ibid.,* xxxiii-xxxiv. Macomb could not later ". . . remember to have given any assurances to Captain Bonneville thro' Mr. Cerré that his leave of absence would be prolonged, because I was under the impression that [he] intended to resign at the end of his leave of absence. . ." Macomb to the Secretary of War, Washington, Dec. 12, 1835. National Archives, Record Group 46.

24 See his letter to Secretary Cass, Sept. 30, 1835, in *Bonneville,* 391-95.

25 Before leaving he sent two parties into the Crow country, one under Walker, the other under Antonio Montero. For Montero, see this series, II, pp. 251-56.

26 Absent from Irving's account of this journey is a meeting between Bonneville and Wyeth in the Grande Ronde Valley, Aug. 31. Two extant letters from Wyeth to Bonneville dated Sept. 1, 1834, show that they now made plans, later abandoned, to cooperate in the Indian trade. See *Bonneville,* 340n, and Wyeth, *op. cit.,* 141-42.

reached on June 22. Within a few days he was joined by a party under Antonio Montero, who had built Portuguese Houses on the Powder River. Walker probably also came to the spot, for Zenas Leonard, who was with Walker, relates that Bonneville selected Walker to remain in the country with fifty-nine men during the following year. Montero received similar orders. Taking the remainder of the men, Leonard among them, Bonneville started for the States. Using the Platte River route, he reached Independence, Missouri, on August 22, 1835, after an absence of three years and four months.

Near the end of September, having first gone to New York to confer, apparently, with his financial backers and to see Astor, Bonneville was again in Washington. There he learned to his astonishment that he had been dropped from Army rolls. Immediately he sought restoration of rank.

A complete record of official correspondence touching upon this matter is on file in the National Archives, and from it one can learn much of Bonneville's case as it rested in the hands of his superiors, as well as information relating to his expedition. Although some opposition came from his fellow officers at Fort Gibson, there was no real obstacle from higher quarters. On January 4, 1836, his name was submitted to the Secretary of War for reappointment, and on January 5 the recommendation was in the hands of President Andrew Jackson, who sent it to the Senate.[27]

In the meantime Bonneville labored to write a narrative of his travels for publication. In March, 1836, when he was unsuccessful in finding a New York publisher, he turned to Washington Irving, who offered to buy the manuscript for $1,000.[28] This became the basis for *The Rocky Mountains.*

---

27 An account of the main aspects of Bonneville's efforts to regain his military status appears in *Bonneville,* xxxv-xxxvi.

28 John F. McDermott, "Washington Irving and the Journal of Captain Bonneville," *Miss. Valley Hist. Rev.,* XLIII (Dec. 1956), 465-66, and Pierre M. Irving, *Life and Letters of Washington Irving* (4 v., New York, 1863), III, p. 114.

Out in the country of the Crows, during all this time, were the trappers whom Bonneville had left under Walker and Montero. Aware that his nomination before the Senate might miscarry and mindful that his business affairs in the West needed his attention, he left for Missouri and obtained on April 19 a trading license from William Clark, Superintendent of Indian Affairs. It shows that he was to trade "At a point of timber on the south side of the Grand river Platte, called Laramais' point, – with the Arapahoes."[29] Unknown to Bonneville, three days later the Adjutant General's Office issued General Order No. 25, declaring that the Senate had reinstated him to his former rank of captain in the Seventh Infantry and ordering him to report for duty at Fort Gibson.

He probably spent little if any time trading with the Arapahoes on the Laramie River. More likely he pressed on rapidly to the Wind River, where he met Walker and perhaps Montero. It was a brief trip. By August he was back at Fort Leavenworth, and before long had returned to Fort Gibson.[30]

Bonneville now resumed an active military role after a lapse of five years. Much of his activity was of a routine sort and will not be summarized here. He participated in the second Seminole War in Florida for three years, and later was stationed at Fort Brooks, Florida; at Baton Rouge, Louisiana; and finally at Pass Christian, Mississippi. In July, 1845, he was promoted to the rank of major and was assigned to the Sixth Infantry. Sometime during 1845 he

29 "Letters Rec'd by the Office of Indians Affiairs, 1836-38." National Archives, Roll 751. His bond was $500 and his capital $1,122. He employed fifteen men.

30 See his letters to Brigadier General Roger Jones, Aug. 8, 1836, and to General Matthew Arbuckle, Oct. 20, 1836. *Bonneville,* xxxviii. Bonneville's return to the mountains that summer was not prompted solely by the uncertainty of his reinstatement. He had made plans to do so the year before; see Leonard, *op. cit.,* 160. Bonneville's return to the settlements was heralded in the press; see *Niles Weekly Register,* LI (Sept. 3, 1836), 16, quoting the *St. Louis Observer;* reprinted in *Bonneville,* xliii.

returned to Fort Smith, Arkansas, where he remained until 1846, when his regiment was ordered into the War with Mexico.

Bonneville and the Sixth Infantry were among the ten thousand troops under General Winfield Scott in the successful invasion of Mexico at Vera Cruz in March, 1847. He fought in the major battles leading to the capture of Mexico City. Although he was promoted to the rank of brevet lieutenant colonel, April 20, 1847, "for gallantry and meritorious conduct in the battles of Contreras and Churubusco,"[31] it is not generally known that he was also court-martialed in October of that same year.

The charge against him was "misbehavior before the enemy," which was supported by ten "specifications" or counts, which are too detailed to be enumerated here. They were attested to by seventeen of his fellow officers. To all charges Bonneville pleaded not guilty. In his defense, he was assisted by Captain F. N. Page as counsel. The trial, held in Mexico City, lasted from October 5 to October 26. Near the end, Bonneville read a thirteen page statement attributing the accusations to ". . . implacable enmity and blind prejudice pent up in the hearts of one or several men. . ." He made much of the fact, which had been brought out in the trial, that in the battle of Churubusco he had been wounded by a ball which so affected him as to render him unfit for active duty. Yet in spite of the testimony for the defense, he was found guilty – even though he was found innocent of seven of the ten specifications. He was sentenced "to be admonished in orders by the General in Chief."[32] Bonneville never entirely recovered from the unnerving effects of his court-martial and the damage he believed had been done to his reputation. As late as 1855 he

---

31 Service Record.

32 See "Court Martial of Benjamin L. E. Bonneville, October, 1847." Records of the Judge Advocate, National Archives, Record Group 153.

continued to seek the testimony and good will of those he felt were sympathetic to him.[33]

Following his court-martial, Bonneville returned to the United States and was assigned to command newly-constructed Fort Kearny on the Oregon-California Trail. He remained here until 1849. His service record fails to show where he was stationed in 1850, but during 1851 and 1852 he took command of Fort Howard on Green Bay, Wisconsin. After a year or so, he was ordered briefly to Fort Columbus, New York, in 1852. Later that year he was transferred to Fort Vancouver (or Columbia Barracks, as it was called at the time) on the north bank of the Columbia. It is ironic indeed that nearly twenty years after his efforts to compete with the Hudson's Bay Company, he was in charge of the very post which had once been the center of much of the opposition against him. Now it was in United States territory and no longer a force in the nearly defunct fur trade.[34]

In May, 1855, Bonneville left Fort Vancouver and was reassigned to duty in the Southwest as commander of the military department of New Mexico with headquarters at Santa Fe. In the areas the United States had won in the recent Mexican War, the military resorted to various measures to keep marauding Indians in check. Campaigns against the Indians were frequent. Among them was the Gila expedition, under the command of Bonneville and Major John S. Simonson, aimed at the Mogollon, Gila, and Coyotero Apaches.[35] The expedition had little to show by way of

33 See letters to Bonneville from Lieut. Edwin Howe, Fort Leavenworth, Aug. 2, 1849; John McCarty (McCarthy), Fort Vancouver, Nov. 9, 1853; and F. N. Page, Jefferson Barracks, March 10, 1853. National Archives, Record Group 94.

34 Following the settlement of the Oregon boundary dispute in 1846, the United States took over Fort Vancouver as an army base in 1849, when it became departmental headquarters of military affairs in the Pacific Northwest. National Park Service, *Soldier and Brave* (New York, 1963), 101-102.

35 See "Field Returns of the Forces of the Gila Expedition under Bonneville's Command, May-June, 1856 [*i.e.,* 1857];" "Field Returns of a Command Stationed

accomplishment in a terrain in which the Indians were at home and could easily evade their pursuers. In numerous ways the expedition seems to have been ill-conceived, and in the diaries of two young officers, John Dubois and Henry M. Lazelle, appears extremely unfavorable criticism of Bonneville and other senior officers. Nowhere, not even in the accusations in his court martial, can one find more damning criticism of Bonneville as a person and of his ability as a commander. The journals of both Dubois and Lazelle are filled with an almost constant barrage of censure that is only partially offset by favorable official reports.[36]

Bonneville remained in command of the military department of New Mexico Territory until October 25, 1859. On March 12, 1860, he received orders to leave with the Third Infantry for Fort Clark, Texas, following the Pecos River below the mouth of the Gallinas River.[37] The journey ended forty-seven days later after a trip which, owing to a scarcity of wood and water and to excessively high temperatures, must have severely tested the stamina of man and beast. The expedition was largely uneventful and peaceful, and only one Indian was captured.

Bonneville remained from the end of July until January, 1861, at Fort Clark, which was commanded by Robert E. Lee, whom Bonneville outranked. He chafed at this predicament and tried to have it remedied, but before he could be

---

at the Depôt on the Rio Grande, N.M., Commanded by Major John S. Simonson RMR for the Month of July, 1857;" and "Field Returns of the U.S. Troops of the Gila Expedition Commanded by B. L. E. Bonneville Colonel 3' Infantry, for the Month of June and Part of July, 1857." National Archives, Record Group 94.

36 See *Campaigns in the West, 1856-1861. The Journals and Letters of Colonel John Van Deusen Dubois,* ed. George P. Hammond (Tucson, 1949), 5-36; and Lazelle's diary, published as "Puritan and Apache: a Diary," ed. Frank D. Reeves, *New Mexico Hist. Rev.*, XXIII (Oct. 1948), 269-301; XXIV (Jan. 1949), 12-53.

37 "Journal of a March of a Battalion of 3rd Infantry, Composed of Reg'l Hd Qrs. and Companies D. F. & H., 3rd Inf. Commanded by Col. B. L. E. Bonneville 3. Inf., from the mouth of the Gallinas N.M. to Fort Clark, Texas, via Pecos River, pursuant to G. O. No. 6, Hd. Qrs. Army March 12, 1860, and D. S. O. No. 52, dated Head Qrs. Dept New Mexico, Santa Fe, April 29, 1860." National Archives, Record Group 94.

reconciled to it, an attack of dysentery led to his being granted leave of absence on January 18, 1861. On April 2, his sick leave was extended for six months. He had felt well enough by the end of February to leave Fort Clark and journey to St. Louis. Here, learning of the outbreak of the Civil War, he went on to Washington to offer his services in any way his health permitted.

There the matter of Bonneville's retirement came before the Board for Retiring Officers, with the result that he was retired from active duty as of September 9, 1861. Before the end of the year, however, he temporarily came out of retirement to serve until late in 1863 as superintendent of the recruiting service in Missouri and later as chief mustering and disbursing officer in Missouri until November 17, 1865. During these years he was also in command, between 1862 and 1865, of Benton Barracks, Missouri, and of Jefferson Barracks from December, 1865, until October 15, 1866. While at Benton Barracks, he was promoted on March 13, 1865, to the rank of brevet brigadier general "for long and faithful service in the Army."[38]

Now seventy years old and with fifty-three years of service to his country behind him, Bonneville retired to farmland, which he had purchased many years earlier from the United States, near Fort Smith. Here he built a substantial three-story house that has since been razed. On November 30, 1871, at the age of seventy-five, he married Susan Neis, then but twenty-two years of age.[39] With her he

[38] Service Record.

[39] The marriage certificate is in Deed Book E, p. 536, Fort Smith District of Sebastian County, Arkansas. Details of Bonneville's home in Fort Smith appear in Anne E. Ford, "A deBonneville Sketch," *Americana,* XXII (April 1928), 148-52. Bonneville had been married many years before, about 1825 or 1826, to Ann (or Anne) Lewis at Jefferson Barracks. A son died in infancy. A daughter, Mary Irving, named for Washington Irving, also died. The mother's death occurred at about the same time. Major, *op. cit.,* XXI, p. 134. According to this source, Bonneville met Miss Lewis at Carlisle Barracks, Penn., and married her there, but nothing in his service record shows that he was ever stationed at this post. The article by Major is, in fact, so filled with errors that it must be used with great caution. The question of Bonneville's first marriage is at this stage of investigation still hazy.

lived out the few remaining years of his life. Sometime in 1875 or 1876, he wrote for James M. Bradley a sketch of his long career.[40] That career was drawing to a close, and at ten o'clock on the morning of June 12, 1878, death came to the man who, up to that moment at the age of 82, had been the oldest retired officer in the U.S. Army.[41]

A survey of Bonneville's life shows that from his young manhood on he was almost constantly associated with the western frontier and the expansion of the country westward. Of those years, only a few were devoted to the fur trade. Yet that comparatively brief period in his life has come to represent him more widely than any other. The reason for this is not hard to find. It rests firmly upon the fact that his name was broadcast at home and abroad through his good fortune in meeting Washington Irving. Had this meeting, which led to the writing of Irving's book about Bonneville, never taken place, it is likely that Bonneville would have been long forgotten, as were countless other Army officers who had as close a connection with the frontier as he. Hiram Chittenden was unquestionably right in pointing to Irving's narrative as "an apt illustration of Diedrich Knickerbocker's profound idea of the power of history to rescue men and events from the 'wide-spread, insatiable maw of oblivion.' "[42] Whatever else might be claimed for him, certainly Bonneville's name will continue to stand in the minds of most people as the subject of the finest literary and historical account contemporaneous with the great days of the western fur trade in the 1830s.

---

[40] *Contr. to the Hist. Soc. of Montana,* I (1876), 105-10.

[41] Robt. Campbell's letter, June 16, 1876, reporting Bonneville's death to the Adjutant General, appears in *Bonneville,* xxxix n. Bonneville's official eulogy is in *Washington Hist. Quar.,* XVII (July 1927), 227-30.

[42] Hiram M. Chittenden, *History of the American Fur Trade of the Far West* (2 v., Stanford, 1954), I, p. 396.

Joseph R. Walker

by Ardis M. Walker
Kernville, California

The story of the Mountain Man is the story of blazed trails and receding horizons and the fate of a young nation identified with Manifest Destiny. A basic history of the conquest of the West can be written in the lives of these men. They fit into the pattern of national evolvement.

Into the maze of these historic times, on December 13, 1798, was born the Tennesseean Joseph Reddeford Walker.[1] He spent his youth, as did many of his contemporaries of the fur trade, on Tennessee's turbulent frontier. Then, in 1819, the family moved westward to Missouri. Here new horizons beckoned. These were to serve as backdrop for Walker's adventures as he trapped and traded to the Pacific shoreline and broke trails west and southwest for nearly a half century.

Living on the Missouri frontier, Joe had daily contacts with the adventurous spirits of the border country – the fur hunters. The lure of their life induced him to join a hunting and trapping expedition to the Rocky Mountains and New Mexico. This party left Missouri in 1820 or 1821.[2] After caching their trade goods on the Arkansas River, Walker and his party continued into New Mexico. There they were imprisoned as intruders, but were soon released to help the

[1] Although his headstone in the Alhambra Cemetery in Martinez, California, gives Roan County, Tennessee, as his birth place, he could have been born in Goochland County, Virginia. His older brother, Joel, born there in 1797, has said that the family moved to Tennessee in 1802. Joel P. Walker, *Pioneer of Pioneers* (Los Angeles, 1953).

[2] Walker's tombstone says 1820; Joel Walker's narrative, cited above, p. 7, says 1821.

Spaniards on a campaign against marauding Indians. This assistance won trade concessions for the Americans.[3]

After going back to the Arkansas for their cached goods, they met another Missouri company bound for New Mexico. Among these traders was Joe's brother Joel, who thus describes the meeting: "I . . . saw as I supposed, an Indian with his hair flying up and down. He came up and to my immense astonishment I saw he was my brother, Captain Walker, who had started the year before trapping."[4]

One group of traders under Stephen Cooper had become separated from the main party. Joe Walker helped locate these stragglers and bring them into camp. He also helped guide the westbound traders to Santa Fe. In New Mexico they found a ready market for their goods. After disposing of their wares, the traders, including Joe Walker, returned to Missouri. These trading companies of 1821 and 1822 really began the great "Commerce of the Prairies" over the soon-to-become famous Santa Fe Trail. In 1822 William Becknell introduced wagons on the route.

As traffic over the Santa Fe Trail increased there developed a demand that the United States government survey and mark the trail and protect the traffic upon it. As a result of the work of Senator Thomas Hart Benton of Missouri and others, a Congressional bill was passed appropriating $10,000 for surveying and marking the road and $20,000 for making treaties with the Indians en route.

Three commissioners were appointed to carry out the project. Among the special persons employed were Joe Walker and his brothers Joel and John. Joe served as hunter and as chainman.[5] When the treaties with the Osages and

[3] Washington Irving, *The Adventures of Captain Bonneville* (New York, 1843), 44; and D. S. Watson, *West Wind: the Life Story of Joseph Reddeford Walker* (Los Angeles, 1934), 6. See also Merton N. Lovell, "Joseph R. Walker, Mountain Man and Guide of the Far West," master's thesis, Brigham Young University, Provo, Utah, 1959.

[4] Joel Walker, *op. cit.*, 7.

[5] Kate L. Gregg (ed.), *The Road to Santa Fe* (Albuquerque, 1952), 32.

Kansas Indians were negotiated, Joe signed as a witness.[6]

Upon reaching the Mexican border, where the 100th meridian crosses the Arkansas River, the party halted. Inasmuch as authorization for continuing the survey into Mexican territory had not been procured, the company broke up here. Commissioner Sibley continued on to Santa Fe to negotiate; the major part of the company, including Joe Walker, returned to Missouri.

After gaining the necessary permission from Mexico, Sibley returned to Missouri and made arrangements to complete the survey. He hired Joe Walker on May 23, 1827, but two days later Joel came and took his place. Apparently Joe had become interested in political matters in western Missouri. The region was becoming thickly populated and a government was needed.

At Fort Osage, where Joe Walker had established the family home, he was busy aiding in community development that would insure more than a loose frontier organization. The new county of Jackson was being formed. Joe later claimed to have chosen the site of the county seat and named it Independence.[7] He was elected the first sheriff of the county.

Independence was becoming the jumping-off place for the Santa Fe Trail. Previously, the expeditions had outfitted at Franklin, farther east. The caravans were manned by coarse, rugged men, and a sheriff who could control this rough element was needed. Joseph Walker was qualified for such a job.[8] He had been reared on the frontier, was accustomed to its ways and physically could command respect, since he was "about six feet high, strong built, dark complexioned, brave in spirit."[9]

Joe served two two-year terms in the office, giving general satisfaction. He refused to run for a third term, wanting

[6] *United States Statutes at Large,* VII, pp. 270, 272.

[7] *The Sonoma Democrat,* Nov. 25, 1876, p. 1.

[8] Merton Lovell, *op. cit.,* 17.

[9] Washington Irving, *op. cit.,* 44.

to go into business for himself; and also, doubtless, he was lured by adventure. Again leading a pack train, he left Independence in February of 1831 and headed into the Southwest on a trading venture to the Cherokee country. It proved to be a fateful journey for Joe Walker and for Manifest Destiny. At Fort Gibson he met up with Bonneville, while the army officer-on-leave was scouring the country for men qualified to insure the success of his historic expedition to the Rocky Mountains.

There have been conflicting opinions among historians as to the true purpose of this expedition. See the discussion in the sketch on Bonneville in this volume.[10] Whether interested in trading in furs or in expanding national boundaries, Bonneville found in Walker a man well suited in talents and temperament to serve as his top aid and consultant. Mountain Man Michel S. Cerré also was hired as an assistant.

After months of tedious preparation, Bonneville took off from Fort Osage on May 1, 1832. His company consisted of approximately 110 men, including his lieutenants, Walker and Cerré, French-Canadian and American trappers, and several Delaware Indians. Being confident that he could carry his baggage more efficiently on wagons than on pack animals, he outfitted accordingly. The company traveled a historic route, northwest across prairies viscous with mud that sucked at wheels and fetlocks, up the Platte and Sweetwater, and over South Pass to Green River.

After an abortive attempt to build a permanent fort or trading post on the banks of the Green River, Bonneville moved his center of operations to the Salmon River, where he set up winter quarters. From here he dispatched three parties for the fall hunt. One night's adventuring by the brigade led by Joe Walker in Montana could well illustrate the circumstances under which these parties operated. In-

[10] Also in *ibid.*, 427.

dians raided the horses and mules while Walker's overconfident horse guards were playing "old sledge" in a nearby willow copse. After a furious bombardment by the Mountain Men, the Indians were forced to retreat without their live booty.

In the face of such harrassment from the Blackfeet and in a country already well depleted of beaver by preceding parties of trappers, the hunters returned to the Salmon River and then took up quarters on Snake River at the mouth of the Blackfoot.[11] In this region Bonneville conducted the spring hunt, and then went to the summer rendezvous of 1833 on the Green River. Hiram M. Chittenden, pioneer historian of the fur trade, said: "Putting everything together, Captain Bonneville did not have as a result of a year's work of his party of over one hundred men more than about twenty-three packs of beaver. . . That would scarcely pay the wages of his men."[12]

Perhaps the commercial aspects of his activities had not excited the imagination of Captain Bonneville nearly as much as the "design of exploring the country to the Rocky Mountains and beyond." Certainly his recent reversals did not dampen his ardor, as he laid plans for his next major move. Evidently Bonneville told Washington Irving that the purpose of this move was "to have this lake (Great Salt Lake) explored and all its secrets revealed."[13] Certainly such a purpose could not have much bearing on the fur trade.

In fact two men who accompanied Walker on the expedition that Bonneville now planned and who had no reason to conceal its true intent, told a different story. George Nidever said: ". . . There were a large number of trappers gath-

[11] W. A. Ferris spent Christmas day, 1832, here with Walker. W. A. Ferris, *Life in the Rocky Mountains,* edited by P. C. Phillips (Denver, 1940), 184.

[12] H. M. Chittenden, *History of the American Fur Trade of the Far West* (Stanford, 1954), I, p. 405.

[13] Irving, *op. cit.,* 187.

ered at the rendezvous in the Green River valley and among them Capt. Walker and Company, bound for California. We joined him. . . ."[14] Zenas Leonard, another member of the party, recalled: "I was anxious to go to the coast of the Pacific, and for that purpose hired with Mr. Walker as clerk for a certain sum per year."[15] Diplomatic reasons would dictate that a captain of the United States Army, Bonneville, designate some one to lead this expedition into a foreign land. As Irving has reported of Bonneville, "This momentous undertaking he confided to his lieutenant, Mr. Walker, in whose experience and ability he had great confidence."

Walker set out from the Green River valley on July 24, 1833. His company, numbering forty of Bonneville's men, with the possible addition of twenty free trappers, was well equipped for a year's journey into the unknown regions of the farthest west. While still in buffalo country, Walker tarried to make jerkey. Then he struck out westward, skirting the northern shore of Salt Lake. During the long, dry struggle across desert wastes, Walker tempered himself and his followers. He moved down the Humboldt. Beaver were scarce; so was vegetation.

But, barren and uninteresting as their route proved to be, it was to become the mainstream of migration and conquest for their countrymen who sought Manifest Destiny beyond western horizons.

As members of the Walker party approached the sink of the Humboldt they ran into scattered bands of Indians. Leonard said of them: "So eager were they to possess themselves of our traps, that we were forced to quit trapping in this vicinity and make for some other quarter. The great

---

[14] W. H. Ellison (ed.), *The Life and Adventures of George Nidever* (Berkeley, Calif., 1937), 32.

[15] J. C. Ewers (ed.) *Adventures of Zenas Leonard, Fur Trader* (Norman, Okla., 1959), 64-65.

annoyance we sustained in this respect greatly displeased some of our men, and they were for taking vengeance before we left the country – but this was not the disposition of Captain Walker."[16] In spite of Walker's admonition, a few of his men killed some Indians while on the hunt. For this they received a sharp reprimand from their commander.

With the party encamped on Humboldt Lake in early September, the Indians became more numerous and more threatening – perhaps because of the unauthorized shooting which had just occurred. Things looked grim enough for Walker to authorize an attack on the besieging Indians, for which he was bitterly criticised by Irving. However, on-the-spot testimony by Leonard and Nidever was to the effect that the action was necessary.

Breaking camp, Walker moved his party to Carson Lake. From here, starved and frozen, they battled for three weeks against granite bluffs and entrapping snow banks to win their way across the Sierra. Living on famine-blue flesh of famished horses – seventeen of them – they worked their way between the watersheds of the Merced and Tuolumne rivers after ascending a southerly tributary of the East Walker River.[17]

Here the Walker odyssey took on epic significance in the words of Leonard; words that came to him out of the memory of an exhausting search that meandered to and fro as the men were frustrated first by one river chasm, then the other, while seeking escape from the divide between rivers. In Leonard's words: "Here we began to encounter in our path, many small streams which would shoot out from under these high snow banks, and, after running a short distance in deep chasms which they have through the ages cut in the rocks, precipitate from one lofty precipice to another,

[16] *Ibid.*, 68.

[17] F. P. Farquhar, *History of the Sierra Nevada* (Berkeley, 1965).

until they are lost in rain below. Some of these precipices appeared to us to be more than a mile high."[18] In this manner was recorded the discovery of incomparable Yosemite.

Other major discoveries were to follow. A few days later Leonard was to add to his journal the first reference to the Big Trees of California. He noted: "In the last two day's traveling we have found some trees of the redwood species; incredibly large – some of which would measure from sixteen to eighteen fathoms around the trunk at the height of a man's head from the ground."

Camped at the mouth of the San Joaquin River, with ears pressed to the ground, they heard the far-off rumble of the Pacific. The inspired Leonard remarked: "The idea of being within hearing of the *end* of the *Far West* inspired the heart of every member of our company with a patriotic feeling for his country's honor. . ." Reaching the Pacific, they encountered Captain Baggshaw of a Boston ship who described for them the country, its settlements and its people. Leonard exclaimed: "Our government should be vigilant. She should assert her claim by taking possession of the whole territory as soon as possible. . ."

Walker moved on across the Santa Cruz Mountains to old Mission San Juan Bautista where he made arrangements to spend the winter. Such arrangements were to insure a winter enlivened by senoritas at fandangos, rodeos, and bull-and-bear fights, to round out a refined rendezvous for the trappers.

On January 13, 1834, Walker pulled stakes and moved from San Juan Bautista to the San Joaquin Valley. He set up a hunting camp by the river of the same name, then journeyed to Monterey to trade for such supplies as would be needed for his trip east to his rendezvous with Bonneville. From this camp the Americans aided Spaniards in catching

---

[18] This and the three Leonard quotations following are from his book cited above, pages 79, 83, 89 and 95.

wild horses. They also joined them in chasing down Indians with stolen horses. Walker traded with the Spaniards for some of the horses.

At last, with "52 men [six having remained in California], 315 horses – and for provisions, 47 beef, and 30 dogs,"[19] the party moved up the San Joaquin Valley. Indians near the mouth of Kern River canyon told them of a pass toward the headwaters of the river that would lead them out onto the east slope of the Sierra. With two of these Indians as guides, they moved on over Greenhorn Mountain and up the South Fork Valley of the Kern to where they could look out onto the desert country to the east of the range. This was Walker Pass, a discovery of major import. Here was the northernmost snow-free pass across the Sierra Nevada. Leonard recounted: "We here made our pilots presents of a horse, some tobacco and many trifling trinkets captivating to the eye of an Indian, when they left us to return to their friends. . . The country on this side is much inferior to that on the opposite side – the soil being thin and rather sandy. . ."[20]

After crossing the pass, the Walker party went north through Owens Valley along the eastern base of the Sierra. A near-tragic detour in a north-easterly direction away from the Sierra cost them 64 horses, 10 cows and 15 dogs, not to mention precious time and almost the last ounce of human energy. Finally striking back toward the Sierra, they hit their out-trail and retraced it to their summer rendezvous.

Walker brought back to Bonneville more visions than of Yosemite and Giant Sequoias. It is safe to assume that his discoveries filled in much of the data needed for producing accurate maps of the country west of the Rockies. Washington Irving in 1836 published his work, *Astoria or Anecdotes of an Enterprise Beyond the Rocky Mountains.* He

19 *Ibid.*, 119.

20 *Ibid.*, 123.

also published an accompanying map. Carl I. Wheat in his *Mapping the American West, 1540-1857* (Worcester, Mass. 1954), calls this map "another of the milestones of western cartography." He adds: "Doubtless Irving picked up his information from Captain Bonneville." He could have added further that, doubtless, Bonneville picked up much of *his* information from Walker. The same would be true of the maps in Irving's book on Bonneville.

Though his men may have enjoyed their reunion at the rendezvous of 1834, Bonneville was not altogether happy. "If the first year of his venture into the fur business had been unsuccessful, the second year was disasterous."[21] Bonneville had taken few furs, and Walker's tour to California had failed, so far as fur gathering was concerned. Bonneville had only ten to fifteen packs of beaver to send back to the States. Cerré, who had come out with supplies from the East, returned after the rendezvous with the year's meager beaver catch.

While Bonneville turned back to the Lower Columbia, Walker led a band to the north. He visited the Bighorn, Yellowstone, and the headwaters of the Missouri. During the winter he traded with the Crows; the spring he spent in trapping in the Wyoming and Montana regions.[22] He came into the rendezvous of 1835 and met Bonneville, who announced that he would take the peltries to the States. He would have much explaining to do to his commercial sponsors for business failure, and to his army superiors for overstaying his leave of absence.

This was Walker's last rendezvous as a Bonneville man. He continued in the mountains, but took service with the big organization popularly called the American Fur Company. He was a brigade leader; but of his paths in 1836 little is known. At the rendezvous of 1837 he became well acquainted with Alfred Jacob Miller, the famous pioneer

[21] Lovell, *op. cit.*, 53.

[22] Leonard, *op. cit.*, 135.

artist who accompanied Capt. William Drummond Stewart, famous Scot adventurer, into the West that year.

Miller made two paintings of Walker: the first, a regular portrait; the second, one of Walker and his Indian squaw mounted on horses. Miller titled the second painting "Bourgeoise W--r, and his squaw." In a note regarding the picture Miller wrote: "The term 'Bourgeois' is given in the mountains to one who has a body of trappers placed under his immediate command. Capt. W--r, being trustworthy and intelligent, received an appointment of this kind, and with his men had many battles with the Indians. . ."[23]

After the rendezvous of 1837 Walker led his detachment of trappers back to the streams for beaver. Again information is scant as to his whereabouts. He appears to have gone into Arizona (probably in 1837-38), where he is reputed to have discovered a metal that later proved to be gold.[24] Here, or elsewhere, he acquired horses with which he showed up at the rendezvous of 1838.[25]

In the fall of 1839 we find Walker at Fort Davy Crockett on the Green River in northwestern Colorado. Here he becomes the leader in an unusual incident. Indians had stolen most of the horses of the trapper band in this sheltered and supposedly safe trapper retreat of Brown's Hole. Instead of endeavoring to recover the stolen stock, a party of the trappers, led by Philip Thompson, resorted to the British Fort Hall on the Snake River and stole some horses from that fort. Moving southward, they encountered some friendly Snake Indians and stole more horses from them.

Returning to Fort Davy Crockett, Thompson and his men were roundly condemned by Joe Walker, Kit Carson,

---

23 M. C. Ross, *The West of Alfred Jacob Miller* (Norman, 1951), plate 78. Just when Walker married this Indian woman and what became of her have not been determined.

24 T. E. Farish, *History of Arizona* (Phoenix, 1915), II, p. 241.

25 Bernard De Voto, *Across the Wide Missouri* (Boston, 1957), 343.

Joe Meek, and others of the more ethical trappers. The Thompson contingent took the loot to a post at the mouth of the Duchesne River. When the wronged Snakes brought their complaint to Fort Crockett, the better whites at the post decided to recover the stolen stock and return it to the owners. Under the command of Walker about 30 men followed the white thieves. Some skilful and bold maneuvers resulted in recovery of the horses and their return.[26]

During the winter at Fort Crockett, Walker proposed a journey to California by boat down the Green and Colorado rivers, trapping for beaver en route. Probably geographical knowledge from the Indians or other trappers induced them not to undertake the project. But Walker appears to have continued to toy with the idea. In 1843 he told Theodore Talbot, who was with Fremont's second expedition, that he had "often endeavored to raise a party to descend Green River but with no success. He thinks that the canions of that river are in a country of high table lands."[27]

The beaver skin trade rapidly declined, and the last rendezvous was held in 1840. In the meantime the Old Spanish Trail, Santa Fe to Los Angeles, had been opened and over it horses and mules had been brought eastward. Retiring trappers saw in this field a substitute for the fur trade. Some trappers, such as Peg-leg Smith, Philip Thompson and others carried on the business by stealing California horses. Walker undertook a legitimate trade.

With pack horses loaded with beaver skins he, Henry Fraeb and others went overland to California. He had a passport visaed by the Mexican charge d'affairs in Washington, which he presented to the officials in California. He and Fraeb sold 417 pounds of beaver to Abel Stearns, Los Angeles merchant, for $1147. They then purchased stock,

---

[26] A full account of events, with sources cited, is found in L. R. and A. W. Hafen, *To the Rockies and Oregon* (Glendale, Calif., 1955), 176-177.

[27] Theodore Talbot, *The Journal of* (Portland, 1931), 48.

paying $2 each for mares and $12 apiece for mules.[28] Moving eastward with a sizeable band, they met the first company of westbound emigrants in the Green River valley. Soon after, in August 1841, Fraeb was killed by Indians on Battle Creek, south-central Wyoming.[29]

Walker was soon in business with Jim Bridger and Louis Vasquez, notable Mountain Men. They continued trapping and trading, using Fort Bridger in southwestern Wyoming as chief base of operations. In the spring of 1843 Walker and Vasquez, traveling east toward Fort Laramie, met Sir William D. Stewart on another of his western hunting ventures. With Stewart was the noted newspaperman, Matthew Field, who wrote of the meeting: "Found the traders all encamped with their furs in piles and their seventy animals grazing in the river bottom. . . [makes mention of] Capt. Walker, a fine old mountaineer – hale, stout-built and eagle-eyed with gray hair."[30]

This year of 1843 saw the "Great Migration" to Oregon. On July 20, 1843, Overton Johnson, westbound on the Oregon Trail, tells of meeting Walker and Vasquez on the Sweetwater carrying furs to Fort Laramie.[31] The leader of one of the westbound parties was Joseph B. Chiles who had been to California before with the emigrants of 1841. His group was now heading for California with mill irons and other accoutrements of the new society they hoped to establish on the Pacific. Near Fort Laramie they engaged Joe Walker to guide them. Says George R. Stewart, "No one living was better qualified to act as a guide on the trail to California."[32]

---

28 L. R. and A. W. Hafen, *Old Spanish Trail* (Glendale, 1954), 242-243. See also the accounts in the Stearns papers, Huntington Library, San Marino, California.

29 See the biography of Henry Fraeb, *Mountain Men*, III, p. 137.

30 Matthew C. Field, *Prairie and Mountain Sketches* (Norman, 1957), 110-11.

31 Overton Johnson and W. H. Winter, *Route Across the Rocky Mountains* (Princeton, 1932), 15.

32 G. R. Stewart, *The California Trail* (New York, 1962), 42.

The party divided at Fort Hall. Chiles with 9 or 10 men "pressed on down the Snake, or Lewis River, with a view to obtain fresh provisions at Fort Boise, to reach California by a direct route talked of by the hunters and, perhaps after reaching Sutter's Fort, to send aid to meet the other party."[33] Walker guided the rest of the company to California by Walker Pass. Just south of Owens Lake they buried their mill irons and abandoned their wagons, the first to roll across the eastern boundary of California.

Joe Walker then acquired more horses in Southern California and departed with them over the Old Spanish Trail in 1844. After reaching the Mountain Meadows (present Utah) he caught up with Fremont, returning on his second expedition. He then guided Fremont on to Bent's Fort.[34] It is significant that Fremont appointed Walker as guide through the Ute country although he already had with him such notable guides and scouts as Thomas Fitzpatrick, Kit Carson, and Alex Godey. Walker and Carson left Fremont at Bent's Fort, Kit going to his home in New Mexico while Joe went north to the Fort Laramie region.

At Fort Laramie members of an Oregon-bound party hired Walker in the summer of 1844 to guide them to Fort Bridger.[35] In this vicinity he appears to have spent the winter of 1844-45. The next summer emigrants again encountered Walker on the Oregon Trail. On July 17, 1845, Joel Palmer met him on the Sweetwater en route to Fort Bridger.[36]

Soon after, Walker accompanied Fremont on his third exploring expedition, that of 1845. On this tour he joined such veterans of the fur trade as Kit Carson, Dick Owens, and Alex Godey on a historic journey. After exploring

---

33 H. H. Bancroft, *History of California* (San Francisco), IV, p. 393.

34 J. C. Fremont, *Report of an Exploring Expedition* (Washington, 1845), 271.

35 L. R. Hafen and F. M. Young, *Fort Laramie* (Glendale, 1938), 105.

36 Palmer's Journal, as reproduced in R. G. Thwaites, *Early Western Travels* (Cleveland, 1906), XXX, p. 70.

Great Salt Lake they pushed across Nevada. Fremont split his forces, leading 15 men himself, while Edward Kern headed the larger force with Walker as guide, which traveled to and along the Humboldt. The two groups joined at a lake which Fremont named Walker Lake, after his guide. Again the company was divided, Fremont crossing the Sierra to the west, while Walker guided the main party southward to avoid the higher mountains. They finally met in the San Joaquin Valley.

Fremont received permission from jittery Mexican officials to remain in California for the winter, provided he kept away from the coastal settlements. Then, as he moved coastward, General Castro asked him to leave the province immediately. Fremont's response was melodramatic, if not downright foolish. He withdrew his party to nearby Hawks Peak, unfurled the American flag and defied the Mexican Government to dislodge him. Finally he withdrew in the night in the direction of Sutter's Fort.

His withdrawal was without the company of his chief guide, Joe Walker. Joe had had enough of the melodramatic and had requested and received his discharge. Here Joe Walker stepped off a stage on which was soon to be enacted a major scene in the drama. He had helped to set the stage for the act of conquest to be played out by Kearny, Stockton, Fremont, Figueroa, Ide and many more. He would loiter in the wings and behind the scenes for other acts to follow.

Joe journeyed into Southern California after leaving Hawks Peak. He would move horses east to be sold to the United States Army now on the prod under alarms of war with Mexico. This Joe Walker adventure was described in an interview by D. F. McClellan, Joe's nephew who journeyed with him. McClellan had helped Walker "and some of his men" drive a herd of horses "south to the Chino ranch, beyond Los Angeles, then in late May set out for the east, going via Cajon Pass and the Spanish Trail to Utah Lake." The interview continues: "Passing by the southern extremity of this, they traveled up the Provo, one of the tributaries of the lake, and thence over a range of the Bear Mountains, ultimately arrived in safety at Fort Bridger, on Black's Fork of Green River. Everyone here was well acquainted with Captain Joe, and here the party remained for some time."[37]

Here in July, Joe met Edwin Bryant in time to give warning of the pitfalls of the cutoff by way of the south end of Salt Lake over which Lansford W. Hastings was luring emigrants to California. The heeding of this advice would have avoided the great tragedy at Donner Lake.[38]

Joe moved on with his herd to Bent's Fort, where, while awaiting the arrival of Colonel Price's regiment, he disposed of his mules to Uncle Sam's army.[39] Then he went east, carrying letters from west-bound emigrants at Fort Bridger to their friends in St. Louis.[40] After visiting friends in Missouri he headed west again. By March 27, 1847, he had met up with Solomon Sublette and Tom Fitzpatrick near Santa Fe.[41]

Then he decided to return to California. After reaching the coast he procured a band of horses and headed them eastward over the Old Spanish Trail. En route he joined the party of Kit Carson and Lieutenant Brewerton, who reported that Walker was taking his horses to trade with the Indians in Utah.[42] After completing this venture he returned again to California.

---

37 *Oakland Daily Transcript*, Jan. 26-29, 1873, as cited by Dale Morgan in his *Overland in 1846* (Georgetown, Calif., 1963), 373.

38 Edwin Bryant, *What I Saw in California* (New York, 1948), 143.

39 W. H. Emory, *Notes on a Military Reconnoissance* (Washington, 1848), 420, 432.

40 J. Roderic Korns, *West From Fort Bridger* (Salt Lake City, 1951), 47.

41 C. L. Camp, *James Clyman, Frontiersman* (Portland, 1960), 268.

42 George Brewerton's *Ride With Kit Carson*, as quoted in L. R. and A. W. Hafen, *Old Spanish Trail, op. cit.*, 324.

With the coming of the gold rush, Joe Walker and his nephew, James Walker, supplied meat to the miners.[43] But no single activity, not even the all-absorbing quest for gold, could halt the restless feet of the aging pathfinder for long. The measure of his wanderings, even after the gold rush, is fabulous. In 1850 he headed an expedition to the Upper Virgin River and visited the Zuni and Hopi villages.[44] In 1851 he returned to California, only to head back to Santa Fe to purchase sheep for sale in California. He found the price too high. However, he did return with a report of brushes with Apaches and Navajoes. It was reported that Walker rested at Chino after being six weeks on the road from New Mexico, from whence he had departed on November 1st.[45]

During the early 1850s the question of a railroad to the Pacific Coast was one of the liveliest subjects considered in Congress. Unable to decide upon a route, the federal government put several corps of engineers into the field to survey four possible lines to find which was the most feasible. In that year Walker, in response to a request from a senate committee of the California Legislature, made a statement "on the practicability of a Railroad from San Francisco to the United States." He recommended a route which would have crossed the Sierra Nevada at Walker Pass, continued across the desert to the vicinity of Las Vegas, crossed the Colorado River near the mouth of the Virgin, then continued across southern Arizona.[46] The route was not adopted.

For three years Walker tried ranching near the San Isidro Ranch of John Gilroy. By 1854 curiosity gained the ascendancy again and Walker led an expedition to explore

---

43 Watson, *op. cit.,* 100.

44 A long account of the trip is given in the *San Francisco Daily Herald,* Sept. 25, 1853.

45 *Los Angeles Star,* Dec. 13, 1851, quoted in Watson, 103.

46 The statement is published and annotated in Pat Adler and Walt Wheelock, *Walker's Railroad Routes, 1853* (Glendale, 1965), 30-34.

the Mono Lake region. On his return to California he took over a cattle ranch near Soledad Mission[47] not far from where he spent Christmas day in 1843 with members of the Chiles party.

In 1859 Walker responded to the call of Colonel Hoffman and guided the troops up the Colorado River in a campaign against the Mojaves.[48] With the trouble over, Joe tarried to examine "likely formations." Among these he found gold, according to a report he made after returning to California in 1860.[49]

In California, gold was still the watchword; and gold could be used as an excuse for further explorations. Walker had run onto prospects during his trapping and trading days. The remembrance of these was enough to draw to him Argonauts who felt they had missed out on the cream of the golden harvest of the Mother Lode, some of whom had drifted south to the Kern River diggings. Here he organized another company at the old camp of Keysville in 1861.

Leaving the Kern River by way of Walker Pass, he crossed an arm of the Mojave Desert and the Death Valley region to the Colorado. Frustrated by Indian harrassment in his attempt to push into the country near Prescott and the Little Colorado, where he and Jack Ralston were reported to have found gold in the 1830s, he continued on eastward into New Mexico. There he enlisted himself and his company to fight belligerent Indians.

After other military services, Walker finally headed south and west across New Mexico, thence on a more westerly course across southern Arizona. He then moved across the Gila Desert and up the Hassayampa to the heart of the Arizona wilderness.[50] About five miles from present Pres-

---

[47] *Daily California Chronicle* (San Francisco), April 15, 1856.

[48] Account of William E. Goodyear, printed in J. S. C. Abbott, *Christopher Carson* (New York, 1873), 313-21.

[49] Watson, *op. cit.*

[50] D. E. Conner, *Joseph Reddeford Walker and the Arizona Adventure* (Norman, 1956).

cott his company felled trees and built a corral in a hollow square that the savages could not break through, in which the sixty head of mules were kept during the night.

From this center of operations they fanned out to prospect for gold. Their first major discovery was made on Lynx Creek where they found gravel that went $4.80 to the pan. Camp was immediately moved to the new discovery, where a miners' meeting was called. The records of this new mining district hint of the sturdy characters and rough times that were to feature the emergence of a new commonwealth. The preamble of the Walker Mining District on Lynx Creek included, among other resolves: "That we denounce the originators of the many falsehoods, circulated by the faint hearted many who have returned to their shin-warming fires as a set unworthy of the name of pioneers. . ."[51]

Reports from the Walker diggings must have been considered with favor. Shortly Fort Whipple was to be built "in the heart of the gold region." And, shortly, Governor Goodwin was to designate a capital for the new Territory at Prescott, a few miles away in the heart of the Walker diggings.

Here in his last wilderness Joe Walker had served as agent of a lesser destiny. He had shattered horizons which had veiled another virgin land. The trails he broke led to the seat of government of a new society. Even into these turbulent years of the rebellion he had served his country ably in the process of consolidation of the new empire it had wrested from Mexico; an empire which he had measured in its entirety and helped to make accessible to the forces of Manifest Destiny. Now the land is his testament. Walker Lake, Walker River, Walker Pass and, in the wake of his latest explorations, Walker Creek and Walker Post Office on Lynx Creek, and the Walker Mining District,

[51] Journal of the Pioneer and Walker Mining Districts, 1863-65, quoted in Conner, *ibid.,* 101.

birthplace of a new state, give mute evidence that he "passed this way."

After returning to California in 1867 to live out his years with his nephew, James T. Walker, on a ranch in Contra Costa County, Joe made a typically modest request. It was that his headstone should say of him, "Camped at Yosemite, November 13, 1833." The land knows the ashes of his camp fires. They are scattered down every stream, over every mountain and across every desert from the Missouri to the "extreme end of the far west." The proper design for his ultimate monument might well be a crest of shining mountains on a field of continent, bordered westerly by the blue Pacific. No man shall ever match his continental vision nor his intimate perspective of the Great West. His headstone adds that he died on November 13, 1872, an appropriate anniversary. It seems unnecessary to say that breaking trail to his Last Rendezvous was no problem for Old Joe Walker.

Nathaniel Jarvis Wyeth

by WILLIAM R. SAMPSON
University of Alberta, Edmonton, Canada

Nathaniel Jarvis Wyeth, the fourth son of Jacob and Elizabeth Jarvis Wyeth, was born on January 29, 1802, at his father's Fresh Pond Hotel near Cambridge, Massachusetts. He did not follow his eldest brother, Jacob, to Harvard, but joined his father in the management of the hotel. On his twenty-second birthday he married his cousin, Elizabeth Jarvis Stone.[1] During the slack season, Wyeth worked to harvest winter's ice from the surface of Fresh Pond to stock the hotel's ice house. His efforts to improve on the back-breaking methods of cutting and shifting the heavy blocks resulted in a series of inventions that made ice a principal export of Boston. With the exception of five frustrating years spent in the fur trade of the Rocky Mountains and Oregon, he was associated with the New England ice trade for the rest of his life.

About 1825 Wyeth devised a horse-drawn ice cutter by means of which the surface of the pond could be grooved into uniform squares which were then broken apart with cutting bars. A historian of the ice trade estimates that this

[1] Lucius R. Paige, *History of Cambridge, Massachusetts, 1630-1877, with a Genealogical Register* (Boston, 1877), 705; Stephen P. Sharples, "Nathaniel Jarvis Wyeth," in *Cambridge Historical Society Publications, Proceedings, 1906-1907* (Cambridge, Mass.), II, pp. 33, 36; John B. Wyeth, *Oregon; or a Short History of a Long Journey. . .*, (*Early Western Travels, 1748-1846, vol.* XXI, edited by Reuben Gold Thwaites, Cleveland, 1905), 23n; Richard O. Cummings, *The American Ice Harvests: A Historical Study in Technology, 1800-1918* (Berkeley, Calif., 1949), 18; Thomas W. Baldwin, comp., *Vital Records of Cambridge, Massachusetts, to the Year 1850* (Boston, 1915), II, p. 437. Nathaniel J. Wyeth was one of the fifth generation of American-born Wyeths. Nicholas Wyeth, the first Wyeth in America, settled in Cambridge about 1645.

basic invention cut the costs of harvesting ice from thirty cents to ten cents a ton and made possible the retail sale of ice by weight rather than by measure. Wyeth soon joined Frederic Tudor's ice company, entering an exclusive agreement to supply Tudor with the harvest from Fresh Pond.[2] Wyeth was joining an important business which provided Boston with a new staple export. The ice trade helped to revitalize Boston's trade with the West Indies and the Far East which had been all but destroyed by the decline of the maritime fur trade and the disruptions of war and depression.

Wyeth turned out the Fresh Pond ice crop for Tudor during the winter of 1826-27, and superintended carting the ice to Boston as well as the fitting and loading of Tudor's vessels. His success in beating the competition during the warm winter of 1827-28 so pleased Tudor that he raised Wyeth's salary to $1200 per year, and with this new financial security Wyeth was able to quit the management of his father's hotel. In 1829, Wyeth was granted a patent on his ice-cutting process; but his exclusive contract with Tudor, who sought to monopolize ice exports, thwarted Wyeth's desire to advance himself by increasing the volume of shipments. He was therefore receptive to new means for expending his restless energies and ambitions.[3]

Wyeth became interested in the schemes of Hall Jackson Kelley, a talented but erratic Boston teacher, mathematician

---

[2] Cummings, *American Ice Harvests,* 18-23. Tudor inaugurated the exportation of New England ice in 1806 when he shipped 130 tons to Martinique. In spite of embargoes, wars, depressions, and warm winters, he extended his trade to include Havana, Jamaica, Charleston, Savannah, and New Orleans. During the 1830s he extended the ice trade to Calcutta and the western Pacific. The tonnage exported from Boston reached 4,000 tons in 1826 (up from 1,200 tons a decade earlier) of which Tudor shipped approximately half. For a detailed study of Tudor's ice business see Henry G. Pearson, "Frederic Tudor, Ice King," in *Proceedings of the Massachusetts Historical Society,* LXV, pp. 169-215.

[3] Cummings, *op. cit.,* 21, 23-24, 26; for Wyeth's first patent, see *Journal of the Franklin Institute,* new series III (June 1829), 417-18.

and engineer, and enrolled in Kelley's American Society for Encouraging the Settlement of Oregon, founded in 1829. In June 1831, Kelley issued a twenty-eight page *Manual of the Oregon Expedition* (also known as *A General Circular to all Persons of Good Character, who wish to Emigrate to the Oregon Territory.* . . .) which outlined his proposals to establish two commercial and agricultural communities on the Columbia River, on which he proposed to settle ". . . a free and enlightened, but redundant population from the American Republic. . ." Wyeth was listed in the *General Circular* as one of thirty-seven agents from whom information on the proposed migration could be obtained. Subscribing emigrants were to pay their own expenses to St. Louis, where they would form into military companies under the leadership of Captain B. L. E. Bonneville and Major Joshua Pilcher. A captain was to be appointed for every fifty male adults, and Wyeth was promised one of the captaincies.[4]

During the summer and autumn of 1831, Wyeth planned and worked for Kelley's proposed expedition to Oregon which was scheduled to leave Boston on the first of January. As the New Year approached, Kelley first consolidated the women and children of the second expedition into the first, and then postponed the departure date until June first. Wyeth became increasingly certain that Kelley's expedition would never leave Boston;[5] and, since he was interested in Oregon for trade not colonization,[6] he determined to organize his own joint-stock company to trade for furs on the Columbia River.

[4] Hall Jackson Kelley, *A History of the Settlement of Oregon and the Interior of Upper California.* . . (Springfield, Mass., 1868), 64, 100; Hall Jackson Kelley, *A General Circular to all Persons of Good Character, who Wish to Emigrate to the Oregon Territory.* . . (Charlestown, Mass., 1831), 3.

[5] Frederick G. Young, ed., *The Correspondence and Journals of Captain Nathaniel J. Wyeth, 1831-6* (*Sources of the History of Oregon,* vol. 1, parts 3-6, Eugene, Oregon, 1899), 8-11. Hereafter cited as Young, *Wyeth Journals.*

[6] Kelley, *History of the Settlement of Oregon,* 65.

Wyeth planned a five year expedition and hoped to enlist fifty men, each of whom was to pay $40 toward the expenses of equipment, arms and transport beyond St. Louis. The men were to share eighty percent of the profits; Wyeth would take sixteen percent for his risks and services, and the remaining four percent was assigned to Wyeth's brother Jacob, who had agreed to serve as the company's surgeon. Wyeth was able to provide about $3,000 of his own money to finance the venture. He raised an additional $5,000 by mortgaging a lot he had recently purchased from Harvard College, and by borrowing, largely from his brothers and from Frederic Tudor, to whom he evidently assigned the patent for his ice cutter and an $800 mortgage on his new house. He was promised an additional $5,000 by the same men to secure the cost of a ship and cargo which were to be sent to the Columbia River by Henry Hall and the firm of Williams and Tucker the following year when Wyeth would have a return cargo, the proceeds of which would pay for the goods received and the freight.

In the meantime, he arranged to make purchases from the cargo of the brig "Sultana," which was scheduled to sail to the Northwest Coast in 1832 on an independent trading voyage for Joseph Baker and Son.[7] While he was arranging for the financing of his Pacific Trading Company, Wyeth collected information on tobacco growing and salmon curing, and procured traps, guns, trading goods, and other equipage for the expedition. To facilitate the transport of his baggage, Wyeth designed and built three amphibious wagons which one member of the party called "Nat-wye-thiums."[8]

The people of Cambridge considered the enterprise to be "extremely notional,"[9] and Wyeth was able to enlist only

---

[7] Young, *Wyeth Journals,* 4, 6-7, 26-27, 30, 37, 46-50, 56.

[8] *Ibid.,* 3, 27-29, 33, 35, 39, 79; John B. Wyeth, *Oregon,* 31-32.

[9] Wyeth, *Oregon,* 32.

twenty men in the Boston area. Early in March 1832, "Captain" Wyeth and his men went into camp on Long Island in Boston Harbor, where for ten days they trained for the rigors of the trip ahead. Each man was provided with a uniform, a musket, an axe and a large clasped knife for eating and common purposes. Even Wyeth's critical kinsman, John B. Wyeth, noted approvingly that "the whole bore an aspect of energy, good contrivance, and competent means."[10] On March 11, the little "Band of Oregon Adventurers" sailed from Boston for Baltimore, where they were joined by four additional recruits, including Jacob Wyeth and John Ball who was to become Oregon's first schoolmaster. From Baltimore, the expedition traveled by railroad and steamboat to St. Louis via Pittsburgh. At St. Louis, which they reached in mid-April, it became all too apparent that Wyeth's enthusiasm for a trading venture to Oregon was greater than his knowledge of the country to be crossed and the equipment needed, and the unsuitable "Nat-wyethiums" were sold for less than half their cost. Kenneth McKenzie and William Sublette, the St. Louis-based suppliers of the Rocky Mountain Fur Company, were outfitting a caravan for the annual fur trade rendezvous in the Rocky Mountains, and, fearing no competition from Wyeth and his greenhorns, they incorporated Wyeth's party into their own.

From St. Louis Wyeth's men took the steamer "Otter" upstream to Independence, where they remained ten days while Wyeth purchased three horses for each of his men and collected a herd of fifteen sheep and two yoke of oxen as a precaution against hunger on the plains. At Independence, some of Wyeth's men began to question the goals and purposes of the expedition and two deserted. Sublette and Robert Campbell led the combined party of some eighty

[10] *Ibid.*, 33.

men out of Independence on May 12. In daily marches of about twenty-five miles, the expedition followed the Santa Fe Trail for several days, then headed northwest to cross the Kansas River in the vicinity of Topeka. By this time three more men had taken "French leave," including Wyeth's young cousin Thomas Livermore, a bugler who had been recruited to provide music for marching.[11]

In late May of 1832 the party reached the "foul and muddy" waters of the Platte opposite Grand Island. Proceeding up the south bank of the Platte, the men soon slaughtered the last of the livestock. The "sharp gnawings of hunger" and debilitating sickness brought on by drinking the warm, thick water of the Platte led to "grumbling, discontent, and dejection."[12] Not until they reached the forks of the Platte almost a week later did the party sight buffalo. Fifty miles above the forks, they crossed the South Platte and followed the North Platte west. At the Laramie River they were forced to halt to construct boats and rafts to carry them across. Sublette constructed bull boats (the buoyant craft of buffalo hide stretched over a framework of pliable willow cuttings and waterproofed with buffalo tallow) and advised Wyeth to do the same. "However, Captain Wyeth was not a man easily diverted by the advice of others,"[13] and he had his men construct a raft to be guided across the swift current by a rope. As Sublette had foreseen, the rope broke; and the raft, loaded with precious blacksmith equipment and gunpowder, hit a snag and unloaded its cargo irretrievably into the swirling waters. At this point Wyeth's kinsman John and others became "entirely convinced that we were engaged in an expedition without being provided with the means to accomplish it."[14]

[11] *Ibid.*, 34-49 *passim;* Kate Ball Powers, Flora Ball Hopkins and Lucy Ball, comp., *Autobiography of John Ball* (Grand Rapids, Mich., 1925), 65.

[12] Wyeth, *Oregon,* 49-50.

[13] John Ball, "Across the Continent Seventy Years Ago," edited by Kate Ball Powers, in *Quarterly of the Oregon Historical Society,* III (March 1902), 88.

From the Laramie crossing, the party followed the Platte and then the Sweetwater to South Pass. Before reaching rendezvous at Pierre's Hole on July 8, they endured intermittent snow, fireless camps, and an attack by Blackfeet which resulted in the loss of a dozen horses. By this time, three men, including Wyeth's brother, were too weak to walk and were permitted to ride. Wyeth remained at Pierre's Hole until July 17 exchanging his worn out horses, some of which he claimed had been purposely injured by his men.[15] While Sublette traded goods for peltry and dispensed his supply of alcohol to trappers and Indians, Wyeth's men "being idle, had time to think, to reflect, and to be uneasy."[16] At a New England-style town meeting, which he called after "considerable altercation," Wyeth read the roll and asked each man if he would go on. Seven of the remaining eighteen, including both Jacob and John B. Wyeth, chose to seek comforts other than those of the unknown, and Wyeth was left with eleven men.

Wyeth attached his diminished party to a group of westbound trappers led by Milton Sublette and Henry Fraeb, and on July 17 the combined party left the main encampment en route for the Salmon River in Idaho. That night they camped about eight miles from rendezvous, and before they could resume their march the next morning they observed two parties of some two hundred Gros Ventres coming over the pass. Their guide Antoine, a Flathead chief, was sent to treat with the approaching Indians, but he instructed a companion to shoot the Gros Ventres chief to avenge the death of his father. The resulting encounter was the well-known and oft-reported Battle of Pierre's Hole, in which Wyeth's men were reported to have taken little or no part.[17] During the day-long battle, in which reinforcements

[14] The incident is described in Wyeth, *Oregon*, 54-56; Young, *Wyeth Journals*, 156; and Ball, "Across the Continent Seventy Years Ago," 88-89.

[15] Young, *Wyeth Journals*, 89.

[16] Wyeth, *Oregon*, 64.

[17] *Ibid.*, 65-72.

were summoned from the main camp, several of William Sublette's men were killed, and Sublette himself was wounded. Milton Sublette and Fraeb moved back to the main camp with Wyeth's men to patch up the wounded and bury their dead. Finally, on the 24th, they were able to move off once more toward the Snake River.[18]

The trappers moved slowly southwestward, trapping beaver and "making meat." After caching six loads of Wyeth's goods and furs, they followed the Portneuf to the Snake River Valley, which they found trapped-out by the Hudson's Bay Company. Sublette and Fraeb parted from Wyeth's company near the junction of the Snake and Owyhee rivers in southwestern Idaho, and Wyeth hurried on across the Blue Mountains to Fort Walla Walla, the Hudson's Bay Company post on the Columbia near the mouth of the Walla Walla River. There Pierre Pambrun provided Wyeth with a decent suit of clothes and the first bread since leaving the forks of the Platte on June first, four and a half months earlier.

Leaving the horses in Pambrun's care, Wyeth and his men set off down the Columbia in a company barge provided by the "hospitable entertainer" Pambrun. They arrived late in October of 1832 at Fort Vancouver where Wyeth was welcomed by John McLoughlin, Chief Factor of the Hudson's Bay Company's Columbia Department. The end of the trip was also the end of the venture. Wyeth learned that the "Sultana" had been wrecked in the South Pacific; and, following the death of Guy Trumbull at Fort Vancouver, the remainder of the band unanimously requested to be released from their engagement.[19] Wyeth, however, re-

18 Young, *Wyeth Journals,* 159-160.

19 *Ibid.,* 160-178 *passim.* For an account of the loss of the "Sultana" see Frances Fuller Victor, "Flotsam and Jetsam of the Pacific – the Owyhee, the Sultana, and the May Dacre," in *Quarterly of the Oregon Historical Society,* II (March 1901), 41-52. All but three of Wyeth's men left Oregon in the Hudson's Bay Company ship "Dryad" in November 1833. One of the remaining men died in 1836, and only Solomon Smith and Calvin Tibbetts remained as permanent settlers in the Willamette Valley.

mained convinced of the possibilities for commercial success in Oregon, and he spent the winter surveying the Lower Columbia and the Willamette Valley to determine the prospects for salmon packing and farming.

The failure of the enterprise forced Wyeth to return to the Rocky Mountains where he hoped to sell the furs he had cached near the Portneuf. He rehired two men from his former party, Wiggin Abbott and John Woodman, to accompany him. Their departure was delayed by a freeze-up of the Columbia River, but on March 3, 1833, the three men joined Francis Ermatinger's Hudson's Bay fur brigade and headed for the Flathead country of Montana. From Fort Colville, Wyeth wrote to George Simpson, governor of the Hudson's Bay Company's North American operations, proposing a five year agreement in which the company would supply Wyeth with goods and men. Wyeth, for his part, promised to limit his trapping activities to the area south of the Columbia, and he would assure the company's monopoly by delivering his catch to company posts.[20]

From Fort Colville, the party traveled to the Missouri, trapping as they went. Wyeth complained of snow, lice and "bad food and starvation,"[21] while John Woodman felt he would be better off alone and took his unlamented leave. During the difficult journey, Wyeth found time to write brief observations of the Flathead, Nez Perce and Blackfoot Indians, which he later expanded in the letters which Henry R. Schoolcraft printed in his six-volume catalog of knowledge relating to the American Indian.[22] In late May, Wyeth and Ermatinger were joined by a party of Bonneville's men. The combined parties, their numbers augmented by a group of Nez Perces, headed up the Salmon River

20 Young, *Wyeth Journals,* Wyeth to Simpson, March 12, 1833, pp. 57-58.

21 *Ibid.,* 63.

22 *Ibid.,* 187-198 *passim.* See N. J. Wyeth, "Indian Tribes of Oregon," in Henry R. Schoolcraft, *Historical and Statistical Information Respecting the History, Condition and Prospects of the Indian Tribes of the United States* (Philadelphia, 1853), I, pp. 204-28.

toward rendezvous on the Green River. In late June, Wyeth was camped on the Upper Salmon River near Bonneville.

Wyeth proposed that the two form a partnership to trap the country south of the Columbia and into California during the following year. Wyeth would lead the party, and Bonneville was expected to provide men and trading goods. It appears that Bonneville accepted the proposal, for on July 4 Wyeth wrote several letters to Boston in which he outlined his forthcoming trapping and trading expedition. For some reason, however, these letters were never sent, and on the following day Wyeth wrote to McLoughlin that he intended to return directly to Boston. Although he gave no reason for this abrupt change of plan, it may have been influenced by Bonneville's small fur returns which would not bring enough at rendezvous to procure the trading goods and equipment which Wyeth needed.[23] Bonneville, nevertheless, was able to send a party under Joseph Reddeford Walker to California later that year. Now traveling with Bonneville, Wyeth reached rendezvous near Bonneville's fort on the Green River on July 17. During the seven days he was at rendezvous, Wyeth wrote to Ermatinger, from whom he had parted in early July, warning that the Hudson's Bay Company would be robbed of both beaver and goods should they attempt to trade with the Americans at rendezvous; for, said Wyeth, "There is here a great majority of Scoundrels."[24]

Unable to retrieve the furs he had cached the previous summer for lack of horses, Wyeth left rendezvous with Milton Sublette and some of his Rocky Mountain Fur Company employees bound for the mouth of the Yellowstone. For the first few days of the trip, they were accompanied by the Scottish adventurer William Drummond Stewart, who was returning to St. Louis from the first of

[23] Young, *Wyeth Journals,* 58-68 *passim;* William H. Goetzmann, *Exploration and Empire* (New York, 1966), 163.

[24] Young, *Wyeth Journals,* 69.

his several trips to rendezvous. After crossing the Wind River Mountains, Wyeth and Sublette camped along the Bighorn River, where their men spent four days building an eighteen foot bull boat.

There, Wyeth persuaded Milton Sublette and Thomas "Broken Hand" Fitzpatrick that he could supply them more cheaply with goods from Boston and New York than could William Sublette with goods bought in St. Louis. On August 14, 1833, Wyeth contracted to supply the Rocky Mountain Fur Company with $3,000 worth of goods at the 1834 rendezvous, for which he was to receive $3,521 above the original cost in beaver pelts which were to be valued at $4.00 a pound.[25] In late August, the parties reached Fort Union, an American Fur Company post on the Missouri just above the mouth of the Yellowstone. Leaving Wiggin Abbott behind with Sublette and Fitzpatrick, Wyeth proceeded down the Missouri in an Indian pirogue accompanied by two Indians, one of whom was Baptiste, a thirteen year old Nez Perce whom he was taking back to Boston. In late September, he stopped at Fort Leavenworth where he reported Fort Union's illicit distillery to the government authorities, and by early November he was back in Boston.[26]

Wyeth found that his detractors had not been silent in his absence. Several critical letters by disaffected members of his original band had been published, and John B. Wyeth, with editorial assistance from Dr. Benjamin Waterhouse who sought to discourage wild schemes for western migration, had published *Oregon; or a Short History of a Long Journey. . . ,* in which he questioned Wyeth's ability to organize and lead an expedition to the West. Wyeth characterized his kinsman's book as *"little lies* told for

[25] *Ibid.*, 74, 76, 83; W. Clement Eaton, "Nathaniel Wyeth's Oregon Expeditions," in *Pacific Historical Review,* IV (June 1935), 103-04.

[26] Young, *Wyeth Journals,* 70, 80, 206-19 *passim,* 254; Hiram M. Chittenden, *The American Fur Trade of the Far West* (Stanford, Calif., 1954), I, pp. 447-48.

gain,"[27] and in spite of such censure, he was able to use his contract with the Rocky Mountain Fur Company as an inducement to persuade Henry Hall and the firm of Messrs. Tucker and Williams to invest heavily in his new venture. The contract amounted to about one-fourth of the value of trade goods which would be taken to the mountains in 1834, and Wyeth felt that with a base on the Columbia, he could effect such savings in wages and transport that he could shortly monopolize the entire trade. Inferior grades of salmon were selling in Boston for $16 a barrel, and Wyeth proposed to pay for the expenses of a vessel and a post on the Columbia with return cargoes of salmon, but the fur trade would provide the profit.

By November 20, the Columbia River Fishing and Trading Company was organized with a capital of $20,000 (later raised to $40,000) of which Wyeth was to provide one-eighth, and in return was to receive a quarter of the profits. He was able to raise only a sixteenth, however, while Hall, Tucker and Williams supplied nine-sixteenths. Wyeth spent a frantic winter arranging for a ship and cargo, purchasing goods to take overland, learning to ascertain longitude and latitude, and attending to Frederic Tudor's ice business. He finally got away from Boston on February 7, and after brief stops in New York and Baltimore, arrived in St. Louis about March 10, where he hired nineteen men for eighteen months at $250, their contracts to expire in the Indian country.[28]

In mid-April of 1834 Wyeth moved up to Independence where he found that the demands of the United States Cavalry and the Santa Fe traders had driven the price of horses and stock higher than he had anticipated. His final departure was delayed by the late arrival of Jason Lee and

[27] Young, *Wyeth Journals,* Wyeth to Rev. Clark Perry, Nov. 12, 1833, p. 80.

[28] *Ibid.,* 60, 75-76, 83, 91, 96-97, 101-02, 105, 123-24; Eaton, "Wyeth's Oregon Expeditions," 104.

his group of Methodist missionaries, whom Wyeth had agreed to escort to the Columbia. Impatient at the delay, Wyeth wrote that "it is like keeping a bag of fleas together to keep the men in this whiskey country."[29] The caravan with seventy men, including the Nez Perce boy Baptiste, Wiggin Abbott, and the naturalists Thomas Nuttall and John Kirk Townsend, finally departed from Independence on April 28 with Wyeth and Milton Sublette in the lead. Within a short time, however, Sublette was forced to turn back because of a leg ailment that eventually caused his death. A few days later the men awoke to find that a large supply train led by William Sublette had passed them during the night.

These two events did not augur well for Wyeth, and, realizing that a race was on to get supplies to rendezvous, he sent a letter ahead notifying Fitzpatrick that he would arrive with the goods for the Rocky Mountain Fur Company about July first.[30] At the Laramie Fork of the Platte, which they reached on June first, some of Sublette's men were starting the construction of Fort William (later to be famous as Fort Laramie on the Oregon Trail), and at Independence Rock they found an inscription by Sublette noting his arrival there three days previously. Crossing South Pass, they proceeded by long marches to the Green River, where Wyeth left the party to locate Fitzpatrick. He found him camped about twelve miles above the mouth of the Big Sandy, but learned to his "astonishment" that the goods which he had brought would not be purchased after all.

Although the Rocky Mountain Fur Company was dissolved at rendezvous and succeeded by the firm of Fitz-

29 Young, *Wyeth Journals*, 130-31.

30 *Ibid.*, 132; John Kirk Townsend, *Narrative of a Journey Across the Rocky Mountains to the Columbia River. . .*, (*Early Western Travels, 1748-1846*, vol. XXI, edited by Reuben Gold Thwaites, Cleveland, 1905), 151.

patrick, Sublette and Bridger, Wyeth was able to collect a $500 forfeit from the new company as well as repayment of the cash advances which he had made to Milton Sublette in St. Louis to settle the accounts of William Drummond Stewart.[31] Wyeth was convinced that William Sublette had bribed Fitzpatrick, and he made plans to "roll a stone into [their] garden that [they would] never be able to get out."[32] That stone was to be a fort on the Snake River from which Wyeth would conduct his fur trade. From Ham's Fork, to which the camp moved in late June, Wyeth sent out messengers to solicit the trade of the Indian tribes of the region. With no prospects of a profitable trade at rendezvous, Wyeth struck camp in early July. In company with Stewart and a following of Indians, he moved his party of forty-one men across to the Bear River where they celebrated the Fourth of July with a "hearty spree."[33] At Soda Springs, near the great bend of the Bear River, Wyeth was joined by McLoughlin's stepson Thomas McKay, with whom he seems to have considered joining forces in an independent trading-trapping operation.[34]

Wyeth crossed to the Portneuf River, near his fur caches of 1832, and reached the Snake on July 14. A few miles upstream from the junction of the two rivers, Wyeth chose the site for his fort, and there on July 27, Jason Lee preached his first sermon since leaving Missouri.[35] A few

[31] Young, *Wyeth Journals,* 130, 138-39; Chittenden, *The American Fur Trade,* I, p. 450.

[32] Young, *Wyeth Journals,* 134, 140, 223-25. Wyeth's threat to "roll a stone" is found in Francis Fuller Victor, *The River of the West* (Hartford, Conn., 1870), 164, cited by Goetzmann, *Exploration and Empire,* 166.

[33] Young, *Wyeth Journals,* 225.

[34] The evidence for this is slender and is based on the conspiratorial tonc of a letter from Wyeth to Francis Ermatinger of July 5, 1834. "I suppose," wrote Wyeth, "that Mckay [sic] has 'thought of it' by this time and perhaps felt of it too, and you too seem to have done more than thought of it." Young, *Wyeth Journals,* 140.

[35] At rendezvous, Lee found that the trappers ignored the Sabbath while the Indians respected it. He feared to propose preaching at rendezvous because it

days later McKay, in company with the missionaries and William D. Stewart, left for the Columbia. By August 5, the log fort was enclosed, and Wyeth ordered a celebration. At sunrise the following morning, a crude flag was raised and saluted with damaged powder. Wyeth named it Fort Hall for the senior partner of the company, and, after the christening, "villainous" alcohol was issued in such quantities as to make the conduct of the men "disgusting and tiger-like" to the sensitive naturalist Townsend.[36] The next day Wyeth left Robert Evans in charge of eleven men at the fort and set out with a trapping party for the Columbia.

Wyeth rejoined the missionaries and Captain Stewart at Fort Walla Walla, where he learned that Tom McKay had left them in the Snake Country to establish an independent trading post on the Boise River. McLoughlin integrated Fort Boise into the network of Columbia Department posts the following year, and it became an all too effective competitor with Fort Hall for the furs and trade of the Snake Country. Wyeth reached Fort Vancouver on September 14, and the following day he took a canoe down the Columbia to meet the brig, "May Dacre," which he had dispatched from Boston the previous January under Captain James Lambert, who had commanded the ill-fated "Sultana." The "May Dacre" had been damaged by lightening and was delayed in Valparaiso, Chile, for extensive repairs. Her arrival in mid-September from Hawaii was too late for that year's salmon run, and Wyeth sent the ship back to Oahu on a trading voyage. He set his men to work constructing Fort William on Multnomah Island (modern Sauvies Island) at the mouth of the Willamette River.[37]

---

would be "rejected with disdain" in favor of trading, drinking or "some such innocent amusement." "Diary of Rev. Jason Lee," in *Quarterly of the Oregon Historical Society*, XVII (Sept. 1916), pp. 139-40.

36 Townsend, *Narrative*, 231.

37 Young, *Wyeth Journals*, 227-33 *passim;* "Diary of Rev. Jason Lee," 251.

Although Wyeth had written from Boston to Governor Simpson withdrawing from the proposed trade agreement with the Hudson's Bay Company, he now sought to salvage the prospects for a profitable venture by concluding a trading agreement with McLoughlin. Dispatches from Simpson arrived in October, informing McLoughlin that Wyeth's proposals of the previous year had been rejected. McLoughlin had come to like the Yankee trader, but he was convinced that Wyeth's enterprise would collapse of its own weight. He felt that, should the company refuse to aid him, Wyeth might establish a trading connection which would enable him to compete more strenuously with the company. As long as Wyeth was dependent on the company, he could be controlled and his activities would not seriously threaten the monopoly of the Hudson's Bay Company.[38] McLoughlin permitted Wyeth to draw supplies from Fort Vancouver, and his generous treatment of Wyeth was the first of a series of disagreements with Governor Simpson which disturbed McLoughlin's relations with the company over the next decade.

After choosing a site for a farm at French Prairie, forty miles up the Willamette from Fort William, Wyeth took some of the laborers brought by Captain Lambert from Hawaii and returned to Fort Walla Walla on a trapping expedition. Instead of going on toward Great Salt Lake, where he had planned to establish two more forts, Wyeth sent his second-in-command, Captain Joseph Thing, to take charge of Fort Hall. Wyeth spent the winter trapping westward, south of the Columbia. He returned to Fort Vancouver in February 1835, where he found Hall Jackson Kelley, who had arrived a sick man with the suspected

[38] Young, *Wyeth Journals*, 84, 125, 233; E. E. Rich, ed., *The Letters of John McLoughlin from Fort Vancouver to the Governor and Committee, First Series, 1825-38* (*Publications of the Champlain Society*, Hudson's Bay Company Series, vol. IV, Toronto, 1941), pp. cvii-cix. Hereafter cited as Rich, *McLoughlin's Letters, First Series*.

horse thief, Ewing Young; the meeting was not a friendly one. Late in the month, Wyeth inspected his farm at French Prairie and enrolled Baptiste in Jason Lee's school at Chemeketa (modern Salem).[39]

In April the "May Dacre" returned, and Wyeth made preparations for the season's salmon catch. By September, however, only half a cargo had been packed, totalling some 300 barrels from which Wyeth realized about $5,000, and the company was sadly depleted by death and sickness.[40] Wyeth left for Fort Hall, which he reached in December. There two of his men, including Wiggin Abbott, had been scalped, and most of the remainder merely awaited their discharge, since their contracts had expired in October. Osborne Russell, one of those who did not renew his contract, wrote that he was "determined not to be so green as to bind myself to an arbitrary Rocky Mountain Chieftain to be kicked over hill and dale at his pleasure."[41] At Fort Hall Wyeth found that about 600 beavers had been traded which would be worth about $4500 in New York,[42] but they were a long way from a market which was even then decreasing due to the introduction of the silk hat.

Toward the end of February 1836, Wyeth returned to Fort Vancouver where he made a last desperate attempt to salvage his distressed fortunes. He made a new proposal to McLoughlin for a trading agreement. McLoughlin agreed, but in June dispatches from Governor Simpson ordered

39 Young, *Wyeth Journals,* 143, 233-51 *passim;* Hall Jackson Kelley, *A Narrative of Events and Difficulties in the Colonization of Oregon, and the Settlement of California. . .* (Boston, 1852), reprinted in Fred Wilbur Powell, ed., *Hall J. Kelley on Oregon* (Princeton, 1932), 186.

40 Young, *Wyeth Journals,* 154, 251; Rich, *McLoughlin's Letters, First Series,* 141; Richard G. Beidleman, "Nathaniel Wyeth's Fort Hall," *Oregon Historical Quarterly,* LVIII (Sept. 1957), 242.

41 Townsend, *Narrative,* 326; Osborne Russell, *Journal of a Trapper,* ed. Aubrey L. Haines (Portland, 1955), 38.

42 Rich, *McLoughlin's Letters, First Series,* 141; Beidleman, "Nathaniel Wyeth's Fort Hall," 242.

him to oppose Wyeth "Vigourously . . . and to Decline Entering into Any Arrangement with him. . ."[43] Wyeth had to admit final defeat, and once more he set out for Boston, this time with no hope of rescuing his Oregon venture, for the depression of 1836 and the effective opposition of the Hudson's Bay Company precluded further financing. After a brief stop at Fort Hall, he proceeded on to the Horse Creek rendezvous where he met the Whitman missionary party and offered the hospitality of Fort Hall to Narcissa Whitman and Eliza Spalding, the first white women to cross the Rockies and the first to make the fort a major reprovisioning and rest stop for travelers on the Oregon Trail.

Wyeth returned to St. Louis via Taos and Bent's Fort and was back in Boston by early fall, having spent over $20,000 and five years of his life in a frustrating attempt to open Oregon to American business. Because of the high fixed charges in maintaining Fort Hall, it was sold to the Hudson's Bay Company along with its equipment and trading goods for $8,179.98 in October 1837.[44] Wyeth did retain Fort William on the Columbia, which he leased to McLoughlin who pastured the company's dairy herd there. When the Provisional Government of Oregon passed a land claim law in July 1843, McLoughlin tried to secure Wyeth's claim to the Fort William site.[45] Although McLoughlin was unsuccessful, Wyeth appreciated his efforts and returned the favor a few years later by refusing to support Oregon's delegate Samuel R. Thurston in his efforts to dispossess McLoughlin of his own Oregon City claim by

43 Rich, *McLoughlin's Letters, First Series,* pp. cxi, 340-42.

44 Young, *Wyeth Journals,* 253, 255; Rich, *McLoughlin's Letters, First Series,* 208; Beidleman, "Nathaniel Wyeth's Fort Hall," 243, 248-49.

45 Young, *Wyeth Journals,* 253-57; William R. Sampson, ed., "John McLoughlin's Business Correspondence, 1847-1848" (unpublished M.A. thesis, University of Wisconsin, 1964), McLoughlin to Wyeth, Oct. 10, 1847, pp. 95-97, and McLoughlin to Wyeth, Feb. 15, 1848, pp. 137-38.

means of a discriminatory clause in the Donation Land Law of 1850.[46]

In Boston, Wyeth returned to Frederic Tudor's ice company at three times his former salary, and during the next fifteen years he received at least fourteen patents for significant improvements in the machinery for cutting and storing ice.[47] However, in 1840 Wyeth severed his connection with Tudor's company because of a lawsuit arising out of an infringement of the ice cutter patent which he had assigned to Tudor in 1832. Wyeth continued in the ice business and was instrumental in securing the construction of a railroad to haul ice from Fresh Pond to the Charlestown docks; but when the Charlestown Branch Railroad Company was absorbed by the Fitchburg Railroad in which Tudor had an interest, the Fresh Pond shippers were bypassed in favor of Walden Pond. Wyeth was able, however, to develop a profitable business shipping refrigerated garden produce from his own and nearby farms to the tropics, and the fruit trees which he had planted in the fall of 1833 added to his income.[48] By 1848, over 60,000 tons of ice were being shipped annually from Boston to the southern states, the Caribbean, and as far as Calcutta. From this trade a profit of $100,000 was realized.[49] It is not surprising then that when Wyeth died in 1856, he was praised as a "public benefactor," who had done more than anyone else to "open

46 *Oregon Spectator* (Oregon City, Oregon), April 3, 1851. [The same correspondence was published in the *Milwaukee Star* (Milwaukee, Oregon) on April 10, 1851, reprinted as "Documents – Correspondence of John McLoughlin, Nathaniel J. Wyeth, S. R. Thurston, and R. C. Winthrop, pertaining to claim of Doctor McLoughlin at the Falls of the Willamette – the site of Oregon City," in *Quarterly of the Oregon Historical Society,* 1 (March 1900), 105-09.]

47 *Journal of the Franklin Institute,* new series 22 (Oct. 1838), 232; 23 (April 1839), 244-45; third series 3 (Feb. 1842), 125-26, 129; 8 (Nov. 1844), 317; 10 (July 1845), 24-25; 18 (Dec. 1849), 501-02, 504; 20 (July 1850), 16.

48 Cummings, *American Ice Harvests,* 38-51 *passim;* Young, *Wyeth Journals,* 117.

49 Nathaniel J. Wyeth, "Ice Trade," *Annual Report of the Commissioner of Patents, for the Year 1848,* Appendix no. 13 (30 Cong., 2 sess., House Exec. doc. no. 59, Washington, 1849), 696-703.

a new field for honorable industry . . . . all the receipts of which are a gain to the country."[50]

Wyeth did not forget the West. In 1839, at the request of Caleb Cushing, he wrote a long memoir on Oregon for the House Committee on Foreign Affairs.[51] Such writings helped to familiarize the East with the physical and political facts of Oregon and, before the expansionist policies of the 1840s, it was men such as Wyeth who made it easier for Congress to support American interests in Oregon. Wyeth's personal failures in Oregon did not destroy his dreams of profitable enterprise there, and in 1847, with the prospects of a northern transcontinental railroad capturing the imagination of easterners, Wyeth suggested to McLoughlin that the two join forces in opening up the country in the region of Fort Hall and Soda Springs, the latter being a good location for a "Watering place" because of the "Salubrity of the Air." The aging and disillusioned McLoughlin replied that he had heard that Mormons had settled in the vicinity and were "very Disagreeable Neighbours." He added that he had already had "too much trouble in opening new Countries to attempt again." He did promise, however, to investigate places on the Northwest Coast from which ice could be obtained for Wyeth's trade.[52]

Wyeth continued to be an important figure in the New England ice and provision trade until his death at his Cambridge home on August 31, 1856, having lived to see Oregon become a territory in the Union. Today he is frequently thought of as a visionary[53] whose projects for opening new

---

50 *Boston Evening Transcript,* September 2, 1856.

51 "Mr. Wyeth's Memoir," Appendix I, 25 Cong., 3 sess., House Reports no. 101 (Washington, 1839), 6-22.

52 Sampson, "McLoughlin's Business Correspondence," McLoughlin to Wyeth, April 20, 1847, p. 29, and McLoughlin to Wyeth, Oct. 10, 1847, p. 97.

53 Wyeth, in a despairing mood, wrote of his "manhoods [sic] troubled stream, its vagaries, its aloes mixed with the gall of bitterness and its results viz. . . despised for a visionary. . .," Young, *Wyeth Journals,* p. 243. Thomas J. Farn-

lands to trade and commerce were plagued by ill-fortune and his own naive expectancy. Yet, his failure in the fur trade is secondary to his role in opening and publicizing the route of the Oregon Trail across South Pass and in guiding such men as Jason Lee to the Columbia. Nathaniel Wyeth, engaged in a commercial enterprise that failed, was the unwitting precursor of a movement which was to help destroy the fur trade while gaining Oregon for the United States.

---

ham, who was in Oregon in 1839, was one of very few who was able to judge Wyeth's activities in the West on the basis of talent not achievement. "From what I saw and heard of Wyeth's management in Oregon," wrote Farnham, "I was impressed with the belief that he was, beyond comparison, the most talented businessman from the States that ever established himself in the Territory." Thomas J. Farnham, *Travels in the Great Western Prairies, the Anahuac and Rocky Mountains, and in the Oregon Territory* (New York, 1843), 73. Wyeth's obituary is in the *Boston Evening Transcript,* September 2, 1856.

Andrew Drips

by HARVEY L. CARTER
Colorado College, Colorado Springs

As a general rule, history is the record of success and the winning side gains the satisfaction of having its version of events accepted while the version of the losing side receives less attention and less credence. However, there are important exceptions to this general rule, wherein the lost cause fares better at the hands of historians. One such exception is to be found in the history of the fur trade of the Far West, where the Rocky Mountain Fur Company has received far more attention and more favorable comment than the American Fur Company, which emerged as the victor. The Ashley men, such as Jedediah Smith, William Sublette, Thomas Fitzpatrick and James Bridger have become familiar figures, while their more successful rivals, William Vanderburgh, Lucien Fontenelle, Etienne Provost, and Andrew Drips are much less well and much less favorably known. Such a state of affairs is somewhat unfair, particularly to Andrew Drips, a man who was engaged in the fur trade before any of the Ashley men, and who continued in it longer than any of them.

Andrew Drips was a son of Thomas Drips and, according to family tradition, was born in Ireland, probably in December 1789. He was brought to the United States as an infant and grew up near Laughlintown, Westmoreland County, Pennsylvania, where the family settled.[1] Nothing is

[1] Mrs. F. M. Barnes and Mrs. J. H. Branch, "Andrew Drips," manuscript in the Missouri Historical Society Library, St. Louis, Missouri. Mrs. Barnes was a daughter and Mrs. Branch was a grand-daughter of Andrew Drips. The only published sketch of the life of Andrew Drips is to be found in Dale L. Morgan and Eleanor T. Harris, *The West of William Marshall Anderson* (San Marino, 1967), 292-96. These authors state, p. 292, that Drips was born in Westmoreland County, Pennsyl-

known of his early years but he served in the Ohio Militia, First Regiment, during the War of 1812.[2]

Drips first came to St. Louis in 1817, where he enlisted in the Missouri Militia. During the year 1819, he was associated with a trader named Joseph Perkins for a short while but entered the Missouri Fur Company, upon its reorganization in September 1820.[3] By 1822, he had become a partner in this company under the direction of Joshua Pilcher, along with William H. Vanderburgh, Lucien Fontenelle, and Moses Carson.[4]

During the campaign against the Arikarees, in 1823, it is probable that Drips was still operating out of Fort Lisa, but with the establishment, in that year, of the new post at Bellevue, about midway between Council Bluffs and the mouth of the Platte, but on the Nebraska side of the Missouri River, he began a residence there which continued for several years. The Missouri Fur Company was dissolved in 1824 but Drips was among those who continued in business along with Pilcher, Fontenelle, Vanderburgh, and Charles Bent.[5] In the years 1825 to 1829, he led several expeditions from Bellevue to trade among the Pawnees.[6] While at Bellevue, he took as a wife an Otoe Indian woman named Macompemay, who was known by the English name of Margaret or

vania. They also indicate that the family name was originally Seldon and that the name Drips was assumed some generations earlier during the course of a migration from the Scottish Highlands to Northern Ireland.

2 Morgan and Harris, *op. cit.*, 292, give the dates of his military service as August 11, 1812, to February 17, 1813, and July 5, 1814, to August 18, 1814. Mrs. Barnes and Mrs. Branch believed that he served under Andrew Jackson at New Orleans but this has not been verified.

3 See *ibid.;* also H. M. Chittenden, *The American Fur Trade of the Far West* (Stanford, 1954), I, p. 392.

4 John E. Sunder, *Joshua Pilcher: Fur Trader and Indian Agent* (Norman, Okla., 1968), 37.

5 *Ibid.*, 62-64. Licenses were granted to this group of traders both in 1825 and 1826.

6 Morgan and Harris, *op. cit.*, 292-93. There are also several brief references to Drips in "The Diary of James Kennerly, 1823-1826," edited by Edgar B. Wesley, in *Missouri Historical Collections,* VI (1928-1931). Kennerly was Indian agent at Fort Atkinson, which was occasionally visited by Drips.

Mary, by whom he had four children, Charles, Jane, Katherine, and William.[7]

When Pilcher decided to go to the mountains in September 1827, in an effort to get a share of the beaver to be found there, he seems to have been accompanied by all his partners. The effort failed and all except Pilcher returned to Bellevue in the summer of 1828.[8] Drips and Fontenelle continued to operate at Bellevue until January 1830, when Drips returned to St. Louis and worked out an arrangement with the Western Division of the American Fur Company, which their former partner, W. H. Vanderburgh had already joined. By this arrangement, Drips and Fontenelle were to lead an expedition to the Rocky Mountains for the company but were apparently allowed to continue some trading and trapping as partners on their own account at the same time.[9]

Drips was back at Bellevue by April 1, 1830, and a month later he and Fontenelle launched their invasion of the Rocky Mountains for the big company. We are able to follow their movements largely through the fact that Warren A. Ferris was a member of their party and left a famous and detailed account of his years as a trapper. Their route was up the Platte; on May 26 they reached Chimney Rock; on June 2 they crossed the Platte "in bull hide canoes and encamped . . . above the mouth of Laramie's Fork, at the foot of the Black Hills." As this was six hundred miles west of Bellevue, the party of fifty had been making about twenty

[7] Charles Drips was born March 27, 1824. Jane Drips was born November 15, 1827. She married first, Leonard Benoist and second, F. M. Barnes. Katherine Drips was born at the Pierre's Hole rendezvous on July 12, 1832. She married William Mulkey. William Drips, born August 12, 1834, died young and was buried along the Platte River. Mrs. Mulkey was responsible for the preservation of a trunkful of her father's papers, which constitute the Drips Papers of the Missouri Historical Society, St. Louis. See Morgan and Harris, *op. cit.*, 292-93; also Mrs. F. M. Barnes and Mrs. J. H. Branch, *op. cit.*, who say that Drips and his Otoe wife were remarried by a justice of the peace September 5, 1841, at what later became Kansas City. Drips' Otoe wife died June 1, 1846.

[8] Morgan and Harris, *op. cit.*, 293, believe it more probable that Drips did not go to the mountains in 1827.

[9] See Alan C. Trottman, "Lucien Fontenelle" in this series, v, pp. 81-99.

miles per day. They saw their first grizzly bear on June 8 and reached Independence Rock on the Sweetwater on June 12. After crossing South Pass on June 21, they turned down Green River, crossing it on June 26 and ascending Ham's Fork. They were looking for a group of free trappers but failed to find them and camped on Bear River on July 8, where they killed many buffalo.[10] On July 16 Ferris accompanied Drips and three others into Cache Valley, where again they failed to find the free trappers and rejoined Fontenelle on Ham's Fork on August 16. They now cached their goods and a week later split into three parties headed by Fontenelle, Michel Robidoux, and Drips. Drips made his fall hunt up Green River to its sources.[11]

As Ferris accompanied Fontenelle, we have only scant knowledge of the movements of Drips. All three parties returned to Cache Valley, where they established winter quarters on October 31, 1830. The free trappers, who had been on the Yellowstone, and the Rocky Mountain Fur Company men also wintered in Cache Valley. After a cold winter, Drips and Fontenelle made their spring hunt on the Snake River. By June 19, 1831, Drips and Fontenelle departed the Flathead country for St. Louis, taking thirty men and twenty Flathead Indians with them.[12]

Expenses had been heavy on this first mountain expedition but returns in furs were sufficient to encourage the outfitting of a second one. Plans were made for Drips to lead an expedition back to the Rocky Mountains in the fall of 1831 but Fontenelle was to remain at Bellevue. The failure of his goods to come up the river at the expected time delayed the departure of Drips until October 1.[13] The late

10 Warren A. Ferris, *Life in the Rocky Mountains*, edited by Paul C. Phillips (Denver, 1940), 1-42.

11 *Ibid.*, 42-50.

12 *Ibid.*, 58, 60, 96.

13 Letter of Lucien Fontenelle to Pierre Chouteau, Jr., Bellevue, Oct. 4, 1831, in the Drips Papers, *loc. cit.* Fontenelle makes an explanation of certain expenses and expresses the belief that Drips will reach his destination, despite his late start and the poor condition of his horses, provided that the weather is fair.

start, the poor condition of his horses, and the lack of forage along the route compelled him to spend the winter "at the foot of the Black Hills," that is, near the mouth of the Laramie River. His party of forty-eight men arrived on Muddy Creek, a tributary of Bear River, on April 24, 1832.[14]

He reached Pierre's Hole by the middle of June probably only trapping a little on his way there, but he was early for the rendezvous and he was in a good position to trade with the Indians as they came in. At the battle of Pierre's Hole, on July 18, his hat was shot through by a bullet that sheared off a lock of his hair.[15]

Drips and Vanderburgh now crossed the Teton Mountains and met Fontenelle and Provost with fifty men and 150 horses on the headwaters of Green River. They also learned that Bonneville was building a fort on Horse Creek, a tributary of Green River.[16] Crossing back to Pierre's Hole, Drips and Vanderburgh now set out on their famous pursuit of Fitzpatrick and Bridger through the Blackfoot country that ended in Vanderburgh's death.[17] A letter of Francis Ermatinger, of the Hudson's Bay Company, to Drips on behalf of certain French-Canadian trappers illustrates some of the financial problems involved when trappers changed from one company to another.[18] After Vanderburgh's death, his men joined Drips, who set out for Snake River on Oc-

---

14 Ferris, *op. cit.*, 141.

15 *Ibid.*, 337. Drips does not mention his near escape in his letter to John B. Sarpy, Pierre's Hole, Rocky Mountains, July 27, 1832, though he mentions that William Sublette was severely wounded. He asks Sarpy to look after his children in St. Louis, his wife having accompanied him to the mountains. He also expresses concern about the non-appearance of Fontenelle with supplies and gives a hint that he and Vanderburgh are impatient to be off, as the Rocky Mountain Fur Company outfit has already taken the field. A letter of the same date from Drips to Pierre Chouteau, Jr., asks him to honor certain notes drawn on him by "Fontenelle, Drips and Co." This indicates that their private operations were conducted with the knowledge and approval of the American Fur Company. These letters are in the Drips Papers, *loc. cit.*

16 Ferris, *op. cit.*, 158-59.

17 Details of this trip may be found in my sketch of William H. Vanderburgh in volume VII of this series and will not be given here.

18 Letter of Francis Ermatinger to Drips, Flathead Camp, Oct. 14, 1832.

tober 24, and spent the winter of 1832-33 at the forks of the Snake River. Drips broke camp on March 24, 1833, and engaged in a successful spring hunt, trapping Lewis Fork, Gray's Hole, Salt River, Pierre's Hole, and Jackson's Hole as he moved toward rendezvous on Green River at the mouth of Horse Creek, where he arrived on June 7, once more the first of several outfits to come in.[19] Bonneville's men congregated at his fort on Horse Creek and the Rocky Mountain Fur Company had to go down Green River a few miles for forage. Drips kept his position at the mouth of Horse Creek.

Fontenelle was late in arriving with supplies. A long letter which he wrote to William Laidlaw at Fort Pierre on July 31 describes the situation.

Randezvous on Green River R[ocky] M[ountains]
July 31st, 1833

After a tedious journey of thirty days I got to this place where I found Mr. Drips and his party consisting of about two hundred persons – near him were encamped Mr. Bonneville and Mr. [Robert] Campbell and their companies – the lat[t]er got out eight days before me and made much of a boast about it. Mr. Drips had to labour under some disadvantages until I got to him as both the others had a large supply of Liquor which as you well know is main main [sic] object with those people with whom we have to deal in this country. It is presumed that my late arrival has cut us off from four or five packs of beaver – it is unfortunate but cannot be bettered – both of them have tried their best to injure the Amer[ican] Fur Co. . . . however Mr. Drips after some difficulty has made more than either of them and to his praise I can say that with about thirty five trappers with him this spring he has made this spring what goes down now at the exception of what he got from Fallon and [James] Vanderburgh – had they not went last fall to the infernal Blackfoot country I really believe that you might have sent in this season upwards of one hundred packs and would have saved the life of a good man [W. H. Vanderburgh] – I am however as much to be blamed as any concerned – we all thought that a fortune was to be easily made in that country . . . Drips has

[19] Ferris, *op. cit.*, 189-207.

become very popular with the people in this country since last year and I had hard work to detain him with me. He would not at all agree with me for the Bargain or rather agreement that I entered into with the Amer[ican] Fur Co. I had to give him (and God knows how I will be able to pay him) fifteen hundred Dollars a year to induce him to stay in the country. . .[20]

At this rendezvous of 1833, Fontenelle and Drips agreed with Fitzpatrick and Bridger to divide the fur country, with the American Fur Company trapping the western and the Rocky Mountain Fur Company trapping the eastern slope.[21]

Drips apparently made his fall hunt in the Snake River country, where he could compete with Bonneville, for the only Indians he saw were of that tribe and he arrived at his wintering ground at the Forks of the Snake on November 2, 1833. He had caught many beaver and lost neither men nor horses. By contrast, both Bonneville and Fitzpatrick had suffered heavy losses from the thievery of the Crows.[22] Drips passed the winter without accident and buffalo were plentiful, assuring a good food supply.[23] His spring hunt in 1834 seems to have been made between the Forks of the Snake and the Wind River Mountains, for Ferris found his camp on "a fine little lake, about ten miles long and one broad" directly east of Green River on the western slope of the Wind River Range on May 29, 1834.[24] Drips broke camp shortly after this and moved southward to the rendezvous on Ham's Fork, where he was joined by Fontenelle, who had been trading among the Utes. William Marshall Anderson on June 29 wrote,

We paid a visit to the American Fur Company's camp, which is at the junction of Black's and Ham's Forks, about 8 miles below [Wil-

20 Letter of Lucien Fontenelle to William Laidlaw, Rendezvous on Green River R.M., July 31, 1833, in the Drips Papers, *loc. cit.*

21 Mrs. Frances Fuller Victor, *The River of the West* (Hartford, 1870), 165-66.

22 Ferris, *op. cit.*, 230.

23 *Ibid.*, 253.

24 *Ibid.*, 264. There are a number of lakes in this vicinity but the only one that is as much as ten miles long is Frémont Lake.

liam Sublette's camp]. This company is conducted by Messrs. Fontenelle and Dripps – they received us very politely and treated us very kindly. Rarities I little expected to meet with here were given us for dinner – rice and plumb puddings – There was a larger and more interesting collection of savages around their trading pen, than I have before met with.[25]

Provost had come in with supplies, which accounts for the puddings, and Drips and Fontenelle could afford to be kind and polite, for the American Fur Company had negotiations under way to absorb the Rocky Mountain Fur Company, which were completed, on August 3, before the end of rendezvous.[26]

Where Drips hunted in the fall of 1834 and the spring of 1835 is not known but it is probable that he remained on the western slope. He was present at the rendezvous of 1835 on Green River below Horse Creek for it was here that Kit Carson had his duel with Shunar, a big and braggart Frenchman "in the party of Captain Drips."[27] A letter of Fontenelle's to Drips, from Fort William [Laramie] on August 1, 1835, advises him, "There are two gentlemen [Rev. Samuel Parker and Dr. Marcus Whitman] going up with the party who are gentlemen and I wish you to treat them as such; the Doctor particularly. He has been of great service to us."[28]

The next that is heard of Drips is on May 8, 1836, when Osborne Russell "Travelled up Bear river to Thomas fork [Talma's Fork] where we found the main Camp likewise Mr. A. Dripps and his party, consisting of about 60 whites and nearly as many half breeds who were encamped with

25 Morgan and Harris, *op. cit.*, 149.

26 *Ibid.*, 173. The new amalgamated company, called Fontenelle, Fitzpatrick and Company, was but a temporary thing and the absorption was completed two years later when Pratte, Chouteau and Company, the St. Louis firm representing the American Fur Company, took control.

27 See Harvey L. Carter, *"Dear Old Kit": The Historical Christopher Carson, with a New Edition of the Carson Memoirs* (Norman, 1968), 63-66.

28 Letter of Lucien Fontenelle to Major Drips, Fort William, Aug. 1, 1835, in the Drips Papers, *loc. cit.*

400 lodges of Snakes and Bonnaks and 100 lodges of Nez Perces and flatheads."[29]

Drips and a small party went to Black's Fork of Green River on May 11 to raise a cache of furs. The Indians separated from the whites and all agreed to meet at rendezvous at the mouth of Horse Creek about July 1. As to the movements of Drips in the fall of 1835 and spring of 1836 nothing is known, but Morgan and Harris conjecture that he hunted to the south and southwest.[30]

Drips remained in the mountains after Pratte, Chouteau and Company took over and must have made his spring hunt in 1837 in the Snake River country once more, for certain entries in the Fort Hall ledgers attest to his presence in that area.[31] The rendezvous of 1837 was again on Horse Creek and Drips arranged to exchange places with Fontenelle, who became field captain for the 1837-1838 hunts while Drips went down to St. Louis with the furs.

He returned in 1838 at the head of the supply caravan to the rendezvous on the Popo Agie. Four missionary couples and a bachelor, bound for Oregon, traveled with him, as well as Sir William Drummond Stewart and Captain John A. Sutter. Of the missionary diarists, both William Gray and Sarah Smith speak of "the kindness of Captain Drips."[32] Mrs. Smith also interestingly describes his two wives.

> Several female Indians are journeying with us. The two wives of Captain Dripps. They are trimmed off in high style, I assure you. The oldest wife rides a beautiful white horse, her saddle ornamented with

---

[29] Osborne Russell, *Journal of a Trapper*, edited by Aubrey L. Haines (Portland, 1955), 41.

[30] Morgan and Harris, *op. cit.*, 294-95. Joe Meek, in Victor, *op. cit.*, 199-200, tells of an excursion that he and Carson and a Flathead Chief named Victor made to the Sweetwater during the rendezvous of 1836.

[31] Fort Hall Account Books; entries for March 11, April 29, May 29, July 21 and 27, 1837, occur under his name. I am indebted to Dr. Richard Beidleman for the use of his microfilm of these accounts.

[32] Clifford M. Drury, *First White Women over the Rockies*, III (Glendale, 1966), 72, 242.

beads and many little gingles. A beautiful white sheepskin covering for the horse, cut in fringes ½ a yard deep, ornamented with collars & a great number of thimbles pierced in the top and hung to the fringe like little balls, making a fine gingle as she rides along. Then comes the rider with her scarlet blanket, painted face & hankerchief on her head, sitting astride. This is the fashion of the country. The second wife acts as an attendant.[33]

Drips remained in the mountains following the rendezvous. Russell found him encamped in Jackson's Hole not long after the rendezvous with sixty men and with Bridger as "Pilot" or guide.[34] From there he moved to Pierre's Hole, where "Doc" Newell joined the party but apparently wintered on Wind River. He was at the rendezvous on Horse Creek in July 1839, "with 4 Carts of Supplies from below."[35]

Drips and Bridger took the furs down to Missouri after the rendezvous. Drips commanded the caravan next year that brought out goods for the final rendezvous in 1840, reaching Green River on the last of June. He brought with him Father Pierre deSmet, who was making the first of his many missionary journeys to the mountains, Joel Walker and family, who were planning to settle in Oregon, and three Protestant missionaries and their wives, also headed for Oregon. Although Fraeb and Bridger returned to the mountains with him, it was clear that the great days of the fur trade were over and Drips did not bring a large supply train.[36]

During 1841-1842, Drips made his home at the settlement called Kansas (later Kansas City) but he was still connected

---

[33] *Ibid.,* 84-85. This is the only reference to Drips having taken another wife and nothing more is known about her. It is evident that his first wife had maintained her prestige. Russell, *op. cit.,* 90, mentioned that Drips brought "20 horse carts loaded with supplies" to the rendezvous.

[34] *Ibid.,* 91.

[35] Robert Newell, *Memoranda,* edited by Dorothy O. Johansen (Portland, 1959), 38. Apparently Drips had met someone who brought out this small amount of supplies for he could not have gone for them himself. He may have picked them up at Fort Laramie.

[36] See LeRoy R. Hafen, "A Brief History of the Fur Trade of the Far West" in this Series, I, pp. 163-64.

in some manner with Pierre Chouteau, Jr. and Company and was not steadily residing at home. Thus it happened that John C. Frémont, looking for a guide for his first expedition did not find him there and employed Kit Carson instead. Frémont had asked Chouteau to recommend some one. He recommended Drips and advised Drips of the fact by letter, which was probably received too late.[37]

Drips was not forgotten by Chouteau, however, and when it appeared that the appointment of a special Indian agent for the Upper Missouri, whose chief responsibility would be to suppress the liquor trade with the Indians, would be to the advantage of the American Fur Company, various strings were pulled that resulted in the appointment of Drips to this position, which he held from August 1842 to June 1846.[38]

In this new capacity, Drips traveled widely and did some very good work in making it more difficult for irresponsible traders to debauch the Indians with liquor. He was up and down the Missouri frequently. Of interest may be the fact that he met John James Audubon at Vermilion River on May 16, 1843. Drips was returning from Fort Pierre with William Laidlaw and the artist, Audubon, was ascending the Missouri gathering materials for his paintings of quadrupeds.[39] Again, he reports the sale of the Union Fur Company to Pierre Chouteau has left some fifty men of bad character footloose on the Upper Missouri.[40] He was concerned with suppressing the liquor traffic not only on the Missouri but also on the Platte and the Arkansas. On the

37 Letter of R. M. Clapp (for Pierre Chouteau, Jr. and Co.) to Andrew Drips, St. Louis, May 30, 1842, in the Drips Papers, *loc. cit.*

38 Letter of T. Hartley Crawford to Major I. F. A. Sanford, War Department, July 2, 1842, and letter of Major Sanford to Andrew Drips, St. Louis, July 10, 1842, in the Drips Papers, *loc. cit.* Major Sanford was son-in-law to Pierre Chouteau, Jr.

39 See *Audubon and his Journals,* edited by Maria R. Audubon and Elliot Coues (New York, 1897), I, p. 499.

40 Letter of Andrew Drips to Thomas H. Harvey, Fort Pierre, May 18, 1845, as quoted in Chittenden, *op. cit.,* I, p. 372.

latter, he received cooperation from Bent and St. Vrain. He recognized and reported the illegal traffic across the border conducted by traders at Hardscrabble and Pueblo but was not able to control it.[41]

However, he was charged with partiality to the Chouteau interests and this led to the termination of his appointment as special agent. There is not much question but that the charge was correct. Charles Larpenteur, who had charge of the liquor department of the American Fur Company at Fort Union during this period, had this to say:

> Major Dripps was, I believe, a good, honest old beaver trapper. He was sent to examine the trading posts, to find out about the liquor trade. He sent his interpreter ahead to let us know he was coming. On his arrival he looked in all places except in the cellar, where there was upwards of 30 barrels of alcohol. The Major was afterward equipped by the American Fur Company and went to the Platte. . .[42]

Pierre Chouteau, Jr., and Company now employed Drips once more as a trader at Fort Pierre. In 1848 the company reorganized its operations on the Upper Missouri. Of twelve shares, Chouteau kept six and gave one each to Drips, Alexander Culbertson, James Kipp, William Laidlaw, and Frederick Labone, with one share to be allocated later.[43]

In 1848, Pierre Papin did not wish to return to Fort Laramie so Drips was chosen to replace him in charge of that trading post, which was within the area affected by the reorganization. When Drips returned to St. Louis with his furs in the spring of 1849, he probably expected to return, but the sale of Fort Laramie to the federal government during his absence ended its use at a trading post.[44]

---

41 Letter of Andrew Drips to Thomas H. Harvey, Fort Pierre, April 11, 1845, as quoted in Chittenden, *op. cit.*, I, p. 369.

42 Charles Larpenteur, *Forty Years a Fur Trader on the Upper Missouri*, edited by Milo M. Quaife (Chicago, 1933), 345.

43 Letter of Pierre Chouteau, Jr., and Company to Major Drips, St. Louis, August 18, 1848, in the Drips Papers, *loc. cit.*

44 LeRoy R. Hafen and Francis M. Young, *Fort Laramie and the Pageant of the West, 1834-1860* (Glendale, 1938), 131-33.

When Chouteau and Company built a new fort, known as Fort John, at Scott's Bluff, Drips had charge of it during the years 1851-1852. In the latter year he returned to Kansas City where he probably lived until 1857, although doubtless he still engaged in trading operations of some sort.[45] After the death of his Otoe wife in 1846, Drips married Louise Geroux, a girl who was half French and half Sioux. They had five children, Andrew Jackson, Thomas, Anna, Julia, and George, all born during the years 1850-1857. The eldest of these was brought up by Katherine Drips Mulkey, who had no children and who also lived in Kansas City.[46]

In 1857 we find Drips engaged in the fur trade once more. His trading post was located on the North Platte near present Torrington, Wyoming, about twenty miles down river from Fort Laramie.[47] From this time until his death, he seems to have divided his time between this post and Kansas City. He died on September 1, 1860, at the home of his daughter, Mrs. Mulkey, in Kansas City, Missouri.[48]

Andrew Drips was older than most of the men engaged in the mountain fur trade by from ten to twenty years. He was an experienced trader when he first came to the mountains. He and Fontenelle contributed more to the triumph of the American Fur Company than any one else. Drips was equally capable at transporting goods, trading with the Indians, directing a band of trappers in the field, or keeping the books for his many transactions.

We have no physical description of him that I know of but there are frequent references to his honesty and integrity. He followed the custom of the Indians in taking more than one wife but it is notable that he called on the wives of

[45] Morgan and Harris, *op. cit.*, 296.

[46] Barnes and Branch, *op. cit.*

[47] LeRoy R. Hafen and Ann W. Hafen, editors, *Relations with the Plains Indians*, in *Far West and the Rockies Series*, IX (Glendale, 1959), p. 72. An entry in Percival G. Lowe's Journal for July 22, 1857, states "Passed Bordeau's trading place and camped below Major Dripp's trading house, nineteen miles from Laramie."

[48] Barnes and Branch, *op. cit.*

the missionaries, who traveled with his train, and that he directed his wives to do so, as well. He provided for his children and it is again notable that they lived among the whites and intermarried with them rather than with the Indians. A portrait of Drips appears herein at page 17.

Few men had a career of forty years in the fur trade and none of the importance and position of Drips lasted that long. He is always referred to as Mr. Drips or Captain or Major Drips, which is an indication that he was held in respect. He was capable of plain talking, as when he wrote "The flour I brought up yesterday is not *eatable*. You can smell it at least 100 yards."[49] Again, when at the rendezvous of 1840, "Black" Harris took a pot shot at "Doc" Newell from about eighty yards with a rifle and missed him, Drips told Harris that if Newell had been killed he would have hanged him.[50]

Andrew Drips deserves a place among the Mountain Men that is well toward the top of the list because of his long and successful career, his mastery of all branches of the business and his ability as a leader of men.

---

49 Letter of Andrew Drips to some unknown person, Sept. 18, 1829, in the Drips Papers, *loc. cit.* I am much indebted to Mrs. Frances H. Stadler, archivist of the Missouri Historical Society, for her cooperation in furnishing materials requested for this sketch.

50 Morgan and Harris, *op. cit.*, 328. I am also indebted to these authors for materials in their sketch of Drips which have not been available to me at first hand.

Joseph L. Meek

by HARVEY E. TOBIE
Portland, Oregon

How can a man maintain integrity of personality while he is enmeshed in extreme environmental complications? A conspicuous test case is the career of Joseph LaFayette Meek. Born February 7, 1810, into ". . . one of the first famaleys of Virginia . . ."[1] he left home early, paused but briefly in Missouri, spent eleven years in the Rocky Mountains, helped found a new settlement in Oregon, became first a leader and then a casualty of the frantic political movements of the fifties and sixties, and stepped into – and suddenly and prematurely out of – the spotlight of a final notoriety. During all these circumstances he was the one and only Joe Meek.

A family genealogist[2] has traced the family back to Cromwellian days in England. Joe Meek's grandfather of the same name moved to Virginia where Joe's father, James, also spent his life. The boy's mother, Spicy Walker Meek, died in 1821. Another prominent connection was made when James' younger brother, Joseph, married Jane Buchanan.

Breaking of these apparently favorable connections came after James Meek married Nancy Yearsley, a widow with children of her own. She attempted to bring order into an oversized and uninhibited family. Soon, young Joe headed

---

[1] Joseph L. Meek to Olive Meek; Harvey E. Tobie, *No Man Like Joe* (Portland, Ore., 1949), 251. Unless otherwise cited, all references and quotations are from this book, which may be consulted for additional information and discussion of debatable points.

[2] Carleton Lee Meek, *Meek Genealogy, 1630-1954;* Daughters of the American Revolution, *Genealogical Record Blank*, 65.

west, where relatives had preceded him. At Lexington, Missouri, he found work with brother Hiram, who operated a sawmill and owned a store. There he also found brother Stephen, five years his elder, who was employed by trader William Sublette, rubbing furs with rum to keep out the moths. Joe enlisted in Sublette's fur trade enterprise and, at age nineteen, left Missouri for the Rocky Mountains, March 17, 1829.

Older and wiser relatives must have felt that the proud Walker-Meek traditions had been severed by an impulsive teen-age enlistment. Even his new employer had tried to discourage him. True, he became an expatriate, but with him were friends with somewhat comparable backgrounds with whom he spent the rest of his life. Distinguished visitors kept passing by. Thus the chain was never completely broken. Among the fifty-four men in the company were his lifelong neighbors and friends George Ebbert, Robert Newell and others.[3]

Except for a few miles on the Santa Fe road, the route of Sublette's brigade was a typical Oregon Trail path to the mountains. The Sweetwater River led them to an appointed destination in some grassy valley at the foot of the mountains, where trappers met for a July 5th celebration and exchange of goods. Two wintering partners failed to arrive. There was, therefore, another reunion and more exchanges, when David Jackson was found at Jackson Hole; and another in August, at Pierre's Hole on the other side of the Tetons, with Jedediah Smith who was returning after disaster on the Smith River. Newell estimated that all parties together totalled about 175 persons. Joe Meek had been a member of the designated search party which located the delayed leader.

Whereas Smith's Hudson's Bay Company rescuers were

[3] George Wood Ebbert to J. Henry Brown, Feb. 1, 1875; Dale L. Morgan, *Jedediah Smith* (Indianapolis, 1953), 429.

well organized for Snake River operations, Smith, Jackson and Sublette were persuaded to divert their energies into the country of thieving Crows and treacherous Blackfeet, where trapping was more profitable than the British leaders realized. What is now Yellowstone Park would become familiar to the Americans. Passing up Henry's Fork of the Snake River, where beaver were "very plenty," to the sources of Madison Fork of the Missouri, Meek and his associates crossed over to the Gallatin and then mastered another rugged passage to reach the Yellowstone.

The new recruit, fleeing from a Blackfoot attack, became lost in an area of snowcapped peaks where he could see, he believed, not only the Yellowstone and the Missouri, but the distant Snake River as well. Hungry, cold, and as frightened as one so characteristically bold could be, he made his way across to the Yellowstone. Waking one morning in a more comfortable area, he was, as any Easterner would have been, astonished to see a vast area of billowing vapor interspersed with craters from which ". . . issued blue flames and molten brimstone . . ." Still, he thought, ". . . if it war hell, it war a more agreeable climate than he had been in for some time . . ."

Fortunately, our young recruit was discovered by other trappers and reunited with the main party, which was heading for the Bighorn River. The horses, especially, experienced some difficulty in making a west-to-east mountain passage by way of the Stinking (Shoshone) branch to the Bighorn. Here, after uniting with Milton Sublette's trapping party, they made their way toward winter quarters on Wind River.[4]

That winter, because "times were hard" for man and beast, the trappers started the year 1830 by moving to Powder River where buffalo were expected. There they all remained until spring. About April 1st, partner Jackson

[4] Morgan, *op. cit.*, 351.

took about half the men back to Jackson Hole and the Snake country while Jedediah Smith led some eighty men onward to their work among the Blackfeet. Enjoying good hunting, they moved over to Tongue River and thence to the Little Bighorn and the Bighorn. Unfortunately, an unexpected late and heavy snow and subsequent flooding led to considerable loss of horses and traps in a high water crossing of Bovey's Fork. Making their way over Pryor Mountains through Pryor's Gap, the party reached Clark's Fork and the Yellowstone. Crossing in bullboats, they worked their way to the Musselshell, and to the Judith River. Though trapping results were excellent, Blackfoot thieving and hostility were great handicaps. The partners reported to the Secretary of War a return-trip casualty which resulted in the crippling of Joe Meek and the death of Glaud Ponto (?), when a cave-in occurred as they were uncovering a cache of furs on the Bighorn.[5]

After a generally successful spring hunt, the two parties came together for a rendezvous on Wind River, perhaps at the junction of the Popo Agie. On July 16, 1830, Captain Billy arrived with supplies, new recruits, including brother Stephen, and wagons.[6] Successful wheel transportation presaged great events in the settlement of the far West, but it would be ten years before Bob Newell, Joe Meek and others would complete the wagon train link to the Oregon Country.

At this rendezvous, an agreement was drawn up ending trapping operations in the area for Smith, Jackson and Sublette, and transferring the mountain operations to the "little booshways," Thomas Fitzpatrick, James Bridger, Milton Sublette, Henry Fraeb and Jean Baptiste Gervais. Though his friends were inclined to make other engagements as

[5] *Ibid.*, 346, 314, 431.

[6] Stephen Hall Meek, *The Autobiography of a Mountain Man*, introduction and notes by Arthur Woodward (Pasadena, Calif., 1948), 4.

suited them, and though equally independent, Joe Meek was inclined to work with these leaders during the years that followed. Already two other companies furnished formidable competition: The Hudson's Bay Company and the American Fur Company. Not fully aware of the extent of the rivalry, Fraeb and Gervais left after the rendezvous for the Snake country, while the other partners returned to their operations in the Blackfoot area, trapping as far as the forks of the Missouri before returning to winter quarters on the Yellowstone. Since the season was unusually inclement and stocks were decreasing alarmingly, Meek was sent with a man he knew as "Legarde" (Baptiste La Geire ?) with dispatches for St. Louis. When his companion was taken prisoner by the Pawnees, Meek, after entrusting his messages to another eastbound express, returned to camp in company with "Cabeneau" (Jean Baptiste Charbonneau ?).

The spring hunt of 1831 led south and east to Tongue River. Theft of fifty-seven steeds by the Crow Indians forced an infantry operation to recover the essential lost property. A working loop took the men to Powder River and the North Platte, and back to Bear River and Cache Valley, where they awaited the supplier. No one came. In this emergency, a search party including Meek and Ebbert, under partner Fraeb, left in August. Finally, the missing supplier was located near the mouth of the Laramie River. Fraeb and his group then worked their way back to the Salmon River where, early in October, the overdue supplies were finally distributed. The three fur companies camped for the winter in watchful proximity near the junction of the Salmon and Lemhi rivers. From winter quarters, Meek and Legarde rode an express over a pass to Bitterroot valley to bargain with some free trappers.

The 1832 spring hunt under Bridger and Milton Sublette proceeded to the Snake River and down Salt River to an encampment on Willow Creek. At Ogden's Hole, Milton was the unfortunate victim of a stabbing which thereafter handicapped his leadership and, in time, led to his premature death. Joe Meek cared for him during his first period of injury, earning a warm friendship, and later, we are told, inheriting Milton's beautiful Indian Mountain Lamb, Umentucken.

About six hundred people were gathered for summer rendezvous of 1832 at Pierre's Hole on the west side of the Tetons. At this notable meeting occurred the famous Battle of Pierre's Hole.

It was late in July before Milton Sublette and his party, including Joe Meek, Fraeb with another group, and the Wyeth party, finally began their Snake country operations. Lack of food and fodder forced a northward swing up Payette River to Payette Lake, in what is now central Idaho. Joe Meek and three other men ventured still farther toward the head of the Salmon River and into the land of the Nez Perce Indians. Later, trapping activities moved from Payette Lake into the Boise basin, Big Lost River, and finally to the winter camp site on the Salmon River. Late in the fall, on an exchange of men, Joe and Stephen Meek and others joined a northern party for operations made difficult by American Fur Company competition and by little wars with the Blackfeet.[7]

During January, 1833, the Rocky Mountain Fur Company camp moved to the junction of the Snake and Portneuf rivers near what is now Pocatello, Idaho. "Fuel war scarce on the Snake River . . .," the weather was very cold, as it had been on the Salmon; and need of food for the horses induced moves by several groups of trappers in watchful competition. About April 6, both Bonneville's men and those led by Milton Sublette and Gervais camped on Big Lost (Godin's) River, waiting for deep snows to melt out

[7] Washington Irving, *The Adventures of Captain Bonneville,* E. W. Todd, ed. (Norman, Okla., 1961), 98-101.

of the passes. Although generally loyal to old associates, Joe Meek was no longer a hired trapper and could hereafter enjoy more independence. He still depended on some concern to furnish his outfit, but his income as a "skin trapper" now depended on what he was able to trap and deliver. He later claimed to have realized as much as $1500 per year. In spite of this greater freedom, he seems to have been working not too far from the main groups in the Snake River and Salt Lake areas, moving toward the rendezvous at Green River.[8]

At the rendezvous, Joe and Stephen Meek joined with Joseph R. Walker, a Bonneville "booshway," for an adventure to the southwest involving about sixty men. Whether by design or not is a matter of dispute; as Stephen Meek said, "We got too far West, and finally started down the Mary's or Humboldt, river for California, over a country entirely unknown to the trappers." Probably Indian battles made it impossible for the party to turn back; and they proceeded rapidly, therefore, as if in flight.

There are some discrepancies between the stories told by Stephen, by Joe, and by Zenas Leonard of the Walker party. Variations in route stated in the Joe Meek account might be partially explainable by the independence of movement a skin trapper might enjoy. Walker's orders, however, would be binding on all who traveled with him. With winter upon them, it is thought that the party traveled through Yosemite Park, or similar terrain, reaching the Merced River, the San Joaquin, and San Juan Bautista Mission.

After a winter in California, which seems to have been enjoyed to the full by the trappers, confusion arising over the distinction between horse trading and stealing led to the early retirement of the Americans to the foothills. In February began the retracing of the route back to the rendez-

8 *Ibid.*, 387, 131-7, 144, 154, 397.

vous. If *The River of the West* is to be believed, even in part, the free trappers, including Joe Meek, must have taken a wide tour through the southwest and united with a Rocky Mountain Fur Company group under Fraeb.[9]

About the middle of June, 1834, the Walker party rejoined Bonneville on Bear River. At Ham's Fork, Green River, occurred the final rendezvous of the R.M.F. Co. Wyeth was back with Jason Lee and party and scientists Nuttall and Townsend. The building of Fort Hall that summer, and Methodist contacts, were both of great importance to Meek and his associates. Their independence was increased by the dissolution of their company, yet Meek seems to have remained loyal to the new "booshway," Jim Bridger.

Bridger's route after the rendezvous of 1834 was northward through the Yellowstone area. Late in the season, Jim and his group were ". . . on Pier's Fork near Horse Prairie. . ." Before settling down for winter at the forks of the Snake, Meek spent three days at new Fort Hall – one day to get drunk, two to get sober, he joked. By the middle of February, after the Fort Hall visit, Meek, Newell, Kit Carson and others started their spring hunt into Blackfoot country. The rendezvous of 1835 at Green River was notable for the presence of Rev. Samuel Parker and Dr. Marcus Whitman. The missionary doctor removed a three-inch arrowhead which Bridger had carried uncomfortably in his back for three years.

Fall trapping centered in the Yellowstone and Teton area. Near Madison River, a lost party of trappers under Joseph Gale was visited on the evening of September 9th by Joe Meek, Kit Carson and a dozen other story tellers and friends. The following morning, Indians who pursued Joe and seven others back to camp, set fire to the thicket in which the trappers were located. Flames united over their

[9] Frances F. Victor, *The River of the West* (Hartford, Conn., 1870), 152.

heads, but greenness prevented fatalities in an incident that all would remember. Bridger's large party came up, and all moved westward till, on the Beaverhead branch of the Jefferson, they competed with a H.B.C. group under Francis Ermatinger. By the end of September they were across the divide, moving toward winter quarters about fifteen miles from Fort Hall, which they reached in November. In February, 1836, sixteen Wyeth men, including diarist Osborne Russell, joined Bridger. Winter did not break up till March, and then swollen rivers handicapped those hunting furs.

Again, the rendezvous was on Green River. Marcus Whitman was back with his wife Narcissa, and Mr. and Mrs. Henry Spalding, W. H. Gray and Miles Goodyear. Within a few years Meek and others would follow these friends into the Oregon country. Now, when they parted, most of the Americans followed Bridger into the land of the Blackfeet. By mid-August they were on the southern shores of Yellowstone Lake, and by the second week of September their location was Rocky Fork, where Meek and Davis Crow had the hair's breadth escape from Indian ambush, a story so well told by Osborne Russell,[10] and by Joe Meek.

Winter quarters in 1836 were first at a big bend of the Yellowstone, then at Clark's Fork, and at other places chosen because of the presence of buffalo. Although trappers were active in February and March, it was April 1, 1837, before the spring hunt could really advance, moving as far as the Musselshell River and trapping mostly on the Bighorn, Yellowstone, and their branches. Meek and his associates arrived early in the vicinity of the summer rendezvous, promptness which was unfortunate. They became involved in a skirmish with Bannock Indians which cost the life of Meek's mate, Umentucken.

---

[10] Aubrey L. Haines, *Osborne Russell's Journal of a Trapper* (Portland, Ore., 1955), 48.

After a festive time on Green River, some trappers went with Bridger into Crow country, some to rugged Yellowstone waters. News of a smallpox epidemic had reached the Crow trading post, Fort Van Buren, and panicky natives left their usual habitats in headlong flight. The Blackfeet were drawn into the vacuum thus created. Winter came and it was unusually cold. Worst of all, winter quarters had been moved from Clark's Fork to an unknown location which some trappers were unable to find till February.

Nor was the March that followed lamblike. Little was accomplished before the end of April, 1838. By May 14th the "whole camp" was at Cross Creeks of the Yellowstone. Here Meek had the fight with a bear which made him famous back in the States. Battling with Indians, whose resistance was made pathetic by ravages of smallpox, trappers moved to Henry's Lake. They crossed over to Pierre's Hole and exploited the tributaries of the upper Snake River on their loop back to Green River. At the old log storehouse on Horse Creek, "Black" Harris had scribbled a note: "Come to Popoazua . . . and you will find plenty trade, whiskey and white women."

On the Popo Agie there was a long and convivial rendezvous period. W. H. Gray was back with his new wife and three other newlywed missionary couples. Bachelor Cornelius Rogers was also enroute to the Whitman mission. Eastward bound was Jason Lee with P. L. Edwards, F. Y. Ewing and some Indian boys. To help enliven the occasion, Sir William Stewart and his hunting party were again present. To offset the entertainment there was news that the wagon train expected to make no more trips to the mountains. Disheartening reality prompted many desertions and some thievery. Doc Newell confided in his *Memorandum* ". . . After a long and tedious time we left for hunting."

Joe Meek, "Cotton" Mansfield, and Caleb Wilkins left early in September for Flathead country, reaching Big Lost

River, continuing to Salmon River and on to the Beaverhead valley, where they joined the Nez Perces in a buffalo hunt. Then Meek recklessly trapped alone on the Gallatin River, and in Gardiner's Hole and Burnt Hole, reporting that "Beaver war plenty." He was one of seven men under John Larison who went to live for a time at Nez Perce chief Kowesote's village on the forks of the Salmon. Here, Meek, Newell, and Wilkins made marriage alliances[11] with three of the chief's daughters whom the Mountain Men later took to Oregon with them.

In March, 1839, Meek and an Englishman named (William?) Allen trapped their way to the Tetons. After Allen was murdered by Blackfeet, Meek proceeded alone to the rendezvous at Horse Creek. There, trading results were very disappointing, and the atmosphere of the gathering was sad and sullen. In July, 1839, Bob Newell went to Fort Hall on business, taking his family, consisting of a wife and two children, and Virginia Meek. Joe, the expert trapper, went to work on Salt River with a Shawnee Indian, Big Jim. After a poor hunt, he, too, went to Fort Hall only to find that Newell, with the families, had left for Fort Crockett during the second week of August. Enroute to find them, Joe reached Bear River, where, on August 28, he met members of the Peoria party from the United States. Suffering much hardship, he completed the trip to Brown's Hole, arriving after September first.

Newell and Meek, with Robert Shortess, returned to Fort Hall for more supplies, being forced to make three days' provisions last eleven days. Leaving Virginia behind, the partners set out again for Fort Crockett. They reached Green River at Black's Fork November 9th, "nothing to eat." However, they soon reached their destination. While Meek wintered at Brown's Hole, on December 7th in what

[11] At different times, after 1837. Census of 1850, ms., Ore. Hist. Soc.

became Bingham County, Idaho, Virginia gave birth to a son, named Courtney Walker Meek after the trader then in charge at Fort Hall.

Early in February a party, including Meek and Newell, returned to Fort Hall, a feat of survival requiring forty-five days. Joe, after spending the spring trapping and trading out of the post, showed up at Green River, but failed to find the old associates or good trading opportunities. Times were indeed hard in a vanishing business. Meek and Newell returned to Fort Hall, Newell as pilot for the Quincy party of missionaries. About the last of August, Meek went trapping again with a small party, mostly in the Teton area and around the forks of the Snake. Arrived at Bear River, he received a message from Newell.

At Fort Hall on September 22nd, Newell explained his plan to drive wagons to Oregon. On September 27th, the party left, with Meek driving one wagon, Wilkins another, and a German called Nicholas (Nicolaus Altgeier?) a third. Newell rode ahead as leader. Members of the party included, among others perhaps, William Craig, John Larison and a Snake Indian. They reached the Whitman mission at Waiilatpu, rested briefly, then the Meek and Newell families proceeded to Fort Walla Walla and, on horseback, to the Willamette Valley where they arrived December 15, 1840. They had contributed most materially, along with William Sublette, Bonneville and Dr. Whitman, to breaking trail for a wagon route to Oregon, where they were to become important influences in the new settlements.

The very fact that Meek and his brothers-in-law took families with them into Oregon proved that they had retained the gentlemanly traditions of the fine families into which they had been born. Joe was acting like a Meek, a Walker, a hero-worshipper of George Washington. There was no Korean-orphan type of irresponsibility in men of this calibre. Asked years later why he had not followed a common mountain practice and left his wife behind, Meek replied with an appropriate gesture, "I could not do that, it *hurt here*." Similarly, the bonds of friendship among mountain men were very strong indeed. Where Jonathan went, David was sure to go. Before 1840, a group of men had agreed that they would live together in Oregon in a community of their own.[12] In a spirit of independence they had originally left the settlements; they would maintain that characteristic in their new homeland.

To prepare themselves for their new roles of importance, what had these men learned during their mountain days? They had explored in detail the Rocky Mountain area, and indeed had traveled widely from the Mississippi to the coast, and almost from border to border. Some of them had been students in what they called the "Rocky Mountain College." There were some trappers, Bridger among them, who were illiterate, but he was a very wise man in wilderness lore. During periods of enforced inactivity these men had taught each other. They had access to the Bible, to the works of Shakespeare, Byron, Scott and many other writers. They talked about these priceless works, recited passages (quite inaccurately at times), named each other and their children after characters in literature, and joked in warped literary idioms. Even in the mountains, there were letters to write, occasional documents to sign. They learned to do these things, or to do them better. In Joe Meek's case, spelling was an exception. For his adult education he was especially grateful to a man named Green. To the end of his days, Joe Meek had an avid intellectual curiosity. ". . . aneything for the Nuse," he wrote, begging Delegate Lane for newspapers.

Love of the beautiful involved more than mountains, lakes or horses. The literary morsels that Meek uttered

[12] Oregon Pioneer Association *Transactions* (1891), 182.

were, like his spelling, more interesting than the correct words. Indians he once described as ". . . old Benj. Johnson's boys . . ." He named a daughter Helen Mar after a character in Porter's *Scottish Chiefs.* Quoting Shakespeare to Dr. McLoughlin, he explained a prank by saying ". . . it is not that I love the *Brutus* less, but my dignity more." "Othello's occupation is gone," he told the Hudson's Bay Commission, forgetting that the Moor's career was war. As did his mountain friends – Joseph Gale, F. X. Matthieu, Angus McDonald – after his own passing, he wrote in poetic parody his heartfelt grief over Newell's death:

> I feel like one who treads alone
> Some banquet hall deserted;
> Whose *lights are gone* whose *spirits flown*
> And all but *me* departed.

The stories for which Joe Meek was famous were gems of original artistry. For the most part, he was the villain rather than the hero of the piece. He told of shooting Indians merely for amusement, or because they looked as if they were about to steal from his traps. Once he sat on a fence and watched while companions committed outrageous acts of vandalism. He could even outlie the Crows.

If praised for bravery, his story was that he couldn't hold his horse, or that his balky mule suddenly decided to run. For us today, also, mules and bears are comic characters. Awkwardness of friends made good story material. Milton Sublette, who thought he was up a tree to escape a bear, was actually on the ground, astraddle the trunk. Doughty allowed a bear to walk over him as he slept. Hawkins was one of the three "bares"; three Daniels invaded a cave of hibernating bruins. A narrow escape caused Meek himself to become ". . . satisfied with bar-fighting." Bridger had to negotiate with the Crows in a state of complete nudity; Gen. Lane spat maggots from his drinking water.

Joe Meek's stories of holiday sprees, normal in his trade, or of alcoholic weekends in Oregon, gave sensation-hunters or puritans an impression which ignored hundreds of days, annually, of drought. One must not forget such unreported recreational activities as wrestling, racing, shooting at targets; nor time spent in letter writing, nor the Rocky Mountain College interludes. Joe's stories of Indian women exaggerate their youth, charm and prowess. He did not, however, admit the abandonment of a squaw. Umentucken was killed in battle, and Helen Mar's mother deserted the drunken trapper.

In the mountains, Joe Meek learned to stay alive. Though he had narrow escapes, in emergencies he "raised a runnin'." He knew neither fear nor hesitation, but educated prudence helped him to survive. "If," said Peter Burnett, reminiscing about the Provisional Government, "we had selected a rash or timid man for sheriff, we must have failed for a time." The personal and collective emergencies of incoming immigrants could best be served by men like Joe Meek. The first stop of an arriving settler was often at the Mountain Man's humble abode. The Virginia plantation tradition of hospitality had not been lost, but only strengthened, by raw wilderness needs. Was an immigrant party in distress? Joe Meek would immediately start a movement to help them. When he moved into a new frame house, he turned the old cabin over to a needy newcomer with a wife and nine children. Did Indian trouble threaten? The Mountain Men rode out to meet the crisis with ample know-how. Washington, D.C., was not too far for Meek to travel in midwinter to seek relief after the Whitman massacre.

It was fortunate for the settlers that Meek and his friends strove for self-improvement. For instance, the story-telling, which became an unrefined art, was useful in Oregon when hot arguments often melted into guffaws as the mountain men told their tales and made droll statements. At early-day picnic celebrations they not only paraded, raced and visited, but made apt speeches, featuring, perhaps, mimicry, literary misquotations, parodies and smiling sarcasm.

As in the mountains, the first task of the 1840 immigrants was to stay alive. They had to turn for help to the Hudson's Bay Company, to the Methodists and to the few ex-trapper settlers, notably Ewing Young. William Doughty already had a cabin at the foot of Chehalem mountain, and George Ebbert had a farm at Champoeg. Though Newell's credit with the Company was good, Meek was denied direct help from the same source. He had to work for Newell and others. Three days' labor on the Young estate, "Self & Horse," brought him six dollars. He also acted as dispatch rider for the Wilkes expedition.

By spring 1842, Joe was helping Doughty put in a crop of wheat, seed for which the latter had originally received from the H.B.C. Similarly, Ebbert and Wilkins helped each other, and all assisted Alvin Smith and other arriving immigrants. "Rocky Mountain Retreat" was the name given to the small original settlement on Tualatin Plains.

When, for various reasons, groups then dominant in Oregon lost, for the most part, their desire for political innovations, leadership in a developing movement for government passed into the hands of the new, independent settlers. Joe Meek's earliest induction into the processes of political evolution came as he was earning five dollars as auctioneer in a series of sales involving the estate of Ewing Young, who had died in February, 1841. So-called Wolf meetings, debating means for civil defense, were dominated by independents. Climactically, on May 2, 1843, a memorable meeting took place at which, after some parliamentary maneuvering made emphatic by Meek's auctioneer's voice and personality, the motion to organize a government carried. The most important office under the circumstances, that of sheriff, was assigned to Joseph LaFayette Meek.

By 1844 a well organized government was in operation, still dominated by independents, and Meek was overwhelmingly elected sheriff. By his conversion at a Methodist camp meeting in 1843, he had apparently taken his stand with that important political element; however, he was not then, or ever, tied to any apron strings. Similarly independent, the legislative committee of 1844 took steps to alter pro-Mission land laws. Unfortunately for the non-conformist element, population about doubled that fall, and again in 1845. Company and Mission interests drew together, and the independents lost heavily in the election of 1845. Meek, nevertheless, was again chosen sheriff by a comfortable, but not a one-sided majority.

By 1845, Joe Meek was a prosperous farmer, who, had he stayed out of politics, might well have been on his way to emulation of the George Washington tradition by becoming a landed gentleman. In the spring of that year, he could boast of his success to brother Hiram; and in the fall he built the first frame house in his county.

On February 5, 1846, Meek publicly resigned as marshal, a new position that had been created for him, hinting strongly of collusion between the Methodist and H.B.C. interests. In this mood, he campaigned for a seat in the legislature and won, leading the ticket in his own county. As the proceedings show, the very first session was considerably dominated by his personality and executive vigor. He took a leading and, narrowly, a winning part in passage of a regulatory liquor measure, rather than the prohibition strongly advocated by opponents. In 1847 he became the prime mover in a "Grand Temperance Movement." He was also, in that year, a leader in a protest movement against claim jumping. He was reelected to the legislature, running second in number of ballots received by successful candidates.

Meek was not destined to furnish top leadership in the

1847 legislature because, when news of the Whitman massacre dominated the proceedings, he became the principal actor in another drama. Driven by his friendship for the Whitmans and by grief over the death of his own daughter, and available because of his relationship with the wife of President Polk, he was glad to be named messenger to the United States.

With his friend and neighbor George Ebbert, experienced express rider and former H.B.C. employe, the ambassador from Oregon left the Willamette Valley January 4, 1848. Determined, to the disgust of political opponents, to take trails familiar to them, they became, enroute, involved for a time in the Cayuse Indian War. It was March 5th before a small company, consisting of Capt. John Owen, Lieut. "Nath" Bowman, John Jones, Jacob Leabo, Dennis Burroughs, David Young, Harvey Evans, M. "Range" Miller, James Stead, Meek and Ebbert left for the Blue Mountains with a temporary escort of volunteers. "Better men," said the leader, "cannot be found." Ahead of them were measles, Indian danger, hunger, heavy snow, and distance. Nevertheless, they reached St. Joseph, Missouri, May 11, 1848, in half the time an emigrant train would have required in better weather. On May 28th, Meek was able to greet his cousin, Mrs. Polk and the President, "cousin Jeems."

On the very next day, the President sent a message to Congress asking for prompt action. Politically, it was impossible for Congress to hurry. Finally, on August 13, 1848, a bill was passed making Oregon a Territory of the United States. Meek had taken with him to Washington a petition signed by 250 persons asking his appointment as Marshal of the new territory. On August 18th, the President signed such a commission. On August 27th, Meek had the honor to deliver to General Joseph Lane of Indiana his commission as Governor. Two days later Meek and Lane started for Oregon overland. On September 10th they left Fort Leavenworth, accompanied by twenty-four mounted riflemen and a wagon train which had to be left at Santa Fe. At San Francisco they took a boat which required eighteen precious days to reach Astoria, Oregon. From that port, with Governor and Marshal taking their turns at the paddles, they traveled by canoe to Oregon City, arriving March 2, 1849, barely in time to establish the new government before a Whig administration took over in Washington.

The change in national politics turned out, eventually, to be a calamity for Marshal Meek, and perhaps for almost everyone concerned. At first, however, the new government was most welcome. The exodus of males to the gold fields had left the communities dangerously unguarded. Unfortunately, the long arm of the federal government was extended with characteristic slowness, while deterrent punishment of Indian depredators had to be delayed in the face of excited public clamor. Finally, on the theory that an on-the-spot trial of a Puget Sound Indian murderer would be an effective warning, Chief Justice William P. Bryant ordered Marshal Meek to transport the entire court personnel, including jurors, to the distant location. Pending receipt of government funds, Meek was obliged personally to provide for the required expenses and was, therefore, eventually about $1000 out of pocket for fulfillment of his duty. In carrying out another court order by hanging the Cayuse murderers against the wishes of the acting Governor, Secretary Kintzing Pritchett, the Marshal showed himself to be virtually the head man in the Territory at the moment.

But the horns of Meek's dilemma widened. More important politically than the anti-Indian hysteria which had been fanned into dangerous flame by the screaming charges of Dr. Whitman's associate, Rev. Henry H. Spalding and his brother-in-law, Meek's neighbor, Rev. John S. Griffin – charges involving Catholics and a foreign company – was a popular outcry about Dr. McLoughlin's holdings at the territorial capital. Independent and moderate in the midst of this in 1849, Meek ran a poor fourth in the race for delegate to Congress. Political excitement increased, with emphasis shifting from anti-Indian and anti-foreign outcries to the capital location question. Several areas combined in logrolling in the territorial legislature to move the seat of government from Oregon City to Salem. With constitutionality of new laws in question, imported Whig Judge Thomas Nelson attempted to hold courts under the old laws, while imported Democratic Judge Orville C. Pratt, an all too vociferous leader of the Salem clique, also conducted courts. Members of both parties came clamoring to Meek for reimbursement for services at court. To make the situation even more impossible, the words "delaying" and "denying" best express the Comptroller's policy in releasing funds for the Marshal's use.

After having sold the ship *Albion* at auction for an actual $3,590.12, but a reported $40,000, paymaster Joe Meek's statement that ". . . thar was barly enough for the officers of the Court" was accurate, but seemed funny. The entire experience of his four-year term was well stated in that famous phrase. Marshall Meek was the chief victim of a methodical mismanagement, and of a fierce political schism. No longer the rich uncle that Hiram's daughter Melissa had assumed him to be in 1848, he left office poor, a fact which belied suspicion of embezzlement. And he was fired. When Democrats returned to office with the election of Franklin Pierce, a "clean sweap" was demanded by a multitude of letter writers. Meek, because he had cooperated with Whig officials, as was his duty, was considered too "soft" to be made an exception in the general house-cleaning.

It was as a deputy under his successor that Meek left a statement characteristic of his personality when he endorsed a document, "The within naimed Witeness caint Be found, having gon Bare hunting." He also served as court crier. On June 5, 1854, the ex-marshal was elected Colonel of the Militia for Washington and Columbia counties. In 1855, he enlisted – not as a Colonel, but as a private – in the Oregon Volunteers for service in the Yakima Indian War, returning as Major. His oldest son, Courtney, also served in this campaign.

Though labeled "soft" and "sorehead" by the ruling faction, in 1857 Meek was still a Democrat, naming his new son, significantly, Stephen Douglas Meek. In 1861, in a letter to his daughter, Olive, Colonel Meek expressed his fervent feeling. If only he were back in Virginia, he would raise a regiment to fight for the Union – not for Abolitionists or Secessionists. "I keep the stars and Stripes flying 80 feet over my hous all the time," he wrote, ". . . and go decidedly for the Union . . ." In 1862 he helped found the Union party, and by this route moved later to become a founder of the Oregon Republican party also. In 1864, and for years thereafter, he was elected coroner.

For his entire lifetime after the great immigrations, Oregon segregation sentiment, which drew a color line mainly against Indians, greatly plagued Joe Meek and his friends and their families. There was sentiment against land-holding by half-breeds; "exterminators" were vociferous and dangerous during periods of Indian war, as were vigilantes in mountain areas. Civil War emotionalists emphasized miscegenation, if they could pronounce the word. Less extreme and more prevalent were social distinctions which sometimes drove "half-Injuns" to drunkenness or greater acts of recklessness. But the well-behaved, normally educated, half-breed majority suffered many rebuffs and much mental anguish. Fond and loyal parents like Meek, Newell, and Wilkins faced problems and suffered heartaches. Joe Meek's oldest son, Courtney, stabbed a local bully in an altercation over non-admission at a dance. The delayed trial and subsequent acquittal were a major concern during Colonel Meek's later years. A lost generation resulted from late marriages of most of the Meek children thus socially restricted.

In 1870 the past life of the Colonel was brought into the foreground by publication of Frances Fuller Victor's *River of the West,* the life and times of Joseph L. Meek. The short time remaining on earth for the subject of the biography was largely occupied with lecture tours to promote the sale of the book and to state positions on controversial affairs, present as well as past.

To the end he was, in personality, much the same as the Joe Meek who left his home at an early age. An element of boyishness persisted to the end. He loved to shock people, and with a prejudiced element he succeeded, thus perpetuating a role he was playing, rather than the real person which his letters and other intimate sources reveal. At the time of his death, the *Willamette Farmer* recognized "deep planted characteristics" for which he would be remembered "when greater men are forgotten." Definitely, Joe Meek should not be remembered as a mere Indian fighter "raised to new dignities," nor, like Lincoln, should he be thought of principally as a great story teller. The mountain experience interrupted, but did not change too much this ". . . ideal chivalry frontiersman," "natural gentleman," ". . . a man of great physical, moral and mental strength . . . a man of great magnetism . . . a born leader of men . . . ," "an exceptionally sweet and true nature . . ." ". . . a lover of the beautiful. . ."

Though prejudiced puritans and frantic partisans recognized some of his good qualities, Meek never quite measured up to their fixed standards. He might pose as a buffoon, but it was impossible for him to play either a subservient or a hypocritical role. In spite of every environmental handicap, he maintained to the end of his life underlying substantial qualities and integrity of personality. In 1848, emerging from a pioneer world and back in boyhood surroundings, he was only momentarily daunted. As he told his biographer,

> "I finally concluded that as I had never tried to act like anybody but myself, I would not make a fool of myself by beginning to ape other folks now. So I said, Joe Meek you have always been, and Joe Meek you shall remain; go ahead Joe Meek!"

Index